APPLIED TIME SERIES ANALYSIS

VOLUME 1

APPLIED TIME SERIES ANALYSIS

VOLUME 1

BASIC TECHNIQUES

ROBERT K. OTNES
Electromagnetic Systems Laboratories, Sunnyvale, California

LOREN ENOCHSON
GenRad Inc.
Acoustics, Vibration and Analysis Division

A Wiley-Interscience Publication
JOHN WILEY AND SONS
New York • Chichester • Brisbane • Toronto

Library of Congress Cataloging in Publication Data:

Otnes, Robert K.
  Applied time series analysis.

  "A Wiley-Interscience publication."
  Bibliography: p.
  CONTENTS: v. 1. Basic techniques.
  1. Time-series analysis.   I. Enochson,
Loren D., joint author.   II. Title.
QA280.086   519.2'32   77-26671

ISBN 0-471-24235-7

Printed in the United States of America

10 9 8 7 6 5 4 3 2

PREFACE

Time series analysis and *digital signal processing* are two related, but by no means identical, subjects. Both disciplines use computers or digital devices; they may use the Fourier transform, digital filtering, power spectral density calculations, and so forth, so that they have in common many of the same tools of the trade.

They differ, however, in their purposes: signal processing falls in the academic area of electrical engineering, and it has as its goal the effective implementation of such devices as *vocoders* in telephone transmission, *radar signal processors*, *sonar signal processors*, and the like. In other words, it is concerned with the design of special-purpose hardware for processing electrical signals.

On the other hand, time series analysis is a statistical discipline, and its techniques are applied in many branches of science and engineering. It may be employed in the analysis of large quantities of data taken during the course of a vibration test or extracted from recorded histories of economic data such as stock market information.

Some examples will clarify the differences. The solution to a digital filtering problem in the signal processing area might be a hardware fixed point filter. If designed for telephone use, it would be optimized so that its performance would be good and yet its cost would be low. It would be fixed purpose, and manufactured in quantity. Its time series counterpart would be a set of routines to be employed on a general-purpose computer, one routine, say, to generate the filter, and the second to do the actual filtering. The particular type or size of filter would vary with the course of the study. Indeed, the same data might be filtered in a number of different ways. Efficiency would not be as major a concern as in the signal processing case. On the other hand, the ability to generate a number of different filter types would be important. The time series analyst would be much more concerned with the effect of the filter on the data than with making the filtering process absolutely optimal in some sense.

As a second example, consider the Fourier transform and its fast implementation. In a signal processing problem, a considerable amount of effort might be spent in the design of a fast piece of hardware. It might be absolutely necessary that the device be able to perform its calculations in a given short interval of time. Because of its fixed point implementation, digital noise problems would be given serious consideration. Every detail of the fast Fourier transform algorithm would be considered so as to possibly speed up and improve the calculations.

The time series analyst would probably use a FORTRAN coded fast Fourier transform algorithm written by someone else. Although he would have to know in general how it works and what its limitations are, he would probably not attempt to write or optimize the routine himself. Rather, he would use it as a part of a larger structure employed in analyzing data.

Thus the key difference between the two subjects is that signal processing is concerned with the details of algorithms such as digital filtering and Fourier transformation, whereas time series analysis is concerned with their *application* in analyzing problems.

This book, as the title implies, is designed for those interested in time series analysis applications rather than the signal processing audience. Thus the emphasis will be on *software* as opposed to *hardware*, FORTRAN or some other higher-level programming language as opposed to machine language, floating point as opposed to fixed point calculations, and flexibility as opposed to optimality. Also, wherever possible, applications are stressed.

It is impossible to separate our subject as it stands today from the computer and computer programming. Hence programming examples and problems are a necessity. FORTRAN was chosen as the language to express the algorithms because of its universality rather than any inherent capability to couch the subtleties found in time series analysis. Appendix A has a small collection of routines that will be useful in solving the problems in the book and perhaps even in solving the reader's own real problems.

The exercises are roughly divided in half: half of them are designed to be solved with paper and pencil. The other half are to be solved on a computer. If the computer exercises are to be done, the reader should first look at Appendix A and obtain and run a copy of the test program and associated routines.

There is a large amount of material included for completeness that could readily be omitted in a course on this subject. For example, much of the material in Chapter 4 on digital filter design could be passed over, as could be much of Chapter 6, which discusses the details of the fast Fourier transform. Some material in Chapter 9 deals with multivariate processes and may be skipped the first time through.

We would like to thank a number of people: Professors Augustine H. Gray, UCSB, Lawrence P. McNamee, UCLA, and Rupert Streets, University of Calgary, for their helpful comments on the rough draft; Steve Barber, Larry Moulton, and Ed Onstead for their assistance with figures; Louise Bosin and Judy Helbling for their extended effort in the preparation of the manuscript; Beatrice Shube, our patient editor; and finally, the seminar and short course students who have helped us debug the preliminary versions of the text.

ROBERT K. OTNES
LOREN ENOCHSON

Palo Alto, California
Los Altos, California
February 1978

CONTENTS

Chapter 3
COLLECTING AND PREPROCESSING DATA

Chapter 4
DESIGN OF DIGITAL FILTERS

Chapter 5
PRACTICAL ASPECTS OF DIGITAL FILTERING

Chapter 6
FOURIER TRANSFORMS

Chapter 7
COVARIANCE AND CONVOLUTION FUNCTIONS

Chapter 8
POWER AND CROSS SPECTRAL DENSITIES

Chapter 9
TRANSFER FUNCTIONS AND COHERENCE FUNCTION

Appendix A
COMPUTER SUBROUTINES FOR TIME SERIES ANALYSIS

Appendix B
BLACKMAN–TUKEY COMPUTATIONAL
PROCEDURE FOR PSD'S

GLOSSARY

a_{1p}	Recursive filter weight, first in cascade implementation
a_{2p}	Recursive filter weight, second in cascade implementation
b	Frequency interval $(=1/NT)$
b_0	Overall nonrecursive scaling factor
b_{0p}	Nonrecursive filter weight, first in cascade implementation
b_{1p}	Nonrecursive filter weight, second in cascade implementation
b_{2p}	Nonrecursive filter weight, third in cascade implementation
B	Signal bandwidth
B_e	Effective resolution bandwidth in PSD calculations
$c(i)$	Convolution function
e	2.7182818...
$\exp(\ )$	$\exp(x)=e^x$
f	Frequency
F	Folding frequency
$h(i)$	Impulse response function
$H(k)$	Fourier transform of $h(i)$ (the transfer function)
i	Time index; time delay index
Im[ ]	Imaginary part of [ ]
j	$\sqrt{-1}$
k	Frequency index
N	Number of points in the sample
n	Number of degrees of freedom

p	Index
P	Period $(=NT)$
q	An index
$r(i)$	Correlation function
Re[ ]	Real part of [ ]
$s_{xx}(i)$	Covariance function or a signal
S	Sampling rate $(=1/T)$
$S_{xx}(k)$	Power spectrum of $x(i)$ at frequency k/NT
t	Time (continuous)
T	Sampling interval
$u(t)$	Boxcar function of width P
$U(f)$	Fourier transform of $u(t)=(\sin \pi fP)/\pi f$
W_N	$=\exp(-j2\pi/N)$
$x(i)$	A time series (frequently the input to a system)
$X(k)$	Fourier transform of $x(i)$
$y(i)$	A time series (frequently the output from a system)
$Y(k)$	Fourier transform of $y(i)$
$z(i)$	A time series (sometimes complex)
$Z(k)$	Fourier transform of $z(i)$
α	Weight for first-order filter
β	Regression coefficient
τ	Time delay
η	Dummy variable of integration
ϕ	Phase angle; probability density function
Φ	Probability distribution function
σ	Standard deviation
ζ	Damping term in a digital filter
Σ	Summation
π	3.14159265...
Π	Product
ω	Frequency in radians
ω_n	Natural frequency in radians

CHAPTER 1

PRELIMINARY CONCEPTS

1.1 INTRODUCTION

This and the following chapter are included to review the basic underlying mathematical and statistical concepts required for reading this book.

The emphasis of this chapter is on the mathematical techniques that are employed in time series analysis. The most important of these is the Fourier transform in its various forms. The Fourier transform and its fast implementation on digital devices have become increasingly important in recent times and are the basic tools employed in this book.

The concepts of linear systems, transfer functions, and convolution are all linked together, and are quite important for an understanding of the material to follow.

There are exercises at the end of each chapter. Some of these require writing short computer programs for their solution. If the reader plans to solve these problems, it would be best to immediately read Appendix A, which has computer subroutines that will simplify the writing of the programs. Additionally, there is a test case and its results. It is recommended that the test case be run and the answers checked before attempting to use the routines.

1.2 REVIEW OF COMPLEX ARITHMETIC

As is standard in engineering notation, the square root of -1 will be written as j (as contrasted with the i used in mathematics):

$$j = \sqrt{-1} \tag{1.1}$$

A *complex number* c consists of j and two real numbers a and b in the form

$$c = a + jb \tag{1.2}$$

The *real part* of c is a, and the *imaginary part* is b. These are written in the form

$$\mathrm{Re}[c] = \text{real part of } c = a$$

$$\mathrm{Im}[c] = \text{imaginary part of } c = b \tag{1.3}$$

If a, b, g, and h are real, then the complex numbers $(a + jb)$ and $(g + jh)$ may be added or multiplied according to the formulas

$$(a + jb) + (g + jh) = (a + g) + j(b + h)$$

$$(a + jb) \cdot (g + jh) = (ag - bh) + j(ah + bg) \tag{1.4}$$

The *complex conjugate* of a complex number c is denoted by

$$c^* = \mathrm{Re}[c] - j\,\mathrm{Im}[c]$$

For $c = (a + jb)$, then

$$cc^* = (a + jb)(a - jb)$$

$$= (a^2 + b^2) + j(ab - ab)$$

$$= a^2 + b^2 \tag{1.5}$$

Thus the product cc^* is always real.

The *absolute value* of c, written $|c|$, is defined to be

$$|c| = \sqrt{cc^*} \tag{1.6}$$

or

$$|a + jb| = \sqrt{a^2 + b^2} \tag{1.7}$$

Complex division is defined in the following manner:

$$\frac{a + jb}{g + jh} = \frac{a + jb}{g + jh}\,\frac{g - jh}{g - jh}$$

$$= \frac{ag + bh}{g^2 + h^2} + j\frac{bg - ah}{g^2 + h^2} \tag{1.8}$$

provided $g^2 + h^2 \neq 0$.

It is interesting to note that

$$\left|\frac{a+jb}{g+jh}\right| = \frac{|a+jb|}{|g+jh|} \tag{1.9}$$

That is, the absolute value of a quotient is equal to the quotient of the absolute values. The proof of this is left to the reader.

Euler's Relation

The following formula is known as Euler's relation:

$$e^{j\theta} = \exp(j\theta) = \cos\theta + j\sin\theta$$

It is used over and over again in this book. A proof of this relationship may be found in many standard texts on trigonometry or calculus, so it is not repeated here. For $\theta = \pi$, the relation may be written as

$$e^{j\pi} + 1 = 0$$

which surely is one of the most beautiful expressions in mathematics, linking five of the very basic quantities.

A complex number $(a+jb)$ may be put into *polar coordinates* r and θ according to the rule

$$r = |a+jb|$$

$$\theta = \arctan\left(\frac{b}{a}\right) \tag{1.10}$$

so that

$$a+jb = r\exp(j\theta) \tag{1.11}$$

Some of the important functions to be discussed will be complex valued functions of a complex variable. For example,

$$f(z) = z^2 + z + 1 \tag{1.12}$$

for $z = (x+jy)$ and x and y real could also be written as

$$f(x,y) = (x+jy)^2 + (x+jy) + 1$$

$$= (x^2 - y^2 + x + 1) + j(2xy + y) \tag{1.13}$$

Frequently it is convenient to speak of the *poles* and *zeroes* of the function $f(z)$. If $f(x)$ is a rational polynomial in z such that

$$f(z) = \frac{N(z)}{D(z)} \tag{1.14}$$

and $N(z)$ and $D(z)$ are polynomials in z, then the zeroes of $f(z)$ are the solutions of

$$N(z) = 0 \tag{1.15}$$

and the poles of $f(z)$ are the solutions of

$$D(z) = 0 \tag{1.16}$$

For example, if

$$f(z) = \frac{3z^2 - 15z + 18}{z^2 - 5z + 4} \tag{1.17}$$

Then the zeroes are 2 and 3 and poles are 1 and 4. The poles and zeroes of rational polynomial function with real coefficients determine the function to within a constant. Specifically, if $f(z)$ has real coefficients, the zeroes of $f(z)$ are $z_1^n, \ldots, z_N^n$, and the poles are $z_1^d, \ldots, z_D^d$, then there is a real coefficient c such that

$$f(z) = c \frac{\prod_{i=1}^{N}(z - z_i^n)}{\prod_{k=1}^{D}(z - z_k^d)} \tag{1.18}$$

The preceding example would then become

$$f(z) = \frac{3z^2 - 15z + 15}{z^2 - 5z + 4} = 3\frac{(z-2)(z-3)}{(z-1)(z-4)} \tag{1.19}$$

The famous fundamental theorem of arithmetic states that any polynomial such as $N(z)$ or $D(z)$ has solutions in the field of complex numbers.

1.3   THE FOURIER TRANSFORM

Fourier transformation is the principal tool used in this book. Though much of the required material on it is outlined in the following sections, it is recommended that a reader totally unfamiliar with it read a basic text on the subject, such as Hsu [1967].

The type of Fourier transformation most likely to be familiar to the reader is that which transforms the time function $x(t)$ into the frequency function $X(f)$ through the use of the following integral realtionship:

$$X(f) = \int_{-\infty}^{\infty} x(t) \exp(-j2\pi ft)\, dt \tag{1.20}$$

Sometimes this is written as

$$X(f) = F\big[x(t)\big] \tag{1.21}$$

The original independent variable is t for time, usually in seconds, and has the range $(-\infty, \infty)$. The new independent variable f is usually in units of hertz, abbreviated Hz. The range of f is also $(-\infty, \infty)$. Sometimes ω is used rather than f; the relationship between ω and f is given by

$$\omega = 2\pi f$$

The variable ω is in *radians* per unit time.

The dimensions of ω and f are both $1/t$. That is, when t is in seconds (usual case), then the dimensions of ω and f are the reciprocal of seconds. As will be seen, there is a tendency for the $X(f)$ function to have properties that are like the reciprocals of the corresponding properties of $x(t)$, and vice versa.

For an arbitrary $x(t)$, it does not follow that there will always be an $X(f)$. In fact, it is possible to exhibit large classes of functions which are not Fourier transformable. In practice this is not a serious problem. The functions dealt with in this book will be transformable.

The Fourier transform is reversible. The definition given above can be inverted to read

$$x(t) = \int_{-\infty}^{\infty} X(f) \exp(j2\pi ft)\, df \tag{1.22}$$

This relationship is occasionally written as

$$x(t) = F^{-1}\big[X(f)\big] \tag{1.23}$$

It would perhaps be better practice to denote the result of this equation as $\hat{x}(t)$, because there are pathological cases where $x(t)$, the original function, and $\hat{x}(t)$, the result of Fourier transforming $x(t)$ and then inverse transforming it, will yield a function $\hat{x}(t)$ that is slightly different from $x(t)$. In mathematical terminology, $x(t)$ and $\hat{x}(t)$ are equal *almost everywhere*. The "almost everywhere" means that there is a set of points on

which they disagree, but no interval on which they are not the same.*
Again, in the type of functions to be considered herein, the problem will
not be important.

If ω is employed rather than f, the above becomes

$$x(t) = \frac{1}{2\pi} \int_{-\infty}^{\infty} X(\omega) \exp(j\omega) \, d\omega \qquad (1.24)$$

Delta Functions

Delta functions are a topic that must be introduced in conjunction with the
Fourier transform. The delta functions $\delta(t)$ or $\delta(f)$ may be thought of as
functions that have infinite height, zero width, and unit area! When
presented in this manner they do not make good mathematical sense. Two
additions to their employment render them more rational:

1. Ultimately they should be employed within integrals.
2. They should be approximated by a sequence of functions which in the
   limit has the desired properties.

The first statement leads to a more mathematical definition of the delta
function:

$$x(t_0) = \int_{-\infty}^{\infty} x(t)\delta(t - t_0) \, dt \qquad (1.25)$$

Note that the left side of this equation is a constant. Thus the application of the delta function and integration on the right side may be viewed
as a process that evaluates $x(t)$ at a specific value t_0.

The sequence of functions referred to in the second statement above
could be of the form

$$d_i(t) = \begin{cases} i & -\frac{1}{2i} \leqslant t < \frac{1}{2i} \\ 0 & \text{elsewhere} \qquad i = 1, 2, \ldots \end{cases} \qquad (1.26)$$

This function has height i and width $1/i$. Because it is rectangular, its
area = height × width = $i \cdot (1/i) = 1$.

Define the sequence $x_i(t_0)$ by the integral

$$x_i(t_0) = \int_{-\infty}^{\infty} x(t)d_i(t - t_0) \, dt \qquad (1.27)$$

---

*This is not a precise definition of the almost everywhere terminology. For those interested in
these problems, Dym and McKean [1972] is recommended.

If this is examined, it will be found to simplify to

$$x_i(t_0) = i \int_{t_0 - 1/2i}^{t_0 + 1/2i} x(t) \, dt \qquad (1.28)$$

For reasonably well behaved $x(t)$ and large enough i, over the small interval $(t_0 - 1/2i, t_0 + 1/2i)$, $x(t)$ could be approximated by $x(t_0)$, the value at the center of the interval. Thus the preceding equation would become

$$x_i(t_0) \cong ix(t_0) \int_{t_0 - 1/2i}^{t_0 + 1/2i} dx = ix(t_0)t \Big|_{t_0 - 1/2i}^{t_0 + 1/2i} = x(t_0) \qquad (1.29)$$

When the above discussion is formalized, it is found that the sequence $x_i(t_0)$ in the limit will go to the value $x(t_0)$.

This is the type of procedure employed when formality is required. Note that the function $d_i(t)$, as defined above is not unique. There are many sequences that will work as well. For example, consider the sequence $e_i(t)$ defined by

$$e_i(t) = \begin{cases} 0 & t < -\dfrac{1}{i} \\[2mm] ti^2 + i & -\dfrac{1}{i} \leqslant t < 0 \\[2mm] -ti^2 + i & 0 \leqslant t < \dfrac{1}{i} \\[2mm] 0 & \dfrac{1}{i} \leqslant t \end{cases} \qquad (1.30)$$

This, when plotted, is found to be an equilateral triangle with height i and base $2/i$. As before, the area of each triangle in the sequence is unity.

Rather than using such sequences and limiting procedures, the integral definition given above is employed in subsequent analysis.

The first application of delta functions is their use in the frequency domain. Suppose it is desired to inverse transform $\delta(f - f_0)$. This would be written and computed as follows:

$$\int_{-\infty}^{\infty} \delta(f - f_0) \exp(j2\pi ft) \, df = \exp(j2\pi f_0 t) \qquad (1.31)$$

That is, the delta function evaluates the exponential at the constant f_0. This resulting inverse transform is a complex function of time. If Euler's relation is applied, the result becomes

$$\exp(j2\pi f_0 t) = \cos 2\pi f_0 t + j\sin 2\pi f_0 t \tag{1.32}$$

From this it is straightforward to find the Fourier transforms of $\cos 2\pi f_0 t$ and $\sin 2\pi f_0 t$. This is done by first finding the inverse Fourier transform of $\delta(f+f_0)$:

$$\int_{-\infty}^{\infty} \delta(f+f_0)\exp(j2\pi ft)\,df = \exp(-j2\pi f_0 t)$$

$$= \cos 2\pi f_0 t - j\sin 2\pi f_0 t \tag{1.33}$$

Next, consider taking the inverse Fourier of the sum of two delta functions:

$$\int_{-\infty}^{\infty} \frac{\delta(f-f_0)+\delta(f+f_0)}{2}\exp(j2\pi ft)\,df$$

$$= \tfrac{1}{2}(\cos 2\pi f_0 t + j\sin 2\pi f_0 t) + \tfrac{1}{2}(\cos 2\pi f_0 t - j\sin 2\pi f_0 t)$$

$$= \cos 2\pi f_0 t \tag{1.34}$$

That is, the Fourier transform of $\cos(2\pi f_0 t)$ is the two delta functions $\delta(f-f_0)$ and $\delta(f+f_0)$, each multiplied by $\tfrac{1}{2}$. Note that this function is real; the j does not appear.

Figure 1.1 is a representation of this transform. Delta functions are usually shown as arrows, because it is not possible to plot their infinite heights. Also, their multipliers are usually placed to one side.

The implication of this plot is that a cosine wave in the time domain goes into two delta functions in the frequency domain, and that the delta functions are located at the frequency plus and minus, corresponding to the frequency of the cosine. That is, all the information about $\cos 2\pi f_0 t$ when it is transformed to the frequency domain is concentrated at $\pm f_0$ Hz.

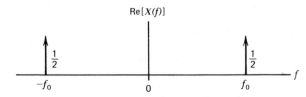

Figure 1.1   The Fourier transform of a cosine function.

If a similar procedure is followed for $\sin 2\pi f_0 t$, its transform is found to be

$$\frac{\delta(f-f_0)-\delta(f+f_0)}{2j} \tag{1.35}$$

The transforms of $\cos 2\pi f_0 t$ and $\sin 2\pi f_0 t$ should be compared in detail by the reader. The following points will be observed:

1. The transform of $\cos 2\pi f_0 t$ is completely real, whereas that of $\sin 2\pi f_0 t$ is completely imaginary.
2. Both transforms are composed of delta functions centered at f_0 and $-f_0$ Hz.
3. The cosine transform is symmetric, whereas the sine transform is antisymmetric (see below for definition).

Taking a somewhat different but related tack, consider the inverse transform of $\delta(f)$:

$$\int_{-\infty}^{\infty} \delta(f)\exp(j2\pi ft)\,dt=\exp(0)=1 \tag{1.36}$$

That is, the Fourier transform of a constant is a delta function at 0 Hz. The same fact could be observed by setting f_0 equal to zero in the Fourier transform of $\cos 2\pi f_0 t$.

Symmetric and Antisymmetric Functions

A function $x(t)$ is *symmetric* (or *even*) if

$$x(t)=x(-t) \tag{1.37}$$

Similarly, $x(t)$ is *antisymmetric* (or *odd*) if

$$x(t)=-x(-t) \tag{1.38}$$

Any real function can be broken into two separate functions, one of which is symmetric and the other of which is antisymmetric. For example, suppose that $x_s(t)$ and $x_a(t)$ are the symmetric and antisymmetric parts of $x(t)$. Then they can be computed from

$$x(t)=x_s(t)+x_a(t)$$
$$x(-t)=x_s(t)-x_a(t) \tag{1.39}$$

Solving these yields

$$x_s(t) = \frac{x(t) + x(-t)}{2}$$

$$x_a(t) = \frac{x(t) - x(-t)}{2} \tag{1.40}$$

For example, if $x(t)$ is a cubic in t,

$$x(t) = a_0 + a_1 t + a_2 t^2 + a_3 t^3 \tag{1.41}$$

then

$$x(-t) = a_0 - a_1 t + a_2 t^2 - a_3 t^3 \tag{1.42}$$

so that

$$x_s(t) = a_0 + a_2 t^2$$

$$x_a(t) = a_1 t + a_3 t^3 \tag{1.43}$$

If the function $x(t)$ is written as $x_s(t) + x_a(t)$ and the exponential in the Fourier transform is written as $(\cos 2\pi ft - j\sin 2\pi ft)$, then the definition of the transform can be rewritten as follows:

$$X(f) = \int_{-\infty}^{\infty} x(t) \exp(-j2\pi ft)\, dt$$

$$= \int_{-\infty}^{\infty} [x_s(t) + x_a(t)][\cos 2\pi ft - j\sin 2\pi ft]\, df$$

$$= \int_{-\infty}^{\infty} x_s(t) \cos 2\pi ft\, dt + \int_{-\infty}^{\infty} x_a(t) \cos 2\pi ft\, dt$$

$$-j\int_{-\infty}^{\infty} x_s(t)\sin 2\pi ft\, dt - j\int_{-\infty}^{\infty} x_a(t)\sin 2\pi ft\, dt \tag{1.44}$$

Three additional facts are needed here:

1. The integral of an antisymmetric function is 0.
2. The product of two symmetric or of two antisymmetric functions is symmetric.
3. The product of an antisymmetric and a symmetric function is antisymmetric.

From the above it can be seen that the products $x_a(t)\cos 2\pi ft$ and $x_s(t)\sin 2\pi ft$ are antisymmetric, and hence their integrals are 0. Thus

$$\int_{-\infty}^{\infty} x(t)\exp(-j2\pi ft)\,dt = \int_{-\infty}^{\infty} x_s(t)\cos 2\pi ft\,dt$$

$$-j\int_{-\infty}^{\infty} x_a(t)\sin 2\pi ft\,dt \qquad (1.45)$$

Finally, if $x(t)$ is symmetric so that $x_a(t)=0$ for all t, then this last result reduces to

$$\int_{-\infty}^{\infty} x(t)\exp(-j2\pi ft)\,dt = \int_{-\infty}^{\infty} x(t)\cos 2\pi ft\,dt \qquad (1.46)$$

The reason for emphasizing this is that the transforms of symmetric functions are always real, and also may be written as a cosine transform. Both these points are used extensively in examples. In particular, it is much easier to examine the transforms of symmetric functions because they are real functions themselves and hence much easier to plot.

Important Fourier Transform Relationships

Tables 1.1 and 1.2 summarize those properties of the Fourier transform that are important in this work. They form only a small portion of the total Fourier transform theorem type of information that is currently available in the literature, but they are sufficient to solve the problems to be encountered.

Relationship 4 in Table 1.1 is going to be used quite heavily, so it is worthwhile looking at its derivation. Suppose as usual that $X(f)$ is the Fourier transform of $x(t)$, and that it is desired to find the transform of $x(t-t_0)$, that is, $x(t)$ delayed or shifted by an amount t_0. The definition of the transform is

$$F[x(t-t_0)] = \int_{-\infty}^{\infty} x(t-t_0)\exp(-j2\pi ft)\,dt \qquad (1.47)$$

If the substitution $\tau = t - t_0$ is made, then $d\tau = dt$ and the above becomes

$$F[x(t-t_0)] = \int_{-\infty}^{\infty} x(\tau)\exp[-j2\pi f(\tau + t_0)]\,d\tau \qquad (1.48)$$

The infinite limits do not change because they are shifted only by a finite amount t_0.

The exponential term involving t_0 can be factored outside the integral to

Table 1.1
Fourier Transform—Functional Relationships

Function	Fourier Transform
1. $x(t)$	$X(f)$
$F^{-1}[X(f)]$	$F[x(t)]$
$\int_{-\infty}^{\infty} X(f)\exp(j2\pi ft)\,df$	$\int_{-\infty}^{\infty} x(t)\exp(-j2\pi ft)\,dt$
2. $y(t)$	$Y(f)$
3. $x(t)y(t)$	$\int_{-\infty}^{\infty} X(\eta)Y(f-\eta)\,d\eta$
$\int_{-\infty}^{\infty} x(\tau)y(t-\tau)\,d\tau$	$X(f)Y(f)$
4. $x(t-t_0)$	$X(f)e^{-j2\pi ft_0}$
$x(t)e^{j2\pi f_0 t}$	$X(f-f_0)$
5. $\dfrac{dx(t)}{dt}$	$j2\pi f X(f)$
6. $\int_{-\infty}^{t} x(\tau)\,d\tau$	$\dfrac{1}{j\omega} X(f)$ provided $X(0)=0$
7. $\int_{-\infty}^{\infty} x^2(t)\,dt$	$\int_{-\infty}^{\infty} \lvert X(f)\rvert^2\,df$
	(Parseval's relation)

Table 1.2
Fourier Transform—Specific Transform Paris

$x(t)$	$X(f)$
1. $x(t)=\begin{cases} 1 & -P/2 \leqslant t < P/2 \\ 0 & \text{otherwise} \end{cases}$	$\dfrac{\sin \pi fP}{\pi f}$
2. $\cos 2\pi f_0 t$	$\tfrac{1}{2}[\delta(f-f_0)+\delta(f+f_0)]$
3. $\sin 2\pi f_0 t$	$\dfrac{1}{2j}[\delta(f-f_0)-\delta(f+f_0)]$
4. $x(t)=\begin{cases} 1 & t \geqslant 0 \\ 0 & t<0 \end{cases}$	$\dfrac{1}{2}\delta(f)+\dfrac{1}{j2\pi f}$
5. $x(t)=1$ all t	$\delta(f)$
6. $x(t)=\delta(t)$	$X(f)=1$ all f
7. $\exp(j2\pi f_0 t)$	$\delta(f-f_0)$
8. $\exp\left(\dfrac{-t^2}{2a^2}\right)$	$\sqrt{2\pi a^2}\,\exp\left(\dfrac{-(2\pi fa)^2}{2}\right)$
9. $\dfrac{2\sin 2\pi Bt}{2\pi t}$	$X(f)=\begin{cases} 1 & -B \leqslant f < B \\ 0 & \text{otherwise} \end{cases}$

yield

$$F[x(t-t_0)] = \exp(-j2\pi f t_0) \int_{-\infty}^{\infty} x(\tau) \exp(-j2\pi f \tau) d\tau$$

$$= \exp(-j2\pi f t_0) X(f) \qquad (1.49)$$

That is, after the exponential term is factored out, the remaining integral is simply the definition of $X(f)$.

In summary, a delay in the time domain corresponds to multiplying by a complex exponential in the frequency domain. This fact is the single most important Fourier theorem when dealing with sampled data.

1.4   THE BOXCAR FUNCTION AND ITS FOURIER TRANSFORM

Transform pair 1 in Table 1.2 is also worth special consideration. As used in this book, it is denoted by $u(t)$ in the time domain, and defined by

$$u(t) = \begin{cases} 1 & -\dfrac{P}{2} \leqslant t < \dfrac{P}{2} \\ 0 & \text{otherwise} \end{cases} \qquad (1.50)$$

As shown in Figure 1.2a, it has a rectangular shape, symmetric about $u(t)$ axis, and is of width P sec.

The derivation of its Fourier transform $U(f)$ is straightforward:

$$U(f) = \int_{-\infty}^{\infty} u(t) \exp(-j2\pi f t) dt$$

$$= \int_{-P/2}^{P/2} \exp(-j2\pi f t) dt$$

$$= \frac{1}{-j2\pi f} \exp(-j2\pi f t) \Big|_{-P/2}^{P/2}$$

$$= \frac{\sin \pi f P}{\pi f} \qquad (1.51)$$

This turns out to be symmetric. It is the product of the two antisymmetric functions $\sin \pi f P$ and $1/\pi f$. The maximum value occurs at $f=0$. This

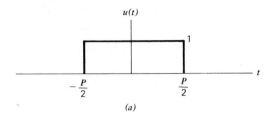

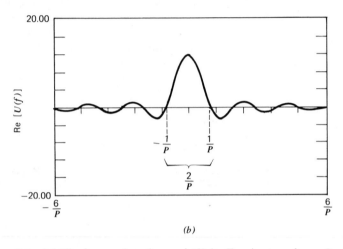

Figure 1.2   (a) The boxcar function and (b) its Fourier transform, $P = 12$.

can be found through the use of L'Hospital's rule:

$$\lim_{f \to 0} \frac{\sin \pi f P}{\pi f} = \lim_{f \to 0} \frac{d/df(\sin \pi f P)}{d/df(\pi f)}$$

$$= \lim_{f \to 0} \frac{\pi P \cos \pi f P}{\pi}$$

$$= P \qquad (1.52)$$

The first zero crossings occur at

$$\pi f P = \pm \pi$$

or

$$f = \pm \frac{1}{P} \qquad (1.53)$$

Thus the width of the central lobe is $2/P$, so that the width in the frequency domain is inversely proportional to the width in the time domain.

This inverse property between the two domains may be best observed by looking at three more transform pairs in Table 1.2.

1. In transform pair 5, the constant 1, which is infinitely broad, is transformed into a delta function in frequency domain. The latter is infinitely narrow.
2. Conversely, pair 6 shows that a delta function in the time domain, again infinitely narrow, is transformed into a constant in the frequency domain, which is infinitely broad.
3. Pair 8 shows that a bell-shaped curve in the time domain goes into a bell-shaped curve in the frequency domain. If the two points of inflection on each curve are taken to be the width of each of them, the time domain curve has width $2a$, and the frequency domain curve has width $1/\pi a$, so that the two widths are inversely proportional.

1.5 LINEAR SYSTEMS

This section is concerned with functions $x(t)$ and $y(t)$ that have a *linear relationship* between them. In particular, functional relationships of the form

$$D^{(1)}[y(t)] = D^{(2)}[x(t)] \qquad (1.54)$$

where $D^{(1)}$ and $D^{(2)}$ are linear differential operators are considered. For example, $D^{(1)}$ might be of the form

$$D^{(1)} = \left[a\frac{d^2}{dt} + b\frac{d}{dt} + c \right] \qquad (1.55)$$

A similar expression is assumed to hold for $x(t)$. This means that $x(t)$ and $y(t)$ are related by a *linear differential equation with constant coefficients*.

As discussed below, there are two more ways of expressing the same relationship. They involve the definition of the *impulse response function*, and its Fourier transform, the transfer function.

A specific example will help illustrate these terms. Suppose the relationship is defined by the equation

$$\frac{d^2y(t)}{dt} + 2\zeta\omega_n\frac{dy(t)}{dt} + \omega_n^2 y(t) = x(t) \qquad (1.56)$$

Here

$$D^{(1)} = \left[\frac{d^2}{dt} + 2\zeta\omega_n \frac{d}{dt} + \omega_n^2 \right] \qquad (1.57)$$

and

$$D^{(2)} = 1$$

The Fourier transform of this equation may be taken using the relations in Table 1.1 and found to be

$$(2\pi f)^2 Y(f) + (j2\pi f)2\zeta\omega_n Y(f) + \omega_n^2 Y(f) = X(f) \qquad (1.58)$$

where $X(f)$ and $Y(f)$ are the Fourier transforms of $x(t)$ and $y(t)$, respectively. Letting $\omega_n = 2\pi f_n$, factoring out the $Y(f)$ terms, and rearranging yield

$$H(f) = \frac{Y(f)}{X(f)} = \frac{1}{\omega_n^2 \left[1 - \left(\frac{f}{f_n} \right)^2 + \frac{j2\zeta f}{f_n} \right]} \qquad (1.59)$$

The ratio $Y(f)/X(f)$ for any linear system is defined to be the *transfer function* between the two functions and is denoted by $H(f)$.

Alternatively, the relationship may be expressed by saying that there is a *filter* operating between $x(t)$ and $y(t)$: $y(t)$ is *filtered* $x(t)$, and $H(f)$ is the transfer function of the filter.

The gain of the filter is the absolute value of the transfer function. In this example the expression for the gain is

$$|H(f)| = \left| \frac{Y(f)}{X(f)} \right| = \frac{1}{\omega_n^2 \sqrt{\left[1 - \left(\frac{f}{f_n} \right)^2 \right]^2 + \left(\frac{2\zeta f}{f_n} \right)^2}} \qquad (1.60)$$

This *phase angle* or simply the *phase* of the transfer function is defined to be the function $\varphi(f)$ given by

$$\varphi(f) = \arctan\left[\frac{\text{Im}[H(f)]}{\text{Re}[H(f)]} \right] \qquad (1.61)$$

$\varphi(f)$ as defined is in radians. It is very often converted to degrees by multiplying by $180/\pi$, in which case it is denoted as $\varphi_d(f)$.

For the example under consideration,

$$\varphi(f) = \arctan\left(-\frac{2\zeta f/f_n}{1-(f/f_n)^2}\right) \tag{1.62}$$

Figure 1.3 shows plots of the gain and phase of this filter for $f_n = 100$ and $\zeta = 0.1$. The gain function for this example peaks at about 100 Hz. Actually, the maximum occurs at the frequency f_p, often referred to as the *peak frequency*, and given by

$$f_p = f_n\sqrt{1-2\zeta^2} \tag{1.63}$$

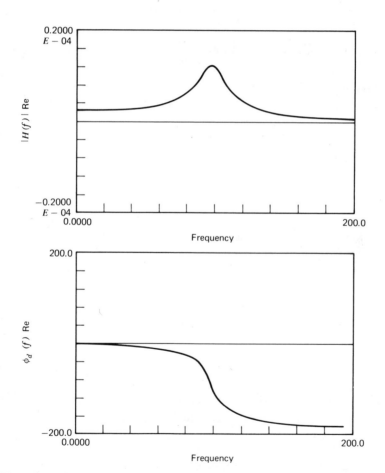

Figure 1.3 Gain and phase of the filter defined by (4.1) for $f_n = 100$ and $\zeta = 0.1$. The subscript d on the phase indicates degrees.

For this example, $f_p = 100\sqrt{1 - .02} \approx 98.99$ Hz. For ζ close to 0, which is often the case in physical systems, f_p and f_n are nearly alike.

The definition of the transfer function could be written in the form

$$|Y(f)| = |H(f)| \cdot |X(f)| \tag{1.64}$$

which emphasizes that the absolute value of the Fourier transform of $y(t)$ is the simple product of the absolute value of the Fourier transform of $y(t)$ and the absolute value of $H(f)$. Taking the inverse Fourier transform of $Y(f) = H(f)X(f)$ yields the *convolution* of $x(t)$ and a new $h(t)$ function which is the inverse Fourier transform of $H(f)$.

$$y(t) = \int_{-\infty}^{\infty} h(\tau)x(t - \tau)\,d\tau \tag{1.65}$$

In the example, $h(t)$ is found from

$$h(t) = \int_{-\infty}^{\infty} e^{j2\pi ft} \frac{1}{\omega_n^2 \left[1 - \left(\dfrac{f}{f_n} \right)^2 + j2\zeta \dfrac{f}{f_n} \right]} \, df$$

$$= \begin{cases} 0 & t < 0 \\ \dfrac{1}{2\pi f_n \sqrt{1 - \zeta^2}} e^{-2\pi f_n \zeta t} \sin\left(2\pi f_n \sqrt{1 - \zeta^2}\, t \right) & t \geqslant 0 \end{cases} \tag{1.66}$$

This function, the inverse Fourier transform of $H(f)$, is often referred to as the *impulse response function*. If $x(t)$ is a delta function, then $y(t)$ is equal to $h(t)$.

Thus, in terms of the convolution integral,

$$y(t) = \frac{1}{2\pi f_n \sqrt{1 - \zeta^2}} \int_0^t e^{-2\pi f_n \zeta \tau} \sin 2\pi f_n \sqrt{1 - \zeta^2}\; \tau \cdot x(t - \tau)\, d\tau \tag{1.67}$$

The finite limits occur because both $h(t)$ and $x(t)$ are taken to be 0 for negative t in this case.

At this point it is best to stop and summarize the results. If $x(t)$ and $y(t)$ are related by a linear differential equation, then there exist functions $h(t)$ and $H(f)$ such that

1. $H(f)$ is the Fourier transform of $h(t)$.

2. In the frequency domain, $Y(f) = H(f)X(f)$.
3. In the time domain,

$$y(t) = \int_{-\infty}^{\infty} h(\tau)x(t-\tau)\, d\tau$$

4. If $x(t) = \delta(t)$, then $y(t) = h(t)$.
5. The original differential equation equivalently may be expressed as an integral equation.

1.6 CONVOLUTION AND CAUSALITY

In the preceding section it was noted that when $y(t)$ and $x(t)$ are related by a linear operator such as a linear, constant coefficient, differential equation, then there exists a function $h(t)$ such that

$$y(t) = \int_{-\infty}^{\infty} h(\tau)x(t-\tau)\, d\tau \tag{1.68}$$

This type of integral has a special name, *convolution*. A standard non-mathematical definition of that term is "a winding or coiling together."

In order to see what is happening, suppose it is desired to evaluate $y(t)$ at $t = t_0$:

$$y(t_0) = \int_{-\infty}^{\infty} h(\tau)x(t_0-\tau)\, d\tau \tag{1.69}$$

Furthermore, suppose that specific functions are taken for $h(t)$ and $x(t)$:

$$x(t) = \begin{cases} t & t \geq 0 \\ 0 & t < 0 \end{cases}$$

$$h(t) = \begin{cases} 2 & t \geq 0 \\ 0 & t < 0 \end{cases} \tag{1.70}$$

These are shown in Figure 1.4a; Figure 1.4b shows the two functions in the τ domain. As would be expected, $h(\tau)$ appears identical to $h(t)$. On the other hand, $x(t_0-\tau)$ is reversed on its axis and shifted t_0 units (t_0 is assumed to be positive in this example). The one value $y(t_0)$ would be computed by multiplying the two functions as shown and then integrating them.

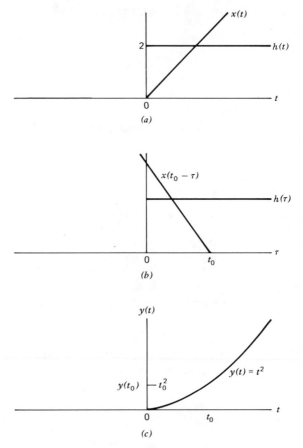

Figure 1.4 Computation of the convolution of $h(t)$ and $x(t)$ at t_0 as given in the example. (*a*) The original functions. (*b*) The functions in the τ domain. $x(t)$ is reversed and shifted t_0 units. (*c*) The complete result of convolving $x(t)$ and $h(t)$ in the example.

This integration would be performed as follows:

$$y(t_0) = \int_0^{t_0} 2(t_0 - \tau)\, d\tau$$

$$= 2t_0\tau - \tau^2 \Big|_0^{t_0} = 2t_0^2 - t_0^2 = t_0^2 \tag{1.71}$$

and in fact, for any t, $y(t) = t^2$ for the functions specified in this example. The resulting $y(t)$ is plotted as Figure 1.4c.

An important theorem about convolution is that it is commutative. This means that the roles of $x(t)$ and $h(t)$ in the definition may be reversed.

$$y(t) = \int_{-\infty}^{\infty} h(\tau)x(t-\tau)\,d\tau$$

$$= \int_{-\infty}^{\infty} h(t-\tau)x(\tau)\,d\tau \qquad (1.72)$$

There is a dual rule with respect to multiplication of functions in the time domain. If $y(t)$ is now defined to be the product of $h(t)$ and $x(t)$, then the Fourier transforms of $h(t)$, $x(t)$, and $y(t)$ are related by convolution in the frequency domain. That is, if

$$y(t) = h(t)x(t)$$

then

$$Y(f) = \int_{-\infty}^{\infty} H(\eta)X(f-\eta)\,d\eta$$

$$= \int_{-\infty}^{\infty} H(f-\eta)X(\eta)\,d\eta \qquad (1.73)$$

This relationship will be found to be important in studying the implications of finite testing. By a *test* we mean conducting an experiment or test (e.g., structural vibration test) in which time series data is recorded by some method for subsequent analysis.

Changing the topic back to that of differential equations which result in impulse response functions, we note there is a condition that must be put upon $h(t)$ to make it correspond to many physical situations, namely, that of making $h(t)$ *causal*. This is done by restricting $h(t)$ to be nonzero only for time greater than or equal to 0. That is,

$$h(t) = \begin{cases} 0 & t < 0 \\ \text{whatever} & t \geqslant 0 \end{cases} \qquad (1.74)$$

This condition is equivalent to requiring that $y(t)$ does not show a response before there is input from $x(t)$.

1.7   THE EFFECTS OF FINITE SAMPLE LENGTH

Most of the functions discussed so far are defined for an infinite span of time, and therefore would correspond to a test of infinite duration.

Because testing can not be done for an infinite length of time, it is quite natural to ask, what is the effect of finite record length?

Perhaps the most thorough answer to this question is found in a paper by Dennis Gabor [1946], who is perhaps better known for his work on holography.

Finite record length is modeled here through the use of the boxcar function $u(t)$. Suppose $x(t)$ is defined for the interval $-\infty < t < \infty$, and that its Fourier transform is $X(f)$. If observation were restricted to the finite segment $-P/2 \le t \le P/2$, then this truncation of the $x(t)$ function could be represented by a new function $x_P(t)$, where

$$x_P(t) = x(t)u(t) \tag{1.75}$$

That is, by multiplying by the boxcar function, the resulting function $x_P(t)$ is 0 outside the range $-P/2 \le t < P/2$, and hence corresponds to a sample of length P.

The Fourier transform of $u(t)$ is known, and that of $x(t)$ is assumed to have been given. From these it is possible to derive a functional form for $x_P(t)$. Because $x_P(t)$ is the product of two functions in the time domain, then its Fourier transform, according to formula 3 in Table 1.1, must be the convolution in the frequency domain of $X(f)$ and $U(f)$. Denoting $X_P(f)$ as the Fourier transform of $x_P(t)$, we have

$$F[x_P(t)] = X_P(f) = \int_{-\infty}^{\infty} X(\eta)U(f-\eta)\,d\eta$$

$$= \int_{-\infty}^{\infty} X(\eta)\frac{\sin\pi(f-\eta)P}{\pi(f-\eta)}\,d\eta$$

$$= \int_{-\infty}^{\infty} X(f-\eta)\frac{\sin\pi\eta P}{\pi\eta}\,d\eta \tag{1.76}$$

Therefore, in general, the effect of having a finite record length is equivalent to convolving the original infinite length transform with a $(\sin x)/x$ function. As will be seen, this results in "smearing."

Consider the important example of a cosine wave with unit amplitude and frequency f_0. Its Fourier transform for the infinite span $(-\infty, \infty)$ was found to be

$$X(f) = \frac{1}{2}\left[\delta(f-f_0) + \delta(f+f_0)\right] \tag{1.77}$$

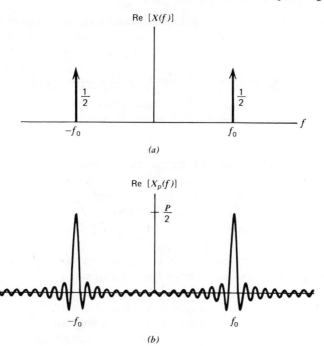

Figure 1.5 Fourier transform of the function $\cos 2\pi f_0 t$. (*a*) No truncation. (*b*) With truncation at $-P/2, P/2$.

The Fourier transform of the truncated record of the cosine is therefore

$$\int_{-\infty}^{\infty} \frac{1}{2}\left[\delta(f-f_0)+\delta(f+f_0)\right] \frac{\sin\pi(f-\eta)P}{\pi(f-\eta)} d\eta$$

$$= \frac{\sin\pi(f-f_0)P}{2\pi(f-f_0)} + \frac{\sin\pi(f+f_0)P}{2\pi(f+f_0)} \qquad (1.78)$$

This is shown in Figure 1.5. Part *a* of the figure shows the original delta functions, and part *b* shows the delta functions convolved with the $(\sin x)/x$ functions induced by the truncation of the infinite record length. The following should be noted:

1. The $(\sin x)/x$ functions are centered about $\pm f_0$, so that the maxima* are located at $\pm f_0$. That is, most of the information is still concentrated near $\pm f_0$ Hz.

*This is an approximation, because the tail of one $(\sin x)/x$ function is added on top of the main lobe of the other, thus distorting the shape. For large enough P, this is not serious.

2. On the other hand, $X_P(f)$ is nonzero except at crossover points. This is the smearing effect. Rather than being concentrated at $\pm f_0$ Hz, the information is smeared out into the whole frequency range.
3. The height of each main lobe of the $(\sin x)/x$ function is $P/2$, whereas its width is $2/P$. Thus as the length of record is made larger, so that P is increased, the heights of the main lobes increase and their widths decrease. In the limit as P goes to infinity, the $(\sin x)/x$ functions become delta functions.

An infinitely long sinusoid function can be said to have a pure tone, in that all of its information is concentrated at the two delta functions. A finite record length of the sinusoid is smeared by convolution with the $(\sin x)/x$, so that it is not a pure tone. Thus any practical test will have frequency information which is smeared relative to the infinite record length models.

Another effect of finite record length is the uncertainty in measuring the frequency. Because the information has been smeared, it is not possible in practice to find the exact maxima of the main lobe, and hence an estimate of the frequency of a finite sample of a sinusoid cannot be exact.* Clearly, the uncertainty depends on both the record length and the frequency of the sinusoid. Higher frequencies are easier to resolve because there is less interference between the two $(\sin x)/x$ functions when they are well separated.

1.8   SAMPLED DATA AND THE NYQUIST FREQUENCY

The term *sampled data* as employed here means data that is sampled at equal interval T, where T is in seconds. The sampled function $x(i)$ is related to its continuous counterpart through the equation

$$x(i) = \int_{-\infty}^{\infty} x(\tau)\delta(iT - \tau)\, d\tau \qquad (1.79)$$

The sampled function $x(i)$ thus consists of a sequence of discrete values corresponding to the time value iT.

The Fourier transform of $x(i)$ is also denoted by $X(f)$, but the definition

---

*If there are no other signals or noise present, then three equidistant points are sufficient to determine the frequency: $f = \dfrac{1}{2\pi T} \arccos\{[x(t) + x(t - 2T)]/2x(t - T)\}$ is exact provided that $x(t - T) \neq 0$ and that the sample values are exact.

is different for the sampled data case

$$X(f) = T \sum_{i=-\infty}^{\infty} x(i) \exp(-j2\pi f i T) \qquad (1.80)$$

This definition could be thought of as an approximation to the earlier definition, but it is probably better to think of both of them as being two forms of the same transformation (there are two more for a total of four; see Otnes and Enochson [1972, p. 12]).

One of the major problems with sampling is the phenomenon of *aliasing*. If a sinusoid whose frequency is greater than $1/2T$ is sampled at interval T, it appears as a lower frequency. That is, rather than appearing at its true frequency, it appears at its aliased (lower) frequency. As an illustration of this, consider

$$x(t) = \sin 2\pi f_0 t$$

with

$$f_0 = \frac{p+q}{2T} \qquad (1.81)$$

where p is an integer, and q is a fractional part less than one. For example, suppose $T = 0.005$, and $f_0 = 1025$ Hz. Then

$$\frac{1}{2T} = 100$$

$$p = 10 \qquad (1.82)$$

$$q = 0.25$$

The $x(t)$ term could be expanded by substituting the above for f_0 and iT for t to yield

$$\sin 2\pi f_0 t = \sin 2\pi \left(\frac{p+q}{2T} \right)(iT)$$

$$= \sin \pi (p+q)i$$

$$= \sin \pi p i \cos \pi q i + \cos \pi p i \sin \pi q i$$

$$= \cos \pi p i \sin \pi q i \qquad (1.83)$$

because $\sin \pi p i = 0$ for all i.

There are now two possibilities depending on whether p is even or odd:

1.   If p is even, then $\cos\pi pi = 1$ for all i, so that

$$x(i) = \sin\pi qi$$

2.   For p odd,

$$x(i) = (-1)^i \sin\pi qi$$

In the first case, the reduced angle πqi could be rewritten as

$$\pi qi = \pi qi\,\frac{2T}{2T} = 2\pi\left(\frac{q}{2T}\right)iT \tag{1.84}$$

so that the effective frequency would be $q/2T$, defined to be f_0'.

In the example given above, p is 10 and hence even, so the reduced frequency is $(0.25)(100) = 25$ Hz. This means that a sine wave at frequency 1025 Hz when sampled at interval $T = 0.005$, or 200 sps (samples per second), would be indistinguishable from a sine wave at 25 Hz!

The frequency $1/2T$ plays a special role in digital data, so hereafter it is designated by the special symbol F (for *folding*):

$$F = \frac{1}{2T} = \frac{S}{2} \tag{1.85}$$

where S is the sampling rate in samples per second. It is often referred to as the *Nyquist folding frequency* in honor of Nyquist, who wrote a major article on the subject [Nyquist, 1924].

Returning to the second case above where p is odd, we have

$$x(i) = (-1)^i \sin\pi qi = \cos\pi i \sin\pi qi$$

$$= \cos\pi i \sin\pi qi - \sin\pi i \cos\pi qi$$

$$= -\sin(\pi i - \pi qi) = -\sin\pi i(1 - q) \tag{1.86}$$

If the numerator and denominator are multiplied by $2T$, the angle becomes

$$\pi i(1 - q) = \pi i(1 - q)\frac{2T}{2T}$$

$$= 2\pi\left(\frac{1}{2T} - \frac{q}{2T}\right)iT$$

$$= 2\pi(F - f_0')iT \tag{1.87}$$

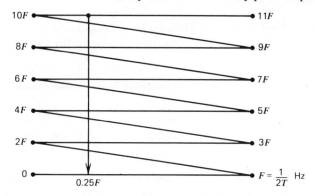

Figure 1.6   The first 11 pleats of a Nyquist aliasing diagram.

Thus, rather than being referenced to 0 Hz, odd cases are referenced to the folding frequency.

Figure 1.6 shows these results in the form of a folding diagram. The frequency axis is folded back onto the range 0–F Hz in pieces of length F Hz. To show how this works the example given above is illustrated: 1025 Hz with a sampling rate of 200 sps corresponds to 10.25F. This drops down to appear as 0.25F, as would 1.75F, 2.25F, 3.75F, 4.25F, 5.75F, 6.25F, 7.75F, 8.25F, 9.75F, etc.

It is often quite helpful to draw up such a diagram for a particular test in order to discover from where a given signal might be aliased. Suppose, employing the same example, that a sinusoid appeared at 80 Hz, which could not be explained by the known physical situation. In this example, with $F = 100$ Hz, a signal to 80 Hz could have been one at 120 Hz* which was aliased so as to appear at the lower value.

The Sampling Theorem

A major question that arises when sampling a time function is, how well does the set of sampled data represent the original function? The answer, as supplied by the *sampling theorem*, is very well if certain specifications are met. The theorem is essentially due to Shannon [1949].

These specifications, stated as hypotheses, are as follows:

Hypotheses

1. $x(t)$ is defined for $-\infty < t < \infty$.

---

*For many applications, 110-V, 60-Hz AC is converted to DC through the use of a power supply. Typically these devices use full wave rectification which changes to AC to DC plus harmonics of 120 Hz, with the harmonic of 120 Hz having the largest amplitude. If these are not properly removed, they may appear in the data.

2. $X(f)$, the Fourier transform of $x(t)$ exists.

3. $X(f)$ is bandlimited in the sense that $|X(f)|=0$ for $|f|>F$ Hz.

If these conditions are met, then the following may be stated:

Conclusion

Let T' be any sampling interval such that $T' \leqslant 1/2F$. Then $x(t)$ can be reconstructed uniquely from the sequence $x(i)$, with disagreement, if any, occurring at isolated points.

The proof is not given here, but the basic ideas come from the fact that because $X(f)$ exists, then the set of $x(i)$ defined by

$$x(i)=\int_{-F}^{F} X(f)\exp(j2\pi fiT)\,df \qquad (1.88)$$

are sufficient so that $X(f)$ can be created from them:

$$X(f)=T \sum_{i=-\infty}^{\infty} x(i)\exp(-j2\pi fiT) \qquad (1.89)$$

As $X(f)$ can be reconstructed from the $x(i)$ terms, then $x(t)$ can be reconstructed from the $x(i)$ sequence. The expression for $x(i)$ can be viewed as a convolution in the time domain corresponding to the multiplication in the frequency domain of $X(f)$ by a boxcar function:

$$
\begin{aligned}
x(t) &= \int_{-F}^{F} X(f)\exp(j2\pi fiT)\,df \\[2mm]
&= \int_{-F}^{F} T \sum_{i=-\infty}^{\infty} x(i)\exp(-j2\pi fiT)\exp(j2\pi ft)\,df \\[2mm]
&= T \sum_{i=-\infty}^{\infty} x(i)\int_{-F}^{F} \exp\big[j2\pi f(t-iT)\big]\,df \\[2mm]
&= T \sum_{i=-\infty}^{\infty} x(i)\frac{2\sin\big[2\pi F(t-iT)\big]}{2\pi(t-iT)} \qquad (1.90)
\end{aligned}
$$

Note that if $t=kT$, then

$$\frac{2\sin\big[2\pi F(kT-iT)\big]}{2\pi(kT-iT)} = \begin{cases} 2F & i=k \\ 0 & i\neq k \end{cases} \qquad (1.91)$$

so that

$$x(kT) = Tx(k)2F = x(k) \tag{1.92}$$

Thus the derived expression for $x(t)$ agrees exactly with $x(i)$ when $t = iT$. In between, it acts as an interpolation scheme which reconstructs $x(t)$ from all the $x(i)$. As would be expected, the $x(i)$ terms for i corresponding to being near t are more heavily weighted than those far away.

1.9   DISCRETE FOURIER TRANSFORM OF LENGTH N

Two forms of the Fourier transform have been discussed:

$$X(f) = \int_{-\infty}^{\infty} x(t) \exp(-j2\pi ft) \, dt$$

$$X(f) = T \sum_{i=-\infty}^{\infty} x(i) \exp(-j2\pi fiT) \tag{1.93}$$

A third form is now introduced which has both X and x discrete and with limited range. For $x(i)$, $i = 0, 1, \ldots, (N-1)$, it is defined by

$$X(k) = T \sum_{i=0}^{N-1} x(i) \exp\left(\frac{-j2\pi ik}{N} \right) \tag{1.94}$$

It is this form that is the most important in the applications considered in this book. Not only is it possible to calculate this form of the Fourier transform and its inverse on a digital computer, but, as will be seen in Chapter 6, for certain values of N, it may be implemented in a manner that allows it to be calculated much faster than the formulas would indicate at first glance.

This form can be related to the transform for the infinite range with discrete $x(i)$ by

1. Defining $x(i) = 0$ $i < 0$, $i > N - 1$.
2. Defining $f_k = k / NT$.

When this is done,

$$X(f_k) = T \sum_{i=0}^{N-1} x(i) \exp(-j2\pi f_k iT)$$

$$= T \sum_{i=0}^{N-1} x(i) \exp\left[-j2\pi \left(\frac{k}{NT} \right) iT \right]$$

$$= T \sum_{i=0}^{N-1} x(i) \exp\left(\frac{-j2\pi ik}{N} \right) \tag{1.95}$$

The inverse Fourier transform is defined in a similar manner:

$$x(i) = b \sum_{k=0}^{N-1} X(k) \exp\left(\frac{j2\pi ik}{N}\right)$$

where

$$b = \frac{1}{NT}$$

and

$$f_k = kb = \frac{k}{NT} \tag{1.96}$$

The range for k is also $k = 0, \ldots, N-1$. Care must be taken in interpreting these frequencies. The folding frequency occurs at $1/2T$, so that the k corresponding to the folding frequency is found from

$$\frac{k}{NT} = \frac{1}{2T} \tag{1.97}$$

or

$$k = \frac{N}{2} \tag{1.98}$$

The proof of the inversion can be shown as follows:

$$b \sum_{k=0}^{N-1} X(k) \exp\left(\frac{j2\pi ik}{N}\right)$$

$$= b \sum_{k=0}^{N-1} \left[T \sum_{p=0}^{N-1} x(p) \exp\left(-\frac{j2\pi pk}{N}\right) \right] \exp\left(\frac{j2\pi ik}{N}\right)$$

$$= bT \sum_{p=0}^{N-1} x(p) \sum_{k=0}^{N-1} \exp\left(-j\frac{2\pi k(p-i)}{N}\right) \tag{1.99}$$

Now, $bT = 1/N$, and

$$\sum_{k=0}^{N-1} \exp\left(-j\frac{2\pi k(p-i)}{N}\right) = \begin{cases} N & i = p \\ 0 & i \neq p \end{cases} \tag{1.100}$$

This can be shown in two steps. If $i = p$, then

$$\sum_{k=0}^{N-1} 1 = N \tag{1.101}$$

On the other hand, for $i \neq p$,

$$\sum_{k=0}^{N-1} \exp\left(-j\frac{2\pi k(p-i)}{N}\right) = \frac{1 - \exp(-j2\pi(p-i))}{1 - \exp\left(\dfrac{-j2\pi(p-i)}{N}\right)} = 0 \quad \text{for } i \neq p \tag{1.102}$$

That is, the folding frequency corresponds to the midpoint of the $X(k)$ sequence.

Detailed examination of this form of the Fourier transform will reveal some very peculiar facts. The first of these is that the formulation assumes that both $x(i)$ and $X(k)$ are circular (periodic) in the sense that evaluations of the functions for i and k outside the range $0, \ldots, N-1$ will yield results modulo N.

For example, suppose $i = pN + q$, where p and q are integers and $0 \leqslant q \leqslant N-1$. When the inverse transform expression is evaluated for this value of i

$$b \sum_{k=0}^{N-1} X(k) \exp\left(\frac{j2\pi ik}{N}\right)$$

$$= b \sum_{k=0}^{N-1} X(k) \exp\left(\frac{j2\pi i(pN+q)}{N}\right)$$

$$= b \sum_{k=0}^{N-1} X(k) \exp\left(\frac{j2\pi iq}{N}\right) \exp\left(\frac{j2\pi ipN}{N}\right) \tag{1.103}$$

then the rightmost exponential term simplifies to unity

$$\exp\left(\frac{j2\pi ipN}{N}\right) = \exp(j2\pi ip) = 1 \tag{1.104}$$

and it is seen that

$$x(i) = x(q) \tag{1.105}$$

for this case. A similar relation can be shown to hold for the Fourier transform of $x(i)$.

Figure 1.7 illustrates the circularity for $N = 16$.

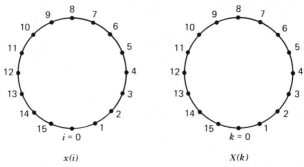

Figure 1.7 Circularity of $x(i)$ and $X(k)$ for $N=16$. The folding frequency corresponds to $k=8$.

Because the k on the range 0–$N/2$ corresponds to the frequency range 0 to the folding frequency, it is only natural to ask, what is the meaning of the $X(k)$ for k greater than $N/2$? The answer is that these correspond to negative frequencies. This may be seen from the following. Suppose k is replaced with $-p$ in the definition of $X(k)$, so that

$$X(-p)= \sum_{i=0}^{N-1} x(i)\exp\left(\frac{-j2\pi i(-p)}{N}\right) \qquad (1.106)$$

The exponential term can be multiplied by $\exp(-j2\pi iN/N)$, because the latter is simply unity, to yield

$$T\sum_{i=0}^{N-1} x(i)\exp\left(-\frac{j2\pi i(-p)}{N}\right)\exp\left(-\frac{j2\pi iN}{N}\right)$$

$$=T\sum_{i=0}^{N-1} x(i)\exp\left(-\frac{j2\pi i(N-p)}{N}\right)=X(N-p) \qquad (1.107)$$

Thus

$$X(-1)=X(N-1)$$

$$X(-2)=X(N-2) \qquad (1.108)$$

and so forth, so that the second half of the transform corresponds to the transform for negative values of k.

For $x(i)$ real, which is the usual case, $X(-k)=X^*(k)$, as would be expected.

A second major difficulty is convolution. Suppose $y(i)$ is given, and its

Fourier transform is found from

$$Y(k) = T \sum_{i=0}^{N-1} y(i) \exp\left(-\frac{j2\pi ik}{N}\right) \qquad (1.109)$$

If the frequency function $Z(k)$ is defined by

$$Z(k) = X(k)Y(k) \qquad (1.110)$$

it would be natural to expect that $z(i)$, the inverse Fourier transform of $Z(k)$, would be the convolution of $x(i)$ and $y(i)$.

Such does turn out to be the case. The problem is that the resulting convolution is also circular. In particular, the formula for convolution is

$$z(i) = T \sum_{p=0}^{N-1} x(p)y(i-p)$$

$$= T \sum_{p=0}^{N-1} x(i-p)y(p) \qquad (1.111)$$

The $(i-p)$ must be interpreted modulo N. This is shown in Figure 1.8. Both $x(i)$ and $y(i)$ are represented as sets of points on circles. The $y(i)$ circle has been reversed. In order to find $z(i)$, $y(i)$ is turned clockwise until $x(0)$ corresponds to $y(i)$. All corresponding pairs are then multiplied together; these products are summed and finally multiplied by T to yield the single value $z(i)$.

As an example of this, consider the convolution of the two functions

$$x(i) = \begin{cases} \dfrac{1}{T} & i = 7 \\ 0 & i \neq 7 \end{cases}$$

$$y(i) = 1 - \frac{i}{15}$$

$$i = 0, \ldots, 15$$

$$N = 16 \qquad (1.112)$$

They are shown in Figure 1.9 along with the resulting $z(i)$. As indicated in the figure, $z(i)$ turns out to be

$$z(i) = T \sum_{p=0}^{N-1} x(p)y(i-p)$$

$$= y(i-7) \qquad \text{modulo 16} \qquad (1.113)$$

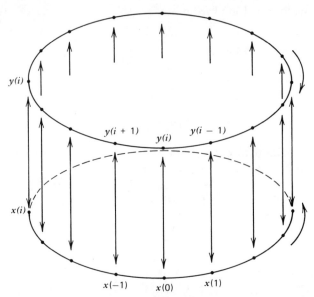

Figure 1.8 Circular convolution. The $y(i)$ term is reversed relative to $x(i)$ with $y(i)$ placed opposite $x(0)$. The single value $z(i)$ is computed by summing all the products of opposing terms and then multiplying by T.

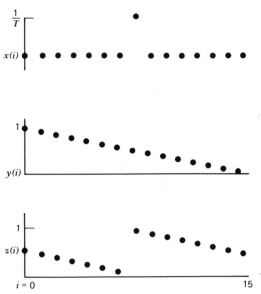

Figure 1.9 Convolution of $x(i)$ and $y(i)$ as defined in the text. $N = 16$ for this case.

so that

$$z(0)=y(9)$$

$$z(1)=y(10)$$

$$\vdots \qquad \vdots$$

$$z(7)=y(0)$$

$$\vdots \qquad \vdots$$

$$z(15)=y(8) \tag{1.114}$$

That is, $z(i)$ is the same as $y(i)$, delayed seven points.

This brings up a serious problem with this form of the Fourier transform. The circularity of the convolution causes a wraparound effect. If an attempt is made to model causal systems using this form in the manner stated, it is possible that the wraparound will result in severe distortions of the data. This problem can be overcome with zero padding, a topic that is discussed in Chapter 6.

Computing the Discrete Fourier Transform

The discrete Fourier transform is easy to implement in slow form. Figure 1.10 shows a small program for computing the transform of 16 real time points.

Lines 4–14 are employed in generating a data function. The parameters f_0 and ϕ are input, and a sinusoid is generated, which has values

$$x(i)=\cos\left(\frac{2\pi i f_0}{N}+\phi\right) \qquad i=0,\ldots,15 \tag{1.115}$$

The parameter N is fixed at the value 16. This is adequate for tutorial purposes, and acts as a safety feature in order that excessive amounts of computer time are not used. The sampling interval T is taken to be unity, so that $F=\frac{1}{2}$ and the frequencies correspond to

$$f_k=\begin{cases} \dfrac{k}{16} & k=0,\ldots,8 \\[2mm] \dfrac{1}{2}-\dfrac{k}{16} & k=9,\ldots,15 \end{cases} \tag{1.116}$$

The double DO loop in lines 15–26 does the computation of the Fourier

```
C        SLOW FOURIER TRANSFORM
         DIMENSION XC(16),XS(16),X(16)
         FACT=2.*3.14159265
5        READ (5,10) ICASE,FO,PHI
10       FORMAT (I6,2F15.6)
         IF (ICASE.LE.0) STOP
         WRITE (6,15) ICASE,FO,PHI
15       FORMAT (23H1SLOW FOURIER TRANSFORM,/,
         117HOTEST CASE NUMBER,I6,/,
         26HOFO  =,F15.6,/,
         36HOPHI =,F15.6,/,
         436HO    K              REAL       IMAGINARY,//)
         DO 20 I=1,16
20       X(I)=COS(FACT*FLOAT(I-1)*FO+PHI)
         DO 30 KK=1,16
         K=KK-1
         SUMC=0.
         SUMS=0.
         DO 25 II=1,16
         I=II-1
         ANG=FACT*FLOAT(I*K)/16.
         SUMC=SUMC+X(II)*COS(ANG)
25       SUMS=SUMS-X(II)*SIN(ANG)
         XC(KK)=SUMC
         XS(KK)=SUMS
30       WRITE(6,10) K,SUMC,SUMS
         GO TO 5
         END
```

Figure 1.10 FORTRAN code for generating a sinusoid and computing its Fourier transform.

```
         SLØW FØURIER TRANSFØRM

         TEST CASE NUMBER         1

         FO  =        0.2500000

         PHI =        0.000000

             K            REAL          IMAGINARY

             0         0.000002         0.000000
             1        -0.000001         0.000001
             2        -0.000001        -0.000001
             3        -0.000000        -0.000001
             4         8.000000         0.000001
             5        -0.000001        -0.000001
             6         0.000004        -0.000001
             7        -0.000001         0.000001
             8        -0.000001         0.000000
             9         0.000001         0.000001
            10         0.000001         0.000001
            11         0.000000         0.000003
            12         8.000000        -0.000001
            13         0.000001         0.000001
            14         0.000002         0.000001
            15        -0.000001        -0.000001
```

Figure 1.11 Printout resulting from running the test case for FO=0.25, PHI=0.

transform and the printing of results. The storage in XC and XS of the results is not necessary, but will make some of the exercises easier.

One way of making this code more efficient would be to compute the sines and cosines recursively. This technique is discussed in Chapter 4.

Figure 1.11 shows one result for running the test program with values $f_0 = \frac{1}{4}$ and $\phi = 0$. Note the real part is the same for $K = 4$ and 12, as would be expected.

1.10   THE z TRANSFORM

The definition of the z transform may be given in a number of ways. Perhaps the most consistent is to first restate the type 2 Fourier transform of $x(i)$:

$$X(f) = T \sum_{i=-\infty}^{\infty} x(i) \exp(-j2\pi f i T) \qquad (1.117)$$

and then replace $\exp(j2\pi f T)$ with z, so that the above becomes

$$X(z) = T \sum_{i=-\infty}^{\infty} x(i) z^{-i} \qquad (1.118)$$

This transform can be employed in the solution of a wide variety of problems in digital signal processing.

It is certainly a simplification in notation: $\exp(j2\pi f T)$ has 10 symbols compared to one for z. However, it is much more than a notational convenience; it has been developed into a complete system for solving sampled data problems. For the reader interested in pursuing the subject, Steiglitz [1974] is recommended.

The problems in time series analysis by and large can be solved using z-transform methods, and in many cases the methods of solution are simpler. But for the applications of interest in this work, it does not seem that their introduction really clarifies what is happening. Thus, except for occasional notational convenience, they are not employed.

EXERCISES

1.1.   Prove (1.9).

1.2.   Find the Fourier transform of the following:

   a. e^{-at} $t \geqslant 0$
        0 $t < 0$

Answer:

$$\frac{1}{a+j2\pi f}$$

b. $e^{-a|t|}$

Answer:

$$\frac{2a}{a^2+(2\pi f)^2}$$

c. $\left(\frac{a}{P}\right)t+a \qquad -P<t<0$

$\left(\frac{-a}{P}\right)t+a \qquad 0<t<P$

$0 \qquad\qquad\quad$ otherwise

(triangular pulse)

Answer:

$$\frac{ap\sin^2\pi fP}{(\pi fP)^2}$$

d. $\dfrac{1+\cos\pi t/P}{2} \qquad -P<t<P$

$0 \qquad\qquad\qquad$ otherwise

Answer:

$$\frac{\sin 2\pi fP}{2\pi f}+\frac{P^2 2\pi f\sin 2\pi fP}{\pi^2-(2\pi fP)^2}$$

(cosine bell)

1.3. Often functions with discontinuities have Fourier transforms with delta functions, as for example, pair 4 in Table 1.2. Use this transform and relationship 4 in Table 1.1 and show an alternative way of computing the Fourier transform of the boxcar function. What happens to the delta functions?

1.4. Consider the differential equation

$$\frac{dy(t)}{dt}+ay(t)=x(t)$$

Assume $x(t)=0$ for $t<0$.
a. Compute the Fourier transform of the equation.
b. Find the transfer function between the two functions.

c. Compute the gain of the transfer function.

d. Compute the phase of the transfer function.

e. Plot the gain and phase as a function of frequency.

f. Compute the impulse response function under the assumption that it is realizable.

1.5. Compute the convolutions of $x(t)$ and $h(t)$ as given. In all cases, $x(t)$, $h(t)$ and the answers are 0 for t less than zero.

a. $x(t)=t, \ h(t)=t$ $\qquad\qquad$ $[t^3/6]$

b. $x(t)=e^t, \ h(t)=e^t$ $\qquad\qquad$ $[te^t]$

c. $x(t)=t+1, \ h(t)=t-1$ $\qquad\quad$ $[t^3/6-t]$

d. $x(t)=e^t, \ h(t)=\sin t$ $\qquad\quad$ $\left[\frac{1}{2}\{e^t-\sin t-\cos t\}\right]$

1.6. Evaluate the integral

$$\int_{-\infty}^{\infty} \frac{\sin \pi \eta P}{\pi \eta} \cdot \frac{\sin \pi(f-\eta)Q}{\pi(f-\eta)} d\eta$$

Answer:

$$\frac{\sin \pi f_p}{\pi f} \qquad P<Q$$

$$\frac{\sin \pi fQ}{\pi f} \qquad P>Q$$

Computer Problems

1.7. Keypunch and run the program shown in Figure 1.10 for the following values:

Case Number	f_0	ϕ
2	0.25	−1.5707963
3	0.5	0.0000000
4	0.3125	0.7853982

Explain the answers.

1.8. Add additional code to the program so that it will also compute and print the inverse Fourier transform after computing the Fourier transform. Run all four cases.

1.9. Modify the program so that

$$x(i)=\begin{cases} 1 & i=0,1,2,14,15 \\ 0 & \text{otherwise} \end{cases}$$

and run it to compute the Fourier transform. Comment on the result.

CHAPTER 2

PROBABILITY AND STATISTICAL CONCEPTS

2.1 INTRODUCTION

Certain statistical concepts continually arise in applications of time series analysis. The purpose of this chapter is to define key parameters such as mean, variance, and probability density since they will be needed in much practical work. We often must deal with data that is corrupted by unwanted noise. This noise leads to certain inaccuracies in computing the various parameters from the time series data. We discuss only those concepts directly pertinent to time series analysis. The emphasis of this text is not to provide a source book in statistics, however, and we mainly define terms, not prove theorens about statistics. For the readers who require a more complete footing in basic statistics, we refer them to Dixon and Massey [1968] for a "cookbook" type approach, complete with very comprehensive tables, or to Fraser [1957] for a more mathematical discussion. The mathematically precise definitions of the statistical parameters are more involved than those given here, and the definition of a random process would require an elaborate mathematical scaffolding because of the variables which may be examined. Fortunately, in the applications considered here, the pathological functions considered by mathematicians do not occur. Hence several simplifying assumptions can be made without impairing the validity of the results:

1. That the functions being considered are bounded and were continous before digitization.

2. That the random process underlying the function is ergodic and stationary.

The technical definition of a random variable basically requires that the variable be measurable in the sense of measure theory. Assumption 1 guarantees this because bounded, continuous functions form a subset of functions that are measurable. The remainder of this section is spent in an intuitive discussion of assumption 2.

Probability Density Function (PDF), Mean, and Variance

Suppose that a large number of identical noise generators have been turned on at some remote time in the past and left to run. Associated with the output of all the generators is a function $f(x,t)$, the probability density function, with the following characteristics. For a certain time, say, t_0, the probability that the output of the qth signal generator $x_q(t_0)$ lies between values a and b is given by the integral

$$P\left[a \leqslant x_q(t_0) < b\right] = \int_a^b f(x,t_0)\,dx \qquad (2.1)$$

Note that the integration is performed with respect to the range of the random variable. The expected value of any function involving x, denoted by $E[g(x)]$ where $g(x)$ is the expression whose expectation is sought, is defined to be

$$E\left\{g\left[x(t_0)\right]\right\} = \int_{-\infty}^{\infty} g\left[x(t_0)\right] f(x,t_0)\,dx \qquad (2.2)$$

In particular, the *true* or *population* mean and variance are given by

$$\mu(t_0) = \int_{-\infty}^{\infty} x(t_0) f(x,t_0)\,dx \qquad (2.3)$$

$$\sigma^2(t_0) = \int_{-\infty}^{\infty} \left[x(t_0) - \mu(t_0)\right]^2 f(x,t_0)\,dx \qquad (2.4)$$

The *standard deviation* is the positive square root of the variance.

If the random process is *stationary*, the parameters $\mu(t_0)$ and $\sigma^2(t_0)$ are independent of time. That is,

$$\mu(t_0) = \mu(t_1) = \mu \qquad (2.5)$$

$$\sigma^2(t_0) = \sigma^2(t_1) = \sigma^2 \qquad (2.6)$$

where t_0 and t_1 are arbitrary. Because stationarity is assumed, the mean and variance hereafter are written without the qualifying t_0.

The assumption of *ergodicity* permits ensemble averages to be replaced with time averages. In the noise generator example, the generators were exactly alike, so that even if an individual generator were producing a different, unique random function, the output of any one of them would be sufficient to define the statistics for all. Thus the expression for the mean in (2.3) may be replaced with

$$\mu_x = \lim_{P \to \infty} \frac{1}{2P} \int_{-P}^{P} x(t) \, dt \qquad (2.7)$$

which is the time average based on a single record of the process. A similar expression for the variance is

$$\sigma_x^2 = \lim_{P \to \infty} \frac{1}{2P} \int_{-P}^{P} [x(t) - \mu]^2 \, dt = E(x^2) - E^2(x) \qquad (2.8)$$

The mean square value is

$$\psi_x^2 = \mu_x^2 + \sigma_x^2 \qquad (2.9)$$

As described above, ergodicity refers to the property that time averages may be substituted for averages over the set of realizations of the random process involved.

Central to the theme of this book is the concept of *power spectral density* (PSD), defined formally below. For the moment we consider it to be a spreading or decomposition of the total mean square power as a function of frequency.

We note that there will be a "true" power spectral density function associated with a random process. We remark that if the process is zero mean Gaussian, then it is completely determined (statistically) by its power spectrum or equivalently by its autocovariance function, to be defined shortly.* Since many process which arise in practice are Gaussian, this makes the power spectrum an extremely important parameter.

*We are skirting an issue here that is beyond the scope of this text. The statistical characteristics of a process are known if we know all multidimensional probability density functions defining the joint probabilities at all time differences for a process. For example, the autocovariance function at time difference τ defines the correlation characteristics between the process amplitudes at time t and $t + \tau$. For Gaussian data, the covariance and two variances completely define the joint (two-dimensional) probability density between the amplitude values at time t and at time $t + \tau$. In general we must extend this to higher and higher orders.

When we collect data in a practical experiment or test, we can only compute estimates of the power spectrum (and other parameters). With ergodicity we can get estimates from time averages of a single segment of a time history. Hence we define an estimate of the PSD from a finite time segment. If we digitize this segment and deal with sampled data and discrete formulas we have no essential difference, from a statistical standpoint, between the continuous and discrete versions. This statement applies so long as we satisfy the requirements of the sampling theorem to avoid significant aliasing.

2.2 SAMPLE VALUES AND ESTIMATES

Because only a sample of the random variable is taken, rather than a record length which is defined for infinite time, the sample mean and sample variance are estimates of the population parameters and are denoted by symbols different from those used for the theoretical parameters. In particular, the sample mean for digital data is calculated from

$$m = \bar{x} = \frac{1}{N} \sum_{i=0}^{N-1} x(i) \tag{2.10}$$

The unbiased sample variance s^2 is obtained from

$$s^2 = \frac{1}{N-1} \sum_{i=0}^{N-1} \left[x(i) - \bar{x} \right]^2 \tag{2.11}$$

Criteria exists for determining the confidence intervals for the sample mean and sample variance. Detailed formulas and tables are to be found in Bendat and Piersol [1971]. For the record lengths encountered in time series data analysis, the statistical variation of these two parameters is usually low and hence not a problem.

If the divisor of the expression for s^2 were $1/N$ rather than $1/(N-1)$, then the expected values of s^2 would be $[(N-1)/N]\sigma^2$, so that the result would be biased. For large N the error would be small, however. In time series analysis we usually deal with values of N that are at least 100 and often as large as 10,000 or more. Hence the question of bias in s^2 induced by the division by N is rarely significant.

A comment on statistical notation is appropriate here. Population parameters are traditionally denoted by Greek letters, for example, μ and σ^2 for mean and variance. Estimates of the parameters are traditionally denoted by the corresponding Latin letters, for example, m and s^2. To confuse things, averages of a random variable are often denoted with a raised bar; for example, the average of x is $\bar{x}$. In time series analysis the bar is often reserved for time averages and the expected value notation $E(x)$ used for more general averaging situations. Finally, a caret placed above parameters has become reasonably standard as notation for an estimate. This is particularly useful when one begins to run out of letters. Hence we denote a power spectrum estimate by $\hat{S}_x(k)$. Occasionally we are forced into employing all the notations discussed and trust that the context will make the intention clear to the reader.

Let us state somewhat more precisely some attributes of statistical estimates. These are bias, variance, and consistency.

Bias: an estimate $\hat{\phi}$ of a parameter ϕ is biased if the average value of $\hat{\phi}$ is not equal to ϕ.

$$\text{Bias} = \Delta\phi = E(\hat{\phi}) - \phi \tag{2.12}$$

The sample variance with a divisor of N is an example of a biased estimator.

Variance: the variance of an estimate is

$$\sigma_{\phi}^2 = E\left[\hat{\phi} - E(\hat{\phi})\right]^2 \tag{2.13}$$

Therefore, the mean square error is defined as

$$\Psi_{\phi}^2 = \sigma_{\phi}^2 + \Delta_{\phi}^2 = E\left[\hat{\phi} - \phi\right]^2 \tag{2.14}$$

Consistency: an estimate is consistent if its variance decreases with an increase in sample size (record length). In equation form,

$$\lim_{N \to \infty} \sigma_{\phi}^2 = 0 \tag{2.15}$$

An example of an inconsistent estimate is the unsmoothed sample power spectrum. If the absolute value squared of a Fourier transform (often called the periodogram) is computed as a power spectrum estimate, it is not consistent. In this case the variability remains constant as record length increases.

Furthermore, the usual estimates of spectral functions are examples of biased estimates. The bias that arises here is interpreted as a frequency band smearing error due to inadequate spectral resolution. This idea is discussed in detail in Chapter 8.

An important example of a variance computation is that for a sinusoid. Suppose that x is a sinusoid

$$x(t) = A\sin(2\pi f_c t + \phi) \qquad -\infty < t < \infty \tag{2.16}$$

Then

$$\sigma_x^2 = \lim_{P \to \infty} \frac{1}{P} \int_{-P/2}^{P/2} A^2 \sin^2(2\pi f_c t + \phi)\, dt$$

$$= A^2 \lim_{P \to \infty} \frac{1}{P} \int_{-P/2}^{P/2} \sin^2(2\pi f_c + \phi)\, dt$$

$$= A^2 \lim_{P \to \infty} \frac{1}{P}\left[\frac{P}{2} + \{\text{sine term} \leqslant 1\}\right] = \frac{A^2}{2} \tag{2.17}$$

Note that Ψ_x^2 and σ_x^2 are identical for those functions, since the mean is 0.

2.3 NORMAL DISTRIBUTION

Suppose the variable x has mean μ and variance σ^2. Then it is *normally* distributed or has a *Gaussian* distribution if its probability density function $\phi(x)$ is given by

$$\phi(x) = \frac{1}{\sqrt{2\pi\sigma^2}} \exp\left[-\frac{1}{2}\left(\frac{x-\mu}{\sigma}\right)^2 \right] \tag{2.18}$$

The probability distribution function for such a Gaussian variable, $\Phi(x)$, is defined by

$$\Phi(x) = \int_{-\infty}^{x} \phi(\xi)\,d\xi \tag{2.19}$$

In words,

$$\Phi(x_0) = \text{probability that } -\infty < x \leqslant x_0$$

$$\Phi(x_1) - \Phi(x_0) = \text{probability that } x_0 < x \leqslant x_1$$

$$(\text{provided } x_1 > x_0)$$

$$1 - \Phi(x_0) = \text{probability that } x_0 < x < \infty \tag{2.20}$$

There is an important theorem associated with Gaussian random variables which we state without proof: "any linear transformation of a Gaussian variable is Gaussian." In particular, if x is Gaussian with mean μ_x and variance σ_x^2, then

$$z = ax + b \tag{2.21}$$

is Gaussian with

$$\mu_z = a\mu_x + b \tag{2.22}$$

and

$$\sigma_z^2 = a^2\sigma_x^2 \tag{2.23}$$

A special version of (2.21) is termed "standardization," which is

$$z = \frac{1}{\sigma_x}(x - \mu_x) \tag{2.24}$$

By (2.22) and (2.23) we see that

$$\mu_z = 0$$

$$\sigma_z^2 = 1$$

It is this that allows the tabulation of the Gaussian variable that appears in the appendix. No matter what the mean and variance of the original data, we can look up probabilities in the table and transform to the values of the original variable by inverting (2.24):

$$x = z\sigma_x + \mu_x \qquad (2.25)$$

Some commonly used values of Φ for $\mu = 0$ and $\sigma = 1$ are

$$\frac{1}{\sqrt{2\pi}} \int_{-1}^{1} \exp\left(-\frac{x^2}{2}\right) dx = 0.682$$

$$\frac{1}{\sqrt{2\pi}} \int_{-2}^{2} \exp\left(-\frac{x^2}{2}\right) dx = 0.954$$

$$\frac{1}{\sqrt{2\pi}} \int_{-3}^{3} \exp\left(-\frac{x^2}{2}\right) dx = 0.997 \qquad (2.26)$$

We assume the reader is familiar with looking up tabulated values and do not pursue this here.

The concept of the normal distribution is theoretical; in actual practice it is not usually possible to have truly normal data. The principal problem is one of range. Most data functions have a finite range of values; normally distributed data must have an infinite range.

Suppose a 2-cm rod is measured by a group of people, each using the same ruler, and that the resulting measurements are normally distributed. Let the true mean of the measurements be 2 cm and the variance be 0.25 cm^2. The probability of a measurement of -0.5 cm or less is

$$P(x \leqslant -0.5) = \frac{1}{\sqrt{2\pi\sigma^2}} \int_{-\infty}^{-0.5} \exp\left[-\frac{(x-\mu)^2}{2\sigma^2}\right] dx$$

Making the substitution $z = (x-\mu)/\sigma$ gives

$$P(x \leqslant -0.5) = \frac{1}{\sqrt{2\pi}} \int_{-\infty}^{\frac{-0.5-2}{0.5}} \exp\left(-\frac{z^2}{2}\right) dy$$

$$\approx 0.0000001 \qquad (2.27)$$

Thus there is a finite (albeit small) probability of a negative measurement of the length of the rod. This, of course, is an absurdity. However, the normal distribution is entirely justified because it is a reasonable approximation to whatever the true distribution may be.

There are a number of reasons for assuming normality (i.e., that the data are normally distributed). The principal ones are as follows:

1. There is a large body of knowledge about the normal distribution. This makes it easy to model a given situation and then make statements about the resulting statistics.

2   The central limit theorem [Cramer, 1946] shows that the sum of variables of any distribution whatsoever tends to be normally distributed if "enough of them" are added together. Filtering data (see Chapter 3) turns out to be the equivalent af adding a number of observations together so that filtered data "tends to be" normally distributed.

Some of the important properties of the normal distribution function are the following:

1. The density and distribution of normal variable x are completely determined by the mean μ_x and variance σ_x^2.

2. The moments of x are

$$E[x^n] = \begin{cases} \mu & n=1 \\ \mu^2 + \sigma^2 & n=2 \\ \mu(\mu^2 + 3\sigma^2) & n=3 \\ \cdots & \cdots \end{cases} \tag{2.28}$$

3. The central monents are

$$E[(x-\mu)^n] = \begin{cases} 0 & n=1,3,\ldots \\ 1 \cdot 3 \cdots (n-1)\sigma^n & n=2,4,\ldots \end{cases} \tag{2.29}$$

The third moment about the mean is termed "skewness" and the fourth monent is termed "kurtosis." Skewness is 0 for any symmetric distribution. If kurtosis is higher than the Gaussian value of $3\sigma^4$, it is an indication that there is considerable data out at high amplitude values. This is reflected in "thicker" tails than the Gaussian density function would have. Various examples of probability density estimates are given in the section on examples and application of probability density function of this chapter.

One final property of random variables associated with the PDF is *independence*.

A pair of random variables x and y are statistically independent if their joint (two-dimensioned) PDF. $p(x,y)$ can be factored. That is,

$$p(x,y)=p(x)p(y) \qquad (2.30)$$

In words, this says that from a statistical standpoint the two variables x and y have no influence on one another. This idea is discussed further in the section on correlation and regression. We now proceed to a second important distribution.

Chi-Square Distribution

Suppose that $x_1, x_2, \ldots, x_n$ are independent Gaussian variables with zero mean and unit variance. Define χ_n^2 by

$$\chi_n^2 = \sum_{i=1}^{n} x_i^2 \qquad (2.31)$$

Then χ_n^2 is said to be a chi-square variable with n degrees of freedom (d.f.) and to have the chi-square distribution. The density function for χ_n^2 is

$$p(\chi_n^2) = \left[2^{n/2} \Gamma\left(\frac{n}{2}\right) \right]^{-1} (\chi_n^2) \exp\left[-\chi_{n/2}^2 \right] \qquad \chi^2 \geqslant 0 \qquad (2.32)$$

where $\Gamma(n/2)$ is the gamma function.

The main use of the chi-square distribution in time series data analysis is in assessing the variability of sample variance and power spectral densities. If $x(i)$ has zero mean, and N independent samples of $x(i)$ are used to compute the sample variance s^2, then the probability is $(1-\alpha)$ that the true variance is between two limits

$$B_1 \leqslant \sigma^2 \leqslant B_2 \qquad (2.33)$$

where the limits B_1 and B_2 are defined by

$$B_1 = \frac{ns^2}{\chi^2_{n;\,1-(\alpha/2)}}$$

$$B_2 = \frac{ns^2}{\chi^2_{n;\,(\alpha/2)}} \qquad n = N - 1 \qquad (2.34)$$

Note that B_1 and B_2 are functions of s^2, α, and χ^2. The interval (B_1, B_2) is referred to as a confidence interval; and one speaks of the $[(1-\alpha)\,100]\%$ confidence interval.*

*We have taken liberties with the term confidence as employed in statistics; strictly speaking it is not a probability. Please consult Fraser [1957] for an amplification of this concept.

As an example,[†] suppose that $N=31$ independent observations are taken from a normally distributed random variable, and that a 90% confidence interval on the sample variance is desired. Suppose further that the sample mean is $\bar{x}=58.61$ and the sample variance $s^2=33.43$. Then the theoretical variance σ^2 is bounded by

$$\text{Prob}\left[\frac{30\,s^2}{43.77}<\sigma^2<\frac{30\,s^2}{18.49}\right]=0.90$$

where

$$\chi^2_{30:0.05}=43.77=\chi^2_{30}\text{ such that }P\left(\chi^2_{30}\right)=0.05$$

$$\chi^2_{30:95}=18.49=\chi^2_{30}\text{ such that }P\left(\chi^2_{30}\right)=0.95$$

When simplified, the above bounds become

$$22.91\leqslant\sigma^2\leqslant54.22$$

Note that on the average the true variance is outside such an interval once out of every 10 tries.

Other distributions are important in basic statistics. In particular, this includes two distributions: (1) the Student "t" distribution useful in making inferences and computing confidence limits with regard to mean values; and (2) the "F" distribution which is employed in testing pairs of independent mean square values for equivalence. We refer the reader to Bendat and Piersol [1971] for a discussion of the basic facts regarding these two distributions.

2.4   CORRELATION AND REGRESSION

The statistical concepts of correlation and regression are closely related to the time series analysis (and engineering) concepts of coherence and frequency response function. Hence we review them here.

First we require the definition of covariance which is the average cross product of two random variables about their mean values. In equation form,

$$\text{cov}(x,y)=\sigma_{xy}=E\left[(x-\mu_x)(y-\mu_y)\right]\tag{2.35}$$

A fundamental fact is that if two variables are independent, that is if

†Taken from Blackman and Tukey [1958].

$p(x, y) = p(x)p(y)$, then

$$\sigma_{xy} = 0 \tag{2.36}$$

Note that the converse is not true. However, in a very important special case of two variables possessing a joint (two-dimensional) Gaussian distribution, then the joint Gaussian distribution factors to the product of the individual one-dimensional distributions. Hence in the case of Gaussian data we have the important result:

"zero covariance implies independence"

or

$$\sigma_{yx} = 0 \Rightarrow \Phi(x, y) = \Phi(x)\Phi(y) \tag{2.37}$$

For perhaps 90% of all practical data analysis problems, the above may be taken as a general fact.

Correlation is a normalized covariance, namely,

$$\rho_{xy} = \frac{\text{cov}(x, y)}{\left[\text{var}(x)\text{var}(y)\right]^{1/2}} = \frac{\sigma_{xy}}{\sigma_x \sigma_y} \tag{2.38}$$

It is a simple matter to demonstrate that the correlation coefficient is always bounded by ± 1. That is,

$$-1 \leqslant \rho_{xy} \leqslant 1 \tag{2.39}$$

This result also holds true for sample values if the sample covariance is defined as

$$S_{xy} = \frac{1}{N-1} \sum_{i=0}^{N-1} \left[x(i) - \bar{x}\right]\left[y(i) - \bar{y}\right] \tag{2.40}$$

The *cross spectral density* function (CSD), $S_{xy}(f)$, is a decomposition of covariance with frequency analogous to PSD being a decomposition of variance.

Regression analysis is closely related to covariance and correlation. A "regression line" is usually defined as a linear relation between two variables.

$$y = \beta_0 + \beta_{xy} x \tag{2.41}$$

If we collect data, and solve for estimates of β_0 and β_{xy}, denoted by b_0 and

b_{xy}, on a least squares error criterion, then we find the result is

$$b_{xy} = \frac{s_{xy}}{s_x^2} \qquad (2.42)$$

$$b_0 = \bar{y} - b_{xy}\bar{x} \qquad (2.43)$$

The resulting line

$$(y - \bar{y}) = b_{xy}(x - \bar{x}) \qquad (2.44)$$

is termed the regression* line of y on x. In general there also exists the regression of x on y where

$$b_{yx} = \frac{s_{xy}}{s_y^2} \qquad (2.45)$$

We note that

$$b_{xy}b_{yx} = \frac{s_{xy}^2}{s_x^2 s_y^2} = r_{xy}^2 \qquad (2.46)$$

The regression line has an important interpretation in the case of a joint Gaussian distribution. It is the major axis of an ellipse of constant probability and the regression coefficient is the slope of the line.

Multiple Regression

The two-variable regression above is easily generalized to p variables (we assume zero mean without loss of generality)

$$y = \beta_1 x_1 + \beta_2 x_2 + \cdots + \beta_p x_p \qquad (2.47)$$

If we assume we have N observations, $N > p$ for all variables and arrange them in matrix-vector form: thus

$$\mathbf{X} = \begin{bmatrix} x_{11} & x_{12} & \cdots & x_{1p} \\ x_{21} & x_{22} & \cdots & x_{2p} \\ \vdots & \vdots & & \vdots \\ x_N & x_{N2} & \cdots & x_{Np} \end{bmatrix} \qquad \mathbf{Y} = \begin{bmatrix} y_1 \\ y_2 \\ \vdots \\ y_N \end{bmatrix} \qquad (2.48)$$

$$\mathbf{B} = \begin{bmatrix} b_1 \\ b_2 \\ \vdots \\ b_N \end{bmatrix}$$

*The term regression results from some early studies of the relation of heights of offspring to their parents. It was found that the heights "regressed" to the average, that is, tall fathers and mothers had shorter sons and daughters and short fathers and mothers had taller sons and daughters.

Then the solution **B** for the estimate of the β_i [Anderson, 1958] is

$$\mathbf{B} = (\mathbf{X^*X})^{-1}\mathbf{X^*Y} \tag{2.49}$$

where the asterisk denotes transpose.

Certain other multivariate parameters become important in multiple frequency response function analysis, but we defer their discussion until they are required in Chapter 9.

2.5 POWER SPECTRAL DENSITY FUNCTION

As can be seen from the preceding discussion, the second moment statistics, which are variance for a single variable and covariance for a pair of variables, are all-important for variables processing a Gaussian distribution. Furthermore, the frequency decomposition of time histories is very important in time series analysis. This information is crucial in estimating such important parameters as resonant frequency and damping ratio. Another application is estimating seasonal fluctuations in economic time series such as unemployment index. The detection of periodic fluctuations in ocean temperatures and the determination of the cycle of rhythmic contractions of a cow's stomach reacting to certain drugs are further examples of uses of the PSD.

An expression for the mean square value over a finite time is

$$\psi_x^2 = \frac{1}{t_2 - t_1} \int_{t_1}^{t_2} x^2(t)\, dt \tag{2.50}$$

Dimensionally, ψ_x^2 is proportional to the mean square energy per unit time, which is by definition, power.

The power spectral density of the function x, written $S_x(f)$, is an extension of this concept. The interpretation of $S_x(f)$ is that the integral

$$\psi_x^2(f_1, f_2) = 2 \int_{f_1}^{f_2} S_x(f)\, df \qquad 0 \leqslant f_1 \leqslant f_2 \tag{2.51}$$

is the mean square value between the frequencies f_1 and f_2. Thus

$$\psi_x^2 = \int_{-\infty}^{\infty} S_x(f)\, df \tag{2.52}$$

The appropriate expression for S_x is given by

$$S_x(f) = \lim_{P \to \infty} \frac{1}{P} \left| \int_{-P/2}^{P/2} x(t) e^{-j\omega t}\, dt \right|^2 \tag{2.53}$$

Difficulties may arise if (2.53) is used without care to compute estimates of PSD's. Statistically inconsistent estimates result when no frequency smoothing is performed. Also mathematical precautions are necessary, as discussed earlier. These two considerations, along with the fact that only inefficient computational procedures were available in the past, led to the dismissal of (2.53) as a suitable spectrum estimation procedure. However, the fast Fourier transform (see Chapter 6) eliminates the computational objection; proper frequency domain smoothing provides consistent estimates; and finite record lengths eliminate the mathematical problems.

An equivalent expression, usually referred to as the Wiener–Khinchine theorem, is

$$S_x(f) = \int_{-\infty}^{\infty} s_x(\tau) e^{-j\omega t} d\tau = 2 \int_0^{\infty} s_x(\tau) \cos 2\pi f \, d\tau \qquad (2.54)$$

where the term $s_x(\tau)$, the time autocovariance function of x, is defined as

$$s_x(\tau) = \lim_{P \to \infty} \frac{1}{P} \int_{-P/2}^{P/2} x(t) x(t+\tau) \, dt \qquad -\infty < \tau < \infty \qquad (2.55)$$

where we tacitly assume that $x(t)$ is a zero mean process.

Demonstration of the equivalence of these two methods for computing S_x is beyond the scope of this work, but is discussed in several references [Bendat and Piersol, 1971; Wiener, 1949]. A third method of defining S_x is available. However, it is based on the concept of filtering, and discussion must be postponed until after filtering has been introduced. The function s_x requires further discussion. Under the condition of ergodicity assumed earlier, it is equal to a generalization of our previous definition of covariance

$$s_x(\tau) = E[x(t)x(t+\tau)] = \int_{-\infty}^{\infty} x(t)x(t+\tau) p(x,t,\tau) \, dx \qquad (2.56)$$

where $p(x,t,\tau)$ is an appropriate probability density function.

Suppose $n(t)$ is uncorrelated random noise with a zero mean. Then its autocorrelation is given by

$$s_n(\tau) = N\delta(\tau)$$

and

$$S_n(f) = N \qquad \text{for all } f \qquad (2.57)$$

That is, the PSD of uncorrelated random noise is a constant. This type of data is known as *white noise*, because the power is uniform (flat) through any given band and therefore is like white light, which is more or less uniform in the visible portion of the optical spectrum.

Although useful as a mathematical tool for clarifying the concept of the PSD, true white noise, it must be noted, is not physically realizable because its variance is infinite. Devices that supposedly generate white noise actually produce noise whose PSD is flat out to a certain frequency and then drops off for higher frequencies.

Suppose that x is a sine wave with frequency f_c, amplitude A, and phase ϕ. That is,

$$x(t) = A \sin(2\pi f_c t + \phi) \tag{2.58}$$

The autocovariance function is computed as follows:

$$
\begin{aligned}
s_x(\tau) &= \lim_{P \to \infty} \frac{1}{P} \int_{-P/2}^{P/2} A^2 \sin(2\pi f_c t + \phi) \sin\left[2\pi f_c(t+\tau) + \phi\right] dt \\
&= \lim_{P \to \infty} \frac{1}{P} \left(\frac{A^2}{2}\right) \int_{-P/2}^{P/2} \left[\cos 2\pi f_c \tau - \cos(2\pi f_c \tau + 4\pi f_c t + 2\phi)\right] dt \\
&= \lim_{P \to \infty} \frac{A^2}{2P} \left[t \cos 2\pi f_c \tau + \frac{1}{4\pi f_c} \sin(2\pi f_c \tau + 4\pi f_c t + 2\phi) \right]_{-P/2}^{P/2} \\
&= \lim_{P \to \infty} \left\{ \frac{A^2}{2} \cos 2\pi f_c \tau - \left(\frac{A^2}{8\pi f_c}\right)\left(\frac{1}{P}\right) \right. \\
&\qquad \left. \times \left[\sin(2\pi f_c \tau + 2\pi f_c T + 2\phi) - \sin(2\pi f_c \tau - 2\pi f_c T + 2\phi)\right] \right\} \\
&= \frac{A^2}{2} \cos 2\pi f_c \tau \tag{2.59}
\end{aligned}
$$

This is true because the term within the brackets is always less than 2. In the limit, this term must go to 0, since it is divided by P, which goes to infinity.

Note that the arbitrary phase angle ϕ has disappeared in the final result. Because the phase angle was arbitrary, the function could just as well have been a cosine wave. Thus the autocorrelation of a sinusoid, regardless of its phase, is always a cosine with zero phase. In general, phase information is lost in the autocorrelation process.

2.6   HOW TO COMPUTE MEAN AND VARIANCE

The computation of mean and variance is in principle very simple. However, as is sometimes the case in digital computer arithmetic, there exist nonobvious and nontrivial problems. For example, the usual implementation of the formula for the computation of the sample mean from discrete data is

$$\bar{x}_k = \left(\sum_{i=0}^{k-1} x(i) \right) + x(k) \qquad k = 0, 1, \ldots, N-1$$

$$\bar{x} = \frac{1}{N} \bar{x}_{N-1} \tag{2.65}$$

That is, we accumulate the data values in sequence. A numerical problem can occur in that the sum of k values can be substantially larger than $x(k)$, so that roundoff can occur which is the same order of magnitude as $x(k)$. This is a problem in floating point arithmetic or block floating of fixed point numbers, as is often accomplished in minicomputers. An alternative formula, usually more accurate, is to compute partial sums in the following manner. Assume the number of data points to be a power of 2, $N = 2^m$. There will be m stages of computation.

$$\bar{x}_1(i) = \frac{1}{2} [x(2i) + x(2i+1)] \qquad i = 0, \ldots, \frac{N}{2} - 1$$

$$\bar{x}_2(i) = \frac{1}{2} [\bar{x}_1(2i) + \bar{x}_1(2i+1)] \qquad i = 0, \ldots, \frac{N}{4} - 1$$

$$\vdots$$

$$\bar{x} = \bar{x}_m(0) = \frac{1}{2} [\bar{x}_{m-1}(0) + \bar{x}_{m-1}(1)] \tag{2.66}$$

That is, we repeatedly add up the original data array a pair of values at a time. As an example, consider the following case where $N = 8$ and $m = 3$. The data consist of $x(0), x(1), \ldots, x(7)$. There are three stages to the computations:

1. Compute

$$\bar{x}_1(0) = \frac{1}{2} [x(0) + x(1)]$$

$$\bar{x}_1(1) = \frac{1}{2} [x(2) + x(3)]$$

$$\bar{x}_1(2) = \frac{1}{2} [x(4) + x(5)]$$

$$\bar{x}_1(3) = \frac{1}{2} [(6) + x(7)]$$

2. From these compute

$$\bar{x}_2(0) = \tfrac{1}{2}\left[\bar{x}_1(0) + \bar{x}_1(1)\right]$$

$$\bar{x}_2(1) = \tfrac{1}{2}\left[\bar{x}_1(2) + \bar{x}_1(3)\right]$$

3. Finally, compute the sample mean:

$$\bar{x} = \bar{x}_3(0) = \tfrac{1}{2}\left[\bar{x}_2(0) + \bar{x}_2(1)\right]$$

This method tends to avoid roundoff error if the data are random as a function of the index i. In floating or block floating point arithmetic, the array could be renormalized after each iteration and data values would never be immersed in roundoff noise. Similar comments would apply to any summation of a sequence of values.

The above comments would naturally also apply to computing a sum of squares or sum of cross products in general. There are several other methods of rewriting variance computations. The formula least sensitive to roundoff error is

$$s_x^2 = \frac{1}{N-1} \sum_{i=0}^{N-1} \left[x(i) - \bar{x}\right]^2 \qquad (2.67)$$

The subtraction of $\bar{x}$ from each data value reduces the "dynamic range" of the resulting values, which makes the resulting summation less likely to be significantly affected by roundoff errors. An alternative formula is

$$s_x^2 = \frac{1}{N-1}\left[\left(\sum_{i=0}^{N-1} x^2(i)\right) - N\bar{x}^2\right] \qquad (2.68)$$

The problem with this formula is that $\sum x^2(i)$ and $N\bar{x}^2$ can both be large numbers whereas their difference, s_x^2, can be small. This amounts to the fact that the roundoff error of the difference of the right side of (2.68) can easily be the same order of magnitude as s_x^2.

These problems mean that one quantity can effectively be shifted out the right side (least significant) of the accumulating register. This phenomenon is known as *underflow*.

In later chapters many additional numerical problems are discussed. In almost all cases they will be related to this problem of underflow and roundoff error accumulation.

2.7 PROBABILITY HISTOGRAMS

Sample probability density functions or histograms also may be obtained from the data. The sample density functions are not unique for a given data group as are $\bar{x}$ and s^2, but depend on the values of certain parameters used to determine them. The histogram is computed in the following manner: an interval of the range of x, say, $a < x < b$, is subdivided into k subintervals of equal length (called "class intervals") so that the entire range of x is broken up into $(k+2)$ intervals. All the data are examined, and the number of occurrences in each interval is tabulated. The histogram consists of a plot showing the number of occurrences for each of the intervals.

More formally, let $\{N_j\}$ be the set of integers obtained by counting the occurrences of $\{x(i)\}$ in the jth interval. Let $c = (b-a)/k$, and $d_j = a + jc$. Then $\{N_j\}$ is defined by the table below.

Figure 2.1 illustrates these terms. The $\{N_j\}$ terms are also called pockets. One method of doing this sorting on a digital computer is to examine each x_i, $i = 1, \ldots, N$ in turn, making the following checks:

j	N_j
0	[number of x such that $x < a$]
$\vdots$	$\vdots$
j	[number of x such that $d_{j-1} \leqslant x < d_j$]
$\vdots$	$\vdots$
k	[number of x such that $d_{k-1} \leqslant x < b$]
$(k+1)$	[number of x such that $x \geqslant b$]

1. If $x(i) < a$, add 1 to N_0.
2. If $x(i) \geqslant b$, add 1 to N_{k+1}.
3. If neither of the two preceding requirements are met, then $a \leqslant x(i) < b$; therefore compute

$$j = \left[\frac{x(i) - a}{c} \right] + 1 \qquad (2.69)$$

The [ ] notation is defined as follows: The expression $j = [a]$ means that for any real number a the integer j is such that $j \leqslant a < j+1$. That is, j is the largest integer less than or equal to a. Once j is computed as in (2.69), the

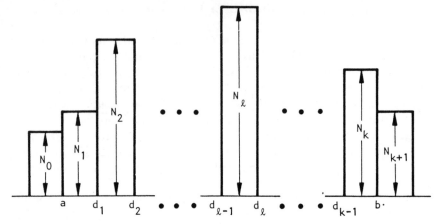

Figure 2.1   Histogram construction.

next step is simply that of adding 1 to N_j. This technique is easy to implement on most digital computers.

Three forms of sequences based on the above are used. The first is the histogram, which is simply the sequence $\{N_j\}$ without change. The second sequence is $\{P_j\}$, where

$$P_j = \text{sample probability that } \left[d_{j-1} \leqslant x < d_j \right]$$

$$= \frac{N_j}{N} \qquad j = 0, 1, \ldots, k+1 \tag{2.70}$$

The third is the sample probability density function (PDF) which takes the form of the sequence $\{p_j\}$, $j = 0, \ldots, k+1$, where

$$P_j = \frac{N_j k}{N(b-a)} \tag{2.71}$$

This can be interpreted as the derivative of the distribution function at the midpoint of each interval.

Before the above procedure can be effected, values for a, b, and k must be chosen. The question naturally arises, what is a reasonable criterion for the choice of these three parameters? There is no good single answer to this problem. Much of the choice must rest on assumptions about the underlying distribution being examined and the manner in which the data were collected. Data obtained using a system like the hypothetical data-acquisition system of Chapter 2 have two limitations imposed on them, namely, that the data are restricted in range, and within that range there are only a finite number of possible levels. If the digitizer has only 128 levels, then it is clearly senseless to choose $k > 128$, as some of the levels must be empty. Also, it is easy to visualize a situation in which the apportionment of ADC counts (or their converted equivalents) to the subintervals of the sample PDF would cause a biasing of answers.

Suppose a digitizer with 16 levels is used and that the output is analyzed without any conversion to engineering units. Suppose further that each of the levels $0, \ldots, 15$ is equally likely, so that the a priori probability of the ith count occurring is $1/16$. If k is taken to be the 12 and a and b are 0 and 15, respectively, then the following distribution of counts would take place.

Pocket	Range	Levels Contained
1	0–1.25	0, 1
2	1.25–2.50	2
3	2.50–3.75	3
4	3.75–5.00	4
5	5.00–6.25	5, 6
6	6.25–7.50	7
7	7.50–8.75	8
8	8.75–10.00	9
9	10.00–11.25	10, 11
10	11.25–12.50	12
11	12.50–13.75	13
12	13.75–15.00	14

The expected contents of pockets 1, 5, and 9 will be twice as large as those of the other pockets, so that the sample PDF obtained would tend to be highly biased at those values, and thus, imply an incorrect result.

The above example shows that reasonable care should be exercised when setting up the calculations for the PDF and that the criteria employed should be scrutinized in order to avoid the pitfalls of biasing. One criterion for establishing the parameters arises from an attempt to determine the answer to a different but related problem; namely, that of deciding whether or not the data are normal (Gaussian) in distribution.

The Chi-Square Goodness-of-Fit Test for Normality

The PDF for the normal distribution, denoted by ϕ is given by (2.18).

$$\phi(x) = \frac{1}{\sqrt{2\pi\sigma^2}} \exp\left(-\frac{(x-\mu)^2}{2\sigma^2}\right)$$

The *probability distribution function* is the integral of the density function

$$\text{prob}[x \leqslant X] = \frac{1}{2\pi\sigma^2} \int_{-\infty}^{X} \exp\left(-\frac{(t-\mu)^2}{2\sigma^2}\right) dt$$

$$= \frac{1}{2\pi} \int_{-\infty}^{(X-\mu)/\sigma} \exp\left(\frac{-t^2}{2}\right) dt$$

$$= \Phi\left(\frac{X-\mu}{\sigma}\right) \tag{2.72}$$

The probability that the variable lies between α and β is given by

$$p[\alpha \leqslant x < \beta] = \Phi\left(\frac{\beta-\mu}{\sigma}\right) - \Phi\left(\frac{\alpha-\mu}{\sigma}\right) \tag{2.73}$$

The normal distribution is assumed as a hypothesis in many analyses, and it arises naturally out of many theoretical calculations. It is often desirable, therefore, to see if the collected data can indeed be reasonably assumed to be Gaussian. One procedure for making a check of the hypothesis is known as the chi-square goodness-of-fit test. The general procedure involves the use of the chi-square statistic as a measure of the discrepancy between an observed PDF and the theoretical density function. An hypothesis of equivalence is then tested by studying the sampling distribution of chi square. The number of occurrences that would be expected to fall within the ith class interval, if the data are Gaussian, is called the expected frequency in the class interval and is denoted by F_j. The discrepancy between the observed frequency and expected frequency is $(N_j - F_j)$. To measure the total discrepancy, each interval must be used, since

$$\sum_{j=0}^{k+1} N_j = \sum_{j=0}^{k+1} F_j = N \tag{2.74}$$

The sum of the discrepancies must be 0. Note that F_j, in general, will not be an integer. The F_j are computed as follows:

$$F_0 = N\Phi\left(\frac{a-m}{s}\right)$$

$$\vdots$$

$$F_j = N\left\{\Phi\left(\frac{a+jc-m}{s}\right) - \Phi\left[\frac{a+c(j-1)-m}{s}\right]\right\}$$

$$F_{k+1} = N\left[1 - \Phi\left(\frac{b-m}{s}\right)\right] \tag{2.75}$$

The sample chi square is obtained as follows:

$$X^2 = \sum_{j=0}^{k+1} \frac{(N_j - F_j)^2}{F_j} \tag{2.76}$$

Under suitable assumptions, this sample chi square will have an approximate χ^2 distribution and may be compared with the theoretical chi-square distribution denoted by $\chi^2_{n;\alpha}$.

The distribution for χ^2, which was introduced earlier in this chapter, is discussed in many references, such as Bendat and Piersol [1971]. It depends on the number of independent squared variables in χ^2 (the number of degrees of freedom (d.f.), n). The value of n is equal to $(k+2)$ if all pockets including the end ones are used, minus the number of different independent linear restrictions imposed on the observations. There is one such restriction, for once the frequencies of the first $(k+1)$ class intervals are known, the frequency in the last class interval is known because their sum is N. There are two additional restrictions caused by fitting the theoretical normal density function to the frequency histograms for the observed data. These arise because the sample mean and sample variance, rather than the true mean and variance, are used to calculate the $\{F_j\}$. The effect of this is to subtract another 2 d.f. from the data. Thus if all $\{N_j\}$ are used, then

$$n = (k+2) - 3 = k - 1 \tag{2.77}$$

The value for n actually used may be smaller than this, as pockets for which $F < 2$ should be combined with other pockets. The details of this are described below.

Once the proper d.f., n, is established for χ^2, a hypothesis test may be performed as follows. Let it be hypothesized that the variable x is normally distributed. After grouping the sampled observations into the $(k+2)$ class intervals and computing F_j for each interval based on the sample mean and variance, compute X^2 as indicated in (2.76). Any deviation of the sample PDF from the normal distribution will cause X^2 to increase. The hypothesis that data are normally distributed is accepted if

$$X^2 \leqslant \chi^2_{n;\alpha} \tag{2.78}$$

In this case, that acceptance is at the α level of significance. If X^2 is greater than $\chi^2_{n;\alpha}$, the hypothesis is rejected at the α level of significance. Significance levels of 5, 10, and 20% (corresponding to confidence levels of 95, 90, and 80%) are commonly employed. The particular level selected is largely a matter of personal choice. The authors tend to favor α equal to the traditional value of 5%, given no additional information.

Based on the assumption that a chi-square goodness-of-fit test for normality is to be made, an expression for the number of class intervals for a given N has been derived [Kendall and Stuart, 1961]. This expression assumes that the data are uncorrelated and that $\alpha = 0.05$:

$$\text{Number of class intervals} = 1.87\,(N-1)^{2/5} \qquad (2.79)$$

This function is tabulated in Table 2.1. As stated earlier, as soon as the number of class intervals becomes comparable with the number of digitizer count levels, large biases may result.

Table 2.1

**Minimum Optimum Number (k) of Class Intervals
for Sample Size N when $\alpha = 0.05$**

N	k	N	k
200	16	20,000	94
400	20	40,000	129
600	24	70,000	162
800	27	100,000	187
1,000	30	200,000	247
1,500	35	400,000	326
2,000	39	700,000	407
4,000	57	1,000,000	470
7,000	65	1,140,000	500
10,000	74		

A standard rule of thumb used by statisticians when applying the chi-square test is that every interval should have an expected frequency of at least 2. This requirement enables one to determine reasonable values for a and b. The end pockets have the smallest expected occupancy. Thus the parameter a should satisfy the following equation:

$$2 = N \left\{ \frac{1}{\sqrt{2\pi}} \int_{-\infty}^{(a-m)/s} e^{-t^2/2}\,dt \right\} \qquad (2.80)$$

This can be solved implicitly for a. After a value is found for a, the parameter b is simply

$$b = 2m - a \qquad (2.81)$$

The parameter k is given by

$$k = [\text{number of class intervals}] - 2 \qquad (2.82)$$

After these three parameters are established, it is then possible to calculate the sample PDF and the expected normal occupancy.

The next step is to make the comparison to see if the data are to be accepted or rejected insofar as normality is concerned. As mentioned earlier, the usual procedure for comparing X^2 with $\chi^2_{n;\alpha}$ is that of computing α', where α' is defined by

$$\alpha' = \text{Prob}\left[X^2 > \chi^2_{n;\alpha'} \right] \tag{2.83}$$

The α' parameter is a function of X^2 and n only. Compute it, compare it with the preselected value α, and conduct the test for normality on the following basis:

$$\alpha' \leqslant \alpha \qquad \text{Reject}$$

$$\alpha' > \alpha \qquad \text{Accept} \tag{2.84}$$

One method for computing α' is the following:

$$\alpha' = 2\Phi(X) - 1 - \sqrt{\frac{2}{\pi}} \, e^{-X^2/2}$$

$$\times \left[\sum_{r=1}^{(n-1)/2} \frac{X^{2r-1}}{1\cdot 3\cdot 5 \ldots (2r-1)} \right] \qquad \text{for } n \text{ odd} \tag{2.85a}$$

or

$$\alpha' = 1 - e^{-X^2/2}\left[1 + \sum_{r=1}^{(n-2)/2} \frac{X^{2r}}{2\cdot 4\cdot 6 \ldots (2r)} \right] \qquad \text{for } n \text{ even} \tag{2.85b}$$

More efficient and accurate algorithms exist but the above are generally adequate for time series analysis problems.

2.8   PEAK PROBABILITY DENSITY FUNCTIONS

There is a serious nomenclature problem regarding the definition of peaks, maxima, and minima. There are at least three distinct problems that are of interest when discussing the occurrence of extreme values in a given record:

1. Distribution of the largest (or smallest) value in a record of length p.
2. Distribution of the largest value occurring between two zero crossings.
3. Distribution of the peak values.

As an example of the first type, suppose that N values of the function $\{x_i\}$ are recorded and that they are independent with density function $f(x)$ and distribution function $F(x)$. Then the density function of the largest value of x is

$$f(x_{max}, N) = Nf(x)[F(x)]^{N-1} \tag{2.86}$$

The distribution function of x_{max} is

$$F(x_{max}, N) = [F(x)]^N \tag{2.87}$$

The expected value of x_{max} is

$$E[x_{max}] = \int_{-\infty}^{\infty} xNf(x)F^{N-1}(x)\,dx \tag{2.88}$$

Suppose x_i consists of N independent, uniformly distributed random variables with the range of x being $[-\frac{1}{2}, \frac{1}{2}]$. Then

$$f(x_i) = \begin{cases} 1 & -\frac{1}{2} \leqslant x_i \leqslant \frac{1}{2} \\ 0 & \text{elsewhere} \end{cases}$$

$$F(x_i) = \begin{cases} 0 & x < -\frac{1}{2} \\ x + \frac{1}{2} & -\frac{1}{2} \leqslant x \leqslant \frac{1}{2} \\ 1 & x > \frac{1}{2} \end{cases}$$

$$F(x_{max}, N) = \begin{cases} 0 & x_{max} < -\frac{1}{2} \\ \left(x + \frac{1}{2}\right)^N & -\frac{1}{2} \leqslant x_{max} \leqslant \frac{1}{2} \\ 1 & x_{max} > \frac{1}{2} \end{cases}$$

$$E[x_{max}] = \int_{-1/2}^{1/2} xN\left(x + \frac{1}{2}\right)^{N-1} dx$$

$$= \frac{N-1}{2(N+1)} \tag{2.89}$$

Although $E[x_{max}]$ as given in (2.88) may be difficult to evaluate in theory, the finding of x_{max} in a sample set of data is quite easy. Indeed, even if there is no specific interest in x_{max} or x_{min}, it is a good idea to have them found by the computer program anyway, because they are frequently useful when a set of data is checked for wild points.

The second type of peak analysis encountered is concerned with the set of largest values between zero crossings. These are simple to find. The following algorithm is typical of one that might be employed. As usual, it is assumed that $\{x_i\}$ has N points:

1. Compute a table of $\{I_k\}$, $k=1,\ldots,K$, where I_k is in the table if

$$x_{I_k} \leqslant 0 \quad \text{and} \quad 0 < x_{(I_k+1)}$$

or

$$0 < x_{I_k} \quad \text{and} \quad x_{(I_k+1)} \leqslant 0$$

2. If $0 < x_{I_k}$, find the minimum of x_i, $i = (I_k+1),\ldots,I_{k+1}$; otherwise, find the maximum value.
3. Continuing, if $x_{I_k} < 0$, find the maximum of x_i, $i = (I_k+1),\ldots,I_k+1$; otherwise, find the minimum of this same set.

With the minima and maxima thus found two things could be done. First, use techniques from the preceding section and find the separate sample PDF's for both the sets of minima and maxima. Second, set the minima positive and combine them with the maxima. Statistical properties of zero crossings are well-known for many types of data, so that the maximum (or minimum) between zero crossings is relatively amenable to analysis. A somewhat more difficult problem is presented in the third case being considered in this section, that of peak values.

In this sense, a peak value is the largest value between any two relative minima. For example, as shown in Figure 2.2, there is only one type 2 peak (which is peak C), but there are three type 3 peaks (A, B, and D). The procedure for locating these values is as follows;

1. For the maxima, find all x_p such that

$$x_p - x_{p-1} > 0$$

$$x_p - x_{p+1} > 0$$

2. Similarly, for the minima, find those values x_q for which

$$x_q - x_{q-1} < 0$$

$$x_q - x_{q+1} < 0$$

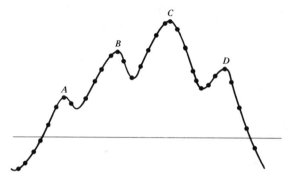

Figure 2.2   Various types of peak values.

As before, these sets of maxima and minima would be processed using the type of techniques outlined in the previous sections.

2.9   MULTIDIMENSIONAL DENSITY FUNCTIONS

If $\{x(i)\}$ and $\{y(i)\}$ are any two data functions, it is possible to compute their joint sample PDF or joint histogram. This is accomplished by dividing the range of each into k_1 and k_2 intervals, as shown in Figure 2.3. In general, more computer storage is required for the two-dimensional than for the one-dimensional case. For example, (k_1+2) cells would be required for $\{x(i)\}$ by itself and (k_2+2) cells for $\{y(i)\}$. Thus $(k_1+2)(k_2+2)$ cells might be a necessary number of pockets for their joint distribution. This might very well be excessive, especially if there are more than two functions to be processed. If there are r separate functions, then there are $(r)(r-1)/2$ ways of comparing them. Suppose that $k_1=k_2=\cdots=k_r=k$; then a total of

$$\frac{(r)(r-1)}{2}(k+2)^2$$

storage cells would be necessary. If $r=50$ and $k=100$, this is 12,744,900, whereas the one-dimensional sample PDF's with the same parameter requirements would need only 5100 cells of computer memory. (See Figure 2.3.)

A meaningful display of the results may be difficult to achieve. Computer listings of the sample joint PDF's tend to be difficult to read because of the overwhelming number of digits presented to the eye. Graphic representation is also difficult. Contour plots have been used with partial

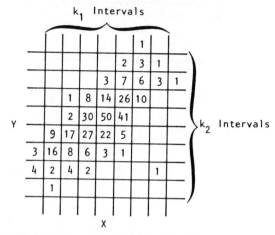

Figure 2.3 Sample joint probability density histogram.

success, but their generation is not trivial. New developments in three-dimensional display devices should increase the usefulness of joint PDF's. Presently, however, the lack of completely satisfactory methods to display the results severely complicates the generation of sample PDF's and impedes their interpretation.

2.10 EXAMPLES AND APPLICATIONS OF PROBABILTY DENSITY FUNCTIONS

Figure 2.4 shows the sample PDF of 1001 samples of uniform white noise generated on a digital computer. The theoretical PDF would be

$$f(x) = \begin{cases} 1 & -\tfrac{1}{2} \leqslant x < \tfrac{1}{2} \\ 0 & \text{otherwise} \end{cases} \tag{2.90}$$

The theoretical mean and variance therefore are

$$\mu = \int_{-\infty}^{\infty} x f(x)\,dx = 0$$

$$\sigma^2 = \int_{-\infty}^{\infty} (x - \mu)^2 f(x)\,dx$$

$$= \int_{-1/2}^{1/2} x^2\,dx = \frac{x^3}{3}\bigg|_{-1/2}^{1/2} = \frac{1}{24} + \frac{1}{24} = \frac{1}{12} = 0.08333333$$

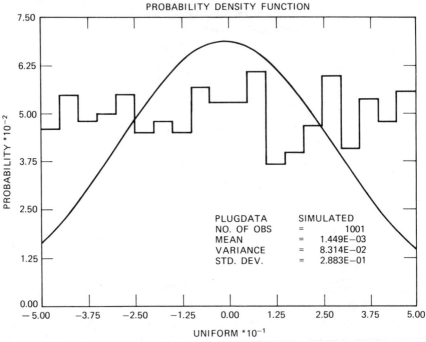

Figure 2.4 Sample PDF of a sequence of uniformly distributed white noise.

These values agree nicely with values obtained for the sample as shown in the upper right hand corner of the figure.

The sample PDF P_j is the ratio of the number of occurrences in the jth pocket divided by the total number of occurrences:

$$P_j = \frac{N_j}{N} = \text{sample probability that } \left[d_{j-1} \leqslant x < d_j \right] \qquad (2.91)$$

The expected value of P_j, therefore, is

$$E\left[P_j \right] = \int_{-\infty}^{\infty} P_j f(x)\,dx$$

$$= \int_{d_{j-1}}^{d_j} f(x)\,dx \qquad (2.92)$$

For the case of uniform noise being examined,

$$E\left[P_j \right] = \int_{d_{j-1}}^{d_j} dx = d_j - d_{j-1} \qquad (2.93)$$

PROBABILITY DENSITY FUNCTION

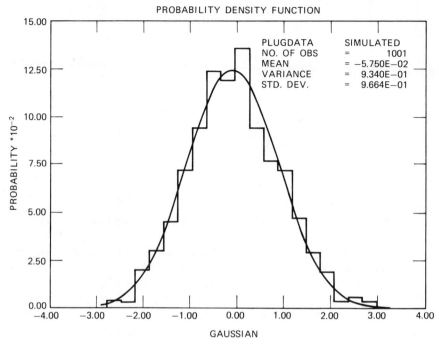

Figure 2.5 Sample PDF of a sequence of white noise with Gaussian distribution.

In particular, the difference is approximately 0.05 in this case.

Note that the Gaussian curve based on the sample mean and variance is superimposed on the sample PDF. Naturally, they do not agree very well, and the χ^2 test failed.

Figure 2.5 shows a similar test made with Gaussian noise generated by a digital pseudo-random number generator. The expected mean and variance are 0 and 1, respectively. The sample variance of 0.934 might seem a little low, but it is within reasonable distance of the expected value. The data was accepted as Gaussian at the 95% confidence level (test parameters: sample $X^2 = 18.39$; Prob[χ^2, 1000, 0.05] = 0.69825).

The next case consisted of a digital sine wave generated using the expression:

$$x(i) = \sin(0.15i) \qquad i = 0, \ldots, 1000 \qquad (2.94)$$

For a random sine wave with fixed coefficients, the statistical parameters are

$$\mu = 0$$

$$\sigma^2 = \tfrac{1}{2}$$

$$f(x) = \begin{cases} \dfrac{1}{\pi\sqrt{1-x^2}} & 1- \leqslant x \leqslant 1 \\ 0 & |x| > 1 \end{cases} \tag{2.95}$$

Note that the PDF is greater than 1 on part of the interval $(-1,1)$. However, the integral of the PDF overall or any part of the interval will be less than or equal to 1.

Figure 2.6 shows the sample PDF. The shape of the histogram and the mean and variance are in good agreement with (2.95).

The next example takes up an interesting case: passing white Gaussian noise through a narrow bandpass filter. The output of such a filter tends to look like a simple sine wave over reasonably short sections of the data. However, if a sample PDF is computed, it will not look like the PDF of a sinusoid. This is illustrated in Figure 2.7, which shows a sample PDF of 60 data points output from a bandpass filter whose distance between half power points was 1% of the total frequency band available (i.e., 1% of the Nyquist frequency) and whose center frequency was located at 15% of the Nyquist frequency. As the figure shows, the sample PDF does not resemble the one shown in Figures 2.6 or 2.5.

Figure 2.8 shows a simple PDF of the same data, but over a much longer sequence. In this case the sample PDF appears to approximate the Gaussian one rather nicely. Actually it failed the χ^2 test of the Gaussian hypothesis assuming independent data values. It very likely would have passed if N ($= 10,001$ in this case) had been adjusted to take into account the fact that the observations were not independent. This would have reduced N to 1% of its original value, namely 100 for this example. This would have correspondingly lowered the value of the sample χ^2 of the difference of the sample PDF and the Gaussian distribution based on the sample mean and variance.

In fact, when the central limit theorem is applied, Gaussian noise, or for that matter, noise with any distribution whatsoever, tends to become Gaussian when passed through a linear filter.

Applying the χ^2 test accurately in such a case may not be simple, owing to the fact that it is not easy to compute the true number of independent estimates in the sample.

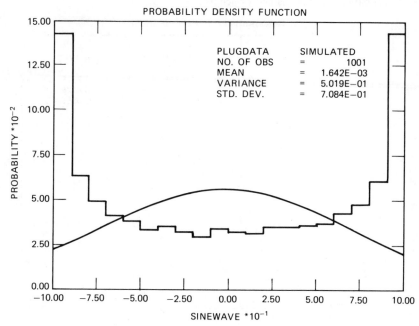

Figure 2.6 Sample PDF of a sine wave.

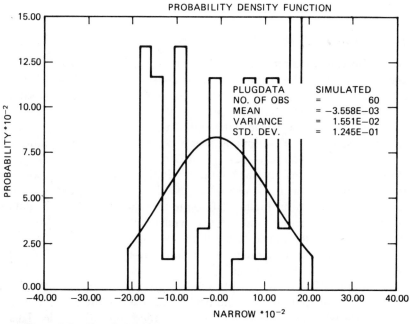

Figure 2.7 Sample PDF of a small segment of a narrow band process.

71

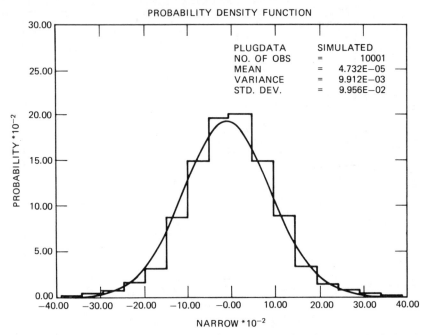

Figure 2.8 Sample PDF of a large sample of a narrow band process. Includes the data shown in Figure 2.4.

Data Validation with Probability Histograms

One way to validate a set of data would be to plot it all and look at it. For large sets of data this is tedious, time-consuming, and expensive. An economical way to help in the validation is through the use of sample PDF's. Properly interpreted, the sample PDF's yield considerable information about the nature of the data and tend to highlight many types of problems. Sample PDF output is cheap compared to a full listing and plotting for large amounts of data.

Wild points are readily shown up by PDF's. Figure 2.9 shows data generated in a manner so as to have wild points. The corresponding sample PDF is shown in Figure 2.10. Note that the majority of the data is closely bunched together, and the two wild points are located far to the right. In between, the pockets are all empty. This is typical for data with wild points since the wide range of the data due to wild points forces the real data into one or two pockets.

The sample PDF of data with another type of problem is shown in Figure 2.11. Note that both the end pockets have a considerable number of occurrences, whereas there is no data past them on either side. This is symptomatic of "clipping." Clipping can be produced in a variety of ways.

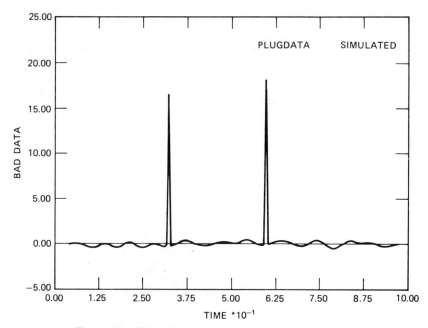

Figure 2.9 Time history generated with two wild points.

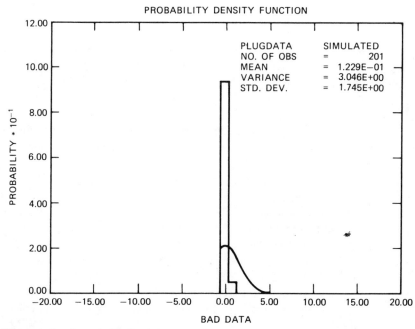

Figure 2.10 Sample PDF of the data shown in Figure 2.9. Note how the majority of the data is bunched together.

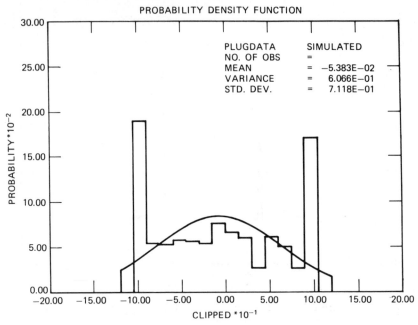

Figure 2.11   Sample PDF of clipped data.

The two most common are by overdriving an analog amplifier past the point where it is linear, or by setting up the analog to digital convertor so that it does not properly cover the entire data range for a given channel.

As for the validation procedure, the following is recommended. It is assumed that a user-written calibration program will be used to generate data:

1. Do the calibration and include with it the computation, the sample PDF, and basic statistical parameters for each output data file produced.

2. Before any further processing is done, review the sample PDF results. The review should take note of the following.
    a. The time (or whatever the independent variable is) should be checked to see that its range is proper and that the number of points counted by the sample PDF agrees with what was intended.
    b. The statistics for each dependent variable should be checked. The sample PDF's for the types of problems described above or any other that become apparent, the mean, variance, maximum, and minimum should be reviewed to see if they correspond to physical reality.

The above procedure will not guarantee that the data is good, but it should help to quickly and economically find the obvious types of problems.

EXERCISES

2.1. Prove that $E(s^2) \neq \sigma^2$ if $s^2 = \frac{1}{N}\Sigma_{i=0}^{N-1}(x_i - \bar{x})^2$.

2.2. Prove that if $x(t)$ is a sinusoid of amplitude A and arbitrary phase its variance is $A^2/2$.

2.3. Prove the claim in (2.8) that

$$\sigma_x^2 = E(x^2) - E^2(x)$$

Answer:

$$\sigma^2 = E(x - \mu)^2 = E(x^2 - 2x\mu + \mu^2)$$

$$= E(x^2) - 2E(x)\mu + \mu^2$$

$$= E(x^2) - 2\mu^2 + \mu^2$$

$$= E(x^2) - \mu^2$$

2.4. Prove that correlation is bounded by unity:

$$-1 \leqslant \frac{\text{cov}(x, y)}{\sigma_x \sigma_y} \leqslant 1$$

Answer:

$$\text{cov}(x, y) = E(x - \mu_x)(y - \mu_y) = E(xy - x\mu_y - y\mu_x + \mu_x\mu_y)$$

$$= E(xy) - \mu_x\mu_y - \mu_y\mu_x + \mu_x\mu_y$$

$$= E(xy) - \mu_x\mu_y$$

$$\text{cov}^2(x, y) = E^2(xy) - 2E(xy)\mu_x\mu_y + \mu_x^2\mu_y^2$$

$$\leqslant E(x^2)E(y^2) - E(x^2)\mu_y^2 - E(y^2)\mu_x^2 + \mu_x^2\mu_y^2.$$

2.5. Derive the autocovariance function of a sinusoid.

2.6. In (2.17), what is the equation for the sine term?

Computer Problems

2.7. Generate uniform noise and duplicate Figure 2.5.

2.8. Generate Gaussian noise and duplicate Figure 2.6.

2.9. Generate a sine wave and duplicate Figure 2.7.

CHAPTER 3

COLLECTING AND
PREPROCESSING DATA

3.1 INTRODUCTION

This chapter outlines some of the major problems that are encountered in the initial stages of time series analysis. The types of data that will be considered fall into two distinct categories.

1. *Continuous* or *analog* data.
2. Data originally digital.

The second type is perhaps the easier with which to work. Stock market data, labor statistics, annual rainfall, and a host of other examples all fall in this category. Though the finding and transcribing of this type of data can be tedious, the acquisition does not pose any problems from a statistical or applications point of view.

Continuous data, on the other hand, does have a number of problems associated with it. These include

- Measuring the data.
- Transmitting and/or recording it.
- Conversion from analog to digital format.

The measurement topic is discussed in Magrab and Blomquist, [1971]. It essentially involves devising or selecting a *transducer*, a device that converts the physical quantity being measured into an electrical voltage.

Usually, but not always, the resulting voltage is proportional to the physical quantity being measured. Included in this category are microphones, hydrophones, accelerometers, and pressure sensing devices.

Transducers usually are designed to have a transfer function which is linear within an allowable range. It is impossible to make a perfectly linear device. The range has to be bounded and most transducers to a greater or lesser degree have *hysteresis*. The latter term means that if the input varies from an initial point to a final point and retraces its values back to the initial point, then the two paths of the output, which should be identical, will not coincide exactly. A plot of this type is called the *hysteresis curve* of the instrument. For a well-designed piece of apparatus, the error will be negligible.

Even if the transducer is linear, it may have a transfer function that attenuates the input over certain frequency ranges. For example, some microphones have transfer functions which look almost like bandpass filters. That is, they pass a broad band of information, but attenuate frequencies near 0 or above a certain cutoff point. Within the bandpass the transfer characteristics may vary slightly. These facts are emphasized because in some cases it may be desirable to compensate for the attenuation.

3.2 DATA ACQUISITION

Figure 3.1 shows a typical system for acquiring analog data in a digital form.

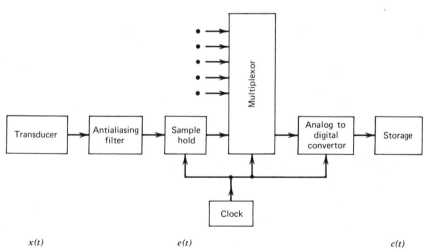

Figure 3.1 A digital data acquisition system. The clock circuit controls all the operations.

The output from the transducer first goes to an antialiasing filter. If the effective sampling rate for this function is going to be S, then in order to prevent aliasing of higher-frequency information, the filter should eliminate everything above $S/2 = F$ Hz. In other words, the ideal antialiasing filter would have a transfer function of the form

$$H(f) = \begin{cases} 1 & -F < f < F \\ 0 & \text{otherwise} \end{cases} \tag{3.1}$$

It is not possible to build a filter that perfectly implements this characteristic. There are two types of the problems that arise:

- The above form is noncausal. In order for it to be causal, there must be a delay in the form of a nonzero phase angle.
- The perfect block shape which eliminates everything outside the range $|f| > F$ is not possible. The edges or corners of the function must be rounded, and though the information greater than $|F|$ may be greatly attenuated, it is not possible to totally eliminate it.

Another problem is that if two functions are to be compared, as is often the case, then the two antialiasing filters employed should be as much alike as possible. Otherwise, different amplitude or phase characteristics may cause errors to arise when calculating transfer or correlation functions or relative delays between the two inputs.

A typical form for the lowpass filter employed for antialiasing is the Butterworth, whose absolute value squared is given by

$$|H(f)|^2 = \frac{1}{1 + \left(\dfrac{2\pi f}{2\pi B}\right)^{2M}} \tag{3.2}$$

When plotted, this will be found to have the following characteristics:

- For $f = 0$, $|H(0)|^2 = 1$.
- For $f = B$, $|H(B)|^2 = \frac{1}{2}$.
- Between $0 < f < B$, $|H(f)|^2$ tends to be flat until B is approached.
- For $f > B$, $|H(f)|^2$ becomes small rapidly with increasing f.

This can be seen by noting that for f much greater than B,

$$|H(f)|^2 \approx \left(\frac{B}{f}\right)^{2M} \tag{3.3}$$

For example, if $f = 8B$, and $M = 6$,

$$|H(8B)|^2 \approx \left(\tfrac{1}{8}\right)^{12} = 1.46 \cdot 10^{-11} = -108.4 \text{ dB} \qquad (3.4)$$

The phase characteristic of a Butterworth filter is approximately linear across the passband. This means that the phase corresponds to a simple delay.

Filtering is discussed more fully in the next two chapters. Though mainly concerned with digital filters, the terminology is applicable to the analog type in most cases.

The next device after the antialiasing filter in Figure 3.1 is the sample and hold circuit. It acts very much like an approximation of the theoretical sampling operation:

$$x(i) = \int_{-\infty}^{\infty} x(t)\delta(iT - t)\,dt \qquad (3.5)$$

It is not possible to get a perfect delta function-like action. Instead, the delta function is replaced with an aperture function which has finite width. If the aperture is rectangular, then the above would become

$$x(i) = \frac{1}{a} \int_{iT - a/2}^{iT + a/2} x(t)\,dt \qquad (3.6)$$

where the parameter a is the width of the aperture. This has the effect of computing the average of $x(t)$ from $iT - a/2$ to $iT + a/2$. Naturally, a must be smaller than T, the smaller the better.

The value of $x(i)$ is held at the sample and hold circuit, usually in the form of a voltage on a charged capacitor, until the *multiplexor* selects it to be sent to the analog to digital convertor. The multiplexor may be thought of as a rotary switch as shown in Figure 3.2, with a sampling rate S for each function. For a multiplexor with s segments, $s \cdot S$ sampled functions per second would be output from it. Many early multiplexors were rotary

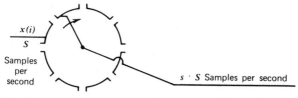

Figure 3.2 Idealized multiplexor, here shown as a rotary switch with eight segments, one each for each of eight functions being processed.

electromechanical switches as shown. Modern ones are made up of solid-state electronics.

Sometimes rather than having a different sample and hold circuit for each function before the multiplexor, economy forces the use of a single sample and hold circuit after the multiplexor. This means that rather than all the functions being sampled at one time, as would be the case where there is one sample and hold for each input, the functions are sampled sequentially. This results in a small delay between the functions; the closer together they are on the multiplexor, the smaller the delay.

A *frame* of data consists of one sample from each of the functions as taken during one rotation of the multiplexor. Associated with each frame is the time at which it was digitized. Later in the processing a time function usually is generated and added to each frame.

From the multiplexor the sampled data, still in analog form, goes to the digitizer to be converted to a digital format. Before this format is discussed, it will be worthwhile to review methods of representing data digitally.

3.3   DIGITAL REPRESENTATION OF INFORMATION

The term *bit*, due to J. W. Tukey, means *binary integer*. A bit then is a quantity that has only two possible values, 0 or 1. Numbers and quantities may be represented as a collection of bits. There are two principal ways of doing this, with binary or with *binary coded decimal* (BCD) representations.

In the binary representation the n bits

$$b_0, b_1, b_2, \ldots, b_{n-1}$$

could be interpreted* as the integer

$$(-1)^{b_0} \sum_{p=1}^{n-1} b_p 2^{n-1-p}$$

For $n = 10$, the following would be typical examples

| | Digital | |
Binary	$b=0$	$b=9$
0000000000	0	0
0000000001	1	0.001953125
1000000001	-1	0.001953125
0111111111	511	0.998046875
1111111111	-511	-0.998046875

*There are a number of other ways of setting up the definition.

It is possible to modify this definition by introducing a *binary point*. The binary point effectively multiplies the number by 2^{-b}, where b is a positive (or negative) integer. Thus for $b=9$, the same set of bits could be interpreted in a very different manner as shown.

The BCD representation uses groups of four bits to stand for a single decimal digit.

0000	0
0001	1
0010	2
0011	3
0100	4
0101	5
0110	6
0111	7
1000	8
1001	9

As an example, a digital voltmeter might read $+9.75$ on its front panel, while outputting the same in BCD via electrical connections at the rear in the following manner:

$$0 \quad 1001 \quad 0111 \quad 0101$$

BCD is not as efficient as binary. Thirteen bits are needed to get the range ± 999 in BCD, but only 11 bits are required to represent the range ± 1023 in binary. Binary has the disadvantage that at some stage it must be converted to decimal in order to make it intelligible.

Computer storage consists of a large array of bits recorded on some media, such as core, disk, tape, or drum. These bits are grouped into sets of standard length called *words*. Typical word size ranges from 4 to 60 bits. The length varies with the scale of the computer.

Computer	Number of Bits in a Word
Micro	4–16
Mini	12–32
Standard	32–60

Storage on magnetic tape is done in terms of *characters or bytes*. Seven-track tape may be thought of as a rectangular array of bits, seven across the width of the tape and hundreds of bits per inch along the length. Each set of seven bits forms one *character* and its *check sum*. The latter is the least significant bit of the sum of the other six.*

---

*There are two different ways of computing the check sum, resulting in what are known as *odd* and *even* parity.

When used with a computer having 36-bit words, these words would be stored on magnetic tape as six adjacent characters.

With nine-track tape, there are nine bits across the width of the tape; eight of them form one byte and the ninth acts as a check sum as in the seven-track case. Thus for a 32-bit computer, one word would be stored as four adjacent bytes on tape.

Within the computer, the words have two types of interpretation insofar as numerical representation of information is concerned: *fixed point* and *floating point*. Fixed point representation is the type described earlier where the bits are interpreted as representing a number times a scale factor; the whole word is used for the representation, and the scale facter is understood rather than actually existing in the machine.

Floating point, on the other hand, carries the binary point with it. Two standard floating point word formats will be discussed.

On machines such as the Univac 1108, which has 36-bit words, the words are broken down into three parts: *sign, characteristic*, and *mantissa*. The definition of sign is obvious. The characteristic has the scale information, and the mantissa has the actual numerical information. The bits are assigned as follows:

	Bits	Function
s	0	Sign
$c_1,\ldots,c_8$	1–8	Characteristic
$m_1,\ldots,m_{27}$	9–35	Mantissa

A number would be interpreted as

$$(-1)^s\left(2^{\left(\Sigma_{p=1}^{8} c_p 2^{(8-p)}\,-\,128\right)}\right)\sum_{q=1}^{27} m_q 2^{-q}$$

Sign   Characteristic   Mantissa

Thus the characteristic has the range $2^{-128}=2.9387\ldots\cdot10^{-39}$ to $2^{128}=1.7014\ldots\cdot10^{38}$. The mantissa is less than 1, so it has the range 0 to $1-2^{-27}$. Unity in this scheme is

010 000 001 100 000 000 000 000 000 000 000 000

201400000000_8

The lower figure is the upper one written in *octal*. The binary digits are grouped together in bunches of three each and rewritten as follows:

$$000 \to 0$$
$$001 \to 1$$
$$010 \to 2$$
$$011 \to 3$$
$$100 \to 4$$
$$101 \to 5$$
$$110 \to 6$$
$$111 \to 7$$

Octal representation decreases the number of digits that have to be written in the ratio three to one; in this case, 36 to 12.

Another example of floating point representation is that found on the IBM 360-370 series computers as well as on Xerox, SEL, and some Univac machines. These devices have 32-bit words set up as follows for floating point:

	Bits	Function
s	0	Sign
$c_1, \ldots, c_7$	1–7	Characteristic
$m_1, \ldots, m_{24}$	8–32	Mantissa

A number is represented in the form

$$(-1)^s 16^{\left(\Sigma_{p=1}^{7} c_p 2^{(7-p)} - 64 \right)} \sum_{q=1}^{24} m_q 2^{-q}$$

Note that the scaling is done with a power of 16 rather than a power of two. The range of the scaling, therefore, is $16^{-64} = 8.636 \ldots \cdot 10^{-78}$ to $16^{63} = 7.237 \ldots \cdot 10^{75}$ so that the range of this *hexadecimal* scaling is much greater than that shown previously for the 36-bit word with power of two scaling.

However, this 32-bit format turns out to be far less accurate than the 36-bit one. In addition to the basic difference of three bits in the mantissa, the two formats differ in their *normalization*. A floating point number is normalized if the most significant bit of the mantissa is moved to the farthest left position. In the case of the 36-bit word, m_1 will always be 1, with a few exceptions.* This means that the full 27 bits of the mantissa are always available. In the 32-bit format with power of 16 scaling, this is not

---

*The number 0, for example.

always possible. The first 15 integers in binary are

	Binary	Hexadecimal
1	0001	1
2	0010	2
3	0011	3
4	0100	4
5	0101	5
6	0110	6
7	0111	7
8	1000	8
9	1001	9
10	1010	A
11	1011	B
12	1100	C
13	1101	D
14	1110	E
15	1111	F

All these would have the same scale factor, namely, 16. That is, if a binary point is assumed now on the left, these numbers cannot be further left adjusted. The effect of this is to lower the number of bits on the average that are available for storing information.

For some 32-bit machines a similar thing happens in rounding. That is, after the completion of a floating point multiply, the rounding off of the product is also done in a power of 16 arithmetic procedure.

The result of the above is that this type of machine does not have as good accuracy as the 36-bit machine. Converted to decimal, the number of significant decimal digits for the 36-bit floating point word is

$$\log_{10} 2^{27} = 8.13$$

Statistical studies have shown that on the average nearly three bits out of the 24 in the mantissa of the 32-bits word are lost owing to the hexadecimal scaling and rounding. This means that the number of decimal digits is

$$\log_{10} 2^{21} = 6.32$$

In other words, there is a difference of nearly two decimal digits between the 32- and 36-bit formats.

As it turns out, six decimal digits are not nearly enough for some calculations that are made in time series work; in these cases, it is necessary to employ *double precision*.

3.4   ANALOG TO DIGITAL CONVERSION

In order to avoid confusion in the following, a single input function is considered in analyzing the digitization process. However, this one function will have several representations:

$x(t) =$ original physical quantity

$x_e(t) = x(t)$ converted to volts by the transducer

$C(t) = x_e(t)$ converted to *continuous* counts

$c(i) = x_e(t)$ converted to rounded counts

$e(i) =$ error term $= C(iT) - c(i)$

The $C(t)$ function is an invention employed here to make the plotting of graphs more intelligible. $C(t)$ and $c(i)$ are both in units of *counts*. $C(t)$ is simply $x_e(t)$ after a linear transformation of the form

$$C(t) = Ax_e(t) + B \qquad (3.7)$$

For example, if the nominal range for $x_e(t)$ is -5 to 5 V, and this is to correspond to a range of 0–1023 counts for $C(t)$, then $A = 102.3$ and $B = 511.5$.

Figure 3.3*a* shows a $C(t)$ function and the corresponding $c(i)$ values actually output from the digitizer. The relationship between the two functions is

$$c(i) = \left[\, C(iT) + 0.5^- \,\right] \qquad (3.8)$$

The brackets in this case are defined to mean "the smallest integer greater than or equal to the expression inside the brackets." The 0.5^- is a term added to make the operation *rounding*. Without it, the brackets would *truncate*.

The error term $e(i)$ is defined to be the difference between $c(i)$ and $C(t)$:

$$e(i) = C(iT) - c(i) \qquad (3.9)$$

If the digitizer is working properly, $e(i)$ is limited to the range $(-\frac{1}{2}, \frac{1}{2})$ counts. Figure 3.3*b* shows the error sequence for the $C(t)$ and $c(i)$ functions given in part *a* of the figure. The above equation can be reversed to yield

$$c(i) = C(iT) + e(i) \qquad (3.10)$$

In this sense, $c(i)$ is $C(iT)$ plus the error term or *noise*.

The next problem is to characterize the function $e(i)$. There is no best

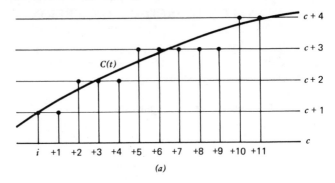

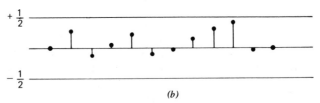

Figure 3.3 (*a*) The function $C(t)$ is shown passing through four count levels. Superimposed on $C(t)$ and shown in whole counts is $c(i)$, the digitized version of $C(t)$. (*b*) The error term in counts, $e(i)$.

way of doing it. For some cases $e(i)$ behaves like a random variable, whereas for others it may be very highly correlated or even periodic.

Consider, for example, the $C(t)$ function to be a sinusoid at the folding frequency defined by

$$C(t) = 511.25\left[\cos\left(\frac{\pi t}{T}\right) + 1\right] + 0.25 \tag{3.11}$$

Then $C(iT)$ will be (note change in the independent variable)

$$C(iT) = 511.25\left[\cos(\pi i) + 1\right] + 0.25$$

$$= 1022.5 + 0.25 = 1022.75 \quad \text{for } i \text{ even}$$

$$= 0.25 \quad \text{for } i \text{ odd} \tag{3.12}$$

Therefore,

$$c(i) = \begin{cases} 1023 & \text{for } i \text{ even} \\ 0 & \text{for } i \text{ odd} \end{cases}$$

$$e(i) = \begin{cases} -0.25 & \text{for } i \text{ even} \\ 0.25 & \text{for } i \text{ odd} \end{cases} \tag{3.13}$$

Thus the error term is also a sinusoid at the folding frequency and hence is periodic.

The other extreme is when the $e(i)$ term is completely random. This can happen under a variety of circumstances. Because this case is very interesting, it is studied in detail.

The following assumptions are made:

1. $e(i)$ is random. That is, $E[e(i)e(i+p)]=0$ for $p \neq 0$.
2. $e(i)$ is uniformly distributed.

The second assumption means that all values of $e(i)$ between $-\frac{1}{2}$ and $\frac{1}{2}$ are equally likely. Thus the probability density function $p(e)$ is given by

$$p(e)=\begin{cases} 1 & -\frac{1}{2} \leqslant e < \frac{1}{2} \\ 0 & \text{otherwise} \end{cases} \tag{3.14}$$

The computations for μ_e and σ_e^2, the mean and variance of $e(i)$, are given by

$$\mu_e = E[e] = \int_{-\infty}^{\infty} ep(e)\,de = 0$$

$$\sigma_e^2 = E[(e-\mu_e)]^2 = \int_{-\infty}^{\infty} (e-\mu_e)^2 p(e)\,de = \int_{-\frac{1}{2}}^{\frac{1}{2}} e^2\,de$$

$$= \frac{e^3}{3}\bigg|_{-\frac{1}{2}}^{\frac{1}{2}} = \frac{1}{12} \tag{3.15}$$

The mean of 0 and variance $\frac{1}{12}$ are in counts and counts squared. In order to convert the variance into physical units, an appropriate multiplying factor must be used. If one count corresponds to p physical units, then the variance would be $p^2/12$. For example, if the range 0–1023 counts corresponds to 0–5 V, then each count corresponds to $5/1023 = 4.8876 \cdot 10^{-3}$ V/count and the variance would be $1.9907 \cdot 10^{-6}$ volts squared. The full range of the digitizer is frequently a power of 2. If the total range of the digitizer corresponds to E physical units, then

$$\sigma_x^2 = \left(\frac{E}{2^n}\right)^2 \frac{1}{12} = \frac{E^2 2^{-2n}}{12} \tag{3.16}$$

where n is the number of digits in the digitizer word. Note that this error decreases exponentially with increasing n. For each extra bit in the digitizer word, the error decreases by a factor of 4 (or 6 dB). Thus in theory the noise level can be made to be arbitrarily small by increasing n. This result is described fully in Oliver, Pierce, and Shannon [1948].

In actual practice, the cost of the digitizer, among other things, is a function of the number of bits. Values of n from 6 to 18 are the current extremes of the range, with 10 and 12 being the most common in time series work. The six-bit digitizers are found in megacycle rate devices such as radar signal processors, whereas the 18-bit ones are likely to be quite slow. Eighteen bits corresponds to an accuracy of nearly $5\frac{1}{2}$ decimal digits. It is very difficult to build and maintain a device to this level. In fact, the same is often said of the 15-bit digitizer.

Table 3.1 shows ranges in counts and decimal digits for six digitizers of power of 2 type.

Table 3.1

Range in Counts and Decimal Digits for Several Binary Digitizing Schemes

Number of Bits	Range in counts	Decimal Digits
6	63	1.8
8	255	2.4
10	1,023	3.0
12	4,095	3.6
15	32,768	4.5
18	262,143	5.4

The power spectral density of the error or noise term may be quickly computed. Because the noise is assumed to be uncorrelated, it will have a flat spectrum. In particular, the product of the power spectral density and the width of the interval from 0 to the folding frequency must be equal to the variance. This follows from the formula

$$\sigma_x^2 = 2\int_0^F S_x(f)df = 2S_x(f)F \tag{3.17}$$

provided that $S_x(f)$ is constant. Hence

$$S_x(f) = \frac{\sigma_x^2}{2F} = T\sigma_x^2 \tag{3.18}$$

For a digitizer range corresponding to E physical units, the PSD of the digitizing noise is

$$S_e(f) = \frac{E^2 2^{-2n}T}{12} \tag{3.19}$$

It is interesting to compare this with the theoretical PSD of a sinusoid. It may be shown that the maximum amplitude sinusoid has a peak at $A^2P/4$. In this case $A = E/2$ so the amplitude of the peak becomes $E^2P/16$. The ratio of the peak of the sinusoid PSD to the average value of the noise PSD therefore is

$$\left(\frac{E^2P}{16}\right) \Big/ \left(\frac{E^2 2^{-2n} T}{12}\right) = \frac{3}{4}\frac{P2^{2n}}{T} \tag{3.20}$$

Because $P = NT$, this further reduces to

$$\tfrac{3}{4}N2^{2n}$$

If $N = 1024$ and $n = 10$, not unreasonable values, then the ratio when converted to decibels is approximately 90 dB. This is an asymptotic value. Computer roundoff noise and other factors lower the ratio to 60 dB, which is a typical result obtained by digital spectral analyzers using the above parameters. This is one method of defining *dynamic range* of a PSD analyzer.

3.5   OTHER ERRORS

The following are some of the more common problems with a data acquisition system:

- Extraneous electrical noise picked up from the environment.
- Noise added by amplifiers.
- Distortion caused by signal levels too high.
- Excessive noise level owing to the signal being too low.
- Folded higher-frequency information owing to the antialiasing filters: the filters either are of poor quality or do not exist.
- Aperture error in the sampling device.
- Jitter in the sampling device.
- Nonlinearities in the digitizer.
- Dropout in the digitizer.
- Digitizer noise.
- Operator error.

In order to avoid or minimize these problems, there are three basic steps that should be taken:

1. Before equipment is ordered, the test should be looked at from its end result: what is the nature of the problem being solved? What are the parameters that are to be calculated? How accurate must they be in order to provide definitive answers? After these questions are answered, the equipment can then be specified. It is not always possible to answer the above questions in practice, but the experimentor should ask them of himself, or he will find that the nature of the experiment has been determined by the equipment rather than the solution being sought.

2. The system should be as automatic as possible. Usually a data acquisition system is controlled by a computer. The computer should be configured and programmed so that it is in charge of the experiment. As a result, it can print out key parameters such as sampling rates and calibration factors. If these are not recorded by an independent source it is all too possible to make an error either in setting the parameters into the system or in writing down their values.

3. The system should be made to be self-checking, and a set of checks should be run periodically: for critical experiments this should be done both before and after a test run. It is relatively easy to add a digital to analog convertor (DAC) to the system. With one or more DAC's, a closed loop test can be run: the system generates some data digitally in its computer and converts it to analog via the DAC's; the output of the DAC's is then input to system as data and sampled and digitized; the original and final functions are then compared. This type of closed loop check can detect nonlinearities, some forms of dropout, improperly set digitizing rates, and other such problems. Where it is possible to implement, it is strongly recommended.

Aperture Error

The *aperture error* mentioned above is caused by the fact that the sampling of the continuous function is not done with a delta function, but rather with finite width functions such as that described in Section 3.2. For the moment, suppose that the rectangular aperture operation is applied to the continuous function $x(t)$ resulting in $y(t)$:

$$y(t) = \frac{1}{a} \int_{t-a/2}^{t+a/2} x(\tau) \, d\tau \tag{3.21}$$

This is the convolution of $x(t)$ with the boxcar function

$$u^*(t) \begin{cases} \dfrac{1}{a} & -\dfrac{a}{2} \leqslant t < \dfrac{a}{2} \\ 0 & \text{otherwise} \end{cases} \tag{3.22}$$

The asterisk is added because this boxcar is different from the standard one given in Chapter 1. In the frequency domain $Y(f)$ is the product of $X(f)$ and $U^*(f)$:

$$Y(f) = X(f)U^*(f) \tag{3.23}$$

where $U^*(f)$ is defined by

$$U^*(f) = \frac{\sin \omega a/2}{\omega a/2} \tag{3.24}$$

Suppose that $a = T$. That is, the aperture is exactly as wide as the sampling interval that will be employed in digitizing. The resulting $U^*(f)$ function is shown in Figure 3.4.

As can be seen in the figure, there is some attenuation on the principal range of 0–F Hz. The value of $U^*(f)$ at the folding frequency is down to $2/\pi$ from unity. Because $U^*(f)$ is effectively the transfer function of the aperture operation, it is clear that there will be attenuation of the higher frequency information in this case.

This problem can be alleviated by decreasing a, the width of the aperture. It should also be remembered that the rectangular aperture function is an idealization of the true function. The true aperture is probably rounded at the corners and with a broader base than top.

Jitter is the process whereby sampling does not take place at the precise instant it should. That is, rather than sampling at $t = iT$, the sampling is done at $iT + J(t)$, where $J(t)$ is a random process. For example, one type

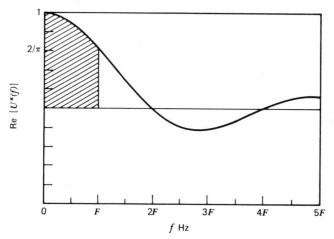

Figure 3.4 Aperture boxcar function for $a = T$.

of function would have

$$p[J(f)] = \begin{cases} 1/T & -\dfrac{T}{2} \leqslant J(t) < \dfrac{T}{2} \\ 0 & \text{otherwise} \end{cases} \tag{3.25}$$

This simply has the acutal time of sampling as being uniformly distributed in the interval of width T about the point iT.

The analysis of jitter is a complex problem. The standard reference [Balakrishnan, 1962] characterizes it as follows. Define $y(t)$ as $x(i)$ with jitter:

$$y(i) = x[i + J(i)] \tag{3.26}$$

Balakrishnan demonstrates that the one-sided power spectral density of $y(i)$, labeled $G_y(f)$, is

$$G_y(f) = |C(f)|^2 G_x(f) + \frac{R_x(0) - a^2}{F} \tag{3.27}$$

where

$G_x(f) = $ the one-sided PSD of $x(i) = 2S_x(f)$

$C(f) = $ the characteristic function of the distribution of $J(i)$

$R_x(0) = $ the autocorrelation of $x(i)$ evaluated at zero

$$a^2 = \int_0^F |C(f)|^2 G_x(f)\, df \tag{3.28}$$

This is done under the assumption that

$$E[J(n)J(m)] = 0 \qquad \text{for} \quad n \neq m \tag{3.29}$$

That is, the jitter is uncorrelated with itself. The purpose of the a^2 term is to keep the total power the same. When $G_y(f)$ is integrated to find the total power $[R_y(0)]$, it will reduce to $R_x(0)$, so that the total power is unchanged by the jitter.

The $C(f)$ function, defined to be the characteristic function of the probability density function of $J(i)$, is explicitly

$$C(f) = \int_{-\infty}^{\infty} \text{Prob}[J] \exp(2\pi f J)\, dJ \tag{3.30}$$

Balakrishnan considers three distributions for $J(i)$:

1. For Gaussian jitter with variance σ^2,

$$|C(f)|^2 = \exp(4\pi^2 f^2 \sigma^2)$$

2. For uniformly distributed jitter such that

$$\text{Prob}[J(t)] = \begin{cases} \dfrac{1}{\gamma T} & -\dfrac{\gamma T}{2} < J(t) < \dfrac{\gamma T}{2} \\ 0 & \text{otherwise} \end{cases}$$

then

$$|C(f)|^2 = \left(\frac{\sin \pi \gamma f T}{\pi \gamma f T} \right)^2$$

3. For

$$\text{Prob}[J(i)] = \begin{cases} P & J(i) = -\gamma T \\ (1-P) & J(i) = \gamma T \end{cases}$$

then

$$C(f) = (1-P)^2 + P^2 + 2P(1-P)\cos 4\pi \gamma f T$$

The first two cases are the most important. Both of them are characterized as follows:

• The $|C(f)|^2$ term tends to attenuate $G_x(f)$ for increasing f. That is, the error is larger at higher frequencies.
• There is a flat, white noise component added in the process, the $(R_x(0) - a^2)/F$ term.

Balakrishnan notes that it is not possible to make any statement for case 3 about attenuation with increasing frequency. Cases 1 and 2, however, seem to be good models for a variety of practical situations.

3.6 CONVERSION TO PHYSICAL UNITS

Two common procedures for converting to engineering units are discussed in this section. These are *step calibration* and *sinusoidal calibration*.

In both cases it is assumed that prior to recording data the transducer is effectively disconnected from the circuit, after which calibration voltages are injected into it. This happens because it is usually impossible to stimulate the transducer itself with the exact force required for the standardization.

In the step calibrations, a series of voltage steps are employed. For example, if the range of the voltage applied to the transducer is 0–5 V, then steps of 0.0, 2.5, and 5.0 V could be employed.* Each step would last a specified span of time, say, 1 sec each. These steps would each be digitized. For programming convenience, it would be best to arrange matters so that they are clearly distinguishable. For example, the steps could be put in separate records if digital magnetic tape is the recording media, the starting and stopping of the record being accomplished by *interrupts* from the device producing the steps.

The first item in the computational procedure is to average each of the steps separately to arrive at a smoothed single value for the step. Label these $a_1, a_2, \ldots, a_N$ (N steps assumed).

Second, values in physical units for each of the steps would be input to the computer, one for each a_k. Label these $p_1, \ldots, p_N$.

Suppose that data are now input to be processed. The data will be in counts as output by the digitizer. This is the sequence $c(i)$ as discussed earlier. The calibrated data sequence $x(i)$ is obtained by combining all of this information.

Linear interpolation is commonly used in calibration and consists of the following: find K such that

$$a_K \leqslant c(i) < a_{K+1}$$

Then

$$x(i) = p_K + (p_{K+1} - p_K) \frac{c(i) - a_K}{a_{K+1} - a_K} \tag{3.31}$$

The end points can be taken care of with the same formulas with the following modifications:

1. For $c(i) < a_1$, take $K = 1$.
2. For $c(i) > a_N$, take $K = N - 1$.

In both cases the interpolating formula will extrapolate.

*The actual procedure often is to replace the transducer with calibration resistors, one for each step.

Sinusoidal calibration is done by injecting a sine wave of known amplitude into the system and recording and digitizing many periods of it.

In processing it, the mean is computed as usual by

$$\bar{d} = \frac{1}{N} \sum_{i=1}^{N} d(i) \tag{3.32}$$

where the sequence $d(i)$ is the digitized sine wave and $\bar{d}$ is the average of it. As before, the sample variance is

$$s_d^2 = \frac{1}{N-1} \sum_{i=1}^{N} \left(d(i) - \bar{d} \right)^2 \tag{3.33}$$

These calculations yield three points:

$$a_3 = \bar{d} + \sqrt{2s_d} \qquad \text{positive peak of the sine wave in counts}$$

$$a_2 = \bar{d} \qquad \text{zero of the sine wave in counts} \tag{3.34}$$

$$a_1 = \bar{d} - \sqrt{2s_d} \qquad \text{negative peak of the sine wave in counts}$$

Physical units corresponding to these would be input, and the preceding formulas would be used for interpolation or extrapolation.

This procedure would be exact if there were no noise and if only a set of whole cycles were digitized. It is usually impossible to eliminate the noise and to start and end at the same place in the cycle. Therefore, many cycles have to be taken to eliminate or at least reduce these problems.

3.7   WILD POINT EDITING

Most data acquisition systems occasionally introduce spurious values into the data. This can occur for a variety of reasons, such as loss of signal in the transmission link, failure of the digitizer, and failure of formatting equipment. The wild points that could be generated by these failures can cause numerous problems in subsequent analyses. A single wild point, if at the digitizer maximum value, can can seriously bias a PSD by raising the overall noise level. Two such points close to each other tend to introduce a number of spurious frequencies into the PSD.

Because of this, it is best to include the detection and elimination of wild points in the overall data reduction scheme. Unfortunately, it is hard to detect them adequately. There are no general procedures for automatic elimination of wild points.

Thus it is prudent to have an editing program or programs that facilitate manual correction, if such is necessary. Such a set of computer programs would operate as follows: a first pass would be made through the data to detect wild points. Once they are found, descriptive information would be output on the printer in the form of either a tabulation or a printer plot. Having reviewed these printouts, the analyst would then generate input into the next program to eliminate the bad points, replace them, or simply not use them at all. The last is preferable, if possible.

A number of automatic editing schemes for removing wild points have been proposed, none of which seem to be entirely satisfactory. Two such schemes are included here as an illustration of the type of thing which is done. The first procedure is shown in Figure 3.5.

This scheme uses two digital RC filters for smoothing. These filters are discussed in detail in Chapter 4. Their object is to produce smoothed (lowpass filtered) estimates of the original function. It is implicit in all of these schemes that the desired data is "smooth" and the wild points are "rough." The sequences $[x(i)]^2$ and $\overline{x^2}(i)$ are defined by the following operation:

$[\overline{x}(i)]^2$ results from smoothing the data and then squaring it.

$\overline{x^2}(i)$ results from squaring the data and then smoothing it.

The purpose of the operations within the area bordered by the dotted lines is to generate a continuously updated value of the sample variance, $s^2(i)$. This is formed from $[\overline{x}(i)]^2$ and $\overline{x^2}(i)$ as follows:

$$s^2(i) = \overline{x^2}(i) - \left[\overline{x}(i)\right]^2 \tag{3.35}$$

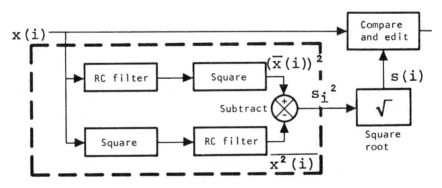

Figure 3.5 Wild point editing scheme.

The standard deviation is computed from $s^2(i)$ by taking its square root. The next step is to check the next data point, $x(i+1)$. It is accepted as being good if

$$\bar{x}(i) - ks(i) < x(i+1) < \bar{x}(i) + ks(i) \qquad (3.36)$$

The parameter k is set by the user to a value appropriate for the data. Typically, it would range from 3 to 9, with 6 being a reasonable choice as a value with which to start.

The replacement for a bad $x(i+1)$, labeled $\hat{x}(i+1)$, could be calculated by the formula

$$\hat{x}(i+1) = 2x(i) - x(i-1) \qquad (3.37)$$

This effectively amounts to linear extrapolation.

It is necessary to augment this procedure with additional complications. A preset limit for the number of successive extrapolations must be incorporated to avoid extrapolating forever. That is, after several bad point detections in succession, the extrapolation might wander far enough off track to reject good data when it finally arrives.

The second wild point editing scheme is reportedly due to J. W. Tukey, and is referred to as the "Tukey 53H" procedure. The basic idea is to generate an estimate of the smooth part of the curve, and then subtract it from data; the wild points are much easier to identify with the smooth or trend portion deleted

The procedure uses the fact that the *median* is a *robust* estimator of the mean. The median is simply the middle value in a set of data after the data has been ordered. As an example, you might estimate the mean height of a set of 101 high school students in the following way: have each of the students punch his height into a regular 80-column card; the cards would be read into a computer and the mean and median found; the mean would be computed in the usual manner; the median would be obtained by putting all the heights in ascending order and then picking the center one. The two parameters probably would be fairly close if there were no serious keypunching errors. On the other hand, if one of the students punched his height as 100 ft, consider what would happen: the mean would be biased higher by about 1 ft, but the median value would be relatively unchanged.

The Tukey 53H procedure makes use of this robustness in computing the estimate of the smooth part of the signal by applying the median concept twice. The procedure is as follows:

1. Construct a new sequence $x'(i)$ from $x(i)$ by finding the median of $x(1),...,x(5)$. This becomes $x'(3)$. Delete $x(1)$ and add $x(6)$ to the set. The median of this new set becomes $x'(4)$. This is continued until all

points are exhausted. Thus there are four less $x'(i)$ terms than there are $x(i)$ terms. The median is always selected from a group of *five* adjacent points.

2. The sequence $x''(i)$ is constructed from $x'(i)$ in much the same manner, except that the span over which the medians are computed is of length *three*.

3. In the final step, the sequence $x'''(i)$ is computed from $x''(i)$ in the following manner:

$$x'''(i) = \tfrac{1}{4}x''(i-1) + \tfrac{1}{2}x''(i) + \tfrac{1}{4}x''(i+1) \tag{3.38}$$

This is a *Hanning* smoothing filter.

As noted above, the sequence $x(i) - x'''(i)$ is then analyzed to see if $|x(i) - x'''(i)| > k$, where k is a predetermined value. If so, it is replaced with an interpolated value.

3.8   TREND REMOVAL

It is sometimes necessary to remove a linear or slowly varying trend from a particular time history. Such trends are likely to be found in the data, for example, when one or more of the components has been integrated. Integration introduces two types of errors. First of all, if the calibration zero point was incorrect, there will be a small error term with each time sample. When integrated, this constant term will become a straight line. Such a linear trend may produce large errors in PSD and related calculations.

The second type of error comes about because the integration procedure tends to amplify power corresponding to low-frequency noise. Such noise is usually present in the data. When integrated, it takes the form of a random but slowly varying trend. Just how rapidly the trend varies depends to some extent upon the sampling interval.

The varying trend can best be removed by using highpass filtering, a topic to be discussed in Chapter 4. Polynomial trends may be removed using least squares techniques. That is done in the following manner: suppose, as usual, that $x(i)$ is a function sampled at the constant interval T for $i = 0, \ldots, N-1$ and that it is desired to fit a polynomial of the form

$$\hat{x}(i) = \sum_{k=0}^{K} (iT)^k c_k \tag{3.39}$$

The set of points $\hat{x}(i)$ is to be an estimate of the polynomial content of

$x(i)$. The standard procedure consists of defining a function $E(c)$ of the polynomial coefficient terms in the following manner:

$$E(c) = \sum_{i=0}^{N-1} \left(x(i) - \sum_{k=0}^{K} (iT)^k c_k \right)^2 \qquad (3.40)$$

$E(c)$ is an error term which can be minimized through the use of standard differential techniques, that is, by taking partial derivatives with respect to each of the c_k terms, setting the results equal to 0, and then solving the resulting $K+1$ equations simultaneously. The equations are

$$\frac{\partial E}{\partial c_j} = \sum_{i=0}^{N-1} 2 \left[x_i - \sum_{k=0}^{K} (iT)^k c_k \right] \left[-(iT)^j \right] = 0 \qquad j=0,\ldots,K \quad (3.41)$$

These can be rearranged to be put in standard simultaneous equation form:

$$\sum_{k=0}^{K} c_k \sum_{i=0}^{N-1} (iT)^{k+j} = \sum_{i=0}^{N-1} (iT)^j x(i) \qquad j=0,\ldots,K \qquad (3.42)$$

For large K values, it becomes tedious to solve for c. Fortunately, the need for solutions for K larger than 3 or 4 are rare. If a program is required only to remove low-order polynomials, then the computer memory that would be used to solve the above by means of matrix inversion* techniques can be used for a direct calculation of the coefficients. For example, the solution for $K=0$ is

$$c_0 = \frac{1}{N} \sum_{i=0}^{N-1} x(i)$$

For $K=1$, the solutions are

$$c_0 = \frac{2(2N-1)\sum_{i=0}^{N-1} x(i) - 6\sum_{i=0}^{N-1} ix(i)}{N(N+1)}$$

$$c_1 = \frac{12\sum_{i=0}^{N-1} ix(i) - \dfrac{N-1}{2}\sum_{i=0}^{N-1} x(i)}{TN(N^2-1)} \qquad (3.43)$$

A tremendous simplification in the calculations can be made if N is odd. Of course, if N is even, the last point can be dropped from the calculations. It turns out that for an odd number of points, and the range of the

---

*Note: it is almost always preferable to use simultaneous equation solution techniques than to actually invert the matrix.

independent variable running from $-N/2, \ldots, i, \ldots, N/2$, many terms in the calculations are 0, in particular, all those having antisymmetric arguments. This reduces the number of calculations and also improves them from an arithmetic point of view.*

In the following, the summation sign Σ is defined by

$$\Sigma = \sum_{i=-(N-1)/2}^{(N-1)/2}$$

For the first case, $K=1$:

$$d_0 = \frac{\Sigma x(i)}{N}$$

$$d_1 = \frac{\Sigma ix(i)}{\Sigma i^2}$$

For $K=2$,

$$d_0 = \frac{\Sigma i^2 \Sigma i^2 x(i)}{(\Sigma i^2)^2 - N\Sigma i^4}$$

$$d_1 = \frac{\Sigma ix(i)}{\Sigma i^2}$$

$$d_2 = \frac{\Sigma i^2 \Sigma x(i) - N\Sigma i^2 x(i)}{\left[(\Sigma i^2)^2 - N\Sigma i^4\right]}$$

For $K=3$,

$$d_0 = \frac{\Sigma x(i)\Sigma i^4 - \Sigma i^2 \Sigma i^2 x(i)}{N\Sigma i^4 - (\Sigma i^2)^2}$$

$$d_1 = \frac{\Sigma i^4 \Sigma i^3 x(i) - \Sigma i^6 \Sigma ix(i)}{\left[(\Sigma i^4)^2 - \Sigma i^2 \Sigma i^6\right]}$$

$$d_2 = \frac{\Sigma i^2 \Sigma x(i) - N\Sigma i^2 x(i)}{\left[(\Sigma i^2) - N\Sigma i^4\right]}$$

$$d_3 = \frac{\Sigma i^4 \Sigma ix(i) - \Sigma i^2 \Sigma i^3 x(i)}{\left[(\Sigma i^4)^2 - \Sigma i^2 \Sigma i^6\right]}$$

*We caution the reader to use care in distinguishing the N in these formulas that follow. For the moment, we deviate from our standard indexing of 0 to $N-1$. Here we use $N+1$ points.

and for $K=4$, (compute d_4 first, then d_3, etc.)

$$d_0 = \left(\Sigma x(i) - d_2 \Sigma i^2 - d_4 \Sigma i^4 \right)/N$$

$$d_1 = \left\{ \Sigma i x(i) \left[\Sigma i^2 \Sigma i^6 - \left(\Sigma i^4 \right)^2 \right] - \left[\Sigma i^4 \Sigma i^2 \Sigma i^3 x(i) \right. \right.$$

$$\left. \left. - \Sigma i^4 \Sigma i x(i) \right] \right\} \Big/ \left\{ \Sigma i^2 \left[\Sigma i^2 \Sigma i^6 - \left(\Sigma i^4 \right)^2 \right] \right\}$$

$$d_2 = \left[\Sigma i^2 \Sigma x(i) - N \Sigma i^2 x(i) - d_4 \left(\Sigma i^2 \Sigma i^4 - N \Sigma i^6 \right) \right] \Big/ \left[\left(\Sigma i^2 \right)^2 - N \Sigma i^4 \right]$$

$$d_3 = \left[\Sigma i^2 \Sigma i^3 x(i) - \Sigma i^4 \Sigma i x(i) \right] \Big/ \left[\Sigma i^2 \Sigma i^6 - \left(\Sigma i^4 \right)^2 \right]$$

$$d_4 = \left\{ \left[N \Sigma i^4 x(i) - \Sigma i^4 \Sigma x(i) \right] \left[\left(\Sigma i^2 \right)^2 - N \Sigma i^4 \right] \right.$$

$$\left. + \left[\Sigma i^2 \Sigma x(i) - N \Sigma i^2 x(i) \right] \left(\Sigma i^4 \Sigma i^2 - N \Sigma i^6 \right) \right\} \Big/$$

$$\times \left\{ \left(\Sigma i^2 \Sigma i^4 - N \Sigma i^6 \right)^2 - \left[\left(\Sigma i^4 \right)^2 - N \Sigma i^8 \right] \left[\left(\Sigma i^2 \right)^2 - N \Sigma i^4 \right] \right\} \quad (3.44)$$

where

$N+1 =$ number of equally spaced samples of $x(i)$ (N must be even)

$$\Sigma i^2 = \frac{N(N^2-1)}{12}$$

$$\Sigma i^4 = \frac{N(N^2-1)(2N^2-7)}{240}$$

$$\Sigma i^6 = \frac{N(N^2-1)(3N^4-18N^2+31)}{1344}$$

$$\Sigma i^8 = \frac{N(N^2-1)(5N^6-55N^4+239N^2-381)}{11520}$$

$$i = \frac{N}{2}, \ldots, \frac{N}{2} \qquad (3.45)$$

The fitted function is then equal to

$$\hat{x}(i) = \sum_{k=0}^{K} i^k d_k \qquad i = \frac{N}{2}, \ldots, \frac{N}{2} \qquad (3.46)$$

Note that all of the arithmetic is integer: the time increment T does not appear. The use of integer arithmetic also improves the accuracy.

Computing the coefficients is done in two stages:

1.   The moments $\Sigma x(i)$ to $\Sigma i^K x(i)$ are first calculated.
2.   The $d_0, \ldots, d_k$ terms are computed using the formulas.

Double precision is recommended for these calculations, and is mandatory for 32-bit machines.

Although the $d_0, \ldots, d_K$ form is convenient to compute and use, the meaning of the terms is obscure; many analysts prefer the $c_0, \ldots, c_K$ form. One reason for this is that d_0 is *not* the mean value except for $K=0$ or 1.

The transformation from d to c coefficients is as follows: first, define M by

$$M = -\frac{NT}{2} \tag{3.47}$$

Second, replace i with $[(M+iT)/T]$ where now $i=0,\ldots,N$. Then the formula for $\hat{x}(i)$ becomes

$$\hat{x}(i) = \sum_{k=0}^{K} \left(\frac{M+iT}{T}\right)^k d_k \qquad i=0,\ldots,N \tag{3.48}$$

This may be written as follows for the case $K=4$:

$$d_0 + \left(\frac{M+iT}{T}\right)d_1 + \left(\frac{M+iT}{T}\right)^2 d_2 + \left(\frac{M+iT}{T}\right)^3 d_3 + \left(\frac{M+iT}{T}\right)^4 d_4 \tag{3.49}$$

Expanding and collecting like powers of $(iT)^k$ yields

$$= \left(d_0 + \frac{Md_1}{T} + \frac{M^2 d_2}{T^2} + \frac{M^3 d_3}{T^3} + \frac{M^4 d_4}{T^4}\right)$$

$$+ iT\left(\frac{d_1}{T} + \frac{2Md_2}{T^2} + \frac{3M^2 d_3}{T^3} + \frac{4M^3 d_4}{T^4}\right)$$

$$+ (iT)^2\left(\frac{d_2}{T^2} + \frac{3Md_3}{T^3} + \frac{6M^2 d_4}{T^4}\right)$$

$$+ (iT)^3\left(\frac{d_3}{T^3} + \frac{4Md_4}{T^4}\right) + (iT^4)\frac{d_4}{T^4} \tag{3.50}$$

Equating term by term, we get

$$c_0 = d_0 + \frac{Md_1}{T} + \frac{M^2 d_2}{T^2} + \frac{M^3 d_3}{T^3} + \frac{M^4 d_4}{T^4}$$

$$c_1 = \frac{d_1}{T} + \frac{2Md_2}{T^3} + \frac{3M^2 d_3}{T^3} + \frac{4M^3 d_4}{T^4}$$

$$c_2 = \frac{d_2}{T^2} + \frac{3Md_3}{T^3} + \frac{6M^2 d_4}{T^4}$$

$$c_3 = \frac{d_3}{T^3} + \frac{4Md_4}{T^4}$$

$$c_4 = \frac{d_4}{T^4} \tag{3.51}$$

These formulas can be used for K less than 4 by setting the appropriate d_k terms equal to 0.

Fitting and Removal of the Mean

Fitting and removal of the mean is by far the commonest form of polynomial filtering and removing. It is routinely done when computing correlation functions and power spectral densities. The calculation looks absurdly simple:

$$c_0 = m = \frac{1}{N} \sum_{i=0}^{N-1} x(i) \tag{3.52}$$

As it turns out, it is rather easy to get an answer that is biased too low if single precision arithmetic is employed on some machines. One example that comes to mind is an application where the analyst was summing up about 14,000 terms with mean approximately 100 on a 32-bit machine in single precision floating point. There was severe underflow. After a certain point in computing the sum, all new data was simply lost.

Because the cost of computing the mean in double precision is small compared to computing the PSD of the function in single precision, it is recommended that double precision be employed routinely when calculating the mean. An exception would be where N is small, say, 1024, in which case single precision should be adequate.

EXERCISES

3.1. Use the following code to simulate quantizing a sine wave on a 10-bit digitizer:

```
        DIMENSION E(1000)
        ⋮
        ⋮
C       PHI AND FACT INPUT
        ⋮
        ⋮
        DO 10 I = 1, 1000
        ANG = FLOAT(I - 1)*FACT + PHI
        CT = 511.5*(SIN(ANG) + 1.)
        CI = FLOAT(IFIX(CT + 0.49999))
10      E(I) = CT - CI
```

a   Describe the characteristics of the CT variable.

b. Do the same for CI.

c. Run the program with the additional features of computing the mean and variance of E, and the correlation coefficient for adjacent values of E for the following values of FACT and PHI:

FACT	PHI
0.0015708	0.0000
3.0753802	0.5218
1.5826000	0.7538

Explain your answers.

3.2 Write a program to simulate jitter when a sine wave is digitized. The following is recommended:

a. $x(i) = \sin(2\pi f_0 iT)$ is to be generated. Pick $T = 1$, and $f_0 = 0.5/8$. That is, f_0 is at $\frac{1}{8}$ of F.

b. Generate the jitter by making iT of the form

$$(iT)_{new} = (iT)_{original} + q[u(i) - 0.5]$$

where $u(i)$ is uniformly distributed random noise generated by TDRAND and q is a scaling factor on the range $0 \leqslant q \leqslant 1$. $q = 0$ corresponds to no jitter.

c. Generate a sequence of length 64 and use FFTRAN to compute its Fourier transform. Remember to put $x(i)$ in the real part and to zero out the imaginary part before taking the transform.

d. Run this simulation for $q = 0$, 0.5, and 1. Comment on the results.

3.3. When sinusoidal calibration is performed, the results will be perfect, except for digitization error, if a whole number of cycles is used. Compute upper bounds for the maximum error in computing $\bar{d}$ and $\bar{s}_d^2$ as a function of N, T, and the frequency of the calibration sinusoid. What happens to the errors as N becomes large?

3.4. The following problem tests the arithmetic on the computer being employed insofar as underflow is concerned. Write a test program that does the following sequence:

a. Computes the $x(i) = 99.5 + u(i)$, where $u(i)$ is a random number generated by TDRAND. What is the expected value of a particular realization of this sequence?

b. Compute

$$\bar{x}_k = \frac{1}{N_k} \sum_{i=1}^{N_k} x(i)$$

for $k = 1, 2, \ldots, 12$

$$N_k = \left[10^{(k+1)/2} \right]$$

c. What is the expected mean and variance of $\bar{x}_k$ as a function N_k?

d. Plot the resulting $\bar{x}_k$ as a function of N_k and explain the results.

e. If computer time permits, rerun the program with the summation portion converted to double precision.

3.5. Prove (3.40).

CHAPTER 4

DESIGN OF
DIGITAL FILTERS

4.1 BASIC CONCEPTS

This chapter discusses design of digital filters and gives specific illustrations of how general common types can be implemented.

The first- and second-order infinite impulse response (IIR) filters are the basic building blocks employed in higher-order filtering, so they are discussed in some detail, followed by discussion of higher-order filters of the lowpass, highpass, bandpass, and band reject types.

As an introduction to digital filtering, consider first the continuous domain filter defined by the differential equation

$$\ddot{y}(t) + 2\zeta\omega_n\dot{y}(t) + \omega_n^2 y(t) = x(t) \tag{4.1}$$

As defined in Chapter 1 where this equation was first discussed, the $x(t)$ function is the input to the filter, and $y(t)$ is the output. This is usually a *bandpass* filter centered at approximately ω_n radians or $f_n = \omega_n/2\pi$ Hz.

Assuming zero initial conditions, taking the Fourier transform of the above equation yields

$$-\omega^2 Y(f) + 2\zeta\omega_n j\omega Y(f) + \omega_n^2 Y(f) = X(f) \tag{4.2}$$

where $\omega = 2\pi f$, so that the transfer function $H(f)$ is

$$\frac{Y(f)}{X(f)} = H(f) = \frac{1}{-\omega^2 + 2\zeta\omega_n j\omega + \omega_n^2} \tag{4.3}$$

106

The transfer function is in general complex valued. Usually the independent variable frequency in the transfer function is real. Exceptions occur in the case of the zeroes and poles of the filter. A more general form of the filter transfer function could be written with

$$H(f) = \frac{N(f)}{D(f)} \tag{4.4}$$

where $N(f)$ and $D(f)$ are both simple polynomials in f. The zeroes are the solutions of the equation

$$N(f) = 0 \tag{4.5}$$

and the poles are the solutions of the equation

$$D(f) = 0 \tag{4.6}$$

As outlined in Chapter 1, the zeroes and poles determine a rational polynomial function such as $H(f)$ to within a constant.

In the example, there are no zeroes. The poles are the solutions of

$$\omega_n^2 \left[1 - \left(\frac{f}{f_n} \right)^2 + \frac{j2\zeta f}{f_n} \right] = 0 \tag{4.7}$$

If this is rewritten as

$$f^2 - j2\zeta f_n f - f_n^2 = 0 \tag{4.8}$$

then the solutions are

$$f_1, f_2 = \frac{j2\zeta f_n \pm \sqrt{(-j2\zeta f_n)^2 + 4f_n^2}}{2}$$

$$= f_n \left[j\zeta \pm \sqrt{1 - \zeta^2} \right]$$

$$= \pm f_n \sqrt{1 - \zeta^2} + j\zeta f_n \tag{4.9}$$

Thus the transfer function for the example could be rewritten in the form

$$H(f) = -\frac{1}{(2\pi)^2 (f - f_1)(f - f_2)} \tag{4.10}$$

In general, the form of the transfer function when written in this manner is

$$H(f) = c \frac{\prod\limits_{l=1}^{L} (f - f_{zl})}{\prod\limits_{k=1}^{K} (f - f_{pk})} \tag{4.11}$$

where the f_{zl} are the zeroes and the f_{pk} are the poles.

Remember also that the inverse Fourier transform of $H(f)$ is $h(t)$, and that $y(t)$ and $x(t)$ can be related by the integral equation

$$y(t) = \int_{-\infty}^{\infty} h(\tau) x(t - \tau) d\tau \tag{4.12}$$

where the integral is the convolution of $h(t)$ and $x(t)$.

It is important to compare the first equation in this chapter to this last equation. The former is a *differential* equation relating $x(t)$ to $y(t)$, whereas the latter is an *integral* equation which defines the same relationship between the two functions. As will be seen when discussing digital filters, an analogous set of relationships occurs.

In particular,

- Differential equations have as their counterpart *difference equations*.
- Convolution as shown in (4.8) becomes equivalent infinite summations.

Some other important points to be remembered are as follows:

- Filter types are generally categorized by their gain, that is, the function $|H(f)|$.
- The poles and zeroes of the transfer function determine the transfer function to within a constant. Additionally, the poles are indicative of the *stability* of the filter.

A *stable* filter, roughly speaking, is one that has a response to an impulse function that is bounded by a decreasing exponential.

4.2   FIRST-ORDER FILTERS

The most general form of the first-order digital filter is defined by a difference equation of the form

$$y(i) = \sum_{k=0}^{K} b_k x(i - k) - a_1 y(i - 1) \tag{4.13}$$

The current output of the filter is defined by linearly combining K past inputs, the current input, and the single past output. In other words, this is a first-order filter because a single previous output (times a constant) is subtracted from the combined input to form the new output value. In general, it is the number of such previous output terms employed in the calculations that determines the order of the filter.

The coefficients for several important cases of this filter are shown in Table 4.1. As indicated in the table, the lowpass filter has the form

$$y(i) = (1-\alpha)x(i) + \alpha y(i-1) \tag{4.14}$$

Table 4.1

Coefficients to Produce Five Types of Filters from the General First-order Type Shown in (4.13)

	b_0	b_1	a_1
Integrator	T	0	-1
Differentiator[a]	$\dfrac{1}{T}$	$-\dfrac{1}{T}$	0
Lowpass filter	$(1-\alpha)$	0	$-\alpha$
Highpass filter	$(1-\alpha)$	0	α
Cornell filter[b] (highpass)	$\left(1-\dfrac{\alpha}{2}\right)$	$-\left(1-\dfrac{\alpha}{2}\right)$	$-(1-\alpha)$
		$0 < \alpha < 1$	

[a]It is perhaps cheating a bit to call the differentiator a first-order filter, for it has no a_1 term.
[b]The Cornell filter was devised by C. B. Notess.

The standard tools for analyzing filters are the transfer function and its gain and phase. The computation of the transfer function can be approached in several ways. For the first time working with a digital filter, it is worthwhile to take the long way around. After starting with the definition of the Fourier transform,

$$Y(f) = T \sum_{i=-\infty}^{\infty} y(i)\exp(-j2\pi fiT) \tag{4.15}$$

the next step is to replace $y(i)$ with the right side of the preceding equation:

$$Y(f) = T \sum_{i=-\infty}^{\infty} \left[(1-\alpha)x(i) + \alpha y(i-1)\right] \cdot \exp(-j2\pi fiT) \tag{4.16}$$

The right side of this equation may be broken apart into two summations:

$$Y(f) = (1-\alpha)T \sum_{i=-\infty}^{\infty} x(i)\exp(-j2\pi fiT)$$

$$+ \alpha T \sum_{i=-\infty}^{\infty} y(i-1)\exp(-j2\pi fiT) \qquad (4.17)$$

The first half of this contains the definition of the Fourier transform of $x(i)$:

$$(1-\alpha) \sum_{i=-\infty}^{\infty} x(i)\exp(-j2\pi fiT) = (1-\alpha)X(f) \qquad (4.18)$$

The second part is almost, but not quite the same thing as the Fourier transform of $y(i)$. If the variable is changed to $l = i - 1$, it can be rewritten as

$$\alpha T \sum_{i=-\infty}^{\infty} y(i-1)\exp(-j2\pi fiT)$$

$$= \alpha T \sum_{l=-\infty}^{\infty} y(l)\exp(-j2\pi f(l+1)T)$$

$$= \alpha \exp(-j2\pi fT)T \sum_{l=-\infty}^{\infty} y(l)\exp(-j2\pi flT)$$

$$= \alpha \exp(-j2\pi fT)Y(f) \qquad (4.19)$$

By making the change of variable, it was possible to factor out an exponential term and end up with the product of an exponential and the Fourier transform of $y(i)$; it does not matter whether the dummy variable in the definition of $Y(f)$ is i or l.

If all these results are collected, the Fourier transform becomes

$$Y(f) = (1-\alpha)X(f) + \alpha \exp(-j2\pi fT)Y(f) \qquad (4.20)$$

Solving for the ratio $Y(f)/X(f)$ yields

$$H(f) = \frac{Y(f)}{X(f)} = \frac{1-\alpha}{1 - \alpha \exp(-j2\pi fT)} \qquad (4.21)$$

The calculations gone through above could have been simplified greatly by using the theorem from Chapter 1:

If $X(f)$ is the Fourier transform of $x(i)$, then the Fourier transform of $x(i-k)$ is $X(f)\exp(-j2\pi fkT)$.

This may be applied directly to the difference equation. For example, the $H(f)$ expression just derived follows direction from the defining difference equation; it is only necessary to make one to one replacements:

$$x(i-k) \rightarrow X(f)\exp(-j2\pi fkT)$$

$$y(i-l) \rightarrow Y(f)\exp(-j2\pi flT) \tag{4.22}$$

Thereafter, it remains only to solve for the ratio $Y(f)/X(f)$. This can be done by first rearranging so that all the $Y(f)$ terms are on one side of the equation, and all the $X(f)$ terms are on the other, then dividing both sides of the equation by $X(f)$ times the factor of the $Y(f)$ expression.

The gain and phase of the transfer function of the lowpass filter can be found by first separating the denominator into real and imaginary parts:

$$H(f) = \frac{1-\alpha}{1-\alpha\exp(-j2\pi fT)}$$

$$= \frac{1-\alpha}{(1-\alpha\cos 2\pi fT)+j\alpha\sin 2\pi fT} \tag{4.23}$$

Then the gain is

$$|H(f)| = \sqrt{\frac{(1-\alpha)^2}{(1-\alpha\cos 2\pi fT)^2 + (\alpha\sin 2\pi fT)^2}}$$

$$= \frac{1-\alpha}{\sqrt{1-2\alpha\cos 2\pi fT + \alpha^2}} \tag{4.24}$$

In a similar manner, the phase will be found to be

$$\phi(f) = \arctan\left(\frac{\alpha\sin 2\pi fT}{1-\alpha\cos 2\pi fT}\right) \tag{4.25}$$

The gain of this filter is plotted for several values of α in Figure 4.1.

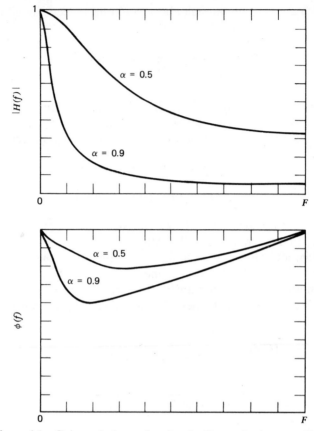

Figure 4.1   Gain and phase plots for the first-order lowpass filter.

Note that $|H(0)| = 1$ for all values of α. The $a_0 = (1 - \alpha)$ coefficient was selected just for the purpose of normalizing the gain of the filter at 0 Hz to unity.

The impulse response function $h(i)$ for this filter could be found by taking the inverse Fourier transform of $H(f)$:

$$h(i) = \int_{-F}^{F} H(f) \exp(j2\pi fiT)\, df$$

$$= \int_{-F}^{F} \frac{(1 - \alpha) \exp(j2\pi fiT)}{\left[1 - \alpha \exp(-j2\pi fT) \right]}\, df \tag{4.26}$$

Rather than performing this nontrivial integration, it is possible to find

$h(i)$ as the response to the sequence $1/T, 0, 0, 0, \ldots$. By definition, $h(i) = 0$ for $i < 0$. Then

$$h(0) = \frac{1-\alpha}{T} + 0$$

$$h(1) = (1-\alpha)0 + \alpha \frac{1-\alpha}{T} = \alpha \frac{1-\alpha}{T}$$

$$h(2) = (1-\alpha)0 + \alpha \left(\alpha \frac{1-\alpha}{T} \right) = \alpha^2 \frac{1-\alpha}{T}$$

$$\vdots$$

$$h(i) = \alpha^i \frac{1-\alpha}{T} \qquad (4.27)$$

The reason for α being limited to the range $0 < \alpha < 1$ will become clear when this expression is examined. For α on that range, $h(i)$ is geometrically *decreasing*; for α greater than 1, it is geometrically *increasing*. For example, consider the cases $\alpha = 0.5$ and $\alpha = 2$:

	$\alpha = 0.5$	$\alpha = 2$
$h(0)$	$\dfrac{0.5}{T}$	$\dfrac{-1}{T}$
$h(1)$	$\dfrac{0.25}{T}$	$\dfrac{-2}{T}$
$h(2)$	$\dfrac{0.125}{T}$	$\dfrac{-4}{T}$
$\vdots$		
$h(i)$	$\dfrac{2^{-i}}{2T}$	$\dfrac{-2^i}{T}$

For $\alpha = 2$, $h(i)$ quickly increases in size beyond the capacity of any fixed point arithmetic device to contain it, and thus results in *overflow*. We note that this is an example of instability in a digital filter.

4.3   SECOND-ORDER FILTERS

The second-order filter

$$y(i) = b_0 x(i) - a_1 y(i-1) - a_2 y(i-2) \qquad (4.28)$$

is discussed first. It is not the most general case; the latter could also have zeroes. This means that the above would have $b_1 x(i-1)+b_2 x(i-2)$ terms added into it.

The following are the important facts to keep in mind about the second-order filter. They are proved later in this section.

- The a_1 and a_2 terms determine the nature of the filter to a large degree. They must fall within a relatively small triangular area in the plane of all possible coefficients pairs (a_1, a_2) in order for the filter to be stable.
- The poles of the filter are also determined by a_1 and a_2 and fall into two distinct cases: (1) the poles are real; (2) the poles are complex. The latter is by far the most interesting case.

The first step in showing these statements to be true is to find the transfer function of the defining equation. Employing the shifting theorem, we have

$$Y(f) = b_0 X(f) - a_1 Y(f) \exp(-j2\pi fT) - a_2 Y(f) \exp(-j4\pi fT) \quad (4.29)$$

or

$$H(f) = \frac{Y(f)}{X(f)} = \frac{b_0}{1 + a_1 \exp(-j2\pi fT) + a_2 \exp(-j4\pi fT)} \quad (4.30)$$

Using the notation $z^{-1} = \exp(-j2\pi fT)$, the denominator of the transfer function becomes

$$1 + a_1 z^{-1} + a_2 z^{-2} \quad (4.31)$$

The poles of the filter are found by setting this equal to zero and multiplying both sides by z^2 to get

$$z^2 + a_1 z + a_2 = 0 \quad (4.32)$$

which is then solved for z_1 and z_2:

$$z_{1,2} = \frac{-a_1 \pm \sqrt{a_1^2 - 4a_2}}{2} \quad (4.33)$$

The roots of this equation fall into two categories:

Case 1

If $a_1^2 - 4a_2 \geqslant 0$, the roots are real and unequal except when $a_1^2 - 4a_2 = 0$, in which case they are real and equal.

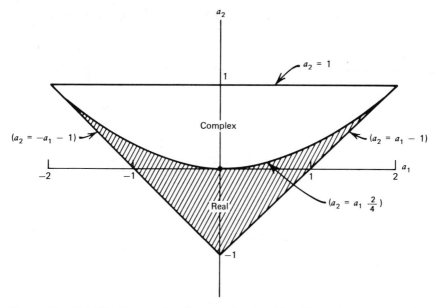

Figure 4.2 Stability diagram for the second-order filter. The point corresponding to the pair of coefficients (a_1, a_2) must fall within the triangle shown in order for the filter to be stable.

Case 2

If $a_1^2 - 4a_2 < 0$, then the roots are complex, and complex conjugates of each other.

The expression inside the radical forms a bound between the two cases when set equal to zero:

$$a_1^2 - 4a_2 = 0$$

This equation is the parabola shown in Figure 4.2.

Real Poles

Case 1 is considered first. The original difference equation can be rewritten as

$$y(i) = b_0 x(i) + (c_1 + c_2) y(i-1) - c_1 c_2 y(i-2) \tag{4.34}$$

where

$$a_1 = -(c_1 + c_2)$$

$$a_2 = c_1 c_2 \tag{4.35}$$

As will be seen below, c_1 and c_2 are the roots of the equation $z^2 + a_1 z + a_2 = (z - c_1)(z - c_2)$. Naturally, these coefficients were not arbitrarily chosen. Given a_1 and a_2, c_1 and c_2 can be calculated from them as follows:

$$c_1 = \frac{a_2}{c_2}$$

so

$$a_1 = -\left(\frac{a_2}{c_2} + c_2\right)$$

or

$$c_2^2 + c_2 a_1 + a_2 = 0 \tag{4.36}$$

so that

$$c_2 = \frac{-a_1 \pm \sqrt{a_1^2 - 4a_2}}{2}$$

and

$$c_1 = \frac{2a_2}{-a_1 \pm \sqrt{a_1^2 - 4a^2}} \tag{4.37}$$

Note that in order for the coefficients c_1 and c_2 to be real, $a_1^2 - 4a_2 > 0$ must hold. This, of course, is the reason for the definition of the c_1 and c_2 terms above; they correspond to the case where the poles are real.

The transfer function of the filter for this case is

$$H(f) = \frac{b_0}{1 - (c_1 + c_2)\exp(-j2\pi fT) + c_1 c_2 \exp(-j4\pi fT)}$$

The denominator may now be factored:

$$= \left[\frac{\sqrt{b_0}}{1 - c_1 \exp(-j2\pi fT)}\right]\left[\frac{\sqrt{b_0}}{1 - c_2 \exp(-j2\pi fT)}\right] \tag{4.38}$$

From this it is clear that $H(f)$ may be rewritten as

$$H(f) = H_1(f)H_2(f) \tag{4.39}$$

where

$$H_1(f) = \frac{\sqrt{b_0}}{1 - c_1 \exp(-j2\pi f T)}$$

$$H_2(f) = \frac{\sqrt{b_0}}{1 - c_2 \exp(-j2\pi f T)} \qquad (4.40)$$

This is the same as applying two first-order filters, one at a time. That is, let $u(i)$ be an intermediate function in the process of computing $y(i)$:

$$u(i) = \sqrt{b_0}\, x(i) + c_1 u(i-1)$$

$$y(i) = \sqrt{b_0}\, u(i) + c_2 y(i-1) \qquad (4.41)$$

then

$$U(f) = H_1(f) X(f)$$

$$Y(f) = H_2(f) U(f) \qquad (4.42)$$

where $U(f)$ is the Fourier transform of $u(i)$, so that

$$Y(f) = H_2(f)\big[H_1(f) X(f) \big] \qquad (4.43)$$

Note that the role of $H_1(f)$ and $H_2(f)$ could have been reversed without affecting the final result.

From the first-order case it is clear that c_1 and c_2 have to be less than unity in absolute value or one of the two subfilters will be unstable. If the absolute value of c_2 is less than unity, then

$$-1 < c_2 < 1$$

or

$$-1 < \frac{-a_1 \pm \sqrt{a_1^2 - 4a_2}}{2} < 1 \qquad (4.44)$$

Multiplying by all terms by 2 and then adding a_1 preserves the direction of the inequality signs and yields

$$a_1 - 2 < \pm\sqrt{a_1^2 - 4a_2} < a_1 + 2 \qquad (4.45)$$

Squaring the two right-hand terms results in

$$a_1^2 - 4a_2 < a_1^2 + 4a_1 + 4$$

or, after simplification

$$a_2 > -a_1 - 1 \tag{4.46}$$

In a similar manner, squaring the two left-hand terms results in

$$a_1^2 - 4a_1 + 4 > a_1^2 - 4a_2 \tag{4.47}$$

so that after simplification

$$a_2 > a_1 - 1 \tag{4.48}$$

Another way of looking at this result is to consider the two lines in the (a_1, a_2) plane

$$a_2 = a_1 - 1$$

$$a_2 = -a_1 - 1 \tag{4.49}$$

and then note that a_2, according to the inequalities must lie above both lines. As shown in Figure 4.2, segments of these two lines form the bottom legs of the stability triangle.

Complex Poles

Case 2 with complex poles turns out to be much more interesting. The filter is redefined as

$$y(i) = b_0 x(i) + [2\exp(-\alpha)\cos\beta] y(i-1) + [-\exp(-2\alpha)] y(i-2) \tag{4.50}$$

The a_1 and a_2 coefficients are

$$a_1 = -2\exp(-\alpha)\cos\beta$$

$$a_2 = \exp(-2\alpha) \tag{4.51}$$

For any a_1 and a_2, the α and β can be found as follows:

$$\alpha = -\tfrac{1}{2}\ln(a_2)$$

$$\beta = \arccos - \left[\frac{a_1}{2\exp(-\alpha)} \right]$$

$$= \arccos - \left[\frac{a_1}{2\sqrt{a_2}} \right] \tag{4.52}$$

There are two restrictions on the a_1 and a_2 terms: because of the equation defining α,

$$0 < a_2 \tag{4.53}$$

Because of the equation defining β,

$$\left| -\frac{a_1}{2\sqrt{a_2}} \right| < 1 \tag{4.54}$$

If either of these two conditions is not met, then the roots are real. Squaring both sides of this yields

$$a_1^2 < 4a_2 \tag{4.55}$$

This is the area *above* the parabola $a_1^2 = 4a_2$.

The quadratic equation for the poles

$$z^2 + a_1 z + a_2 = 0 \tag{4.56}$$

for this second case becomes

$$z^2 - [2\exp(-\alpha)\cos\beta]z + \exp(-2\alpha) = 0 \tag{4.57}$$

Therefore, the two roots are

$$z_{1,2} = \frac{2\exp(-\alpha)\cos\beta \pm \sqrt{4\exp(-2\alpha)\cos^2\beta - 4\exp(-2\alpha)}}{2} \tag{4.58}$$

Factoring out the $4\exp(-2\alpha)$ from within the radical and simplifying, we have

$$z_{1,2} = \exp(-\alpha)\left[\cos\beta \pm \sqrt{\cos^2\beta - 1} \right]$$

$$= \exp(-\alpha)[\cos\beta \pm j\sin\beta]$$

$$= \exp(-\alpha)\exp(\pm j\beta)$$

$$= \exp(-\alpha \pm j\beta) \tag{4.59}$$

With $z = \exp(j2\pi fT)$, this finally becomes

$$j2\pi fT = -\alpha \pm j\beta$$

$$f_{1,2} = \frac{1}{2\pi T}\left[\pm\beta + j\alpha \right] \tag{4.60}$$

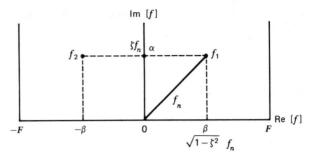

Figure 4.3 Pole positions for the complex second-order filter. The α term is assumed positive (it always is).

The poles for second-order filters with real poles always fall either on the lines $f=0$ or $f=F$. In the latter case, it also appears on the line $f=-F$. The poles repeat outside the range $(-F, F)$.

The pole positions are shown in Figure 4.3. In natural frequency and damping terminology,

$$\alpha = 2\pi\zeta f_n$$

$$\beta = 2\pi\sqrt{1-\zeta^2}\,f_n \qquad (4.61)$$

The next step is to check the expression for the denominator of the transfer function:

$$D(f) = \{1-\exp[-j2\pi T(f-f_1)]\}\{1-\exp[-j2\pi T(f-f_2)]\} \qquad (4.62)$$

Note that when f is equal to either f_1 or f_2, then one or the other exponential argument becomes 0, so that the corresponding exponential becomes unity. The terms then cancel. That is,

$$D(f_1) = D(f_2) = 0 \qquad (4.63)$$

as would be expected.

When the derived expressions for f_1 and f_2 are put into $D(f)$, the latter yield the original coefficients

$$D(f) = \left\{1-\exp\left[-j2\pi T\left(f - \frac{-\beta+j\alpha}{2\pi T}\right)\right]\right\}$$

$$\times \left\{1-\exp\left[-j2\pi T\left(f - \frac{+\beta+j\alpha}{2\pi T}\right)\right]\right\}$$

$$= \left[1-\exp(-j2\pi fT)\exp(-j\beta-\alpha)\right]$$

$$\times \left[1-\exp(-j2\pi fT)\exp(j\beta-\alpha)\right] \qquad (4.64)$$

Multiplying this out, we get

$$D(f) = 1 - \exp(-j2\pi fT)\left[\exp(-j\beta - \alpha) + \exp(j\beta - \alpha)\right]$$
$$+ \exp(-j42\pi fT)\exp(-j\beta - \alpha + j\beta - \alpha)$$
$$= 1 - \exp(-j2\pi fT)\left[2\exp(-\alpha)\cos\beta\right]$$
$$+ \left[\exp(-2\alpha)\right]\exp(-j4\pi fT)$$
$$= 1 - 2\exp(-\alpha)\cos\beta z^{-1} + \exp(-2\alpha)z^{-2} \qquad (4.65)$$

This, of course, is the way that the denominator of the transfer function should turn out.

Impulse Response Function

In order to get the last bound on the stability triangle shown in Figure 4.2, it will be necessary to find the unit impulse response of the second order filter for Case 2, where the poles are complex.

It is left to the reader to verify* that if

$$x(i) = \begin{cases} \dfrac{1}{T} & i = 0 \\ 0 & \text{otherwise} \end{cases} \qquad (4.66)$$

and $y(i) = 0$ for $i < 0$, then the solution of

$$y(i) = b_0 x(i) + 2\exp(-\alpha)\cos\beta y(i-1) - \exp(-2\alpha)y(i-2)$$

is

$$y(i) = \frac{b_0}{T}\exp(-i\alpha)\left[\frac{\cos\beta\cos(i\beta - \beta) + (1 - 2\cos^2\beta)\cos i\beta}{1 - \cos^2\beta}\right]$$

$$i \geq 0 \qquad (4.67)$$

The solution has not been simplified because it is a little easier to check the first few values of $y(i)$ when it is written in this form.

There are some important things to note about the solution:

- The α and β parts are nicely factored apart. This makes it easier to access what role each part plays.
- The α part is exponential.
- The β part is trigonometric.

*Exercise 4.6.

The trigonometric term is periodic and bounded above by $2/(1-\cos^2\beta)$. So far as stability is concerned, it is not as important as the exponential term.

The exponential term has three cases:

1. $\alpha > 0$ Stability.
2. $\alpha = 0$ Marginal stability.
3. $\alpha < 0$ Instability.

That is, for $\alpha > 0$, the $\exp(-i\alpha)$ is exponentially *decreasing*; for $\alpha = 0$, the exponential term drops out; and for $\alpha < 0$, the $\exp(-i\alpha)$ is exponentially *increasing*.

The stability boundary $\alpha = 0$ yields the last of the three sides of the stability triangle. When plugged into the relationship

$$a_2 = \exp(-2\alpha) \tag{4.68}$$

the result is the line

$$a_2 = 1 \tag{4.69}$$

This is the top of the triangle as shown in Figure 4.2.

The Second-Order Filter as an Oscillator

With α equal to 0, the second-order filter with complex poles may be used to generate either sines or cosines. The equation becomes

$$y(i) = 2\cos\beta y(i-1) - y(i-2) \qquad i = 0, 1, 2, \ldots \tag{4.70}$$

with the initial conditions defined as follows:

	Sine Generation	Cosine Generation
$y(-1)$	$-\sin\beta$	$\cos\beta$
$y(-2)$	$-\sin 2\beta$	$\cos 2\beta$

The sine or cosine will be generated at a frequency

$$f = \frac{\beta}{2\pi T}\,\text{Hz} \tag{4.71}$$

As an example, consider the sine case

$$y(0) = 2\cos\beta \cdot (-\sin\beta) - \sin 2\beta = 0$$

$$y(1) = 2\cos\beta (0) - (-\sin\beta) = \sin\beta$$

$$y(2) = 2\cos\beta \sin\beta - (0) = \sin 2\beta$$

$$y(3) = 2\cos\beta \sin 2\beta - \sin\beta$$

$$= 4\cos^2\beta \sin\beta - \sin\beta$$

$$= 4(1 - \sin^2\beta)\sin\beta - \sin\beta$$

$$= 3\sin\beta - 4\sin^3\beta = \sin 3\beta \qquad (4.72)$$

The proof for the general case can be demonstrated inductively. Assume

$$y(i-1) = \sin(i-1)\beta$$

$$y(i-2) = \sin(i-2)\beta \qquad (4.73)$$

Then, if the formula is correct, the next term should be

$$y(i) = 2\cos\beta\sin(i-1)\beta - \sin(i-2)\beta \qquad (4.74)$$

First of all, expand the last term

$$\sin(i-2)\beta = \sin(i-1)\beta\cos\beta - \cos(i-1)\beta\sin\beta \qquad (4.75)$$

When this is substituted into the expression for $y(i)$, the latter becomes

$$y(i) = 2\cos\beta\sin(i-1)\beta - \sin(i-1)\beta\cos\beta + \cos(i-1)\beta\sin\beta$$

$$= \cos\beta\sin(i-1)\beta + \cos(i-1)\beta\sin\beta = \sin i\beta \qquad (4.76)$$

This completes the inductive proof for the sine case. The proof for the cosine case would be similar.

An Exact Second-Order Lowpass Filter

The filter whose transfer function is

$$|H(f)|^2 = \frac{1}{1 + \left(\dfrac{\sin\omega T/2}{A}\right)^4} \qquad (4.77)$$

where $A = \sin \pi BT$, is a lowpass Butterworth filter, [Butterworth, 1931]. The analog form of this filter was discussed in Chapter 3. As shown there, a few special values help define its characteristics:

$$|H(0)|^2 = \frac{1}{1+0} = 1$$

$$|H(B)|^2 = \frac{1}{1+\left(\dfrac{\sin \pi BT}{\sin \pi BT}\right)^4} = \frac{1}{1+1^4} = \frac{1}{2} \qquad (4.78)$$

For f such that $\pi BT < \pi fT < \pi$, $|H(0)|^2$ tends to go to 0. $(\sin \pi fT / \sin \pi \beta T)^4$ is greater than 1, so that $|H(f)|^2$ decreases as πfT increases and reaches a minimum when $\pi fT = \pi / 2$.

The a_1 and a_2 terms for this filter can be found in several ways. The following procedure is the "brute force technique." It is included to emphasize the fact that such techniques are difficult and quite limited.

The transfer function can be rewritten as

$$\frac{1}{1+\left(\dfrac{\sin \omega T/2}{A}\right)^4} = \frac{A^4}{A^4 + \sin^4(\omega T/2)}$$

$$= \frac{A^4}{A^2 + \left(\dfrac{1-\cos \omega T}{2}\right)^2} = \frac{4A^4}{4A^4 + (1 - 2\cos \omega T + \cos^2 \omega T)}$$

$$= \frac{4A^4}{\cos^2 \omega T - 2\cos \omega T + (1 + 4A^4)} \qquad (4.79)$$

The transfer function had to be gotten out of the form having $\sin \omega T/2$, because the factor of $\frac{1}{2}$ in the argument is not directly implementable. The next step is to note that the denominator of the Fourier transform of the difference equation of any two-pole filter can be written in the form $(s + pz^{-1} + qz^{-2})$. These s, p, and q terms will yield the coefficients after they are found. The absolute value squared of the denominator of the transfer function must be as follows:

$$(s + pz^{-1} + qz^{-2})(s + pz + qz^2)$$

$$= (s^2 + p^2 + q^2) + (pq + sp)(z + z^{-1}) + sq(z^2 + z^{-2}) \qquad (4.80)$$

Because

$$\cos\omega T = \frac{z + z^{-1}}{2}$$

$$\cos^2\omega T = \tfrac{1}{4}(z^2 + 2 + z^{-2}) \tag{4.81}$$

the original denominator can be rewritten as

$$\cos^2\omega T - 2\cos\omega T + (1 + 4A^4) = \frac{1}{4}(z^2 + 2 + z^{-2}) - 2\left(\frac{z + z^{-1}}{2}\right) + (1 + 4A^4)$$

$$= \frac{1}{4}\left\{(z^2 + z^{-2}) - 4(z + z^{-1}) + \left[4(1 + 4A^4) + 2\right]\right\} \tag{4.82}$$

Equating term by term and dropping the multiplicative factor of $\frac{1}{4}$ yields three equations in three unknowns:

$$sq = 1$$

$$pq + sp = -4$$

$$s^2 + p^2 + q^2 = (6 + 16A^4) = C \tag{4.83}$$

Some fairly involved calculations yield the following solution:

$$a_1 = qp$$

$$a_2 = q^2 \tag{4.84}$$

where

$$p = \sqrt{\frac{C + 2 - \sqrt{(C+2)^2 - 64}}{2}}$$

$$q = \frac{-\frac{4}{p} + \sqrt{\left(\frac{4}{p}\right)^2 - 4}}{2}$$

and

$$C = 6 + 16A^4 \tag{4.85}$$

Figure 4.4 shows a special FORTRAN routine for computing the a_1, a_2,

```
 1          SUBRØUTINE LP2 (BW,T,A1,A2,BO)
 2          DØUBLE PRECISIØN A,C,P,PP,Q,QQ
 3          A = SIN (3.1415927*T*BW)
 4          C = 8.0D0 + 16.0D0*(A**4)
 5          PP = DSQRT (C*C - 64.0D0)
 6          P = DSQRT ((C - PP)/2.0D0)
 7          QQ = (4.0D0/P)**2 - 4.0D0
 8          Q = -2.0D0/P + DSQRT(QQ)/2.0D0
 9          A1 = P*Q
10          A2 = Q*Q
11          BO = 1.0 + A1 + A2
12          RETURN
13          END
```

Figure 4.4   Code to generate the weights for a second-order lowpass filter.

and b_0 filter weights for this filter. The terms in the code equate to the above as follows:

Text	Code
B	BW
T	T
a_1	A1
a_2	A2
b_0	BO
A	A
$C+2$	C
p	P
q	Q

This is a lot of effort for so simple a result. It is possible that higher-order Butterworth filters could be worked out in this manner, but it scarcely seems worth it. As will be seen shortly there is a much easier way of generating higher-order filters of this type.

4.4   HIGHER-ORDER FILTERS

By a higher-order filter is meant one with three or more recursive terms; for example,

$$y(i) = b_0 x(i) - a_1 y(i-1) - a_2 y(i-2) - a_3 y(i-3) \qquad (4.86)$$

is a third-order filter.

This section discusses four forms of filter implementation:

- Direct.
- Serial or cascade.
- Parallel.
- Ladder.

For the applications being considered, the serial form is by far the most important.

An Mth-order filter written in the direct form has the difference equation

$$y(i) = \sum_{k=0}^{M} b_k x(i-k) - \sum_{m=1}^{M} a_m y(i-m) \qquad (4.87)$$

If Fourier transform techniques are employed exactly as before, the Fourier transform of the difference equation is

$$Y(f) = X(f) \sum_{k=0}^{M} b_k \exp(-j2\pi fkT) - Y(f) \sum_{m=1}^{M} a_m \exp(-j2\pi fmT) \quad (4.88)$$

The transfer function therefore is

$$H(f) = \frac{Y(f)}{X(f)} = \frac{\displaystyle\sum_{k=0}^{M} b_k \exp(-j2\pi fkT)}{1 + \displaystyle\sum_{m=1}^{M} a_m \exp_p(-j2fmT)} \qquad (4.89)$$

Both the numerator and denominator are Mth-order polynomials in $z = \exp(j2\pi fT)$. In particular,

$$N(f) = \sum_{k=0}^{M} b_k z^{-k}$$

$$D(f) = 1 + \sum_{m=1}^{M} a_m z^{-m} \qquad (4.90)$$

As discussed earlier in this chapter, there are roots $f_1, \ldots, f_M$ to the equation

$$D(f) = 0 \qquad (4.91)$$

This means that $D(f)$ can be rewritten as

$$D(f) = a_0 \prod_{i=1}^{M} \left\{ 1 - \exp[-j2\pi T(f - f_k)] \right\} \tag{4.92}$$

where the a_0 term is a scaling parameter.

There are two types of roots:

Imaginary Roots: in this case f_k is of the form $j\alpha_k/2\pi T$ or $j\alpha_k/2\pi T + F$, where $\alpha_k > 0$. Then the term corresponding to this root is

$$\left\{ 1 - \exp\left[-j2\pi T\left(f - \frac{j\alpha_k}{2\pi T} \right) \right] \right\} = \left[1 - \exp(-\alpha_k)z^{-1} \right] \tag{4.93}$$

If the root is of the $jc_k + F$ form, then the result similarly is

$$\left[1 + \exp(-\alpha_k)z^{-1} \right] \tag{4.94}$$

which corresponds to a highpass filter.

Complex Roots: for this case the roots come in pairs. If

$$f_k = \frac{j\alpha_k + \beta_k}{2\pi T} \qquad \beta_k > 0 \tag{4.95}$$

then there is a k' such that

$$f_{k'} = \frac{j\alpha_k - \beta_k}{2\pi T} \tag{4.96}$$

The two terms corresponding to f_k and $f_{k'}$ may be combined to yield

$$\left\{ 1 - \exp\left[-j2\pi T\left(f - \frac{j\alpha_k + \beta_k}{2\pi T} \right) \right] \right\} \cdot \left\{ 1 - \exp\left[-j2\pi T\left(f - \frac{j\alpha_k - \beta_k}{2\pi T} \right) \right] \right\}$$

$$= 1 - 2\exp(-\alpha_k)\cos\beta_k z^{-1} + \exp(-2\alpha_k)z^{-2} \tag{4.97}$$

If this information is combined, it can be asserted that there are two positive integers P and Q such that $M = P + Q$, Q is even, and

$$D(f) = \prod_{p=1}^{P} \left(1 - a_{1p}z^{-1} \right) \prod_{q=1}^{Q/2} \left(1 - a_{1q}z^{-1} - a_{2q}z^{-2} \right) \tag{4.98}$$

where a_{1p}, a_{1q}, and a_{2q} are real. What this means is that the polynomial $D(f)$ can always be factored into a series of factors of degree one or two, where the factors shown have real coefficients.

So far, this is all algebra and can be proved with some elementary theorems from the theory of equations. Its meaning for filter theory is also straightforward. Suppose for simplicity and not too much loss of generality that there is only one term in numerator, so that

$$H(f) = \frac{b_0}{D(f)} \tag{4.99}$$

Define $H_r(f)$ by

$$H_r(f) = \begin{cases} \dfrac{b_0^{1/R}}{1 - a_{1p}z^{-1}} \\[4mm] \dfrac{b_0^{1/R}}{1 - a_{1q}z^{-1} - a_{2q}z^{-2}} \end{cases}$$

$$R = P + \frac{Q}{2} \qquad \begin{matrix} r = q = 1, \ldots, Q/2 \\ p = r - Q/2, \ldots, R \end{matrix} \tag{4.100}$$

The transfer function can be rewritten as

$$H(f) = \prod_{r=1}^{R} H_r(f) \tag{4.101}$$

As can be seen, the $H_r(f)$ functions are transfer functions and correspond to either first- or second-order filters. Thus *any higher-order filter can be broken down into a series of first- and second-order filters.*

The equation for the difference equation for the rth filter is

$$u^{(r)}(i) = b_0' u^{(r-1)}(i) - a_{1r} u^{(r)}(i-1) - a_{2r} u^{(r)}(i-2)$$

where

$$b_0' = b_0^{1/R}$$

$$u^{(0)}(i) = x(i)$$

$$u^{(R)}(i) = y(i) \tag{4.102}$$

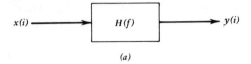

(a)

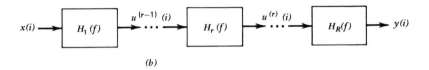

(b)

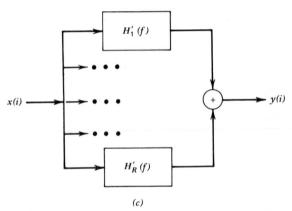

(c)

Figure 4.5 Three ways of implementing the same filter. (a) Direct implementation. (b) Series or cascade implementation. (c) Parallel implementation.

In other words, at the rth stage of the filter, the sequence $u^{(r-i)}(i)$ is the input to the rth stage, and $u^{(r)}(i)$ is the output from that stage. Note that some of the a_{2r} filter weights may be 0.

The direct and series filters are shown in parts a and b of Figure 4.5. The series filter is often referred to as the *cascade* filter.

The filter stages are commutative, and, at least on a computer with a very large number of bits, there is no difference in permuting them. There are $R!$ such permutations. As discussed in the next chapter, as the number of bits decreases, noise is generated by the filter itself as part of the computations, and the order of the sections does matter, because some sections generate more noise than others or attenuate the noise in a different fashion from the others.

It also turns out that the direct form can be implemented in a parallel form under certain conditions. The parallel filter is shown in part c of Figure 4.5. The individual sections are defined by

$$H'_r(f) = \frac{N_r(f)}{D_r(f)} \tag{4.103}$$

where the $D_r(f)$ are the same as for the series implementation.
  The overall transfer function there is

$$H(f) = \sum_{r=1}^{R} H'_r(f)$$

$$= \frac{N_1(f)}{D_1(f)} + \cdots + \frac{N_R(f)}{D_R(f)} \tag{4.104}$$

This last may be put into a rational polynomial form by adding all the terms:

$$H(f) = \frac{\sum_{r=1}^{R} N_r(f) \Pi_{k=1}^{R} D_k(f)/D_r(f)}{\sum_{r=1}^{R} D_r(f)} \tag{4.105}$$

The numerator for this case must be equal to b_0. The problem in implementing this filter is finding the $N_r(f)$ or numerator functions so that this occurs. That is

$$b_0 = \sum_{r=1}^{R} N_r(f) \prod_{k=1}^{R} \frac{D_k(f)}{D_r(f)} \tag{4.106}$$

Partial fraction expansion techniques from calculus will show that this can be done if none of the poles, that is, roots of the overall $D(f)$ function, are equal.
  From these definitions it is clear that all sorts of intermediate forms can be devised which might be part direct, part parallel, and part serial. There does not seem to be any good reason for delving into this.
  A *ladder* filter is one where the operations are spread out to roughly form the shape of a ladder. A portion of such a filter is shown in Figure 4.6. References for the ladder filter are Gray and Markel [1973] and Mitra and Sherwood [1973]. It should be understood that such a representation is not unique. There are many ways by which the simple second-order filter may be rewritten as a ladder filter, and for higher-order filters, the number of possibilities no doubt becomes immense.

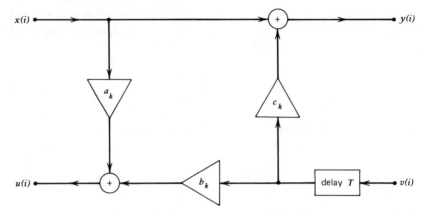

Figure 4.6   One segment of a ladder filter.

With a choice of four different categories of forms for the same filter, with a possibility of myriad subcategories, the question naturally arises, which is best?

The answer to this depends on a number of factors involved with the type of information being processed and the machinery used in the processing. However, when the application area is limited to that of the scope of this book, that is, analysis of test data on general-purpose computers with floating point arithmetic, then the following statements can be made:

- The serial form of the filter is the best all around.
- The direct form is the worst from a numerical point of view, but is best from the point of view of cost of the computation performed in doing the filtering.
- The filters to be discussed are always implementable as a serial filter with at most one first-order stage.
- The potential gains from using a ladder implementation of a filter are probably small on general-purpose computers.
- The parallel implementation does not seem to have much to recommend it.

In summary, unless there are good reasons to the contrary, the serial form is the best one to employ on a large-scale computer.

If fixed point arithmetic is employed, the above comments change drastically:

- The direct form is rarely usable if bandwidth is small.
- The parallel form has the least error. See, for example, Jackson [1970].
- Ordering of the sections of the cascade filter becomes quite important, because it can be used to minimize the total amount of self-noise generated by the filter. The Jackson [1970] reference is basic to this problem also.
- Some sort of ladder implementation probably offers the best potential for having the least amount of self noise.

Stability

When the discussion is limited to the serial implementation of the filter, the problem of design stability becomes simple. In order to see that there is a problem, the third-order filter mentioned at the beginning of this section should be considered. The three coefficients (a_1, a_2, and a_3) define a three-space. The set of all possible stable third-order filters will be found to be in a volume bounded by a tetrahedron. It is not very easy to work out this exact shape. For fourth- and higher-order filters, the problem becomes progressively more difficult for the direct form. A basic solution to the problem is to be found in Jury and Blanchard [1961] or Jury [1961].

For the serial implementation of the same filter, the problem is quite easy. Each section may be considered separately. If each section is stable, then the filter as a whole is stable.

As far as the poles are concerned, this means that they must lie in the upper half of the frequency plane as shown in Figure 4.3. *Caution*: many engineering texts plot $j2\pi f$ rather than f. This results in rotating the plot counterclockwise 90° and puts the stable poles in the left half-plane. Also, in texts dealing with discrete frequency, many if not most authors use the fact that stable poles are inside the unit circle in the z-plane.

The f-plane as opposed to the $j2\pi f$ or z-planes is employed because of the emphasis in this book on power spectral density: when looking at filter characteristics, it is easier to interpret them and corresponding spectral densities when the basic axes are the same.

4.5   BASIC IDEAL FILTERS

By *basic filters* are meant the traditional forms commonly used in processing of data or signals. The ones of main concern are the lowpass, highpass, bandpass, and bandreject, the latter sometimes being referred to as the notch filter.

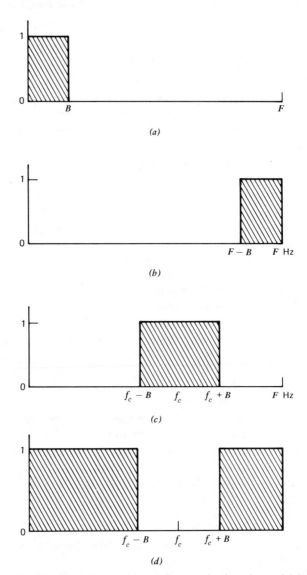

Figure 4.7 The absolute value square of the transfer functions of (*a*) ideal lowpass filter, (*b*) ideal highpass filter, (*c*) ideal bandpass filter, and (*d*) ideal band reject filter. The crosshatched areas indicate which portions of the data are passed.

The ideal versions of the above would have the following characteristics:

- The ideal lowpass filter would pass all information on the frequency range $(0, B)$ Hz, while rejecting all information on the range (B, F) Hz.
- The ideal highpass filter would reverse the characteristics of the ideal lowpass filter.
- The ideal bandpass filter would pass only information in the range $(f_c - B)$ to $(f_c + B)$ Hz.
- The ideal bandreject filter would reject all information in the range $(f_c - B)$ to $(f_c + B)$ Hz, while retaining the information outside this range.

The widths of the passbands are as follows:

Lowpass	B Hz
Highpass	B Hz
Bandpass	$2B$ Hz
Bandreject	$(F - 2B)$ Hz

The ideal forms are shown in Figure 4.7. Though such ideal filter responses are desirable, perfect rejection or acceptance is not possible in practice. There are two reasons for this. The first is that only in the limit as N goes to infinity is it possible to attain the ideal form, so that the filters actually used are only approximations to the ideal forms. Second, only finite amounts of data are present in practice, so that the true transfer function is actually the theoretical one convolved with a $(\sin x)/x$ term which arises from the truncations of the data. On the other hand, filters can be generated and applied that for all practical purposes are identical to their ideal counterparts.

Implementation of Approximations to the Ideal Filters

The filters discussed above would require an infinite number of terms to implement perfectly. Therefore, as with electrical/electronic filters, the ideal forms are approximated through the use of polynomials. In the electrical case, the polynomials are directly in f. For the digital case they are in trigonometric functions of f.

For example, the ideal lowpass shown in Figure 4.7a could be approximated by the Butterworth filter

$$|H(f)|^2 = \frac{1}{1 + \left(\dfrac{f}{B}\right)^{2M}} \tag{4.107}$$

in the electrical case, or by the digital Butterworth filters

$$|H(f)|^2 = \frac{1}{1 + \left(\dfrac{\sin \pi f T}{\sin \pi B T} \right)^{2M}}$$

and

$$|H(f)|^2 = \frac{1}{1 + \left(\dfrac{\tan \pi f T}{\tan \pi B T} \right)^{2M}} \tag{4.108}$$

In all three cases

$$|H(f)|^2 = \begin{cases} 1 & f = 0 \\ \frac{1}{2} & f = B \\ < \frac{1}{2} & f > B \end{cases} \tag{4.109}$$

The approximation of these filters to the ideal case improves with increas-

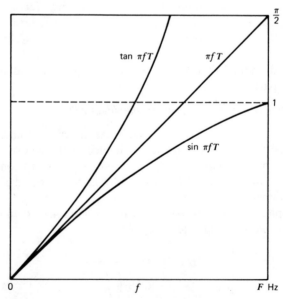

Figure 4.8   Comparison of $\pi t T$, $\tan \pi f T$, and $\sin \pi f T$.

ing M. Increasing M, of course, means increasing the cost of the filter or filtering operation.

The reason that they tend to behave like the ideal lowpass is that on the range of f from 0 to F, $\sin \pi f T$ and $\tan \pi f T$ tend to act like πTf. This is shown in Figure 4.8.

The problem to be solved is that of computing the a_m and b_k weights for the direct filter implementation (or, equivalently, the weights for one of the other implementations) so that transfer function of the filter will result in an approximation to one of the ideal filters.

4.6   SINE BUTTERWORTH LOWPASS FILTER

The sine Butterworth lowpass filter is both one of the simplest higher filters and also one that is usable in a variety of applications. For these reasons it is discussed in detail. In particular, the subroutine LPSB in Appendix A generates the coefficients for filters of this type, so the procedures employed in that routine are discussed at length.

The absolute value squared of the transfer function of the sine Butterworth filter is

$$|H(f)|^2 = \cfrac{1}{1 + \left(\cfrac{\sin \pi f T}{\sin \pi BT} \right)^{2M}} \tag{4.110}$$

There are M poles in this filter and no zeroes.

Implementation of this filter for $M=2$ was discussed at the end of Section 4.3. As noted there, the method employed in that section does not conveniently generalize for values of M greater than 2.

The method to be used in this section has the following steps:

1. The denominator $D(f)=1+(\sin \pi f T/\sin \pi BT)^{2M}$ is set equal to 0, and the solutions (poles) are found.
2. There are $2M$ roots to the equation: M in the upper half-plane, and M in the lower half-plane. The ones in the lower half-plane all correspond to unstable filters; they were added when $H(f)$ was multiplied by $H^*(f)$ to form $|H(f)|^2$. In any event, the M poles in the upper half-plane are the only ones used, and they will yield a stable filter.
3. The most complicated part of the solution is that of finding α_m, β_m in the equation

$$\sin\left(\frac{\beta_m + j\alpha_m}{2} \right) = a_m + jb_m \tag{4.111}$$

which will be found below. The equation solution requires the calculation of a complex arcsine.

4. The poles (α_m, β_m) $m = 1, \ldots, M$, once found, are inserted into quadratic terms of the form

$$1 - 2\exp(-\alpha_m)\cos\beta z^{-1} + \exp(-2\alpha_m)z^{-2} \qquad (4.112)$$

That is, for the mth stage,

$$a_{1m} = 2\exp(-\alpha_m)\cos\beta_m$$

$$a_{2m} = -\exp(-2\alpha_m) \qquad (4.113)$$

For $m = 1, \ldots, M/2$ and M even. For M odd, this is done for $m = 1, \ldots, (M-1)/2$ and a special $(M+1)/2$ term is computed.

The details of this are studied along with the code to calculate the weights. First of all, the $D(f) = 0$ can be written as

$$s^{2M} + 1 = 0 \qquad (4.114)$$

where $s = \sin\pi f T / \sin BT$.

There are $2M$ solutions to this equation. M of them are not used at all (they correspond to the lower half-plane), and of the remaining M, only $M/2$ are used directly.

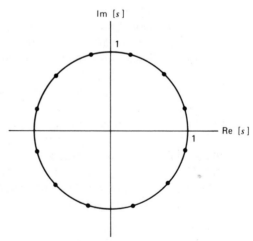

Figure 4.9 Roots of $s^{2M} + 1 = 0$ for $M = 6$. Notice the equal spacing of the roots, and that none of them are real.

The solutions of this equation are always imaginary or complex. Figure 4.9 shows the location of the solutions for $M=6$. As shown in the picture, the roots are equally spaced around the unit circle. The code for generating these numbers of the form:

```
SECTOR = 3.14159265/FLOAT(M)
WEDGE = SECTOR/2.
DO 5 I = 1, M1
FN = I − 1
ANG = FN*SECTOR + WEDGE
    ⋮
```

The M1 parameter is defined as follows:

$$M1 = \begin{cases} M/2 & M \text{ even} \\ \dfrac{M-1}{2} & M \text{ odd} \end{cases}$$

This code successively generates the angles

	I
WEDGE	1
SECTOR + WEDGE	2
2.*SECTOR + WEDGE	3
⋮	
FLOAT(M/2 − 1)*SECTOR + WEDGE	M1

in radians. For example, if $M=6$, and putting the angles in degrees, then $15°$, $45°$, and $75°$ would be the equivalent angles computed.

Denote these roots as $s_1, \ldots, s_{M/2}$. The next step is that of finding the α_m and β_m in

$$\sin\left(\frac{\beta_m + j\alpha_m}{2}\right) = \sin(\pi BT)s_m \tag{4.115}$$

Complex Arcsine Computation

Suppose a similar equation to the above is considered:

$$\sin(u + jv) = a + jb \tag{4.116}$$

It is assumed that a and b are known and it is desired to find u and v. First of all, the double angle formula for sines can be employed to yield

$$\sin(u+jv)=\sin u \cos jv + \cos u \sin jv \qquad (4.117)$$

As $\sin j\theta = j \sinh \theta$ and $\cos j\theta = \cosh \theta$, this can be rewritten as

$$\sin u \cosh v + j \cos u \sinh v = a + jb \qquad (4.118)$$

Equating real and imaginary parts results in two equations in two unknowns, u and v:

$$\sin u \cosh v = a$$
$$\cos u \sinh v = b \qquad (4.119)$$

If these are squared and the identity $\cos^2 u = 1 - \sin^2 u$ is used, they become

$$\sin^2 u \cosh^2 v = a^2$$
$$(1 - \sin^2 u) \sinh^2 v = b^2 \qquad (4.120)$$

Substituting the first of these into the second yields

$$\left(1 - \frac{a^2}{\cosh^2 v}\right) \sinh^2 v = b^2$$

or

$$(\cosh^2 v - a^2) \sinh^2 v = b^2 \cosh^2 v \qquad (4.121)$$

The identity $\cosh^2 v - \sinh^2 v = 1$ is next used to reduce this to the quadratic equation

$$\sinh^4 v + (1 - a^2 - b^2) \sinh^2 v - b^2 = 0 \qquad (4.122)$$

A new parameter C is defined at this point:

$$C = 1 - a^2 - b^2 \qquad (4.123)$$

so the equation is

$$\sinh^4 v + C \sinh^2 v - b^2 = 0 \qquad (4.124)$$

Examination of the C term shows that it is actually only a function of the filter cutoff frequency for the Butterworth implementation. This is solved as a quadratic in $\sinh^2 v$, yielding

$$\sinh^2 v = \frac{-C \pm \sqrt{C^2 + 4b^2}}{2} \tag{4.125}$$

For convenience and later conversion to code, one root is called D. That is,

$$D = \frac{-C + \sqrt{C^2 + 4b^2}}{2} \tag{4.126}$$

Only the plus sign is needed. Writing

$$\sinh^2 v = \left(\frac{e^v - e^{-v}}{2}\right)^2 = D \tag{4.127}$$

the next equation is obtained by taking the square root of both sides:

$$e^v - e^{-v} = 2\sqrt{D} \tag{4.128}$$

Multiplying through by e^v results in

$$e^{2v} - 2\sqrt{D}\, e^v - 1 = 0 \tag{4.129}$$

This is now solved for e^v, yielding

$$e^v = \frac{2\sqrt{D} \pm \sqrt{4D + 4}}{2} = \sqrt{D} \pm \sqrt{D+1} \tag{4.130}$$

Define the parameter E by

$$E = e^v = \sqrt{D} + \sqrt{D+1} \tag{4.131}$$

Clearly, for real v, the sign must be plus. Then the solution for v is

$$v = \ln E = \ln\left[\sqrt{D} + \sqrt{D+1}\,\right] \tag{4.132}$$

Since $\cos u \sinh v = b$,

$$u = \arccos\left(\frac{b}{\sinh v}\right) \tag{4.133}$$

Note that as $\sinh^2 v = D$ the expression for u becomes

$$u = \arccos\left(\frac{b}{\sqrt{D}}\right) \tag{4.134}$$

FORTRAN Code for the Lowpass Filter

The complex arcsine relationship just discussed may now be applied to the equation

$$\sin\left(\frac{\beta_m + j\alpha_m}{2}\right) = \sin(\pi BT)s_m \tag{4.135}$$

so that it may be solved for α_m and β_m.

Then the b_m term for each section (the a_m term need not be calculated) is

$$b_m = \sin \pi BT \cdot \mathrm{Im}\big[s_m\big]$$

$$= \sin \pi BT \cdot \sin \theta_m \tag{4.136}$$

where θ_m is the same as ANG defined above. The $\sin \pi BT$ term is replaced by the parameter FACT in the code, so that this becomes

$$B = FACT*SIN(ANG)$$

where FACT has been previously computed as

$$FACT = SIN(3.14159265*BW*T)$$

where BW is the cutoff frequency B and T is the sampling interval in seconds.

Next, the solution obtained above in terms of the parameters α and β is

$$\frac{\beta + j\alpha}{2} = u + jv \tag{4.137}$$

The factor of 2 in the denominator is very important. The coefficients for a given stage are then

$$a_1 = -2\exp(-\alpha)\cos\beta$$

$$= -2\exp(-2v)\cos 2u$$

$$= -2\exp(-2\ln E)\cos\left[2\arccos\left(\frac{B}{\sqrt{D}}\right)\right]$$

$$= -2E^{-2}\left(\frac{2B^2}{D} - 1\right)$$

$$a_2 = \exp(-2\alpha)$$

$$= \exp(-2v)$$

$$= E^{-4} \tag{4.138}$$

```
      M1 = M/2
      FACT = SIN(3.14159265*BW*T)
      DØ 5 = I-1 M1
      FN = I-1
      B = FACT*SIN(FN*SECTØR+WEDGE)
      C = 1. - FACT*FACT
      D = 0.5*(-C+SQRT(C*C+4*B*B))
      E = SQRT(D+1.)+SQRT(D)
      A1(I) = -2.*(E**-2)*(2.*B*B/D-1.)
    5 A2(I) = E**-4
```

Figure 4.10   FORTRAN code for generating the filter weights.

The required formulas may be summed up as follows:

$$A = FACT \cdot \cos(ANG)$$

$$B = FACT \cdot \sin(ANG)$$

$$C = 1 - A^2 - B^2 = 1 - (FACT)^2$$

$$D = \frac{-C + \sqrt{C^2 + 4B^2}}{2}$$

$$E = \sqrt{D} + \sqrt{D+1}$$

$$a_1 = -2E^{-2}\left(\frac{2B^2}{D} - 1\right)$$

$$a_2 = E^{-4}$$

Thus for the Butterworth implementation, the A term may be deleted. These equations as converted to FORTRAN code are shown in Figure 4.10. The code is rather short considering the lengthy derivation of the terms.

This figure should be compared to the one for subroutine LPSB in Appendix A. LPSB was coded in *double precision*, so that the correspondence is not exact, but they are quite similar.

Figure A.11 in Appendix A shows a test case for $M = 5$. The sampling rate is 200 sps, so that $T = 0.005$ and $F = 100$. The cutoff frequency B was taken to be 5 Hz. This is 5% of F. As it turns out, it is the percentage that is relevant rather than the actual value of B. For example, the following values of B and S yield the exact same set of filter weights.

B	S	F	%
0.5	20	10	5
1	40	20	5
5	200	100	5
100	4,000	2,000	5
500	20,000	10,000	5

This is because B here is always 5% of F, so that the relative position does not change.

With $M=5$, there are three sections to the filter: two stages with two complex poles and one stage with a single pole.

The scaling coefficient b_0, the same for all three stages, is obtained in the following manner. Recall that the formula for the transfer function of the filter in this case is

$$H(f) = \prod_{p=1}^{3} \frac{b_0}{1 + a_{1p}\exp(-j2\pi fT) + a_{2p}\exp(-j4\pi fT)} \qquad (4.139)$$

The passband is from 0 to f_c Hz. It is natural to have unit gain in this band. In particular, it is desirable to have $H(0)=1$. Because $\exp(0)=1$, the above becomes

$$1 = \frac{b_0^3}{\displaystyle\prod_{p=1}^{3}(1 + a_{1p} + a_{2p})} \qquad (4.140)$$

so that

$$b_0 = \sqrt[3]{\prod_{p=1}^{3}(1 + a_{1p} + a_{2p})}$$

$$= \sqrt[3]{(1 + a_{11} + a_{21})(1 + a_{12} + a_{22})(1 + a_{13})}$$

$$= 0.041955 \qquad (4.141)$$

for the parameters given in the test case.

The gain in decibels of the transfer function of this filter is shown in Figure A.11b. Note the following values:

f	$10\log_{10}|H(f)|^2$	$|H(f)|^2$
0	0.0000	1.0
5	-3.0103	0.5
100	-110.5357	$1/1.1313 \cdot 10^{11}$

The half-power point is sometimes called the "3 dB" point because the gain is down approximately 3 dB from its passband value.

4.7 SINE BUTTERWORTH HIGHPASS FILTER

A highpass filter could be generated in much the same way as that for the lowpass filter. The transfer function to be implemented is

$$|H(f)| = \cfrac{1}{1 + \left(\cfrac{\sin(\pi fT + \pi/2)}{\sin \pi BT} \right)^{2M}} \qquad (4.142)$$

The critical values for this function are as follows:

f	$H(f)^2$
0	$< \frac{1}{2}$
$F - B$	$\frac{1}{2}$
F	1

The effective result is that little or nothing is passed on the range 0 to $(F - B)$ Hz, whereas on the range $(F - B)$ to F Hz, the information is passed with relatively little attenuation.

This transfer function is almost identical to the one for the lowpass filter except for the $\pi/2$ term. Thus the previous algorithm can be modified very slightly and also made to generate highpass filters. In particular, the basic angle formula is now

$$\frac{\beta + j\alpha + \pi}{2} = u + jv \qquad (4.143)$$

This implies that

$$\beta = 2u + \pi$$

$$\alpha = 2v \qquad (4.144)$$

Thus the α term does not change. Because the a_{2p} weights have only α_p in them, they do not change. The a_{1p} weights do, however, have a modification:

$$a_1 = -2\exp(-\alpha)\cos\beta$$

$$= -2\exp(-\alpha)\cos\left(2u + \frac{\pi}{2}\right)$$

$$= -2\exp(-\alpha)(\cos 2u \cos \pi - \sin 2u \sin \pi)$$

$$= 2\exp(-\alpha)\cos 2u \qquad (4.145)$$

The only difference between this expression for the a_{1p} weight and that for the lowpass filter is a change in sign. This means that if a set of weights is available for a lowpass filter with cutoff at B Hz, then a highpass filter with cutoff at $F - B$ Hz may be generated by simply changing the signs of the a_{1p} coefficients: Note that the width of the passbands is the same in both cases.

As it turns out, the scaling parameter b_0 also remains the same. Why?

4.8   BANDPASS FILTERS

Bandpass filters tend to pass information in a band centered at frequency f_c, with the bandwidth of size B.

There are a number of ways of implementing such a filter. Perhaps the easiest is through the use of two lowpass filters as shown in Figure 4.11. As shown in the figure, $x(i)$ is processed along two different branches. The upper one multiplies $x(i)$ by $\sin 2\pi f_c iT$, passes it through a lowpass filter, and again multiplies the result by $\sin 2\pi f_c iT$. The lower branch is the same except that $\cos 2\pi f_c iT$ is employed in place of the sine. The output $y(i)$ function therefore is

$$y(i) = \sin 2\pi f_c iT \left\{ h(i)*\left[x(i)\sin 2\pi f_c iT \right] \right\}$$

$$+ \cos 2\pi f_c iT \left\{ h(i)*\left[x(i)\cos 2\pi f_c iT \right] \right\} \qquad (4.146)$$

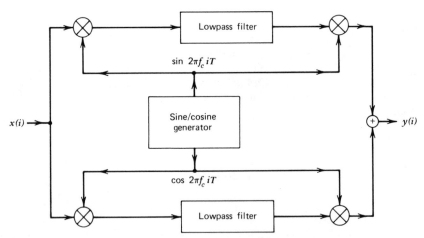

Figure 4.11 A bandpass filter implemented with two lowpass filters and a sine/cosine generator.

where $h(i)$ is the unit impulse response function of the identical filters. If $h(i)$ is the delta function

$$h(i) = \begin{cases} \dfrac{1}{T} & i=0 \\ 0 & \text{otherwise} \end{cases} \qquad (4.147)$$

then the overall action of the filter reduces to

$$y(i) = \sin 2\pi f_c iT \left[x(i)\sin 2\pi f_c iT \right]$$
$$+ \cos 2\pi f_c iT \left[x(i)\cos 2\pi f_c iT \right]$$
$$= x(i)\left(\sin^2 2\pi f_c iT + \cos^2 2\pi f_c iT \right)$$
$$= x(i) \qquad (4.148)$$

That is, in the trivial case where the lowpass filters pass everything, the overall filter reduces to one that also passes everything.

What is really happening is best shown by rewriting the defining equations with complex notation:

$$y(i) = \exp(-j2\pi f_c iT)\left\{ h(i)* \left[x(i)\exp(j2\pi f_c iT) \right] \right\} \qquad (4.149)$$

The innermost $\exp(j2\pi f_c iT)$ multiplies $x(i)$ in the time domain. As discussed in Chapter 1, this is the same as shifting $X(f)$ in the frequency domain. In particular, the Fourier transform of $x(i)\exp(j2\pi f_c iT)$ is

$$T \sum_{i=-\infty}^{\infty} x(i)\exp(j2\pi f_c iT)\exp(-j2\pi fiT)$$

$$= T \sum_{i-\infty}^{\infty} x(i)\exp\left[-j2\pi(f-f_c)iT \right] = X(f-f_c) \qquad (4.150)$$

That is, the information that was at or near frequency f_c is shifted to 0 Hz. The two lowpass filters retain this information and reject information outside the band of interest. Finally, the multiplication by $\exp(-j2\pi f_c iT)$ shifts the information back to its original position.

In order to have a passband of B Hz, the half-power points of the two lowpass filters must be set at $B/2$ Hz.

The sines and cosines may be generated in a variety of ways. On a computer with a large word size, the recursive relationship shown in Section 4.3 may be satisfactory. A more reliable procedure is as follows: accumulate the angle $\lambda(i) = 2\pi f_c iT$ by successively adding $2\pi f_c T$ to the expression for the angle, that is, $\lambda(i) = \lambda(i-1) + 2\pi f_c T$; each time $\lambda(i)$ exceeds 2π, 2π is subtracted from it [thus $\lambda(i)$ is reduced modulo 2π]; by multiplying $\lambda(i)$ by $2048/2\pi$, an index is created which when used in conjunction with a table of the sine function having one cycle in 2048 points will yield the proper result. Actually, the usual practice is to have only the first quarter of the sine wave (513 points in this example) in the table, and to check the value of $\lambda(i) \cdot 2048/2\pi$ to find the proper quadrant.

This algorithm works, but is probably best suited to the situation where the coefficients are hardwired, as in a microprocessor, and it is not possible to have code to generate the filter weights. A few sets of weights for the lowpass case and the above algorithm are sufficient to generate bandpass filters for a large number of filters.

This same type of filter can be implemented in a manner similar to the lowpass case. The transfer function form is different:

$$|H(f)|^2 = \cfrac{1}{1 + \left(\cfrac{\cos 2\pi f T - C}{S}\right)^M} \qquad (4.151)$$

where

$$C = \cos 2\pi f_c T \cos \pi B T$$

$$S = \sin 2\pi f_c T \sin \pi B T$$

The reader should verify that

$$\left|H\left(f_c - \frac{B}{2}\right)\right|^2 = \left|H\left(f_c + \frac{B}{2}\right)\right|^2 = \frac{1}{2} \qquad (4.152)$$

and that the maximum occurs at frequency f_m defined by the equation

$$\cos 2\pi f_m T = \cos 2\pi f_c T \cos \pi B T \qquad (4.153)$$

For small B, this reduces to $f_m \approx f_c$. Thus the passband is from $(f_c - B/2)$ to $(f_c + B/2)$ Hz.

Note the following facts about the transfer function:

- Rather than $\sin \pi f T$, $\cos 2\pi f T$ is employed. The factor of 2 makes more difference than does the cosine term.
- M rather than $2M$ is used as the exponent of the denominator term. As it turns out, M must be even for both the bandpass and band notch filters.

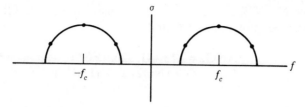

Figure 4.12 Pole positions for a six-pole bandpass filter.

The algorithm given in the preceding section can be modified in a few places and made to generate bandpass filters in this form. First of all, the denominator of the equation is set equal to 0 for the purpose of finding the poles. For convenience, the cosine is replaced with a sine and a phase angle

$$1 + \left(\frac{\sin(2\pi f T + \pi/2) - C}{S} \right)^M \qquad (4.154)$$

This can be rewritten as

$$s^M + 1 = 0$$

where

$$s = \frac{\sin(2\pi f T + \pi/2) - C}{S} \qquad (4.155)$$

There are M solutions to this equation, $M/2$ of which are used. However, each of the $M/2$ solutions yields two poles that are employed in the filter implementation.

This is shown in Figure 4.12 for a six-pole filter ($M=6$). There are only six solutions to the equation $s^6 + 1 = 0$, and only three of these are used; the C and S terms in the defining equation cause these to be reflected around the σ axis.

The principal equation to solve is then

$$\sin\left[\left(\beta_m + \frac{\pi}{2} \right) + j\alpha_m \right] = Ss_m + C$$

$$= a_m + jb_m \qquad (4.156)$$

This is exactly the same form as for the lowpass case except for the $\pi/2$ term and the fact that a_m and b_m are different. In the FORTRAN code, the following changes have to be made:

1. Compute C and S. Because C is already used in the FORTRAN code, it is best to employ names CC and SS

$$ANG2 = 2.*3.14159265*FC*T$$
$$CC = COS(ANG2)*COS(FACT)$$
$$SS = SIN(ANG2)*SIN(FACT)$$

FC corresponds to f_c. The FACT term is not modified.

2. Multiply SECTOR by 2. That is, the SECTOR term becomes

$$SECTOR = 2.*3.14159265/FLOAT(M)$$

3. The computations for A, B, and C are modified as follows:

$$ANG = FN*SETOR + WEDGE$$
$$A = SS*COS(ANG) + CC$$
$$B = SS*SIN(ANG)$$
$$C = 1. - A*A - B*B$$

4. The computations for G and H (terms in the LPSB routine) have to be changed:

$$G = 2.*SQRT(1. - B*B/D)/E$$
$$IF(A.LT.O.)G = -G$$
$$H = -1./(E**2)$$

Figure 4.13 shows LPSB with the above modifications. The routine name has been changed to BNPS, which is more appropriate to its function.
Modification 4 above needs some further explanation. Remember that

$$a_{1m} = -2\exp(-\alpha_m)\cos\beta_m$$
$$a_{2m} = \exp(-2\alpha_m) \tag{4.157}$$

In this case rather than

$$\frac{\beta_m + j\alpha_m}{2} = u_m + jv_m \tag{4.158}$$

```
      SUBROUTINE BNPS (MM,T,BW,FC,A1,A2,BZERO)
      DIMENSION A1(1),A2(1),B0(1),B1(1),B2(1)
     1,FREQ(1),ABZ(1),PHS(1)
      DOUBLE PRECISION A,B,C,D,E,G,H,GN,FACT,WEDGE,SECTOR,ANG
     1,CC,SS,ANG2
      DATA B0 /1./,B1 /0./, B2 /0./
      FACT=2.*3.14159265*T*BW
      ANG2=2.*3.14159265*T*FC
      CC=DCOS(ANG2)*DCOS(FACT)
      CCC=CC
      FREQ(1)=ATAN2(SQRT(1.-CCC*CCC),CCC)/6.2831853
      SS=DSIN(ANG2)*DSIN(FACT)
      M=MM
      M1=M/2
      A=M
      HTRAN=0.
      SECTOR=2.D0*3.14159265D0/A
      WEDGE=SECTOR/2.D0
      DO 5 I=1,M1
      FN=I-1
      ANG=FN*SECTOR+WEDGE
      A=SS*DCOS(ANG)+CC
      B=SS*DSIN(ANG)
      C=1.D0-(A**2+B**2)
      D=0.5*(-C+DSQRT(C*C+4.D0*B**2))
      E=DSQRT(D+1.D0)+DSQRT(D)
      G=2.D0*DSQRT(1.D0-B*B/D)/E
      IF (A.LT.0.D0) G=-G
      H=-1.D0/(E**2)
      A1(I)=-G
      A2(I)=-H
      CALL TTRAN (A1(I),A2(I),B0,B1,B2,2,1,1.,FREQ,ABZ,PHS)
      HTRAN=HTRAN+ABZ(1)
    5 CONTINUE
      BZERO=10.**(-HTRAN/(20.*FLOAT(M1)))
      RETURN
      END
```

Figure 4.13 Bandpass sine filter weight generating routine. FC is the center frequency of the filter and BW is the half bandwidth. Note that the routine has been coded in double precision.

the formula is

$$\beta_m + \frac{\pi}{2} + j\alpha_m = u_m + jv_m \tag{4.159}$$

So that, omitting the m subscript,

$$\beta = u - \frac{\pi}{2}$$

$$\alpha = v \tag{4.160}$$

Thus the coefficients are

$$a_1 = -2\exp(-\alpha)\cos\beta$$

$$= -2\exp(-v)\cos\left(u - \frac{\pi}{2}\right)$$

$$= 2\exp(-\ln E)\sin u$$

$$= 2E^{-1}\sin\left[\arccos\left(\frac{B}{\sqrt{D}}\right)\right]$$

$$= \pm 2E^{-1}\sqrt{1 - \cos^2\left[\arccos\left(\frac{B}{\sqrt{D}}\right)\right]}$$

$$= \pm 2E^{-1}\sqrt{1 - \frac{B^2}{D}}$$

$$a_2 = \exp(-2\alpha)$$

$$= E^{-2} \tag{4.161}$$

There are a few other minor differences in the code for BNPS. The maximum occurs at a frequency at or near FC, namely, at $f_m = \arccos(CC)/2\pi T$. The subroutine TTRAN is used by BNPS to compute the single value at f_m of the transfer function in decibels of each two pole sections of the filter; these are summed and converted to an overall scaling factor.

4.9 BAND REJECT FILTERS

This section discusses a specific type of band reject filter. It is a somewhat limited form, and the results for it do not necessarily indicate the behavior of the other band reject types.

The band reject type of filter is a close relative of the bandpass. In fact, as will be seen, the poles are identical. There is one big difference between the band reject and previous filters: all filters discussed to this point have no zeroes; the band reject has as many zeroes as poles.

The transfer function for the band reject filter is obtained in a very simple manner: the transfer function of bandpass filters is subtracted from unity. That is, the transfer function of the band reject filter is of the form

$$|H(f)|^2 = 1 - \frac{1}{1 + \left(\dfrac{\cos 2\pi fT - C}{S}\right)^M} \qquad (4.162)$$

When the subtraction is completed,

$$|H(f)|^2 = \frac{1 + \left(\dfrac{\cos 2\pi fT - C}{S}\right)^M - 1}{1 + \left(\dfrac{\cos 2\pi fT - C}{S}\right)^M}$$

$$= \frac{\left(\dfrac{\cos 2\pi fT - C}{S}\right)^M}{1 + \left(\dfrac{\cos 2\pi fT - C}{S}\right)^M} \qquad (4.163)$$

The important things to note here are the following:

1. The denominator is the same as for the band pass filter; hence for this case the two filters have the same poles.
2. The transfer function satisfies $|H(f)|^2 \geq 0$; otherwise it would not be a valid function.
3. The stop band has its half-power points exactly where the bandpass filter has its half-power points.

Figure 4.14 shows the transfer function of a bandpass filter and its corresponding band reject filter.

As noted above, the band reject filter has zeroes. Up until now, all the filters discussed could be implemented in cascade form with c series of difference equations of the form

$$y(i) = b_0 x(i) - a_1 y(i-1) - a_2 y(i-2) \qquad (4.164)$$

The band reject filter requires a filter equation of the form

$$y(i) = b_0 x(i) + b_1 x(i-1) + b_2 (x-2) - a_1 y(i-1) - a_2 y(i-2) \qquad (4.165)$$

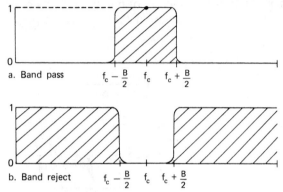

a. Band pass $f_c - \dfrac{B}{2}$ f_c $f_c + \dfrac{B}{2}$

b. Band reject $f_c - \dfrac{B}{2}$ f_c $f_c + \dfrac{B}{2}$

Figure 4.14   A bandpass filter and a band reject filter formed from it.

The problem then is that of finding the proper b_0, b_1, and b_2 terms for each section of the filter. However, this is not difficult to do.

The zeroes, exactly like the poles, are found by setting their defining equation equal to zero and then solving for the values that satisfy the equation. In this case, the equation is

$$\left(\frac{\cos 2\pi f T - C}{S} \right)^M = 0 \tag{4.166}$$

The solution of this is quite easy. All the roots of this equation are equal, and the solution for all of the zeroes is

$$\cos 2\pi f_m T = C$$

$$= \cos 2\pi f_c T \cos \pi B T$$

Thus

$$2\pi f_m T = \pm \arccos C \tag{4.167}$$

The plus or minus sign comes about because of the fact that $\cos(-x) = \cos x$. Hence, although the solutions of the original equation are equal, the solutions for f_m may differ by sign.

The next step is finding the proper b_0, b_1, and b_2 terms. For a single zero (there are two zeroes per cascade section), the expression is

$$1 - bz_m^{-1} = 0 \tag{4.168}$$

so that

$$b = z_m = \exp(j2\pi Tf_m)$$

$$= \exp(\pm j \arccos C) \qquad (4.169)$$

Thus for a cascade section, the two possible signs for f_m will be employed so that the overall factor is

$$(1 - bz^{-1})(1 - b^*z^{-1}) = [1 - \exp(j \arccos C)z^{-1}][1 - \exp(-j \arccos C)z^{-1}]$$

$$= 1 - [\exp(j \arccos C) + \exp(-j \arccos C)]z^{-1}$$

$$+ [\exp(j \arccos C)\cdot(-j \arccos C)]z^{-2}$$

$$= 1 - 2\cos[\arccos C]z^{-1} + \exp(0)z^{-2}$$

$$= 1 - 2Cz^{-1} + z^{-2} \qquad (4.170)$$

The values for b_0, b_1, and b_2, to within a scaling constant, are found by equating the coefficients. Thus

$$b_0 = 1$$

$$b_1 = -2C$$

$$b_2 = 1 \qquad (4.171)$$

This result is good for all second-order sections. Naturally, normalization of the filter will change these values. Normalization is accomplished by evaluating the transfer function of the filter using the above values at either $f = 0$ or $1/2T$. Suppose that this value is $|H'(0)|^2$, where the prime indicates the filter is unnormalized. What is desired is that the normalized filter be such that

$$|H(0)|^2 = 1 \qquad (4.172)$$

This could be accomplished by setting

$$|H(f)|^2 = \left[\frac{1}{|H'(0)|^2} \right] |H'(f)|^2 \qquad (4.173)$$

that is, by multiplying the unnormalized filter by the constant $1/|H'(0)|^2$, which forces $|H(0)|^2 = 1$. Thus the coefficients for each cascade stage become

$$b_0 = 1 \frac{1}{|H'(0)|^{2/M}}$$

$$b_1 = \frac{-2C}{|H'(0)|^{2/M}}$$

$$b_2 = \frac{1}{|H'(0)|^{2/M}} \tag{4.174}$$

The $|H'(0)|^2$ could easily be calculated using the TTRAN subroutine included in Appendix A. The b_0, b_1, and b_2 terms would be put in as 1, $-2C$, and 1. Also, it would not be necessary to write a special routine to generate band reject filters: a routine for generating bandpass filters will yield the recursive parts of the filter; to get the nonrecursive weights, it is only necessary to calculate them as indicated above, which is quite straightforward.

4.10   TANGENT FILTERS

An entirely new family of filters may be generated by replacing the sine term with a similar tangent term. For example, the transfer function of the Butterworth lowpass filter becomes

$$|H(f)|^2 = \frac{1}{1 + \left(\dfrac{\tan \pi f T}{\tan \pi B T} \right)^{2M}} \tag{4.175}$$

When evaluated at 0, B, and F, the following values are found:

$$|H(0)|^2 = 1$$

$$|H(B)|^2 = \frac{1}{2}$$

$$|H(F)|^2 = 0 \tag{4.176}$$

When graphed, it will superficially look like the sine Butterworth filter for the same values of B and M. In detail it will be different. In particular, if both the sine and tangent filters are plotted in decibels, the tangent version will be seen to have superior performance in the stop band: it will fall considerably below the equivalent sine filter when they are put on the same plot.

This improved performance is not without cost; all tangent filters have zeroes. Thus they are more computationally expensive. This is discussed in more detail below.

There are several ways of implementing tangent filters: of these, the zero-pole and bilateral z-transform methods are considered here. First the poles are discussed; the zeroes turn out to be easy to generate.

For the lowpass Butterworth case, it is required to find the poles by solving for the roots of

$$1 + \left(\frac{\tan \pi f T}{\tan \pi B T} \right)^{2M} = 0 \tag{4.177}$$

As with the form, assume that $s_1, \ldots, s_{M/2}$ are roots of unity in the upper half-plane, and that $\beta_m + j\alpha_m$ is the desired solution. That is, the equation to be solved is

$$\tan \left(\frac{\beta_m + j\alpha_m}{2} \right) = \tan(\pi B T)s_m \tag{4.178}$$

It is possible to solve this directly. From the previous result the complex arccosine may be employed after appropriate modifications to the above. Because

$$\tan x = \frac{\sin x}{\cos x} \tag{4.179}$$

the previous equation can be written as

$$\frac{\sin \left(\dfrac{\beta_m + j\alpha_m}{2} \right)}{\cos \left(\dfrac{\beta_m + j\alpha_m}{2} \right)} = \tan(\pi B T)s_m \tag{4.180}$$

The cosine term may be eliminated by squaring both sides, replacing $\cos^2 x$ with $1 - \sin^2 x$, and then solving for $\sin x$.

The considerably simpler bilateral z-transform technique popularized by Kaiser [1963] makes use of the fact that

$$\tan \pi f T = \frac{1}{j} \frac{1 - z^{-1}}{1 + z^{-1}} \tag{4.181}$$

The term bilateral z-transform terminology arises from the fact that the conformal mapping

$$y = \frac{1}{j}\frac{1-1/x}{1+1/x} = \frac{1}{j}\frac{x-1}{x+1} \tag{4.182}$$

is generally referred to as the *bilinear mapping* or *transformation*. Because z^{-1} rather than $z^{-1/2}$ appears in the expression, it is much simpler to work out the formulas for the coefficients. The calculations proceed as follows: set

$$\tan \pi f_m T = \frac{1}{j}\frac{1-z_m^{-1}}{1+z_m^{-1}} = \tan(\pi BT)s_m$$

$$= a_m + jb_m \tag{4.183}$$

That is, set

$$\frac{1}{j}\frac{1-z_m^{-1}}{1+z_m^{-1}} = a_m + jb_m \tag{4.184}$$

After the calculations are performed, z_m^{-1} may be found to be

$$z_m^{-1} = \frac{(1+b_m)-ja_m}{(1-b_m)+ja_m} \tag{4.185}$$

Because the relationship

$$(1-z_m z^{-1})(1-z_m^* z^{-1}) = 1 + a_{1m}z^{-1} + a_{2m}z^{-2} \tag{4.186}$$

must be satisfied,

$$a_{1m} = -z_m - z_m^* = -\frac{(1-b_m)+ja_m}{(1+b_m)-ja_m} - \frac{(1-b_m)-ja_m}{(1+b_m)+ja_m}$$

$$= -2\frac{(1-b_m^2)-a_m^2}{(1+b_m)^2+a_m^2}$$

$$a_{2m} = z_m z_m^* = \frac{(1-b_m)^2+a_m^2}{(1+b_m)^2+a_m^2} \tag{4.187}$$

In summary, the algorithm is as follows:

1. Select M, the number of poles in the filter, and B the cutoff frequency.
2. Compute the a_m and b_m terms:
   ANG = 3.14159265*B*T
   FACT = SIN(ANG)/COS(ANG)
   M1 = M − M/2
   SECTOR = 3.14159265/FLOAT(M)
   WEDGE = SECTOR/2.
   DO 5 I = 1, M1
   FN = I − 1
   ANG = FN*SECTOR + WEDGE
   AM = FACT*SIN(ANG)
   BM = FACT*COS(ANG)
3. Compute the denominator:
   AMS = AM*AM
   DEN = (1. + BM)**2 + AMS
4. Compute a_{1m}:
   A1(I) = −2.*((1. − BM*BM) − AMS)/DEN
5. Compute a_{2m}:
   A2(I) = ((1. − BM)**2 + AMS)/DEN
6. CONTINUE.

This code is summarized in Figure 4.15 in the form of subroutine LPTB. The calling sequence is identical to LPSB. Only two items remain, the zeroes and the normalization factor.

In order to find the zeroes, it is necessary to look again at the original transfer function:

$$|H(f)|^2 = \frac{1}{1 + \left(\dfrac{\tan \pi fT}{\tan \pi BT}\right)^{2M}} \qquad (4.188)$$

When both numerator and denominator are multiplied by $\cos^{2M}\pi fT$, it becomes

$$\frac{\cos^{2M}\pi fT}{\cos^{2M}\pi fT + \dfrac{\sin^{2M}\pi fT}{\tan^{2M}\pi fT}} \qquad (4.189)$$

```
      SUBROUTINE LPTB (MM,T,B,A1,A2,BZERO)
      DIMENSION A1(1),A2(1)
      DOUBLE PRECISION ANG,FACT,SECTOR,WEDGE,FN,AM,BM,AMS,DEN
      M=MM
      ANG=3.14159265*B*T
      FACT=DSIN(ANG)/DCOS(ANG)
      M1=M-M/2
      F=1.
      FN=M
      SECTOR=3.14159265D0/FN
      WEDGE=SECTOR/2.D0
      DO 5 I=1,M1
      FN=I-1
      ANG=FN*SECTOR+WEDGE
      AM=FACT*DSIN(ANG)
      BM=FACT*DCOS(ANG)
      AMS=AM*AM
      DEN=(1.D0+BM)**2+AMS
      A1(I)=-2.D0*((1.D0-BM*BM)-AMS)/DEN
      A2(I)=((1.D0-BM)**2+AMS)/DEN
      F=F*(1.+A1(I)+A2(I))/4.
5     CONTINUE
      BZERO=F**(1./FLOAT(M1))
      RETURN
      END
```

Figure 4.15 Subroutine LPTB for generating lowpass tangent Butterworth filters. $M(=\text{MM})$ must be even.

Thus the zeroes are solutions of the equation

$$\cos^{2M}\pi fT=0 \tag{4.190}$$

The solution of this is $f=\pm F$.

As with the sine band reject, the function for a single section is

$$\begin{aligned} b=z_m&=\exp(j2\pi Tf_m)\\ &=\exp(\pm j2\pi TF)\\ &=\exp(\pm j\pi)\\ &=-1 \end{aligned} \tag{4.191}$$

For the cascade section this becomes

$$\begin{aligned} (1-bz^{-1})(1-b^*z^{-1})&=(1-z^{-1})(1+z^{-1})\\ &=1+2z^{-1}+z^{-2} \end{aligned} \tag{4.192}$$

That is, b_0, b_1, and b_2 are proportional to 1, 2, and 1, respectively.

Normalization is then done in the usual manner.

Tangent Highpass Filter

The tangent highpass filter is of the form

$$|H(f)|^2 = \frac{1}{1 + \left(\dfrac{\cot \pi f T}{\tan \pi B T}\right)^{2M}} \tag{4.193}$$

As a check on this, the transfer function may be evaluated at 0, $(F-B)$, and F:

$$|H(0)|^2 = 0$$

$$|H(F-B)|^2 = \frac{1}{1 + \left(\dfrac{\tan \pi B T}{\tan \pi B T}\right)^{2M}} = \frac{1}{2}$$

$$|H(F)|^2 = 1 \tag{4.194}$$

It is interesting to compare the lowpass and highpass transfer functions when simplified:

Lowpass:

$$\frac{(\sin \pi B T \cos \pi f T)^{2M}}{(\sin \pi B T \cos \pi f T)^{2M} + (\cos \pi B T \sin \pi f T)^{2M}}$$

Highpass:

$$\frac{(-\cos \pi B T \sin \pi f T)^{2M}}{(\sin \pi B T \cos \pi f T)^{2M} + (-\cos \pi B T \sin \pi f T)^{2M}} \tag{4.195}$$

Except for the minus sign, the poles of these two filters are identical. *This implies that except for differences in sign, the recursive filter coefficients are identical for the lowpass and highpass cases.* Another critical point to take into account is when $B = F/2$. As can be seen, the two transfer functions at this cutoff reduce to

Lowpass:

$$\frac{(\sin \pi/4 \cos \pi f T)^{2M}}{(\sin \pi/4 \cos \pi f T)^{2M} + (\cos \pi/4 \sin \pi f T)^{2M}} = \frac{(\cos \pi f T)^{2M}}{(\cos \pi f T)^{2M} + (\sin \pi f T)^{2M}}$$

Highpass:

$$\frac{(-\cos\pi/4\sin\pi fT)^{2M}}{(\sin\pi/4\cos\pi fT)^{2M}+(-\cos\pi/4\sin\pi fT)^{2M}}=\frac{(\sin\pi fT)^{2M}}{(\cos\pi fT)^{2M}+(-\sin\pi fT)^{2M}}$$

The poles for this special case thus are derived from the equation

$$\cos\pi fT=s_m\sin\pi fT \tag{4.196}$$

where s_m is a root of unity. One peculiarity of this special case is that $a_{1m}=0$ for all m. This can be independently seen from the fact that $a_{1m}>0$ for $B<F/2$, and $a_{1m}<0$ for $B>F/2$. Hence it must be equal to 0 for $B=F/2$.

The signs for the high- and lowpass tangent filters can be summarized in the following manner: suppose a_{1m} and a_{2m}, $m=1,\ldots,M/2$ are found for the lowpass case for $B<F/2$. Then a_{2m} is the same for all cases, as is a_{1m} except for its sign:

Lowpass		Highpass	
$B<F/2$	$B>F/2$	$(F-B)>\dfrac{F}{2}$	$(F-B)<\dfrac{F}{2}$
a_{1m}	$-a_{1m}$	$-a_{1m}$	a_{1m}

The unnormalized nonrecursive weights for both cases are

	Lowpass	Highpass
b_{0m}	1	1
b_{1m}	2	-2
b_{2m}	1	1

As a final check on the duality of these two filters, consider the following: if either of the transfer functions is subtracted from unity, the other transfer function is produced. That is,

$$1-(\text{highpass})=(\text{lowpass})$$

$$1-(\text{lowpass})=(\text{highpass})$$

It is interesting to note that the reason for this duality is easily traceable back to the conformal mapping employed, namely,

$$\tan\pi f_m T=\frac{1}{j}\frac{1-z_m^{-1}}{1+z_m^{-1}} \tag{4.197}$$

Bandpass and Band Reject Tangent Filters

One transfer function that can be employed as a bandpass form is

$$|H(f)|^2 = \cfrac{1}{1 + \left(\cfrac{\cos 2\pi fT - D}{E \sin 2\pi fT} \right)^M} \tag{4.198}$$

where

$$D = \frac{\cos 2\pi f_c T}{\cos \pi BT}$$

$$E = \tan \pi BT \tag{4.199}$$

and M is even.

It has the following characteristics:

f	$\lvert H(f)\rvert^2$	$10\log_{10}\lvert H(f)\rvert^2$
0	0	$-\infty$
$f_c - B/2$	$\frac{1}{2}$	$-3.$
f_{max}	1	0
$f_c + B/2$	$\frac{1}{2}$	$-3.$
F	0	$-\infty$

The maximum occurs at frequency f_{max} defined by

$$f_{max} = \arccos D$$

The equation for the poles reduces to

$$E \sin 2\pi f_m T = s_m (\cos 2\pi f_m T - D) \tag{4.200}$$

where s_m is a root of unity exactly as described for the sine Butterworth case. This may be squared and solved for $\cos 2\pi f_m T$ to yield

$$\cos 2\pi f_m T = \frac{D \pm E s_m \sqrt{1 + E^2 s_m^2 - D^2}}{1 + E^2 s_m^2} \tag{4.201}$$

It should be remembered that the s_m terms are complex. This means that there is still quite a bit of simplification yet to do in the equation before it is directly implementable.

After simplification, the equation reduces to the form

$$\cos 2\pi f_m T = a_m + j b_m \tag{4.202}$$

at which point the procedure for the sine Butterworth may be employed.

The form for the tangent band reject is obtained in the same manner as its sine counterpart, namely, by subtracting $|H(f)|^2$ from unity:

$$1 - \cfrac{1}{1 + \left(\cfrac{\cos 2\pi f T - D}{E \sin 2\pi f T}\right)^M} = \cfrac{1 + \left(\cfrac{\cos 2\pi f T - D}{E \sin 2\pi f T}\right)^M - 1}{1 + \left(\cfrac{\cos 2\pi f T - D}{E \sin 2\pi f T}\right)^M}$$

$$= \frac{(\cos 2\pi f r T - D)^M}{(E \sin 2\pi f T)^M + (\cos 2\pi f T - D)^M} \tag{4.203}$$

Thus the poles are the same as for the bandpass case. The zeroes, however, are quite different. They are solutions of

$$(\cos 2\pi f T - D)^M = 0 \tag{4.204}$$

All these are of the form

$$\cos 2\pi f_m T = D \tag{4.205}$$

Some grinding will yield the nonrecursive coefficients to be (to within a constant):

$$b_0 = 1$$

$$b_1 = -2E$$

$$b_2 = 1 \tag{4.206}$$

4.11   OTHER RECURSIVE FILTERS

In addition to the Butterworth filter, which has been the only basic type discussed up to this point, it is also possible to implement filters referred to as

- Chebyshev type 1 (ripple in the pass band).
- Chebyshev type 2 (ripple in the stop band).
- Elliptic (ripple in both the pass and stop band).
- Bessel.
- Gaussian.

Either sine or tangent version of these may be generated, and lowpass, highpass, bandpass, and band reject versions can be selected.

These filters in their analog form are discussed in Guilleman [1957] and Storer [1957]. The corresponding digital version can be implemented in a variety of ways. The authors have for the most part used the procedure discussed for the sine filter, finding the zeroes and poles and employing either a complex arcsine or arctangent mapping to find the coefficients.

In particular, the two Chebyshev types and the elliptic filter were implemented. The complexity of code for implementing the Butterworth, Chebyshev 1, Chebyshev 2, and elliptic filters increases rather rapidly. In terms of the FORTRAN language, and including comments, the number of statements required for each of the four types for projects in which we were engaged is as follows:

Type of Filter Program	Number of Statements
Butterworth	32
Chebyshev 1	100
Chebyshev 2	245
Elliptic	238

plus an additional 400 statements for the sine and tangent mapping and their variations as required for the lowpass, highpass, bandpass, and band reject filters.

4.12   NONRECURSIVE (FIR) FILTERS

Nonrecursive (finite impulse response—FIR) filters were studied by Ormsby [1961]. His article was one of the early milestones in time series analysis. His procedures, now superseded by later IIR and FIR designs, were in use in industry for many years, and in fact are still employed by some organizations. His main contribution was to improve the performance of lowpass filters. The basic design at that time was to use a symmetric filter of the form

$$y(i) = \sum_{k=-M}^{M} b_k x(i-k) \tag{4.207}$$

with

$$b_{-k} = b_k \tag{4.208}$$

and

$$b_k = \frac{\sin 2\pi B k T}{\pi k} \tag{4.209}$$

A symmetric filter such as this has zero phase angle. It is, of course, nonrealizable in the electronic sense, and only realizable in digital "real time" situations with a delay. Ex post facto, however, which was the way it was employed, it is perfectly implementable on a computer.

Ormsby noted that

$$|b_k| \leqslant \frac{2BT}{k} \tag{4.210}$$

so that the size of the weights decreases rather slowly. Hence M must be quite large in some cases in order to achieve good filtering.

The filter weights b_k were derived by taking the inverse Fourier transform of the boxcar function:

$$b_k = T \int_{-B}^{B} e^{j2\pi fkT} df \tag{4.211}$$

The T in front is included in the b_k terms so as to put the coefficients into proper dimension. Otherwise, it would have to be applied at the end of the calculation.

Ormsby improved the filter substantially by changing it from a boxcar to a trapezoidal shape as shown in Figure 4.16. The addition of the triangle starting at B (the cutoff frequency) and ending at f_r (the rolloff frequency) causes the weights to be bounded by $1/k^2$ rather than $1/k$. Thus their size tends to decrease much more rapidly than does the simple boxcar-shaped lowpass filter. Because this form has been superseded by later developments, its weights are not given.

Considerable study has been done on FIR filters since Ormsby. Probably the two most useful pieces of work on this problem are the papers by Parks and McClellan [1972] and McClellan, Parks, and Rabiner [1973]. The Parks–McClellan computer program for generating finite impulse response filters, listings for which are given in their articles, via approximation techniques and the Remez exchange algorithm has been used widely. We have employed it, and feel that it is extremely useful. Indeed, it is the current standard in industry. Rabiner is probably the most prolific writer in the FIR area, and Rabiner and Gold [1975] discuss his results in detail.

Rabiner notes that there are three basic methods for deriving the FIR filter weights:

• Applying a window to the basic boxcar weights in the time domain.
• Frequency constraining.
• Variational techniques that minimize an error criterion.

The last of these will be discussed to some extent in the next section.

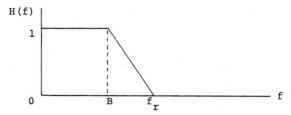

Figure 4.16 Ormsby's improved filter.

Rather than rehashing Rabiner's work, a specific example not previously given in the literature of the windowing method is described in detail here. It employs a window design by R. W. Potter [1971], and was communicated to us by P. Bickford and H. Glaze, while they were both of Time/Data Corporation (Santa Clara, California 95051).

This type of procedure consists of the following:

1.   The b_k weights for the boxcar are computed over the range $-M$ to M (actually, $k=0,\ldots$, or, as the second half are redundant).
2.   The weights are multiplied by a windowing function.

The windowing function improves the performance of the filter in the stop band at the expense of broadening out the passband. Almost any windowing function used for PSD calculations may be employed for this purpose, and the Hanning and Hamming windows discussed in Chapter 7 are often selected.

Potter discusses a number of windows in the referenced work. His P310 window was found to be appropriate for filter implementation. It takes the form

$$w_k = \frac{c_k}{w}\left[d_0 + 2\sum_{p=-3}^{3} d_p \cos\frac{\pi p k}{M}\right] \tag{4.212}$$

where

$$c_k = \begin{cases} \frac{1}{2} & k = \pm M \\ 1 & \text{otherwise} \end{cases} \tag{4.213}$$

$$d_0 = 1$$

$$d_{-1} = d_1 = 0.684988$$

$$d_{-2} = d_2 = 0.202701$$

$$d_{-3} = d_3 = 0.0177127$$

and

$$w = d_0 + 2 \sum_{p=-3}^{3} d = 2.8108034 \qquad (4.214)$$

Code for generating these filter weights is shown in Figure 4.17. The calling sequence is

CALL LPSPBG (M, B, T, BK)

where

M = the span of the filter; $2M + 1$ weights are employed; because of symmetry, only $M + 1$ need be generated

B = the cutoff point of the filter in hertz

T = the sampling interval in seconds

BK = The filter weights; must be of dimension $M + 1$ or greater

The d coefficients [D0, D(1), D(2) and D(3) in the routine] have been divided by 2.8108034 in order to normalize them.

Figure 4.18 shows the result of applying the Potter P310 window to a boxcar lowpass filter. The parameters for this example are

$$T = 1 \qquad (F = 0.5)$$

$$B = 0.1245$$

$$M = 128 \qquad \text{(span of 257 points total in the filter)} \qquad (4.215)$$

As can be seen, the floor of the filter is lowered by an average of about 40 dB through the use of windowing, but the bandwidth is increased by only a small amount. This is considerable improvement over the so-called Kaiser window, as discussed in Rabiner and Gold [1975].

It is easy to extend this routine to the highpass, bandpass, and band reject cases. Indeed, the calculations can be done without modifying the routine:

1. For a highpass filter with passband from B to F, generate a lowpass filter on the range 0–B, and then subtract the central weight from

```
      SUBROUTINE LPSPBG (MM,B,T,BK)
      DIMENSION BK(1),D(3)
      DATA D0/0.35577019/,D(1)/0.2436983/,D(2)/0.07211497/,
     *D(3)/0.00630165/,PI/3.14159265/
C     ROUTINE GENERATES LOWPASS FIR FILTER WEIGHTS
C     METHOD DEVISED BY POTTER, BICKFORD AND GLAZE
C     THERE ARE A TOTAL OF 2M+1 WEIGHTS...LPSPBG GENERATES M+1
C     T IS THE SAMPLING INTERVAL IN SECONDS
C     B IS THE BANDWIDTH IN HZ
C     RESULTS ARE STORED IN BK
      M=MM
C     FIRST GENERATE PLAIN BOXCAR WEIGHTS
      FACT=2.*B*T
      BK(1)=FACT
      FACT=FACT*PI
      DO 5 I=1,M
      FI=I
5     BK(I+1)=SIN(FACT*FI)/(PI*FI)
C     TRAPEZOIDAL WEIGHTING AT END
      BK(M+1)=BK(M+1)/2.
C     NOW APPLY THE POTTER P310 WINDOW
      SUMG=BK(1)
      DO 15 I=1,M
      SUM=D0
      FACT=PI*FLOAT(I)/FLOAT(M)
      DO 10 K=1,3
10    SUM=SUM+2.*D(K)*COS(FACT*FLOAT(K))
      BK(I+1)=BK(I+1)*SUM
15    SUMG=SUMG+2.*BK(I+1)
      M1=M+1
      DO 20 I=1,M1
20    BK(I)=BK(I)/SUMG
      RETURN
      END
```

Figure 4.17 Subroutine LPSPBG for generating lowpass FIR filter weights.

unity and change the signs of the remainder of the weights. That is,

Highpass		Lowpass
b_0'	$=$	$1 - b_0$
b_k'	$=$	$b_k \quad k \neq 0$

2. For a bandpass filter passing data from f_1 to f_2 Hz generate two lowpass filters passing data from 0 to f_1 and 0 to f_2, respectively. Then compute

$$(\text{bandpass weight}) = (\text{lowpass } f_2 \text{ weight}) - (\text{lowpass } f_1 \text{ weight})$$

3. For a band reject filter rejecting everything on the range f_1 to f_2, compute the two lowpass filters as, and then compute

$$(\text{band reject weight}) = 1 - (\text{lowpass } f_2 \text{ weight}) + (\text{lowpass } f_1 \text{ weight})$$

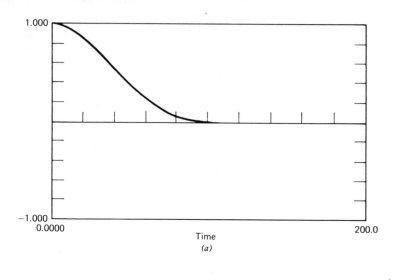

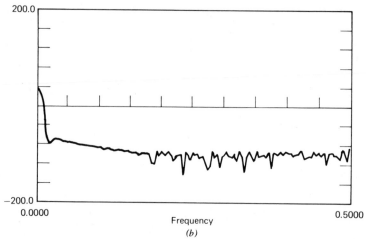

Figure 4.18 Potter P310 window and lowpass filter before and after applying the window. (*a*) Potter P310 window, time domain. (*b*) Potter P310 window, frequency domain. (*c*) Unwindowed lowpass FIR filter. (*d*) Same filter with Potter window applied. Note the change in scale. T = 1, B = 0.1245, M = 128, for a total sum of 257 points.

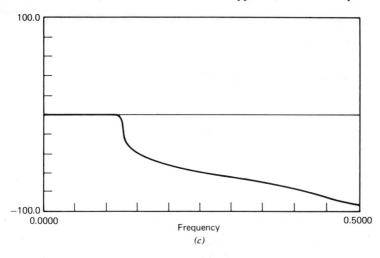

(c)

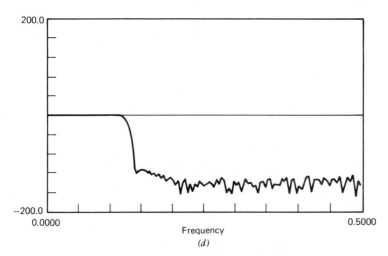

(d)

Figure 4.18   (*Continued*).

4.13   FILTER APPROXIMATION TECHNIQUES

A number of approximation procedures for designing digital filters have
been discussed in the literature including using the Fletcher–Powell algorithm [Jullien and Sid-Ahmed, 1973] and minimax or Chebyshev procedures [Holtz, 1973]. As noted above, the papers of Parks and McClellan
and the associated computer programs are probably the major references.
The method given herein uses the Fletcher–Powell algorithm [Fletcher and

Powell, 1963]. That algorithm has been coded in FORTRAN and is available [IBM, 1968].

Suppose the situation is as follows:

1. $|H(f_i)|^2$ and f_i are given as tables of (nonnegative) numbers for $i = 1, \ldots, N$.
2. λ_i is defined to be $2\pi f_i T$.
3. The filter is to be recursive with M cascaded stages.
4. $|\hat{H}(f_i)|^2$ is the approximation to $|H(f_i)|^2$.

Each stage will be approximated with a rational polynomial expression of the form

$$\frac{\sin^4 \lambda_i / 2 + 2p_m^2 \sin^2 \lambda_i / 2 + \left(p_m^4 + q_m^4\right)}{\sin^4 \lambda_i / 2 + 2r_m^2 \sin^2 \lambda_i / 2 + \left(r_m^4 + s_m^4\right)} \tag{4.216}$$

The reasons for this rather peculiar looking formulation are that

1. It guarantees that $|\hat{H}(f_i)|^2 \geqslant 0$ no matter what the signs of p_m and q_m turn out to be.
2. It guarantees that the filter will be stable.

The transfer function will thus be of the form

$$|\hat{H}(f_i)|^2 = A \prod_{m=1}^{M} \frac{\sin^4 \lambda_i / 2 + 2p_m^2 \sin^2 \lambda_i / 2 + \left(p_m^4 + q_m^4\right)}{\sin^4 \lambda_i / 2 + 2r_m^2 \sin^2 \lambda_i / 2 + \left(r_m^4 + s_m^4\right)} \qquad i = 1, \ldots, N$$

$$\tag{4.217}$$

The A parameter is an overall scaling factor.

The algorithm proceeds as follows:

1. Assume starting values for p_m, q_m, r_m, s_m, $m = 1, \ldots, M$.
2. Compute

$$g_{im} = \sin^4 \frac{\lambda_i}{2} + 2p_m^2 \sin^2 \frac{\lambda_i}{2} + \left(p_m^4 + q_m^4\right)$$

$$h_{im} = \sin^4 \frac{\lambda_i}{2} + 2r_m^2 \sin^2 \frac{\lambda_i}{2} + \left(r_m^4 + s_m^4\right)$$

for $m = 1, \ldots, M$ and $i = 1, \ldots, N$ \qquad (4.218)

As a programming footnote, the $\sin^2 \lambda_i/2$ and $\sin^4 \lambda_i/2$ terms could be precomputed and saved.

3. Compute

$$P_i = \prod_{m=1}^{M} \frac{g_{im}}{h_{im}} \qquad \text{for } i = 1, \dots, N \tag{4.219}$$

4. Compute A^* (estimate of A)

$$A^* = \frac{\sum_{i=1}^{N} |H(f_i)|^2}{\sum_{i=1}^{N} P_i |H(f_i)|^2} \tag{4.220}$$

5. Compute the error

$$E_i = A^* P_i - |H(f_i)|^2 = |\hat{H}(f_i)|^2 - |H(f_i)|^2 \qquad i = 1, \dots, N \tag{4.221}$$

6. Compute the mean square error

$$Q = \frac{1}{N} \sum_{i=1}^{N} E_i^2 \tag{4.222}$$

7. The partial derivative of Q with respect to a parameter ϕ is then

$$\frac{\partial Q}{\partial \phi} = \frac{2}{N} \sum_{i=1}^{N} E_i \frac{\partial |\hat{H}(f_i)|^2}{\partial \phi}$$

The partials $\partial |\hat{H}(f_i)|^2 / \partial \phi$ for each of the parameters p_m, q_m, r_m, and s_m are

$$\frac{\partial |\hat{H}(f_i)|^2}{\partial p_m} = \frac{4 A^* P_i}{g_{im}} \left(p_m \sin^2 \frac{\lambda_i}{2} + p_m^3 \right)$$

$$\frac{\partial |H(f_i)|^2}{\partial q_m} = \frac{4 A^* P_i}{g_{im}} (q_m^4) \tag{4.223}$$

$$\frac{\partial |\hat{H}(f_i)|^2}{\partial m} = - \frac{4 A^* P_i}{h_{im}} \left(r_m \sin^2 \frac{\lambda_i}{2} + r_m^3 \right)$$

$$\frac{\partial |\hat{H}(f_i)|^2}{\partial s_m} = - \frac{4 A^* P_i s_m^3}{h_{im}} \qquad i = 1, \dots, N, \quad m = 1, \dots, m \tag{4.224}$$

From these the terms

$$\frac{\partial Q}{\partial p_m}, \ \frac{\partial Q}{\partial q_m}, \ \frac{\partial Q}{\partial r_m}, \ \frac{\partial Q}{\partial s_m} \qquad m=1,\ldots,M$$

are computed.

8. This information is turned over to the Fletcher–Powell routine which produces a new set of p_m, q_m, r_m, and s_m terms, $m=1,\ldots,M$.

9. The iteration would return to step 2 at this point if it is not done, or continue to the final processing if the results were finally adequate.

10. The poles and zeroes are next found. For the mth stage, the zeroes are defined by

$$\sin^4\frac{\lambda_m}{2} + 2p_m^2\sin^2\frac{\lambda_m}{2} + (p_m^4 + q_m^4) = 0 \qquad (4.225)$$

Solving as a quadratic, this yields

$$\sin^2\lambda_m/2 = -\frac{2p_m^2 \pm \sqrt{4p_m^4 - 4p_m^4 - 4q_m^4}}{2} \qquad (4.226)$$

$$= -p_m^2 \pm jq_m^2$$

so that

$$f_{pm} = \frac{1}{\pi T}\arcsin\left(-p_m^2 \pm jq_m^2\right)^{1/2} \qquad (4.227)$$

Similarly for the poles:

$$f_{zm} = \frac{1}{\pi T}\arcsin\left(-r_m^2 \pm js_m^2\right)^{1/2} \qquad (4.228)$$

Only the M stable zeroes and poles are used.

11. The mathematics and code used in the lowpass sine Butterworth routine can be modified to compute the a_{1m}, a_{2m}, b_{1m}, and b_{2m} terms ($b_{0m}=1$ for all m at this point). The overall scale factor is finally computed and then included in the b terms. For example, if it is desired that

$$|H(f_0)|^2 = A \qquad (4.229)$$

then the b terms would all be multiplied by c, where

$$c = \left\{ \frac{A}{\left| \prod_{m=1}^{M} \frac{1 + b_{1m}e^{-j2\pi f_0 T} + b_{2m}e^{-j4\pi f_0 T}}{1 + a_{1m}e^{-j2\pi f_0 T} + a_{2m}e^{-j4\pi f_0 T}} \right|} \right\}^{1/M} \tag{4.230}$$

The algorithm can readily be modified to compute either a FIR or completely recursive filter by excluding either the r_m and s_m or p_m and q_m terms, respectively.

EXERCISES

4.1. Show that

$$|H(f)|^2 = \frac{1}{\omega_n^4 \left[\left[1 - \left(\frac{f}{f_n} \right)^2 \right]^2 + \left(\frac{2\zeta f}{f_n} \right)^2 \right]}$$

has its maximum at frequency $f_p = f_n (1 - 2\zeta^2)^{1/2}$.

4.2. Compute the transfer function of the filter

$$yi = \tfrac{1}{4}x_{i-1} + \tfrac{1}{2}x_i + \tfrac{1}{4}x_{i+1}$$

Answer:

$$H(f) = \cos^2 \pi f T$$

4.3. Compute the transfer function of the filter

$$y(i) = \frac{1}{2^N} \sum_{n=0}^{N} \binom{N}{n} x \left(i + n - \frac{N}{2} \right)$$

where N is even and

$$\binom{N}{n} = \frac{N!}{(N-n)!n!}$$

Answer:

$$H(f) = \cos^N \pi f T$$

4.4. Compute α for the first-order lowpass filter such that the half-power point of the filter is at B Hz. That is,

$$|H(B)|^2 = \tfrac{1}{2}, \text{ and } |H(0)|^2 = 1.$$

Answer:

$$\alpha = 2A^2 + 1 - 2A\sqrt{A^2+1}$$
$$\text{where } A = \sin \pi TB$$

4.5. It was shown that a second-order filter with real poles could be written as two first-order filters. Show that the same can be done for the second-order filter with complex poles provided that complex coefficients are allowed. Derive the coefficients in terms of α and β.

4.6. Verify that the expression given for the unit impulse response function of the second-order filter with complex poles is correct.
   a. Generate the first five terms ($i=0,\ldots,4$) by using both the difference equation and by evaluating the derived expression for $y(i)$. Compare the results.
   b. Show that the difference equation is satisfied by the solution.

Computer Problems

Some problems require the subroutines LPSB and TTRAN in Appendix A. Subroutine PRPLOT will be useful in displaying the results.

4.7. Write a program to code α for a lowpass first order filter as given in Exercise 4.4. Include in the program code to do the following:
   a. Compute α for $T=0.005$ and $B=3.125$, 6.25, 12.5, 25., 20., and 100. Hz.
   b. Compute $y(i)$ for $x(i)=1,0,0,0\ldots,i=0,\ldots,25$.
   c. Compute and plot the transfer function in terms of gain and phase for $f=0,2,4,\ldots,F$ Hz.

4.8. Write a program to compute a_1, a_2, and b_0 for the general, complex second-order filter. Include in the program code to fix $T=0.005$ and compute the coefficients for (f_n, ζ) pairs as follows:
   a. Hold f_n fixed at 50 Hz, and use values of $\zeta=0.5$, 0.25, 0.1, 0.05, 0.01, 0.001.
   b. Hold ζ fixed at 0.05 and use values of $f_n=25., 10., 5., 2.5$ Hz.
   c. Compute b_0 for the above cases such that the gain of the filter is unity at the peak frequency.
   d. Compute and plot the response of the filter to the sequence $x(i)=1,0,0,0$, for the pairs $(50,0.05)$ and $(50,0.01)$. Does this check with the theoretical answer?

e.   Compute and plot the transfer function gain and phase for the first four (δ_n, ζ_n) pairs given in part a. Comment on the width of the passband.

4.9.   Compile routine LP2 (Figure 4.4) and write a driver program to do the following:

a.   Compute f_n and ζ from A1 and A2 (a_1 and a_2) for T = 0.005 and BW = 32, 16, 8, 4, 2, and 1 Hz. Comment on the results.

b.   Compute and plot the transfer function gain and phase for $f = 0, 1, 2, ..., F$ Hz. Comment on the results.

c.   Compute the response of the filter to $x(i) = 1, 0, 0, 0, ...,$ $i =$ 0, ..., 25. Comment on the results.

4.10.   Compile routine LPSB and write a driver routine to do the following:

a.   Verify that the routine is working correctly. Duplication of the results in Table 5.3 for six-pole filter or the two-pole filter results obtained in Exercise 4.9 are sufficient.

b.   Use subroutine TTRAN to compute the transfer function gain and phase of a six-pole filter for T = 0.005 and B = 32, 16, 8, 4, 2, and 1 Hz. Comment on the results.

c.   Find the poles for each of the 18 coefficient pairs computed in Part b. Plot the pole positions in the complex plane. Comment on the results.

4.11.   Convert subroutine LPSB to a highpass Butterworth filter routine as described in Section 4.7. Do Exercise 4.10 for the converted routine, but use B = 68, 84, 92, 96, 98, and 99 Hz. Compare the results with those obtained in Exercise 4.10 and comment.

4.12.   Compile the bandpass filter generation procedure as shown in Figure 4.13. Use six recursive coefficients and T = 0.005. Compute and plot the transfer function gain and phase for $f = 0, 1, 2, ..., F$ Hz and:

a. $F_c = 50$ Hz and B = 1, 2, 5, 10, 25 Hz.

b.   B = 2, Hz, $f_c = 2$, 4, 10, and 20 Hz.

Comment on the results.

4.13.   Convert the code for Exercise 4.12 to a routine for computing band reject filters and repeat the calculations.

4.14.   Compile routine LPTB for computing lowpass Butterworth filters as shown in Figure 4.14. Repeat Exercise 4.10 using LPTB instead of LPSB. Compare the results of the two problems and comment.

4.15.   a.   Write a routine to compute the gain of the transfer function of a symmetric FIR filter.

   b. Write a routine to compute lowpass filter weights of the form

$$b_k = \frac{\sin(2\pi BkT)}{\pi k} \qquad k=0,\ldots,M$$

   c. Write a program using the code for parts a and b that will plot
       the gain for $T=0.005$, $B=32, 16, 8, 4, 2, 1$ Hz, and $M=$
       $8, 16, 32, 64$. Comment on the results. Compare also with the
       results from Exercise 4.10.

4.16. Implement the Potter, Bickford, and Glaze algorithm in the form of
       subroutine LPSPBG as shown in Figure 4.19, and redo Exercise
       4.18 using this routine. Compare the results from the two problems.

CHAPTER 5

PRACTICAL ASPECTS
OF DIGITAL FILTERING

5.1   INTRODUCTION

This chapter discusses procedures to be used and problems that may occur when digital filtering techniques are actually applied to data. These topics include the following:

- Noise and distortion.
- Instability.
- Various ways of coding the filtering algorithm.
- Data smoothing.
- Decimation.

There is no general rule for selecting a filter because the type required, such as lowpass or bandpass, and the general circumstances accompanying the need for filtering vary considerably from application to application.

On the other hand, a large percentage of applications require a lowpass filter. If this is the case, then the six-pole Butterworth lowpass filter may be taken as a sort of starting point in the selection procedure. Put another way, the user might ask himself the following question: "does this particular application require anything other than a six-pole Butterworth type?" Often it is an adequate if not optimal choice.

5.2 NOISE AND DISTORTION

Noise is generated in many computer operations. In fixed point arithmetic it happens primarily as a result of multiplication. After multiplying, the least significant half of the product is discarded, and the most significant half is retained after either truncation or rounding. The difference between the reduced number and the number before truncation or rounding is a *noise term*. Its level is approximately plus or minus one-half of the least significant bit.

Floating point arithmetic not only produces this type of error, but may also generate noise from underflow during addition. When two floating point numbers are added, and one is relatively much larger than the other, all or part of the smaller number may be lost in the process.

Chapter 4 discussed digital filtering without regard to the problems that arise because the arithmetic used in the implementation is finite. Thus in an actual implementation the performance of a filter deviates from the theoretical performance it would have with perfect arithmetic.

As might be expected, the fewer the number of bits in computer used in the implementation, the greater the problem. Thus minicomputers tend to be somewhat more limited than standard sized ones, since their word length is usually 12–16 bits rather than 24–60 as in larger computers.

There are a number of ways to characterize the problems that arise from the less than perfect arithmetic. The three main ones of interest here are

- Noise.
- Distortion.
- Instability.

These topics are covered in many articles. Three collections, the two IEEE reprints (Rabiner and Rader [1972], Oppenheim et al. [1976]) and the one edited by Liu [1975], are all recommended.

The noise model is shown in Figure 5.1. The filter, visualized as perfect, is shown with a source adding noise into the normal output from the filter so that rather than $y(i)$ alone, $y(i) + n(i)$ is output where $n(i)$ is a noise term.

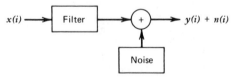

Figure 5.1 Noise model of a perfect filter.

The form of $n(i)$ varies considerably depending on the type of arithmetic employed and the filter implementation.

In summary, these are the major results concerning noise:

- Noise is a function of the number of bits employed in the arithmetic: the fewer the number of bits, the greater the noise.
- The cascade and parallel* implementations are less noisy than the combined. For four or more poles or zeroes, it is always better to use a cascaded form of the filter. This is true for both the FIR and IIR filters.
- The different possible outputs from a filter implemented in cascade form are not commutative. By this is meant the following: if the arithmetic were perfect, then the output of the filter would be the same no matter what order the two pole/zero sections were placed; in an actual implementation, the noise will vary for the same data when the second-order sections are permuted. Thus it is possible to minimize the noise by finding the permutation of the second-order sections which have the least noise output.

The computational noise tends to add in a "floor." This can easily be seen from looking at an idealized fixed point arithmetic case: assume that m bits are allowed in expressing the fractional part of the data. There may be more bits in the computer word, but m of them are set aside for the fractional part. Then it can be argued that, just as in digitization, there will be an error of the order of plus or minus one-half a bit in the last decimal place each time a multiplication takes place. If there are k multiplications, then the variance of the error, assuming that they are uncorrelated, is $k/12$ bits squared.

In terms of data words, this means that the noise floor is $k2^{-2m}/12$ bits squared. In terms of decibels, it is

$$10\log_{10}\left(k2^{-2m}/12\right) = 10\log_{10}k - 20m\log_{10}2 - 10\log_{10}12$$

$$\approx 10\log_{10}k - 10.8 - 6m. \tag{5.1}$$

Thus there is a bottom set for the noise floor by the number of bits in the fractional part of the computer words. This floor is raised by the number of multiplications performed: the larger the filter, the higher the noise floor.

---

*The parallel and ladder implementations will generally be ignored in the following. While offering improvement in performance in some cases, the increased complexity of these forms makes them unsuitable for our purposes.

This result is heuristic and approximate. It assumes things that may not be true in practice, such as the noise being uncorrelated. Also, it is in a sense a lower bound, because, as will be seen, there may be considerably more noise generated by an IIR filter when it tends to become unstable.

One reason the cascade implementation is better than the combined form is as follows: although each stage tends to inject its own roundoff noise into the filtered data it outputs, *it also tends to remove noise generated by previous stages.* Thus there is both noise generation and noise cancellation in a cascaded filter. There is much less tendency for this to happen in the combined form. Perhaps more important is the tendency of the combined form to generate more self-noise.

Distortion

Distortion arises because when the transfer function of the filter as implemented deviates from its theoretical counterpart in a substantial manner. It is common to measure the distortion using a mean-square criterion:

$$\varepsilon^2 = \int_0^F |H(f) - \hat{H}(f)|^2 \, df \qquad (5.2)$$

where

$\varepsilon^2 =$ the mean square distortion

$H(f) =$ The theoretical transfer function

$\hat{H}(f) =$ the transfer function of the filter as implemented in finite word length arithmetic

The most obvious and early manifestation of distortion is the tendency of passband type filters to exhibit a roughness or deviation from the desired transfer function form. That is, as the number of bits is decreased, the filter shape develops a noticeable distortion at the band edge as shown in Figure 5.2. As the number of bits decreases, the distortion becomes more pronounced until the original form is no longer recognizable.

Noise is probably more important than distortion: by the time that distortion becomes noticeable on a linear scale, the noise floor, as measured in decibels, may have risen high enough to make the filter performance poor. Of course, the definition of distortion can also be

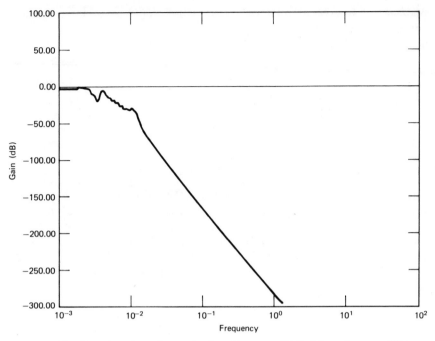

Figure 5.2   Deterioration of transfer function as exhibited by a lowpass filter.

modified so as to be done in logarithmic form:

$$\varepsilon_{dB}^2 = 10 \int_0^F \log_{10}\left|\frac{H(f)}{\hat{H}(f)}\right|^2 df \tag{5.3}$$

in which case it would tend to also reflect the error due to the noise floor.

Measurement of $\hat{H}(f)$

There are at least two ways in which $\hat{H}(f)$ can be measured.

Method 1.   Use the computer and type of arithmetic on which the computations are to be performed to calculate $\hat{H}(f)$ as the Fourier transform of the filter. That is, compute

$$\hat{H}(f) = \prod_{m=1}^{M/2} \frac{b_{0m} + b_{1m}\exp(-j\omega T) + b_{2m}\exp(-2j\omega T)}{1 + a_{1m}\exp(-j\omega T) + a_{2m}\exp(-2j\omega T)} \tag{5.4}$$

Method 2.   For each frequency f_p at which $\hat{H}(f)$ is to be evaluated, compute the sequence

$$x_p(i) = \sin(2\pi f_p i T) \tag{5.5}$$

and filter it to yield $y_p(i)$. After sufficient time for the transient response to die out has passed, compute

$$s_p^2 = \frac{1}{N_p} \sum_{i=q}^{N_p + q - 1} y_p^2(i) \tag{5.6}$$

Ideally, f_p and N_p would be selected so that N_p points will contain an integer number of cycles of the sine wave. The q parameter is selected so that $y_p(i)$ has reached its steady state for $i \geq q$. Also, the series $z_p(i)$ where

$$z_p(i) = x_p(i) y_p(i) \tag{5.7}$$

would be calculated. From this sequence the correlation parameter ρ_p would be obtained:

$$\rho_p = \frac{1}{s_p \dfrac{1}{\sqrt{2}} N_p} \sum_{i=q}^{N_p + q - 1} z_p(i) \tag{5.8}$$

where $1/\sqrt{2}$ and s_p are the standard deviations of the input and output, and are used to normalize the results. Assume that the steady-state output $y_p(i)$ is given by

$$y_p(i) = A_p \sin(2\pi f_p i T + \phi_p) \qquad i \geq q \tag{5.9}$$

Then

$$s_p^2 = \frac{A_p^2}{2} \tag{5.10}$$

and

$$z_p(i) = \sin(2\pi f_p i T) A_p \sin(2\pi f_p i T + \phi_p)$$
$$= \frac{A_p}{2} \left[\cos\phi_i - \cos(4\pi f_p i T + \phi_p) \right] \tag{5.11}$$

When a whole number of cycles is employed, the summation of $z_p(i)$ will add up the rightmost term in its equation to 0. Thus

$$\rho_p = \frac{\sqrt{2}}{s_p N_p} \sum_{i=q}^{N_p - q + 1} \left[\cos\phi_p - \cos(4\pi f_p iT + \phi_p) \right]$$

$$= \left[\frac{\sqrt{2}}{(A_p/\sqrt{2})N_p} \right] \frac{A_p}{2} N_p \cos\phi_p$$

$$= \cos\phi_p \tag{5.12}$$

Therefore, the gain of the filter at f_p is

$$A_p = \sqrt{2}\, s_p \tag{5.13}$$

and the phase is

$$\phi_p = \arccos(\rho_p) \tag{5.14}$$

Naturally, there will be some error if an integer number of cycles is not used, or if the output has not reached steady state, so that reasonable care must be taken in picking the set of frequencies.

Method 2 is preferable. It most closely resembles standard procedures for computing the transfer function of an analog filter. However, it can be tedious and expensive to obtain for a large set of f_p's, especially if the product BT, where B is the width of the passband of the filter, is small. Roughly speaking, the time for the transient response to die down is proportional to $1/BT$. Thus as BT is made smaller, progressively longer time is required to reach the steady state portion of the response.

The first procedure given above is far easier and cheaper to implement. However, it must be regarded as being indicative of noise and distortion rather than definitive of their size.

5.3   DETERIORATION

Though noise and distortion are important in themselves, the *stability* of the digital filter will be the main tool for examining filter performance. Actually, noise, distortion, and instability are just different aspects of the same problem: degeneration of filter performance when using less than infinite precision.

By instability is meant that the filter outputs infinite energy for a finite energy input. For example, the filter

$$y(i) = 2y(i-1) + x(i) \tag{5.15}$$

will respond to the input sequence $1, 0, 0, \ldots,$ with the sequence $1, 2, 4, \ldots, 2^i \ldots$. This filter is clearly unstable.

The stability conditions for the second-order filter were derived in Chapter 4. They are shown again in Figure 5.3. In the infinite plane of all possible second-order filter coefficients, the pairs that will yield stable filters are limited to the small triangle located at the origin. The coefficient pair $a_1 = -0.6$; $a_2 = 0.4$ is shown within the triangle. The distances d_1, d_2, and d_3 are frequently helpful in assessing stability. The closer the point (a_1, a_2) is to an edge of the triangle, the smaller one of the three distances will be. In the example, the distances are

$$d_1 = 0.6$$

$$d_2 = 0.8$$

$$d_3 = 2.0$$

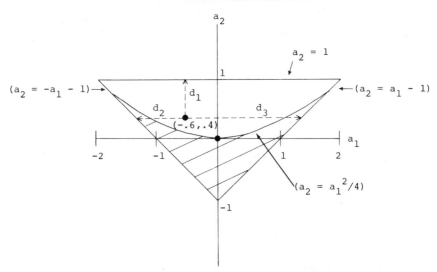

Figure 5.3 The second-order filter coefficient stability triangle. Each recursive coefficient pair (a_1, a_2) defines one point in the plane. If the point is within the triangle, the filter is stable. If it is on the border or outside, then the filter is unstable.

Another way of looking at the problem is that of a threshold. In Otnes and McNamee [1970] it is shown that for lowpass filters there is a point on the frequency scale such that for bandwidths below the point, digital filters tend to lose their form and go unstable. The formula for the threshold is

$$B_{t,N} = \frac{2^{-(t-1-\beta_N)/N}}{2\pi T} \tag{5.16}$$

where

$N =$ the number of poles in the filter

$t =$ the total number of bits available for computation

$\beta_N =$ the integer such that

$$2^{\beta_N - 1} < \left(\left[\frac{N}{\left[\frac{N}{2} \right]} \right] \right) \leqslant 2^{\beta_N} \tag{5.17}$$

Table 5.1 shows this function as adjusted for floating point and calculated for two computers, the IBM 704 (which extends to include the IBM 709, 7090, and the SRU 1106, 1107, 1108, and 1109) and the IBM 360 (whose format is also employed on the IBM 370 and the Xerox 5, 6, 7, etc.). The values given in the table are for the combined form of sine or tangent $T = 0.005$ lowpass Butterworth filter employing the cascade version, effectively uses the line with N equal to 2.

Table 5.1

Threshold Values of $B_{t,N}$ (in Hz) for Several Values of N for Two Computer Floating Point Word Formats

N	IBM 704 Format ($t = 36$ bits)		IBM 360 Format ($t = 32$ bits)	
	B	B_{actual}	B	B_{actual}
2	0.0054	—	0.032	—
3	0.13	0.10	0.32	0.15
4	0.6	0.4	1.0	1.0
5	1.3	1.3	1.0	2.0
6	2.4	2.4	3.2–5.0[a]	3.8

[a]For $N = 6$ the threshold is difficult to calculate because the hexadecimal (4-bit) rounding employed on the IBM 360 causes problems at this point.

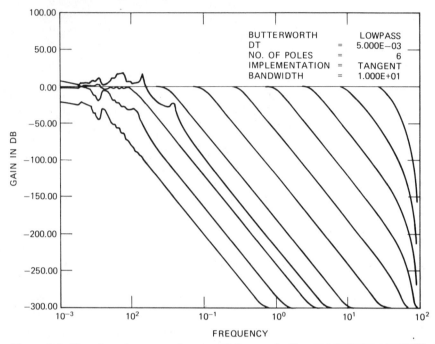

Figure 5.4   Ten six-pole tangent lowpass Butterworth filters with different cutoffs, computed on an SRU 1108. $T = 0.005$, $F = 100$ Hz. The filter with the lowest cutoff has moved out of position over to falling between the seventh and eighth filters.

In addition to the theoretical values for B, cases were run on both types of computers to verify the results. These are shown under the heading B_{actual}. The results are reasonably close to each other.

As an example of this phenomenon consider Figure 5.4. It shows the transfer functions of six-pole filters with B varying from 0.00031623 to 10 Hz as computed on an SRU 1108. These transfer functions were computed by method 1, that is, by evaluating $\hat{H}(f)$ from the finite filter weights on the computer on which the filtering is being performed. This was for the *cascade* implementation. As in Table 5.1, $T = 0.005$, so that the Nyquist folding frequency is 100 Hz, thus allowing the plotted frequencies to be thought of as percentages. The actual cutoffs are shown in Table 5.2. The weights for the filters are given in Table 5.3.

After the sixth filter, the transfer function deteriorates, not only in its gain near 0, which visibly has grown rough, but in the position of the 3-dB point. The cutoff points of filters 7–10 have been moved to the right of where they would be in theory. Any of these last four filters could or would be unstable. In particular, the frequency with the lowest cutoff has

Table 5.2

**Cutoff Frequencies and Appearance of the
10 Filters Shown in Figure 5.4**

Filter	Cutoff (Hz)	Appearance
1	10.	Good
2	3.1625	Good
3	1.	Good
4	0.3162	Good
5	0.1	Good
6	0.0316	Good
7	0.01	Marginal or bad
8	0.0032	Bad
9	0.001	Bad
10	0.0003	Bad

Table 5.3

**Filter Weights for the six-pole Tangent Butterworth Filters Implemented in Cascade
Form for a Range of Cutoff Frequencies from 0.01 to 10 Hz, as Shown in Figure 5.4[a]**

	B	b_0	a_{11}	a_{21}	a_{12}	a_{22}	a_{13}	a_{23}
1	10.00000	0.02046936		0.540254		0.641352		0.851887
			-1.464868		-1.561018		-1.761249	
2	3.16228	0.00231823		0.825146		0.868927		0.949944
			-1.816146		-1.859712		-1.940330	
3	1.00000	0.00024185		0.941106		0.956544		0.983972
			-1.940148		-1.955578		-1.982893	
4	0.31623	0.00002452		0.980991		0.986049		0.994871
			-1.980893		-1.985951		-1.994772	
5	0.10000	0.00000247		0.993949		0.995567		0.998375
			-1.993939		-1.995557		-1.998365	
6	0.03162	0.00000025		0.998083		0.998596		0.999486
			-1.998082		-1.998595		-1.999485	
7	0.01000	0.00000002		0.999393		0.999556		0.999837
			-1.999393		-1.999556		-1.999837	

[a]Sampling rate is 200 sps. Only the overall scaling factor is shown for the nonrecursive terms; there
are three terms per filter section.

moved to falling between the filters with cutoffs at 0.0032 and 0.01 Hz.

The concept of a coefficient plane with stable coefficients for the second-order case may be generalized for higher-order combined filters. For example, the third-order filter,

$$y(i) = b_0 x(i) - a_1 y(i-1) - a_2 y(i-2) - a_3 y(i-3) \qquad (5.18)$$

may be thought of as defining a three-space of the coefficient triplets (a_1, a_2, a_3). There is a stability tetrahedron such that if (a_1, a_2, a_3) falls within it, then the filter is stable. The plane defined by $a_3 = 0$ is of course the same as that for the second-order case.

For an IIR filter with M poles, there is a corresponding M-space which has a stability polyhedron: if the filter coefficient point $(a_1, \ldots, a_M)$ falls within the polyhedron the filter is stable. This could be gone into in great detail, but we do not bother with it here for the simple reason that higher-order combined filters are not in general recommended: if M is higher than 2, then the cascade form of the filter may very well be stable even though the combined form is not. In other words, the cascade form of the filter is always more stable, and freer of noise and distortion than the combined form. Hence it is recommended that the cascade form be used.

Naturally, there are exceptions. The cascade implementation is computationally less efficient than the equivalent combined implementation. Hence if the combined form is stable for a given computer, and a large volume of data is to be processed, then consideration should be given to using the combined implementation.

The combined form weights for the first seven cases of the six-pole lowpass sine Butterworth filter are shown in Table 5.4. Part of the problem can be seen from this table, namely, that whereas stable weights for the

Table 5.4

Filter Weights for a Six-Pole Sine Butterworth Filter Implemented in the Combined Form for a Range of Cutoff Frequencies from 0.01 to 10 Hz[a]

	B	b_0	a_1	a_2	a_3	a_4	a_5	a_6
1	10.000000	0.512018-03	-4.79661	09.6857	-10.5252	06.4863	-2.14663	0.298003
2	3.162300	0.791620-06	-5.61649	13.1553	-16.4476	11.5766	-4.34912	0.581305
3	1.000000	0.904631-09	-5.87863	14.4005	-18.8154	13.8295	-5.42168	0.885697
4	0.316230	0.943210-12	-5.96162	14.8088	-19.6191	14.6205	-5.81099	0.962342
5	0.100000	0.955728-15	-5.98786	14.9394	-19.8789	14.8791	-5.93960	0.987935
6	0.031623	0.959648-18	-5.99616	14.9808	-19.9616	14.9617	-5.98083	0.996169
7	0.010000	0.953604-21	-5.99879	14.9939	-19.9878	14.9879	-5.99393	0.998787
	Limit	0.000000-00	-6.00000	15.0000	-20.0000	15.0000	-6.00000	1.000000

[a]The sampling rate is 200 sps.

cascade case are bounded by

$$|a_1| < 2$$

$$|a_2| < 1 \tag{5.19}$$

the equivalent weights for the combined implementation have a much higher bound. In fact,

$$|a_k| < \binom{M}{k} = \frac{M!}{k!(M-k!)} \tag{5.20}$$

[Note: these are bounds rather than conditions for stability; although a stable filter will always satisfy them, there are unstable filters that also will satisfy the conditions, for example, $a_1 = 1$, $a_2 = -0.5$.]

The point here is that the combined implementation requires more bits in both the integer and fractional part of the number, so that the available number of bits is decreased by two factors when the combined implementation is employed.

The Nonrecursive Coefficients as Indicators of Stability

As discussed in Chapter 4, a scale factor is usually introduced for the purpose of normalizing the filter, that is to say, making the gain unity within the passband. As it turns out, this scaling parameter can yield useful information about stability.

The reason for this is as follows: define $\hat{H}(f)$ to be the transfer function without normalization. Suppose that the maximum value of $|\hat{H}(f)|^2$ in the passband occurs at f_{max}. Then the transfer function $H(f)$ defined by

$$H(f) = \frac{\hat{H}(f)}{|\hat{H}(f_{max})|} \tag{5.21}$$

is normalized. Usually this is done by multiplying the nonrecursive terms by $1/|\hat{H}(f_{max})|$. Denote the nonrecursive weights before normalization by $\hat{b}_0, \hat{b}_1, \ldots, \hat{b}_M$ for the combined form, where $\hat{b}_0$ is by definition unity. Then

$$b_k = \frac{\hat{b}_k}{|\hat{H}(f_{max})|} = b\hat{b}_k \tag{5.22}$$

where b is the normalization factor:

$$b = \frac{1}{|\hat{H}(f_{max})|} \tag{5.23}$$

As will be seen shortly, if the relative size of the passband is decreased, then the value for b correspondingly decreases. When the bandwidth of the filter has decreased to the point where b is effectively a machine 0, two related phenomena occur. The two cases may best be examined by assuming that $x(i)$ is a sine wave at frequency f_{max}:

$$x(i) = \sin(2\pi f_{max} iT) \qquad i \geq 0 \tag{5.24}$$

Also assume that i is large enough so that steady state has been reached. At f_{max}, the recursive weights add up to -1 in the limit as the bandwidth goes to 0 (the reader may verify this by checking that case for $f_{max} = 0$ and then generalizing the result). Thus under the special conditions that the sine was is at f_{max} and that steady state has been reached, the recursive portion of the filter can be expressed in the form

$$-\sum_{k=1}^{M} a_k y(i-k) = \sin(2\pi f_{max} iT + \phi) - \varepsilon_i \tag{5.25}$$

where ε_i is a small sinusoidal term also at frequency f_{max} and ϕ is a phase angle introduced by the filter. Thus

$$y_i = \sum_{k=0}^{M} b_k x(i-k) + \sin(2\pi f_{max} iT + \phi) - \varepsilon_i \tag{5.26}$$

Equivalently,

$$\varepsilon_i = -b \sum_{k=0}^{M} \hat{b}_k x(i-k) \tag{5.27}$$

That is, the input as filtered by the nonrecursive portion of the filter becomes a relatively low-amplitude sine wave which cancels the ε_i term.

Case 1.   Fixed Point

Consider the fixed point case first. When b is less than 2^{-m}, where m is the number of bits in the fractional part of the computer word, then it is effectively 0. *Hence there will be no input to the filter.* Also,

$$|\hat{H}(f_{max})| = \frac{1}{b} = \frac{1}{0} = \infty \tag{5.28}$$

so that the filter is effectively unstable.

Case 2.   Floating Point

The floating point case is a little more complicated, but basically reduces to the same result: although there is greater dynamic range to floating point arithmetic, one number may still be 0 relative to another number when they are added. If the floating point word has m bits in its mantissa, and the numbers x and y are such that

$$|x| > |2^m y| \tag{5.29}$$

then

$$x + y = x \tag{5.30}$$

In other words, y will completely *underflow*, relative to x under addition. So, although the number y may not be small enough to be a machine 0 in floating point, it may still effectively be 0 under addition.

Hence if $b < 2^{-m}$, where m is the number of bits in the mantissa of the floating point word being used, then for data greater than unity, the b term may effectively be 0, and the results from the fixed point case will apply.

Thus examination of the b term will yield information about the relative stability of filter as implemented in the combined form.

For the cascade implementation, the section scale factor b^1 defined by

$$b^1 = b^{2/M} \tag{5.31}$$

is also useful.

The b normalization term may thus be employed as a lower bound on the number of bits needed to implement a filter: b must be such that

$$b > 2^{-m} \tag{5.32}$$

where m is the number of bits employed in the fractional part of the computer word used in implementing the filter. Taking the logarithm to the base 2 of both sides yields

$$m > -\log_2 b \tag{5.33}$$

That is, for a given b, the lower bound on the number of bits needed to implement the filter is a logarithmic function of b. Thus if b is known then a minimum m can be determined. As it turns out, this imposes some interesting relationships on $H(f)$. Suppose that b is not known, and $H(f)$ is known only in a general way. Is it possible to obtain information about b and hence m from $|H(f)|^2$? The answer is yes.

Suppose it is assumed that $H(f)$ is stable and that its zeroes are also in the upper half-plane (left half-plane in $j\omega$ notation). Then it can be shown that the unnormalized transfer function $\hat{H}(f)$ satisfies

$$\int_0^F \log_2 |\hat{H}(f)|^2 \, df = 0 \tag{5.34}$$

Pointed in Gray and Markel [1978], this has some important implications. In particular, $H(f)$ may be evaluated to yield

$$\int_0^F \log_2 |H(f)|^2 df = \int_0^F \log_2 |b\hat{H}(f)|^2 df$$

$$= \int_0^F 2\log_2 b \, df + \int_0^F \log_2 |\hat{H}(f)|^2 df$$

$$= 2F \log_2 b \qquad (5.35)$$

Therefore, after rearranging this last result,

$$\log_2 b = \frac{1}{2F} \int_0^F \log_2 |H(f)|^2 df \qquad (5.36)$$

Hence the number of bits required to implement a given normalized minimum phase filter is given by

$$m > -\frac{1}{2F} \int_0^F \log_2 |H(f)|^2 df \qquad (5.37)$$

One immediate implication is that if the function $|H(f)|^2$ is 0 on any nonzero width interval of f, then the filter cannot be implemented. Some examples will help illustrate the use of the formula.

1. The Mth-order binomial filter (FIR type) has weights

$$b_k = \frac{\binom{M}{k}}{2^M} \qquad k = -M, \ldots, M \qquad (5.38)$$

and its transfer function is such that

$$|H(f)|^2 = \cos^{2M} \pi f T \qquad (5.39)$$

Thus

$$-\int_0^F \log_2 |H(f)|^2 df = -2M \int_0^F \log_2 (\cos \pi f T) \, df$$

$$= M \qquad (5.40)$$

This implies that M bits would be required in the fractional part of the computer word. Because

$$b_0 = b_M = \frac{1}{2^M} \tag{5.41}$$

this would be seen to be true in the sense that for less than M bits, coefficients will be set to 0.

2. The first order lowpass filter is given by

$$y(i) = (1 - \alpha)x(i) + \alpha y(i - 1) \qquad 0 < \alpha < 1 \tag{5.42}$$

Here $b = (1 - \alpha)$. Because

$$m > -\log_2 b \tag{5.43}$$

and if $(1 - \alpha) = 2^{-N}$, then

$$m > N \tag{5.44}$$

These results and the underlying integral formula may be used to derive some basic information about filters.

Consider the unnormalized lowpass filter shown in Figure 5.5. According to the integral relationship

$$\int_0^F \log_2 |\hat{H}(f)|^2 df = 0 \tag{5.45}$$

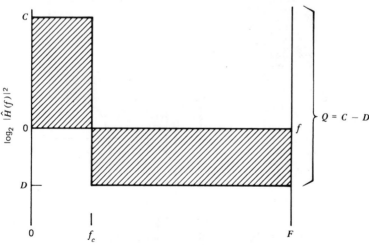

Figure 5.5 An idealized lowpass filter.

it is necessary for

$$C \cdot f_c = - D \cdot (F - f_c) \tag{5.46}$$

The term on the left side represents the area above 0, and the right side is the shaded area below 0.

The equation may be solved for C to yield

$$C = - D \cdot \left(\frac{F - f_c}{f} \right) \tag{5.47}$$

The b term is

$$b = 2^{-C/2} \tag{5.48}$$

As an example, suppose that $f_c = F/4$ and that $C - D = 20$. This corresponds to a range of 60 dB. After some grinding, the value $b = 1/181$ may be obtained.

Figure 5.6 shows this result as compared to an actual filter. A six-pole, six-zero Chebyshev type II filter was generated with the stop band down 60 dB, and cutoff frequency at $f_c = F/4$. The normalization factor was calculated to be $b = 1/132$. The Chebyshev filter, of course, is considerably less sharp than the idealized form in Figure 5.5.

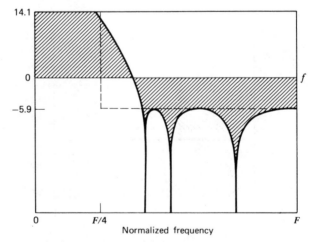

Figure 5.6 Approximate bounding shown with a Chebyshev type 2 filter. The shaded area integrates to 0.

5.4   FILTER IMPLEMENTATION

This section discusses some of the procedures employed in doing the actual filtering.

Figure 5.7 shows subroutine BFILT1. This is a single function filtering routine. It is used in the following manner.

1. All communication is done through the labeled COMMON block FILTR1. The definitions follow:

   X = input data (single point)

   Y = output data (single point)

   B0 = single scaling factor for each stage of the combined ′ implementation

   A1 = the a_{1m} recursive weights

   A2 = the a_{2m} recursive weights

   M = the number of poles in the filter

```
      SUBROUTINE BFILT1
      COMMON /FILTR1/ X, Y, B0, A1(10), A2 (10), M
      DIMENSION Y0(11), Y1(11)
      DO 10 K = 1, 11
      Y0(K) = 0.
10    Y1(K) = 0.
      M2 = M - M/2
      RETURN
      ENTRY FILT1
      Y0(1) = X
      DO 20 K = 1, M2
      K1 = K + 1
      YI = B0 * Y0(K) - A1(K) * Y0(K1) - A2(K) * Y1(K1)
      Y1(K1) = Y0(K1)
20    Y0(K1) = YI
      Y = YI
      RETURN
      END
```

Figure 5.7   Subroutine BFILT1. Note that there are two entry points. The BFILT1 entry is used only once to set up the filtering operation. The FILT1 entry is then used once for each date point to be filtered.

2. BFILT1 is only called once; it does the setup, zeroing out storage, etc.

3. The FILT1 entry is used once for each data point in the sequence to be filtered. The input data is put into the X location, FILT1 is called, and the output point is taken from location Y.

4. The user must put the filter weights into the FILTR1 common block.

An example will clarify what is required. Assume a main program is written as follows. First the common statements:

```
COMMON XX(1000), YY(1000)
COMMON/FILTR1/X, Y, etc.
```
⋮

CALL BFILT1   } Initialization of the filter

⋮

M = 6

T = 0.005
B = 25.   } Generation of the filter weights for a six-pole lowpass sine filter

CALL LPSB(...)

⋮

(Generation of the XX data, whatever it is)

⋮

```
DO 100 I = 1, 1000
  X = XX(I)
  CALL FILT1
  YY(I) = Y
100 CONTINUE
```
} The actual filtering loop

⋮

(Display, or whatever)

The filtering operation could have been put into the main program rather than isolated in the subroutine. But using the subroutine format has a number of convenient features.

Labeled COMMON is used for two reasons: it reduces the overhead time by not having to pass data through calling sequences; secondly, there are no standards on ENTRY statements. Code having multiple entries with arguments will work on some computers, but not on others; using labeled COMMON avoids this problem.

The BFILT1 routine can only be used with filters where each cascade section has the form

$$y^{(m)}(i) = b_0 y^{(m-1)}(i) - a_{1m} y^{(m)}(i-1) - a_{2m} y^{(m)}(i-2)$$

where $y^{(m-1)}(i)$ is the input to this stage of the filter and $y^{(m)}(i)$ is the corresponding output. That is, there is only one nonrecursive term, and it has the same coefficient for all sections.

The more general case has the defining equation

$$y^{(m)}(i) = b_{0m} y^{(m-1)}(i) + b_{1m} y^{(m-1)}(i-1)$$
$$+ b_{2m} y^{(m-1)}(i-2) - a_{1m} y^{(m)}(i-1) - a_{2m} y^{(m)}(i-2)$$

Figure 5.8 shows subroutine BFILT2. It is essentially identical to BFILT1 except that is allows three different nonrecursive terms per stage.

```
      SUBROUTINE BFILT2
      COMMON /FILTR2/ X, Y, BO(10), B1(10), B2(10),
     *     A1(10), A2(10), M
      DIMENSION Y0(11), Y1(11), Y2(11)
      DO 10 K = 1,11
      Y0(K) = 0.
      Y1(K) = 0.
10    Y2(K) = 0.
      M2 = M - M/2
      RETURN
      ENTRY FILT2
      Y0(1) = X
      DO 20 K = 1, M2
      K1 = K + 1
      YI = BO(K) * Y0(K) + B1(K) * Y1(K) + B2(K) * Y2(K)
     1     - A1(K) * Y0(K1) - A2(K) * Y1(K1)
      Y2(K1) = Y1(K1)
      Y1(K1) = Y0(K)
20    Y0(K1) = YI
      Y2(1) = Y1(1)
      Y1(1) = Y0(1)
      Y = YI
      RETURN
      END
```

Figure 5.8   Subroutine BFILT2. Similar to BFILT1, except that greater latitude is allowed on the recursive terms.

Naturally, more storage and movement of data are required.

One problem common to both these routines is that a substantial percentage of the time spent in the routine is employed in shifting the data.

Subroutine BFILT3, Figure 5.9, attempts to get around this problem by permuting the indices rather than actually moving the data. This technique can work very well, especially when implemented in machine language. However, it is not guaranteed to be any faster, or even as fast, when coded in FORTRAN as in the figure. This is because FORTRAN compilers vary

```
      SUBROUTINE BFILT3
      COMMON /FILTR3/ X, Y, B0(10), B1(10), B2(10),
     *     A1(10), A2(10), M
      DIMENSION YM (11,3)
      DO 10 K = 1, 11
      DO 10 I = 1, 3
   10 YM (K, I) = 0.
      M2 = M - M/2
      J1 = 1
      J2 = 3
      J3 = 2
      RETURN
C
C
      ENTRY FILT3
      YM (1, J1) = X
      DO 20  K = 1, M2
      K1 = K + 1
      YMM = B0(K) * YM(K,J1) + B1(K) * YM(K,J2)
     *     + B2(K) * YM(K,J3) - A1(K) * YM(K1,J2)
     *     - A2(K) * YM(K1,J3)
   20 YM(K1,J1) = YMM
      J4 = J1
      J1 = J3
      J3 = J2
      J2 = J4
      Y = YMM
      RETURN
      END
```

Figure 5.9 Subroutine BFILT3. Used in an identical manner to BFILT2. BFILT3 employs a rotating buffer scheme.

considerably: if a particular compiler is poor at indexing variables, then it will not produce good efficient code for this purpose. If speed is important, the procedure could be coded in machine language, or the user could experiment with these FORTRAN examples in order to find which is faster on his machine.

```
      SUBROUTINE BFILT4
      COMMON /FILTR4/ X, Y, B(1001), M
      DIMENSION BUFFER (1001)
      DO 5 I = 1, 1001
5     BUFFER (I) = 0.
      LOC = 1
      M2 = M/2
      RETURN
      ENTRY FILT4
      BUFFER(LOC) = X
      L0 = LOC - M2
      IF (L0. LT. 1) L0 = L0 + M
      Y = BUFFER (L0) * B(1)
      DO 10 I = 1, M2
      LL = L0 - I
      IF (LL. LT. 1) LL = LL + M
      LR = L0 + I
      IF (LR. GT. M) LR = LR - M
      Y = Y+(BUFFER(LL)+BUFFER(LR)) * B(I + 1)
10    CONTINUE
      LOC = LOC + 1
      IF (LOC. GT. M) LOC = LOC - M
      RETURN
      END
```

Figure 5.10   Rotating buffer scheme for a symmetric FIR filter.

Figure 5.10 shows a rotating buffer scheme as applied to a FIR filter. This routine has a large internal vector labeled BUFFER to store up to 1001 points. The filtering operation is assumed to be of the form

$$y(i) = \sum_{k=-M/2}^{M/2} b_k x(i-k) \qquad (5.49)$$

where M is odd. In particular, because it is assumed that the filter is symmetric, the filtering equation can be rewritten as

$$y(i) = b_0 x(i) + \sum_{k=1}^{M/2} b_k [x(i-k) + x(i+k)]$$ (5.50)

Because the data is never moved within the buffer, the amount of time required to calculate where the proper piece of data is located is increased over simpler, nonrotating buffer schemes. As with the recursive equivalent, this procedure can be done very efficiently in machine language, but *may* yield relatively poor code when implemented in FORTRAN.

5.5   DECIMATION

Properly speaking, the word decimation means to lose one-tenth of one's military forces in battle or through punishment.* As used in signal processing, the term has come to mean simply the discarding of unwanted or redundant information with a corresponding compaction of the data.

The most common reason for lowering the sampling rate by decimating the data is economy. Suppose that a test ran for 30 min., and that the sampling rate was 400 sps. This would result in $30 \cdot 60 \cdot 400 = 720,000$ data points. If it was desired to plot this information on a 30-in. plot, there would be 24,000 points/in. If the plotter being used plotted in increments of 0.01 in., a common value, each step would represent 240 data points. It would seem reasonable to reduce the amount of data by systematically throwing away data points. In this case a decimation rate of at least 240 to 1 would be called for.

Filtering is usually performed in conjunction with decimation, and usually a lowpass filter is employed. The filtering is done to prevent higher frequency data from becoming aliased and appearing as a lower frequency.

For example, consider the time history

$$x(i) = \cos\left(\frac{3\pi i}{4}\right)$$ (5.51)

The first 10 points of this are shown in the upper part of Figure 5.11. The function is a cosine wave with frequency at 75% of the Nyquist folding frequency. The points are shown connected to help visualize the process. If

*During the republican era of Rome, decimation was a military punishment for cowardice: the offending unit would be broken down into groups of 10 soldiers; each group of 10 would cast lots amongst themselves, one man losing; typically, the loser would be skinned alive by his comrades.

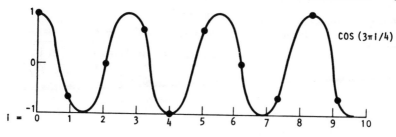

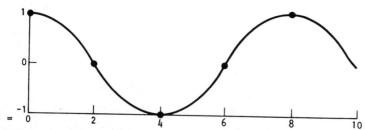

Figure 5.11 A cosine wave before (top) and after (bottom) decimating by throwing away every other point.

every other point starting with $i = 1$ were discarded, a new function would result, as shown in the bottom of the figure. This new function would appear to be much lower in frequency than the one from which it was derived. In particular, it would appear to be 25% of the original folding frequency.

In order to prevent the higher-frequency information from appearing as low-frequency information, it is necessary to lowpass filter in the following manner:

- Suppose the decimation index is p, so that the first point is kept, the next $(p-1)$ points are discarded, the following point is kept, $(p-1)$ points are discarded, etc.
- The original folding frequency was $F = S/2 = 1/2T$ Hz. The new folding frequency will be F/p, one pth of the original.
- Any information on the original range F/p to F Hz will be aliased so as to appear as lower-frequency information after decimation.
- Therefore, before decimation the data should be filtered with a lowpass filter with cutoff below $F' = 1/2pT$ Hz.

The decimation formulas are summarized in Table 5.5.

Table 5.5

Decimation Formulas in Terms of T, S, or F

	In Terms of T	In Terms of S	In Terms of F
Sampling rate and interval	$S = \dfrac{1}{T}$	$T = \dfrac{1}{S}$	$S = 2F$ $T = 1/2F$
Folding (Nyquist) frequency	$F = \dfrac{1}{2T}$	$F = \dfrac{S}{2}$	F
Folding frequency after decimation	$F' = \dfrac{1}{2pT}$	$F' = \dfrac{S}{2p}$	$F' = \dfrac{F}{p}$
New interval/rate	$T' = pT$ $S' = 1/pT$	$T' = p/S$ $S' = S/p$	$T' = \dfrac{p}{2F}$ $S' = \dfrac{2F}{p}$

Selection of Filter

There are several ways of selecting the cutoff point of the lowpass filter employed in decimation. One standard setting is to put the cutoff point at F', so that the power there is down only 3 dB. That is, its power is reduced by half, or its amplitude correspondingly is reduced by about 30%. Information slightly to the right of the new folding frequency will appear on the left of it with amplitude also reduced by about these amounts. A second criterion requires that the amplitude of the aliased data be reduced to a given specification. Thus it might be necessary to pick a filter such that the amplitude of its transfer function at the new folding frequency is at or below a certain level in decibels. For example, it might be required that the aliased power be down 60 dB at F'. By filtering with a lowpass filter that is down 60 dB at F' it is guaranteed that this will be the case. Some information near the folding frequency will be lost in either case: with the 3-dB procedure, data from above F' will be aliased and combined with data below F', thus making it impossible to correctly interpret what is occurring there; when a 60 dB at F' criterion is employed, there is correspondingly less aliasing of a problem, but good data below F' may have been lost in the process.

Once it is determined where the cutoff of the filter is to be relative to F', the next problem is that of choosing either a FIR or an IIR filter, the specific type of filter, and the number of coefficients to be used. Table 5.6 summarizes some of the advantages and disadvantages of FIR and IIR filters.

As noted in the table, when employing a FIR filter, it is not necessary to compute every output point. If a p to 1 decimation is being performed, all

Table 5.6

Advantages and Disadvantages of FIR and IIR Filters as Employed in Decimation

FIR	IIR
Advantages	
1. It is only necessary to compute every pth output point	1. Much less storage required both for weights and data
2. Always stable	2. Usually can achieve a filter that has nearly linear phase across the passband
3. Phaseless filtering is easy to do	3. Often most efficient computationally
4. Can be done in fixed point on minicomputers	
Disadvantages	
1. A large number of weights may be required	1. All output points must be computed (There are formulations which do not require all output points to be computed, however, they usually do not turn out to be more efficient)
2. Possibly noisy	2. Possibly noisy and even unstable
3. May require a great deal of storage for weights and data	3. Not possible to get phaseless filtering (unless the data is run twice through the same filter, going in different directions each time)
	4. Best done in floating point

that is needed is that every pth output point be computed. This is the primary advantage of the FIR filters in decimation.

There is no perfect rule for selecting the proper type of filter. In addition to the decimation rate, the hardware and software to be employed must be considered along with many other factors. Our prejudices are as follows:

- For decimation done on a fixed point device such as special-purpose hardware or a mini- or microcomputer, the FIR type would seem to be preferable.
- On a large-scale computer or on an array processor with floating point and words of 32 or more bits, the IIR filters may be more convenient:

the user knows what he will be getting without having to do an analysis of the filter before employing it in a given situation. Also, the lesser amount of data storage required may be helpful, especially if a large number of functions are being processed.

If this turns out to be the case, it may be necessary to do the decimation in two or more stages. Using more than one stage of decimation is referred to as *cascaded* decimation. Suppose that

$$p = q^2 \qquad\qquad (5.52)$$

Then the natural thing to do would be to decimate in two stages of q to 1 each. For example, suppose that $f_s = 1,000,000$ and it is desired to have $p = 10,000$, that is, a decimation of 10,000 to 1. This would call for a filter cutoff at $1/10,000$ of the folding frequency, a value not possible on many computers. On the other hand, two stages of 100 to 1 each are easily accomplished. This calls for two stages, rather than a single one that would be used if the filter were possible.

Cascading of filters is generally not commutative. For example, a total decimation of 30 to 1 could be accomplished by any one of the following:

1. 30 to 1 decimation.
2. 5 to 1 followed by a 6 to 1.
3. 6 to 1 followed by a 5 to 1.
4. 3 to 1 followed by a 10 to 1.
5. 10 to 1 followed by a 3 to 1.
6. 15 to 1 followed by a 2 to 1.
7. 2 to 1 followed by a 15 to 1.
8. 2 to 1, 3 to 1, 5 to 1.
9. 2 to 1, 5 to 1, 3 to 1.
10. 3 to 1, 2 to 1, 5 to 1.
11. 3 to 1, 5 to 1, 2 to 1.
12. 5 to 1, 2 to 1, 3 to 1.
13. 5 to 1, 3 to 1, 2 to 1.

Figure 5.12 shows the overall filter transfer function for cases 2 through 5 as implemented using Parks–McClellan FIR filters as discussed in the

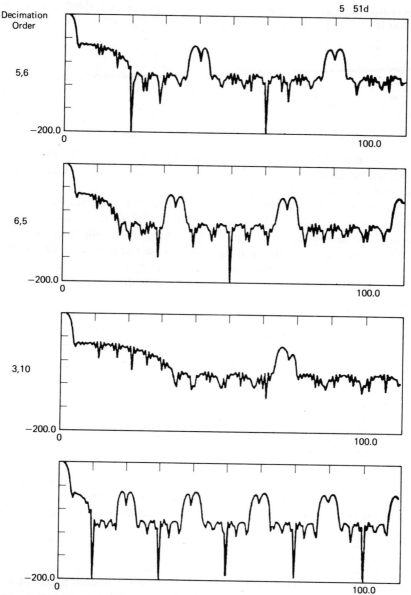

Figure 5.12 Four examples of implementations of 30 to 1 decimation filters.

preceding chapter. The parameters for the filters are as follows (relative to a 100-Hz folding frequency):

Decimation	M	Cutoff Frequency (Hz)
3 to 1	18	13.3
5 to 1	30	8.
6 to 1	36	6.7
10 to 1	60	4.

Each of these filters has a stop band floor at about -46 dB. When operated in cascade, this tends to double except for aliased passbands, which appear as double bumps.

Although the pass bands are identical for the four decimation operations shown, note that the stop bands are very different, so that 5 to 1 followed by 6 to 1 is not the same as 6 to 1 followed by 5 to 1. However, the peak values of the bumps in the stop band in no case rise over -46 dB, so that the overall filter characteristic is at least as good as the original filters.

When antialiasing filtering is done with FIR filters, there are several points that should be considered:

- Only every pth output of the filter is required. Hence the filtering scheme is modified so that $(p-1)$ times out of p the incoming data is merely stored, and no other operation takes place. On the pth entry, one output point is computed.
- The size of M will typically vary from $5p$ to $10p$ or more, depending on how low a stop band characteristic is required.
- Rather than storing the data it is possible to store the *partial sums*; this can result in a great deal of savings in storage.

The savings from the partial sum technique come about from the fact that only approximately M/p partial sum values need be retained as opposed to the $5p$–$10p$ data values that the standard method requires. That is, suppose

$$M = rp$$

Then only r partial sums are necessary. For each new data point input to the filter, r operations are performed: the input value is multiplied by r different coefficients and one addition of such a weighted data point is made to each partial sum. Every p data points a partial sum graduates as an output data point, and a new partial sum is started.

The partial sum technique requires only $1/p$th of the storage that the standard method uses. This can become quite significant if there are many channels being processed.

5.6   UPWARDS DECIMATION

Sometimes it is necessary to increase the sampling rate rather than decrease it. In particular, this can occur when it is desired to obtain matching sampling rates for two time histories whose sampling rates are not integral multiples of one another. This is described fully in Section 5.7. This effectively amounts to interpolating in new data points between the old ones. The process is referred to as upwards decimation. The procedure is as follows:

• Zeroes are added between each original data point. For a 1 to p upwards decimation, $(p-1)$ zeroes are inserted.
• The original data is multiplied by p.
• The new sequence of scaled original data and zeroes is lowpass filtered with a filter whose cutoff frequency is set at the original Nyquist folding frequency.

For example, suppose that the original data was sampled at a rate of 200 sps, and that it was desired to increase this to 1000 sps. This would amount to a 1 to 5 increase. If the original data were $x(0), x(1), x(2)$, etc., then going into the digital filter would be the sequence $5x(0), 0, 0, 0, 0, 5x(1), 0, 0, 0, 0, 5x(2), 0, 0$, etc.

The lowpass filter acts as an interpolator; it lowers the amplitude and fills in smoothed values. The multiplication by p is required because desired power is being eliminated by the filter, the opposite of downwards decimation.

Figure 5.13 should help in giving an intuitive picture of what is occurring. Suppose that in the above example the amplitude of the Fourier transform of the data looked as shown in 5.13a. Adding the four zeroes between each data point causes the change as shown in Figure 5.13b; the overall level is reduced, and the power is spread out systematically throughout the new frequency range. Note that only the range 0 to the Nyquist frequency is shown in each case. Figure 5.13c shows the result of lowpass filtering as described above. The power from F to F' Hz has been removed, thus leaving the amplitude spectrum without the aliased data.

As a further example of the procedure Figure 5.14 shows a data sequence before and after filtering. The original time history was a unit

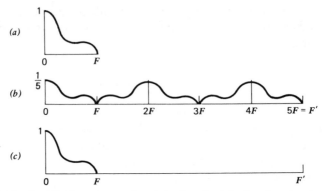

Figure 5.13 Amplitude spectra of a data function during the stages of upwards decimation.

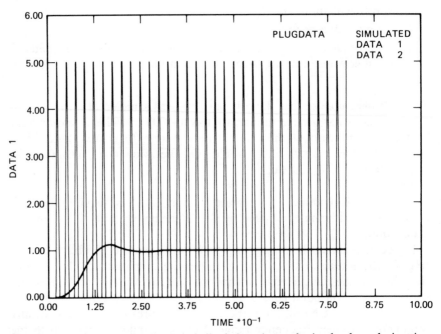

Figure 5.14 The intermediate and final functions obtained when decimating upwards 1 to 5. The comblike function was derived from a unit step function by multiplying by 5 and adding four zeroes between each data point. The second function resulted from passing the function through the proper digital filter.

step, that is, a series of 33 ones. As in the above examples, an upwards decimation rate of 1 to 5 was selected. Four zeroes were added between each data unit, and the sequence was multiplied by 5, resulting in the comblike function shown in the plot. The second function is the result of passing the comb function through a lowpass six-pole filter.

After an initial transient, the filtered data settles down very nicely to unity, so that the data again has the form of a step function.

5.7   REDUCTION TO A COMMON SAMPLING RATE

Sometimes it is required to run a two-function analysis (i.e., cross correlation, cross spectrum, transfer function, etc.) on two functions which are not at the same sampling rate. Using upwards and downwards decimation and multiple passes through the data, it is always possible to make the rates commensurate. However, as will be seen, care must be taken or expenses incurred by the process may be large.

Suppose the sampling rates in question are S_1 and S_2. There are several cases to consider:

Case 1. $S_1 = pS_2$, p as usual an integer

In this case the most reasonable thing to do is to decimate (downwards) the first sequence at a p to 1 rate. The same goal could be accomplished by interpolating the second function at a 1 to p rate, but there are two reasons why this should not be done. First of all, it is more expensive; there will be p times as much data to process. Secondly, the results may be deceptive, for there really is no information above $S_2/2$ contained in the second function if the filtering has been properly performed.

Case 2. $S_1 \neq pS_2$

In this case it is necessary to find the least common multiple (lcm) of S_1 and S_2. That is, the smallest number S_3 such that both S_1 and S_2 divide S_3 without remainder. That is, there exist integers p and q such that

$$S_1 p = S_2 q = S_3$$

If S_1 and S_2 are relatively prime (worst case) then $p = S_2$ and $q = S_1$.

The next step would be to compare p and q to see which is the largest. Suppose that p is the largest. Then the second function would be decimated upwards 1 to q, and then decimated downwards p to 1. The resulting sampling rate would be

$$\frac{S_2 q}{p} = \frac{S_3}{p} = \frac{S_1 p}{p} = S_1$$

This procedure would yield the lower of the two possible sampling rates, which is the desirable approach to take. As an example, suppose

$$S_1 = 800 = 2^5 \cdot 5^2$$

$$S_2 = 1{,}000 = 2^3 \cdot 5^3$$

The lowest common multiple of S_1 and S_2 in this case is

$$S_3 = 2^5 \cdot 5^3 = 4{,}000$$

so that $p = 5$ and $q = 4$. Therefore, the second sequence would be decimated upwards 1 to 4, resulting in the intermediate rate of 4,000 sps, and then decimated downwards 5 to 1, so that its final sampling rate is the same as the first function.

Note that digital filtering would have been performed at both stages, resulting in a change of phase angle or the addition of delay to the second function. This should be remembered when analyzing the cross spectra and other functions where phase or delay may be interpreted.

5.8   COMPLEX DEMODULATION

Section 4.8 on bandpass filters discusses the concept of complex demodulation. Basically, it amounts to multiplying a sequence by the complex exponential term $\exp(j2\pi f_c iT)$. The result is that $X(f)$ is shifted by an amount f_c. This can be seen as follows:

Let

$$X(f) = T \sum_{i=-\infty}^{\infty} x(i)\exp(j2\pi fiT) \qquad (5.53)$$

Define $y(i)$ by

$$y(i) = x(i)\exp(j2\pi f_c iT)$$

That is, it is $x(i)$ multiplied by a sine and cosine term at frequency f_c Hz. The Fourier transform of $y(i)$ thus is

$$Y(s) = T \sum_{i=-\infty}^{\infty} y(i)\exp(-j2\pi siT)$$

$$= T \sum_{i=-\infty}^{\infty} x(i)\exp(j2\pi f_c iT)\exp(-j2\pi siT)$$

$$= T \sum_{i=-\infty}^{\infty} x(i)\exp(-j2\pi(s-f_c)iT) \qquad (5.54)$$

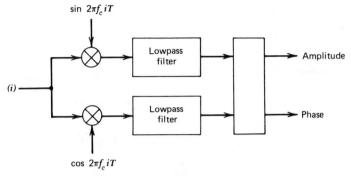

Figure 5.15   Complex demodulation.

If the variable term $(s - f_c)$ is replaced with f;

$$f = s - f_c$$

and is replaced with

$$s = f + f_c \tag{5.55}$$

The equation becomes

$$Y(f + f_c) = T \sum_{i=-\infty}^{\infty} x(i)\exp(-j2\pi fiT)$$

$$= X(f) \tag{5.56}$$

Thus complex demodulation in the time domain amounts to a shift in the frequency domain.

Complex demodulation is usually done in conjunction with a pair of filters as shows in Figure 5.15. The box shown at the right of the figure computes the amplitude and phase of the signal of the inputs. This is done as follows:

Define

$$x_s(i) = x(i)\sin 2\pi f_c iT$$

$$x_c(i) = x(i)\cos 2\pi f_c iT$$

$$y_s(i) = \text{filtered } x_s(i)$$

$$y_c(i) = \text{filtered } x_c(i)$$

$$a(i) = \text{amplitude} = \sqrt{2\big(y_s^2(i) + y_c^2(i)\big)}$$

$$\phi(i) = \arctan\left(\frac{-y_s(i)}{y_c(i)}\right) \tag{5.57}$$

To see how this works, consider the sequence

$$x(i) = A \cos(2\pi f_c iT + \phi_c) \tag{5.58}$$

where ϕ_c is an arbitrary phase angle.

Then

$$x_s(i) = A \cos(2\pi f_c iT + \phi_c) \sin(2\pi f_c iT)$$

$$= \frac{A}{2} \left\{ \sin\left[2\pi(f_c + f_c)iT + \phi_c \right] \right.$$

$$\left. + \sin\left[2\pi(f_c - f_c)iT - \phi_c \right] \right\}$$

$$= \frac{A}{2} \left[\sin(4\pi f_c iT + \phi_c) - \sin \phi_c \right] \tag{5.59}$$

The $y_s(i)$ term, neglecting the phase delay, would therefore be

$$y_s(i) = -\frac{A}{2} \sin \phi_c \tag{5.60}$$

because the filter will delete the higher frequency term. Similarly,

$$x_c(i) = A\cos(2\pi f_c iT + \phi_c)\cos(2\pi f_c iT)$$

$$= \frac{A}{2} \left[\cos\left[2\pi(f_c + f_c) + \phi_c \right] \right.$$

$$\left. + \cos\left[2\pi(f_c - f_c) + \phi_c \right] \right]$$

$$= \frac{A}{2} \left[\cos(4f_c iT + \phi_c) + \cos \phi_c \right] \tag{5.61}$$

Thus under the same arguments given for $y_s(i)$,

$$y_c(i) = \frac{A}{2} \cos \phi_c$$

$$y_s^2(i) + y_c^2(i) = \frac{A^2}{4} \sin^2 \phi_c + \frac{A^2}{4} \cos^2 \phi_c$$

$$= \frac{A^2}{2} \tag{5.62}$$

Hence

$$a(i) = \sqrt{2(y_s^2(i) + y_c^2(i))} = A \tag{5.63}$$

Similarly,

$$\phi(i) = \arctan\left(\frac{-y_s(i)}{y_c(i)}\right)$$

$$= \arctan\left(\frac{\sin\phi_c}{\cos\phi_c}\right) = \phi_c \qquad (5.64)$$

It should be remembered that there will be a delay term in the phase angle. However, a main use of this procedure is computing transfer functions: two identical complex demodulators are set up, one at the input, and the second at the output of the device being analyzed. The gain is computed from the ratio of the input to the output sequences, and the phase is computed from the difference between the two phase angles. If identical filtering is employed in both complex demodulators then the relative phase angle introduced by the filters cancels.

EXERCISES

5.1. The simulation of filtering operations done in fixed point is most easily accomplished in FORTRAN using double precision floating point. Assume that m bits are to be allowed in the fractional part of the fixed point numbers being simulated. Then all calculations may actually be directly done in double precision floating point except rounding and multiplication. These can be done with two subroutines as follows:

Simulation rounding
```
SUBROUTINE SIMRND (AA,M)
DOUBLE PRECISION AA,A,FACT
FACT=2.D0**M
A=AA*FACT+0.5D0
A=A−DMOD (A,1.D0)
AA=A/FACT
RETURN
END
```

Simulation multiplication
```
SUBROUTINE SIMMLT (A,B,C,M)
DOUBLE PRECISION A,B,C,CC
CC=A*B/(2.D0**M)
CALL SIMRND (CC,M)
C=CC
RETURN
END
```

a. Using these two routines, redo Exercise 4.7 in a manner such that all the calculations for parts b and c are done in simulated fixed point. Run the problem with $M = 16$, 12, 8, and 4, $T = 0.005$, and $B = 4$ Hz only. A SIMDIV routine will be needed for the transfer function calculations in order to do the division. Write such a routine after studying SIMMLT.

b. In parallel to the simulated fixed point, run the same calculations in floating point. The floating point results will be used as a standard. Compute an error term by differencing the results obtained from the two different forms of arithmetic, squaring the difference, and then averaging over all of the resulting squared terms. Comment on the derived error terms.

5.2. This problem amounts to implementing the measurement of $\hat{H}(f)$ using method 2 from Section 5.2. The simulated arithmetic from the preceding exercise will be employed. The pieces of code required are as follows:

a. Subroutine SIMSIN to recursively generate $\sin(2\pi f_p iT)$. Use the algorithm given in Section 4.3 under the heading *The Second-Order Filter as an Oscillator*. This routine should be coded in ordinary floating point. The output should be converted to double precision and rounded using SIMRND.

b. Subroutine SIMFIL to compute

$$y(i) = b_o x(i) - a_1 y(i-1) - a_2 y(i-2)$$

in simulated fixed point.

c. A driver program that does the following:
   1. Allows a value of m to be input or taken from a data statement.
   2. Generates either first- or second-order lowpass filter weights (the latter by calling LP2) and converts the weights from ordinary floating point to simulated fixed point including rounding.
   3. Uses SIMSIN to generate a sine wave at a given frequency and SIMFIL to filter the sine wave.
   4. Converts the output of the filter, after neglecting a transient to ordinary floating point and computes the mean square energy. This represents the gain of the transfer function for the frequency of the sine wave being generated.
   5. Runs the overall program with the following values: $T = 0.005$, $B = 4$, $f_p = 2, 4, 8, 16, 32, 64$ Hz, $m = 16, 12, 8, 4$.

d. Run the program for both the first- and second-order filters. Comment on the results.

5.3. Is the following filter stable?

$$y(i) = 2x(i) - 4x(i-1) - 8x(i-2) + 2y(i-1) + 4y(i-2)$$

Explain. Are there any pathological cases?

5.4. The Mth-order binomial filter (FIR) has weights

$$b_k = \frac{\binom{M}{k}}{2^M} \qquad k = -M, \ldots, M$$

Show that $|H(f)| = \cos^{2M} \pi f T$. Where is the 3-dB point (i.e., where $10 \log_{10} |H(f)| = 10 \log_{10} \frac{1}{2}$) in terms of frequency and M? What does a cascaded version of this filter look like? What are the zeroes of the filter?

5.5. Implement BFILT1. Using it, PRPLOT, LPSB, and a driver program similar to the one shown in the example, do the following:

   a. Recode the driver to generate and plot six filtered sequences of 101 points each. Each of them has $T = 0.005$, and input $x(i) = 1, 0, 0, \ldots, 0, \ i = 0, \ldots, 100$.

   b. The filter employed will in each case have six recursive weights (three cascade stages). The cutoff points to be employed are 32, 16, 8, 4, 2, and 1 Hz.

   c. Comment on the results.

5.6. Implement both BFILT2 and BFILT3, and write a test program to check their relative efficiency. Note: some sort of timing must be available on the computer employed in order to do this problem. The procedure might be as follows: generate and store 1000 points of a sine wave; time BFILT2 for filtering the data; time BFILT3 for filtering the data; print the results. If time and skill permit, a further comparison would be to code BFILT3 in machine language and run the timing test for the routine. This is recommended as a project rather than a simple problem.

5.7. Implement and test subroutine BFILT4 using the binomial filter:

   a. Pick $M = 8$, $T = 0.005$, and $N = 1016$.

   b. Generate and filter sine waves of length N. Discard the first and last M points and compute the mean and variance of the output.

   c. Do this for $f = 9.3$, 18.6, 37.2, and 74.4 Hz. Comment on the results.

5.8. Redo Exercise 5.7 using weights generated by subroutine LPSPBG, Figure 4.19. Use $M = 8$, $T = 0.005$, and $B = 18.6$. Comment on the results. Also, compute the transfer functions of the two filters and compare them. Since TTRAN cannot be used in this case, what are the alternatives? Can FFTRAN be used for this purpose? If so, how?

5.9. Write a test program to see the problems in decimation. This could be done in the following manner:

a. Generate 1024 points of uniformly distributed data using TDRAND. Subtract 0.5 from each point so that the expected mean will be 0.

b. Filter the data using BFILT1 and LPSB. Assume $T = 0.005$, six poles in the filter, and $B = 20$ Hz.

c. Decimate the original and filtered data at a rate of 4 to 1 $(p = 4)$.

d. Compute the Fourier transform of each of these sequences. (Note: use FFTRAN separately for each sequence; put the sequence in the real part and zero out the imaginary part; there is a more efficient way of doing this operation, but it is not taken up until the next chapter). Then compute the absolute value squared of transforms.

e. There will now be 129 points in each transform. Why? Plot these results and compare them.

f. Repeat with $B = 12.5$ and 25 Hz. Compare with the results for 20 Hz.

5.10. Suppose that a 10,000 to 1 decimation is required. Attempt to have LPSB generate an appropriate six-pole filter. Are the results usable? What would be a reasonable alternative?

5.11 Generate 64 points of uniformly distributed pseudorandom noise using TDRAND. Do an upwards decimation of 1 to 4 including an appropriate filtering operation. Comment on the results. Compute and plot the absolute value squared of the Fourier transform of the upwards decimated data with and without filtering and comment on the results.

CHAPTER 6

FOURIER TRANSFORMS

6.1 BACKGROUND AND THEORY

Much of time series data analysis is based on the Fourier transform and its efficient computation. In addition to the usefulness of the Fourier transform itself as a data analysis tool, it is an intermediate step in determining PSD's, CSD's, transfer functions, convolutions and filtering, correlations (see Table 6.1), and finally can be used for interpolation. In this chapter, a brief review of some of the theory is given, but emphasis is placed on applications and properties useful in computing other functions. Many books give complete detail which the reader is referred to. A particularly useful one for our purposes is Bracewell [1965].

The fast Fourier transform algorithm is only briefly reviewed; the reader may refer to Otnes and Enochson [1972] for an amplified discussion.

Definition of the Fourier Transform

The definition of the continuous, infinite range Fourier transform that we employ is

$$X(f) = \int_{-\infty}^{\infty} x(t) \exp(-j2\pi ft)\, dt \qquad -\infty < f < \infty \qquad (6.1)$$

where $x(t)$ is usually a time history (but not necessarily so). In this case t is thought of as a time variable and f a frequency variable. An elaborate mathematical scaffolding is necessary for the existence of $X(f)$ when $x(t)$ is a random variable. However, we will be dealing with finite record length and finite amplitude recorded time histories, and the Fourier transform will always exist in such special situations.

Table 6.1

Functions Derived from FFTs

1. PSD

$$S_{xx}(k) = \frac{1}{P} \overline{X^*(k)X(k)} = \frac{1}{P}|\overline{X(k)}|^2$$

2. CSD

$$S_{xy}(k) = \frac{1}{P} \overline{X^*(k)Y(k)}$$

3. Transfer Function

$$H_{xy}(k) = \frac{Y(k)}{X(k)}$$

4. Convolution[a]

$$u(i) = \text{FFT}^{-1}[U(k)], \, U(k) = X(k)Y(k)$$

5. Covariance[a]

$$s_{xy}(i) = \frac{N}{N-i}\text{FFT}^{-1}[S_{xy}(k)],$$

$$S_{xy}(k) = \frac{1}{P}X^*(k)Y(k)$$

[a]For convolution and covariance, at least the last half of $X(k)$ and $Y(k)$ must be zeroes.
The quantities

$$x(i), y(i), u(i) \qquad i = 0, 1, 2, \ldots, N-1$$

are final time histories, and

$$X(k), Y(k), U(k) \quad \begin{matrix} k = 0, 1, 2, \ldots, \frac{N}{2}, \, N \text{ even} \\ k = 0, 1, 2, \ldots, \frac{N-1}{2}, \, N \text{ odd} \end{matrix}$$

are the corresponding FFTs. Bar denotes averaging.

In particular, we are concerned with the finite range, discrete time, Fourier transform usually computed via an FFT algorithm. If we consider a complex valued function, denoted by $z(i)$, $i = 0, 1, 2, \ldots, N-1$, then the definition is

$$Z(k) = T \sum_{i=0}^{N-1} z(i) \exp\left(-j\frac{2\pi}{N}ik\right) \qquad k = 0, 1, 2, \ldots, N-1 \qquad (6.2)$$

Recall that $z(i)$ is shorthand notation for the time point $z(iT)$. The finite record length of $z(i)$ induces a discreteness in the frequency domain and $Z(k)$ is shorthand notation for $Z(kb)$ where

$$b = \frac{1}{NT} = \frac{1}{P} \qquad (6.3)$$

In the discussion of the duality of aliasing and time and frequency domain versions of the sampling theorem, this fact is amplified. The N frequency domain points are adequate to completely reconstruct the N time domain points. Moreover, for band and time limited functions, all other points in between could be constructed by application of the interpolation formula of the sampling theorem. A fundamental fact is that $Z(k)$ is actually a periodic function and if we continue computing for values of k larger than N we merely repeat $Z(k)$. In equation form we have

$$Z(N+k) = Z(k) \qquad (6.4)$$

which is depicted in Figure 6.1.

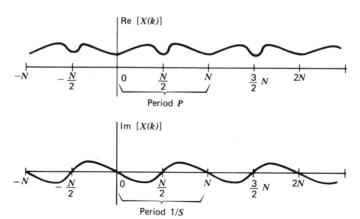

Figure 6.1 Illustration of periodicity of discrete Fourier transform.

Now, in the practical data analysis situation, we record real, not complex, time histories. Hence (6.2) becomes

$$X(k) = T \sum_{i=0}^{N-1} x(i) \exp\left(-j\frac{2\pi}{N}ik\right) \qquad k = \begin{cases} 0, 1, 2, \ldots, \dfrac{N}{2} & N \text{ even} \\[2mm] 0, 1, 2, \ldots, \dfrac{N-1}{2} & N \text{ odd} \end{cases}$$

$$(6.5)$$

That is, we have approximately half as many frequency points as time points. If we were to continue computing for larger values of k we would obtain a reversed complex conjugate of the first part.

In equation form

$$X^*(N-k) = X(k) \qquad (6.6)$$

which is illustrated in Figure 6.2.

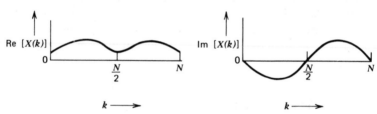

Figure 6.2 Typical symmetric real and antisymmetric imaginary parts of Fourier transform of real functions.

This result follows immediately from (6.5) and takes note of the fact that the cosine and sine functions are even and odd, respectively. Thus

$$\text{Re}[X(k)] = T \sum_{i=0}^{N-1} x(i) \cos\left(\frac{2\pi}{N}ik\right) \qquad (6.7)$$

is an even (symmetric) function $[\text{Re}\,X(k) = \text{Re}\,X(-k)]$ and

$$\text{Im}[X(k)] = -T \sum_{i=0}^{N-1} x(i) \sin\left(\frac{2\pi}{N}ik\right) \qquad (6.8)$$

is an odd (antisymmetric) function $[\text{Im}\,X(k) = -\text{Im}\,X(-k)]$. The detailed proof of this is left for Exercise 6.3.

If we examine more closely the total number of real and imaginary values in the frequency function $X(k)$ we observe that we have the same total number of values as we begin with in the time function. We note two facts:

$$X(0) = X^*(N) = X^*(0) \qquad (6.9)$$

and, for even N,

$$X\left(\frac{N}{2}\right) = X^*\left(N - \frac{N}{2}\right) = X^*\left(\frac{N}{2}\right) \qquad (6.10)$$

Thus both the zero frequency value (DC component) and the Nyquist frequency value are pure real numbers. In the case of an odd number of points, $X([N-1]/2)$ is the point just before the Nyquist point and there is no value computed exactly at the Nyquist frequency. These facts are illustrated in Figure 6.3.

We note that most contemporary minicomputer based Fourier analysis systems have transform algorithms based on a number of data points which is a power of 2 and therefore one need only be concerned with considerations for an even number of points. However, a popular algorithm for larger computer systems that will handle numbers of data points which are powers of 2, 3, 4, and 5 is given in Singleton [1969]. In that case, we must account for the differences which occur with an odd number of data values.

The symmetry equation, (6.6), and the fact that the $k=0$ and $k=N/2$ (N even) are real values, along with (6.9) and (6.10), demonstrate a fact that was previously mentioned. Namely, N real data values transform into N real data values. There are two cases:

- N *even*: N real points go into one real value at the two frequency-index values $k=0$ and $N/2$ plus $(N-2)/2$ real parts and imaginary parts in between for a total of N components.
- N *odd*: N real points go into one real value at $k=0$ and $(N-1)/2$ real parts and imaginary parts for a total of N components.

We must remark that although these details are important in constructing correct computer programs for doing Fourier transforms, they are not important considerations in engineering interpretations of Fourier transforms of scientific test data.

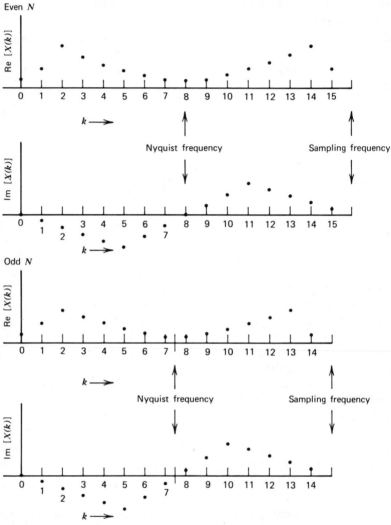

Figure 6.3 Distinction between Fourier transforms for even and odd number of points.

Polar Coordinates (Absolute Value and Phase)

The Fourier transform at a specific frequency is a complex number and is often desired in terms of polar coordinates

$$|X(k)| = \left\{ \text{Re}^2[X(k)] + \text{Im}^2[X(k)] \right\}^{1/2} \tag{6.11}$$

$$\phi_x(k) = \text{Tan}^{-1} \frac{\text{Im}[X(k)]}{\text{Re}[X(k)]} \tag{6.12}$$

where the capitalization of Tan^{-1} denotes principal value.

The quantity $|X(k)|$ is referred to interchangeably as gain, absolute value, or magnitude. The quantity $\varphi_x(k)$ is referred to as phase or argument. Figure 6.4 illustrates the real and imaginary parts and absolute value and phase of a Fourier transform.

Inverse Transform

The inverse Fourier transform is obtained by reversing the sign of the exponential in (6.5) and interchanging the roles of $x(i)$ and $X(k)$, namely,

$$x(i) = b \sum_{i=0}^{N-1} X(k) \exp\left[j2\pi\frac{ik}{N} \right] \qquad i = 0, 1, 2, \ldots, N-1 \qquad (6.13)$$

Note that we only define $X(k)$ for $N/2+1$ or $(N-1)/2$ values but in (6.13) the summation runs over N values so that we must account for the symmetry. The Fourier transform of a real valued function is Hermitian symmetric, defined by (6.6).

For example, the real and imaginary parts of a Fourier transform of a real function might appear as in Figure 6.1. The diagram tacitly assumes N is even. Odd values for N are discussed below.

It should be clear that the complex conjugate symmetric half of the function is redundant, and hence need not appear directly in an equation. A method for avoiding explicit use of the second half is given in the Special Inverse Transform section. Similarly, when the Fourier transform of a real sequence is computed utilizing a complex Fourier transform algorithm, one need not fill in the imaginary part with zeroes. Rather, the real sequence can be divided among the real and imaginary parts of the data array.

Note that the discrete Fourier transform definitions given here include the time interval and frequency interval explicitly in the formulas. Many texts and articles use a slightly modified definition which corresponds to a normalized time interval. Note that if $T = 1$ then the frequency increment is

$$b = \frac{1}{P} = \frac{1}{NT} = \frac{1}{N} \qquad (6.14)$$

In this case the Fourier transform pair becomes

$$X(k) = \sum_{i=0}^{N-1} x(i) \exp\left[-j2\pi\frac{ik}{N} \right] \qquad (6.15)$$

$$x(i) = \frac{1}{N} \sum_{i=0}^{N-1} X(k) \exp\left[j2\pi\frac{ik}{N} \right] \qquad (6.16)$$

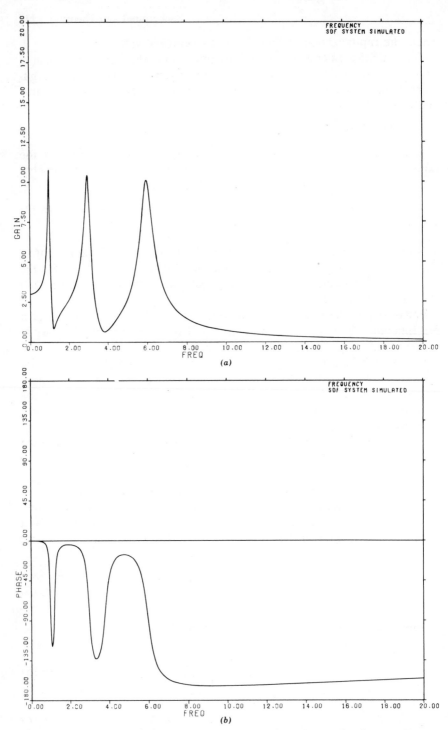

Figure 6.4. Comparison of Cartesian and polar coordinates.

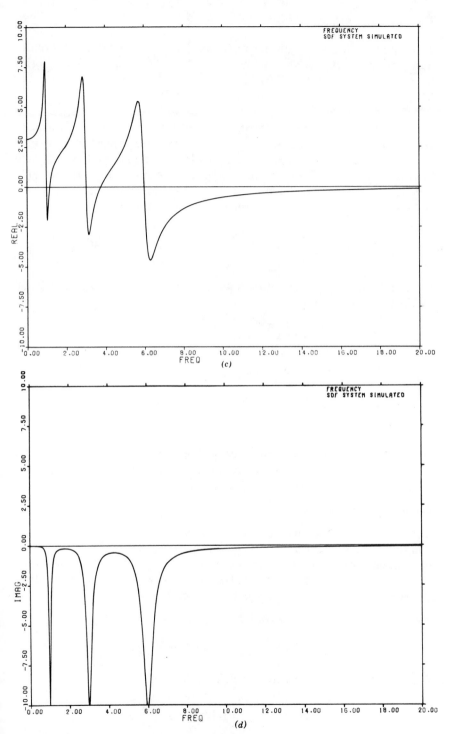

(*a*) Absolute values. (*b*) Phase. (*c*) Real part. (*d*) Imaginary part.

227

We now define some special relations that are very useful in Fourier transform calculations. One of these, the "double-length" formula, forms the basis for the power of 2 FFT.

Two-at-a-Time

The straightforward FFT algorithms are for complex data sequences. However, in normal data analysis, we deal with real time histories. Fortunately, it is simple to employ a complex Fourier transform to obtain real Fourier transforms. Suppose we have two time histories, $x(i)$ and $y(i)$, $i = 0, 1, 2, \ldots, N-1$. Let $x(i)$ and $y(i)$ be the real and imaginary parts of a complex function $z(i)$. Then define the Fourier transform

$$Z(k) = T \sum_{i=0}^{N-1} z(i) \exp\left[-j\pi \frac{ik}{N} \right] \qquad k = 0, 1, 2, \ldots, N-1$$

We can break $Z(k)$ down into the individual transforms, $X(k)$ and $Y(k)$, by the following formulas:

$$X(k) = \frac{Z(k) + Z^*(N-k)}{2} \tag{6.17}$$

$$Y(k) = \frac{Z(k) - Z^*(N-k)}{2j} \qquad k = \begin{cases} 0, 1, 2, \ldots, \dfrac{N}{2} & N \text{ even} \\[2mm] 0, 1, 2, \ldots, \dfrac{N-1}{2} & N \text{ odd} \end{cases} \tag{6.18}$$

Note that we require the property of a real transform processing essentially $N/2$ points in order to obtain this result. Formulas (6.17) and (6.18) are illustrated in Figure 6.5.

Double-Length Transform

The result to be discussed now leads to a capability to perform an "out-of-core" transform by doing two half-length transforms and then combining them appropriately. Consider a single $2N$ point (complex) function $z(i)$, $i = 0, 1, 2, \ldots, 2N-1$. Define two new functions consisting of the even and odd indexed points, respectively.

$$a(i) = z(2i)$$

$$b(i) = z(2i+1) \qquad i = 0, 1, 2, \ldots, N-1$$

Now compute the two Fourier transforms

$$A(k) = T \sum_{i=0}^{N-1} a(i) \exp\left(-j2\pi \frac{ik}{N} \right)$$

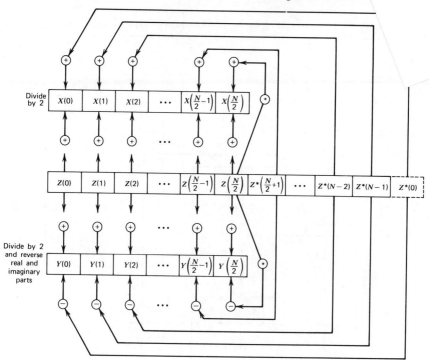

Figure 6.5 Diagram for two-at-a-time split apart formula.

and

$$B(k) = T \sum_{i=0}^{N-1} b(i) \exp\left(-j2\pi \frac{ik}{N}\right) \qquad k = 0, 1, 2, \ldots, N-1$$

These may now be combined to obtain $Z(k)$ by the formulas

$$Z(k) = A(k) + B(k) W_{2N}^k$$

$$Z(N+k) = A(k) - B(k) W_{2N}^k \qquad k = 0, 1, 2, \ldots, N-1 \qquad (6.19)$$

where

$$W_{2N} = \exp\left(-j\frac{2\pi}{2N}\right) = \exp\left(-j\frac{\pi}{N}\right) \qquad (6.20)$$

We note that the Fourier transform of a single N point time history may be obtained from a single $N/2$ point complex transform by (6.19). Formula (6.19) is depicted in Figure 6.6.

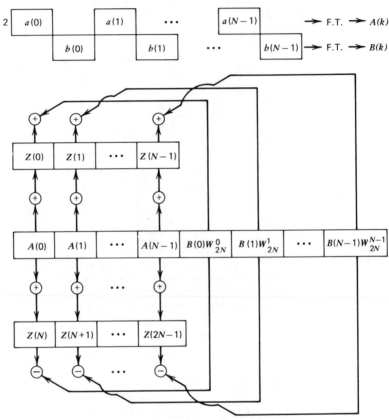

Figure 6.6   Diagram for double-length Fourier transform computation.

Fourier Series

The Fourier series is related to the complex transform in a simple way (see Hsu [1970, pp. 52–54]),

$$x(t) = \frac{1}{2}a_0 + \sum_{k=1}^{\infty} (a_k \cos k\omega_0 t + b_k \sin k\omega_0 t) \tag{6.21}$$

where

$$\omega_0 = \frac{2\pi}{P}$$

The discrete version is

$$x(i) = b\left[\frac{1}{2}a_0 + \sum_{k=1}^{N/2}\left(a_k\cos\frac{2\pi i k}{N} + b_k\sin\frac{2\pi i k}{N}\right)\right] \qquad (6.22)$$

where a_k and b_k are twice the cosine and sine transforms, respectively:

$$a_k = 2T\sum_{i=0}^{N-1}x(i)\cos\frac{2\pi i k}{N} \qquad (6.23)$$

$$b_k = 2T\sum_{i=0}^{N-1}x(i)\sin\frac{2\pi i k}{N} \qquad (6.24)$$

We note that

$$a_k = X(k) + X^*(k) \qquad (6.25)$$

$$b_k = -\left[X(k) - X^*(k)\right] \qquad (6.26)$$

Thus the classical Fourier series of a periodic function is straightforwardly obtained from the complex Fourier transform.

We should comment at this point, however, that there is substantial difference in the mathematical interpretation of the results. The development of a Fourier transform of a random function requires a considerably more elaborate mathematical framework than that of a Fourier series of a function. Questions of existence in terms of convergence of the integrals involved are substantially different. However, we are fortunate that in dealing with practical data analysis questions these subtleties rarely need concern us. Moreover, we accrue the additional advantage that the computational algorithms are suitable whether computing the Fourier series expansion of a deterministic periodic function or the finite discrete Fourier transform of a digitized sample of an infinietly long random process.

Special Inverse Transform

We have noted that the Fourier transform of a real sequence is defined by $N/2$ [or $(N-1)/2$] points due to the complex conjugate symmetry property it possesses, which are illustrated in Figure 6.1. Conversely, the inverse Fourier transform of a complex sequence which is complex conjugate symmetric is real. It is clear that the second half of the function is redundant from an information standpoint. Thus we can obtain an inverse transform by the following formula. Define the function

$$U(k) = Z(k) + Z^*(M-k) + j\left[Z(k) - Z^*(M-k)\right]W_M^{-k/2}$$

$$k = 0, 1, 2, \ldots, M-1 \qquad (6.27)$$

where $M = N/2$ or $(N-1)/2$ and $Z(k)$ is the N point Fourier transform of $z(i)$. Thus in (6.27) we have an $M = N/2$ or $(N-1)/2$ point function and do not require the complex conjugate half of the function. The inverse transform of $U(k)$ is

$$u(i) = b \sum_{k=0}^{M-1} U(k) \exp\left[j \frac{2\pi i k}{M} \right]$$

and finally we obtain $z(i)$ as the real and imaginary parts of $u(i)$. Namely,

$$z(2i) = \mathrm{Re}\, u(i)$$

$$z(2i+1) = \mathrm{Im}\, u(i) \qquad i = 0, 1, 2, \dots, M-1 \qquad (6.28)$$

The advantage of this arrangement is that this is the usual way complex functions are arranged in core storage in a FORTRAN computer program. This computation is illustrated in Figure 6.7.

If two functions are available to be inverse transformed, then the use of (6.17) and (6.18) may be reversed. We solve for $Z(k)$ and $Z^*(N-k)$:

$$Z(k) + Z^*(N-k) = 2X(k)$$

$$Z(k) - Z^*(N-k) = 2jY(k)$$

The above equations are added and subtracted so that we have

$$Z(k) = X(k) + jY(k) \qquad (6.29)$$

$$Z^*(N-k) = X(k) - jY(k) \qquad k = \begin{cases} 0, 1, 2, \dots, N/2 & N \text{ even} \\ 0, 1, 2, \dots, (N-1)/2 & N \text{ odd} \end{cases}$$

$$(6.30)$$

Thus we obtain N points to inverse transform which will result in $x(i)$ and $y(i)$ in the real and imaginary parts of $z(i)$, respectively.

Frequency Spacing and Length Considerations

We discuss two FFT algorithms in Section 6.2, one based on a power of two data points, $N = 2^p$, and a more general one based on power of 2, 3, 4, and 5, $N = 2^n 3^m 4^p 5^q$. If the number of data points is not exactly one of these numbers, then zeroes are padded into the end of the time series. The effect of the zeroes is to change the spacing of the points of the frequency domain function. If the original length is N, and if a transform was

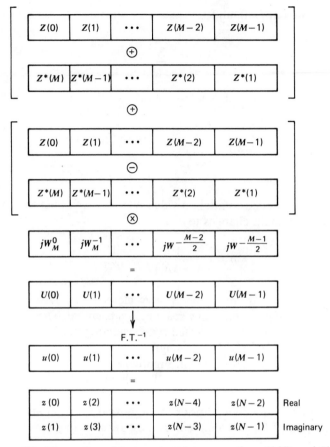

Figure 6.7   Illustration of inverse transform equations (6.27) and (6.28).

computed, then the spacing in the frequency domain is

$$b = \frac{1}{NT} = \frac{S}{N} = \frac{F}{N/2} \qquad (6.31)$$

The computed values are

$$X(k) \begin{cases} k = 0, 1, 2, \dots, \dfrac{N}{2} & N \text{ even} \\[2mm] k = 0, 1, 2, \dots, \dfrac{N-1}{2} & N \text{ odd} \end{cases} \qquad (6.32)$$

where

$$X(k) = X(kb) \qquad (6.33)$$

The first point is at $f=0$, and

$$X(0) = \sum_{i=0}^{N-1} x(i) \tag{6.34}$$

The last point is at $f = F$, if N is even and

$$X\left(\frac{N}{2}\right) = \sum_{i=0}^{N/2-1} \left[x(2i) - x(2i+1) \right] \tag{6.35}$$

Padding with Zeroes

If ΔN zeroes are added to attain a value $N' = N + \Delta N$, then the spacing in the frequency domain changes to

$$b' = \frac{1}{(N+\Delta N)T} = \frac{1}{N'T} \tag{6.36}$$

For large N', ΔN is small and N very close to N'. Hence $b \approx b'$. For small N', the change in frequency spacing is substantial. The interpretation of the results may best be illustrated by considering the Fourier transform of a boxcar function, $u_{P/2}(t)$ of length P. The function $u_{P/2}(t)$ and its transform, $U_{P/2}(f)$ are illustrated in Figure 6.8.

If $NT = P$ and we compute the FFT without padding with zeroes, the result is Figure 6.9.

If N zeroes are added ($N/2$ prior to the boxcar function and $N/2$ after) and the $2N$ point FFT is computed, then the result is Figure 6.10.

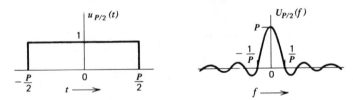

Figure 6.8   Boxcar function and its transform.

Figure 6.9   FFT without zeroes.

Figure 6.10   FFT with N zeroes added.

Hence we interpolate points on the function $U_{P/2}(f)$ when we add zeroes. As more and more zeroes are added, more and more points are interpolated. When nonintegral multiples of N zeroes are added, merely different points of $U_{P/2}(f)$ are computed. Similar types of interpolation occur on any function for which zeroes have been added.

We emphasize later that although the computational spacing, b, changes, the effective *resolution* bandwidth, B_e, remains the same no matter how many zeroes are added.

Record Length

All computers employed for digital time series analysis impose constraints on the number of data points from a digitized time history that can be accommodated in a single segment. Depending on the digitizing rate, then, the record length is restricted to some amount

$$P = NT = \frac{N}{S}$$

Typical maximum values for N in a minicomputer system range from 1024 (2^{10}) to 8192 (2^{13}). Normally, the FFT algorithms are designed for N equal to a power of 2. Typical medium- to large-scale (midi to maxi) computer restrictions on N range from 1024 to 32,768 (2^{15}). Also, the implementation of the power of 2, 3, 4, and 5 algorithm is often done on the larger computer.

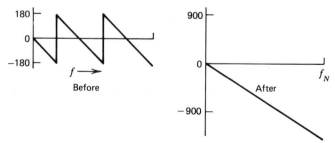

Figure 6.11   Phase straightening.

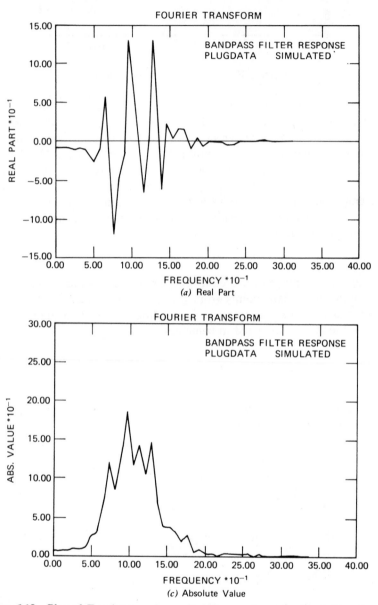

Figure 6.12 Plot of Fourier transform of response of narrow band filter (narrow band noise) in terms of (a) real part, (b) imaginary part, (c) absolute value, and (d) phase.

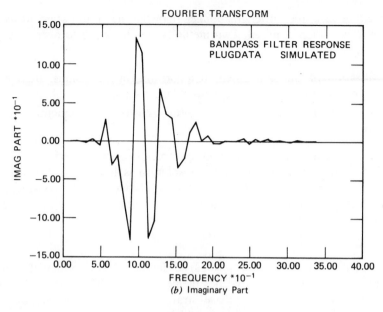

(b) Imaginary Part

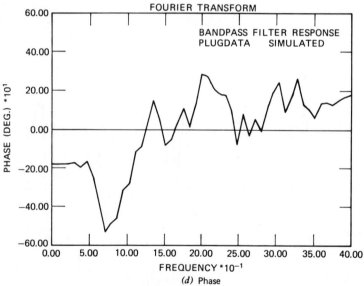

(d) Phase

Figure 6.12 (*Continued*).

In either case, record lengths longer than the maximum segment length $P_s = N_s T$ are often required. Two methods are employed to overcome this limitation.

• Utilization of the double-length algorithm, or extensions, thereof, to obtain a true Fourier transform of a larger segment.
• Computation of an average transform, by way of a segmenting procedure.

In the first case, a finer resolution spectrum is obtained, with resolution $b = 1/NT$. In the second case, the resolution is limited by the segment length and is $b_s = 1/N_s T$. When noisy data is involved, the consideration of degrees of freedom is important and the relationship of the two methods is discussed in Chapter 8.

Phase Straightening

We capitalize the arctangent in (6.12) to denote that the principal value is computed, that is, a value that lies in the range $-180°$ to $180°$. A useful procedure which we term "phase straightening" expands the range of phase and removes discontinuities which occur at $180°$ by assuming the

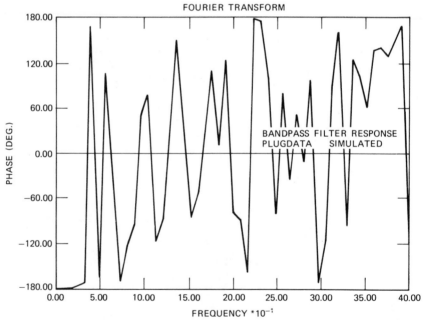

Figure 6.13 Plot of phase of Figure 6.12*d* without phase straightening.

phase function is a reasonably "smooth" function of frequency. One checks for a large jump as would happen when phase might go from $(180-\varepsilon)°$ to $-(180-\varepsilon)°$. This would be a jump $\Delta\phi=(180-\varepsilon)°+(180-\varepsilon)°$ $=360°-2\varepsilon$ when it could just as well be represented by a jump of 2ε since $-(180-\varepsilon)°=180+\varepsilon$. Subroutine TTRAN in Figure A.7 (Appendix A) uses this technique.

The effect of phase straightening is depicted in Figure 6.11. A plot of linear phase (corresponding to a simple time shift) is depicted before and after phase straightening as it would appear in a typical computer plot. Figure 6.12 shows the Fourier transform of narrow bandpass filtered pseudo-random white noise, in terms of real and imaginary parts, gain, and straightened phase. Figure 6.13 is the same phase, but in terms of the principal value of the arctangent (unstraightened). This plot illustrates the much "hashier" appearance of unstraightened phase.

6.2   FAST FOURIER TRANSFORM ALGORITHM

In this section we present a brief derivation of the fast Fourier transform based on a matrix multiplication approach. This derivation will correspond to the *Cooley–Tukey* [Cooley and Tukey, 1965] version of the FFT. A second version of the algorithm, termed the *Sande–Tukey* [Gentleman and Sande, 1966] version is also presented. These two versions may be considered canonical in the sense that all FFT algorithms reduce to one of these two basic forms. For reasons described later, the Cooley–Tukey version is referred to as "decimation in time" and the Sande–Tukey version as "decimation in frequency."

We present three computer programs. The first two were rated second and first, respectively, in a survey [Maynard, 1973] of 10 available programs. The first [Otnes, Nathans, and Enochson, 1969], is by far the simplest to code and will be used by the reader in solving the computer problems in this chapter. It is based on a power of 2. The second [Singleton, 1969] is more extensive and based on powers of 2, 3, 4, and 5. The third allows out-of-core (long record length) transforms and is also due to Singleton [1967].

Matrix Formulation of FFT Algorithm

We now employ the previously introduced notation for the complex exponential which has come into common use.

$$W_N = \exp\left[-j\frac{2\pi}{N}\right] = \cos\frac{2\pi}{N} - j\sin\frac{2\pi}{N} \tag{6.37}$$

We note that the sines and cosines in the Fourier transform equations become

$$W_N^{ik} = \exp\left[-j\frac{2\pi i k}{N} \right] = \cos\frac{2\pi}{N}ik - j\sin\frac{2\pi}{N}ik \qquad (6.38)$$

These values of W_{16} are illustrated in Figure 6.14 and we note that these values are termed *the Nth roots of unity* in the theory of functions of a complex variable. The derivation of some very complicated trigonometric formulas may be obtained from (6.38); we leave this to Exercise 6.11.

In McCowan [1966], an approach to a characterization of an FFT algorithm is presented. This explanation is in terms of factoring a matrix, and this approach is developed further in Theilheimer [1969]. We can motivate the derivation in matrix terms by considering an analogous situation, the decomposition of an aircraft maneuver into its roll, pitch, and yaw components. A rotation of plane coordinates through an angle θ can be written in matrix form as

$$\begin{pmatrix} x' \\ y' \end{pmatrix} = \begin{pmatrix} \cos\theta & -\sin\theta \\ \sin\theta & \cos\theta \end{pmatrix}\begin{pmatrix} x \\ y \end{pmatrix} \qquad (6.39)$$

In three dimensions, any general rotation can be written in terms of three

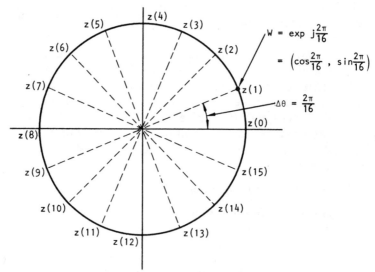

Figure 6.14   Illustration of data points arranged on unit circle in complex plane.

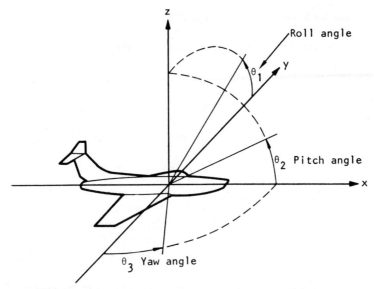

Figure 6.15   Illustration of roll, pitch, and yaw components.

two-dimensional components (see Figure 6.15), roll (rotation in (y,z) coordinate plane), pitch (rotation in (x,z) coordinate plane), and yaw (rotation in (y,z) plane).

Thus the total rotation is the product of three two-dimensional matrices:

$$T(\theta_1,\theta_2,\theta_3)=\underbrace{\begin{bmatrix} \cos\theta_3 & -\sin\theta_3 & 0 \\ \sin\theta_3 & \cos\theta_3 & 0 \\ 0 & 0 & 1 \end{bmatrix}}_{\text{Yaw}}\underbrace{\begin{bmatrix} \cos\theta_2 & 0 & -\sin\theta_2 \\ 0 & 1 & 0 \\ \sin\theta_2 & 0 & \cos\theta_2 \end{bmatrix}}_{\text{Pitch}}$$

$$\times\underbrace{\begin{bmatrix} 1 & 0 & 0 \\ 0 & \cos\theta_1 & -\sin\theta_1 \\ 0 & \sin\theta_1 & \cos\theta_1 \end{bmatrix}}_{\text{Roll}} \tag{6.40}$$

The actual computations necessary for performing a transformation of coordinates can thus be broken down into three two-dimensional matrix vector multiplications rather than one three-dimensional matrix vector multiplication. The number of operations for the single three-dimensional multiplication is

$$\text{Number of operations (3-dimensional)}=3^2=9$$

whereas for three two-dimensional multiplications,

$$\text{Number of operations (3 2-dimensional)} = 3 \times 2^2 = 12$$

For the four-dimensional case,

$$\text{Number of operations (4-dimensional)} = 4^2 = 16$$

$$\text{Number of operations (4 2-dimensional)} = 2^2 + 2^2 + 2^2 + 2^2$$

$$= 2(2+2+2+2) = 16$$

For a five-dimensional rotation,

$$\text{Number of operations (5-dimensional)} = 5^2 = 25$$

$$\text{Number of operations (5 2-dimensional)} = 2(2+2+2+2+2) = 20$$

The potential time savings of this approach when the dimension of the transformation becomes large enough are readily seen. Roughly speaking, this is what happens for FFT algorithms. A discrete, finite Fourier transform of N data points may be viewed as a rotation in N-dimensional space. In mathematical terms, it is an orthogonal linear transformation. The exponent for W also specifies its position in the matrix. In matrix equation form,

$$
\begin{bmatrix}
X_0 \\
X_1 \\
X_2 \\
\vdots \\
X_{N-1}
\end{bmatrix}
$$

$$
=
\begin{bmatrix}
W^{0 \cdot 0} & W^{0 \cdot 1} & W^{0 \cdot 2} & \cdots & W^{0 \cdot (N-1)} \\
W^{1 \cdot 0} & W^{1 \cdot 1} & W^{1 \cdot 2} & \cdots & W^{1 \cdot (N-1)} \\
W^{2 \cdot 0} & W^{2 \cdot 1} & W^{2 \cdot 2} & \cdots & W^{2 \cdot (N-1)} \\
\vdots & \vdots & \vdots & & \vdots \\
W^{(N-1) \cdot 0} & W^{(N-1) \cdot 1} & W^{(N-1) \cdot 2} & \cdots & W^{(N-1)(N-1)}
\end{bmatrix}
\begin{bmatrix}
x_0 \\
x_1 \\
x_2 \\
\vdots \\
x_{N-1}
\end{bmatrix}
\tag{6.41}
$$

or in compact matrix notation,

$$\mathbf{X} = \mathbf{W}\mathbf{x}$$

For the special case $N = 2^3 = 8$, $p = 3$, the explicit matrix is

$$
\mathbf{W} = \begin{bmatrix}
1 & 1 & 1 & 1 & 1 & 1 & 1 & 1 \\
1 & W^1 & W^2 & W^3 & W^4 & W^5 & W^6 & W^7 \\
1 & W^2 & W^4 & W^6 & W^8 & W^{10} & W^{12} & W^{14} \\
1 & W^3 & W^6 & W^9 & W^{12} & W^{15} & W^{18} & W^{21} \\
1 & W^4 & W^8 & W^{12} & W^{16} & W^{20} & W^{24} & W^{28} \\
1 & W^5 & W^{10} & W^{15} & W^{20} & W^{25} & W^{30} & W^{35} \\
1 & W^6 & W^{12} & W^{18} & W^{24} & W^{30} & W^{36} & W^{42} \\
1 & W^7 & W^{14} & W^{21} & W^{28} & W^{35} & W^{42} & W^{49}
\end{bmatrix} \tag{6.42}
$$

This matrix can be factored into $(p+1=4)$ matrices,

$$
\mathbf{W} = \mathbf{W}_3 \mathbf{W}_2 \mathbf{W}_1 \mathbf{W}_0 \tag{6.43}
$$

or, in general, the factorization is

$$
\mathbf{W} = \mathbf{W}_p \mathbf{W}_{p-1} \cdots \mathbf{W}_1 \mathbf{W}_0 \tag{6.44}
$$

The last matrix, $\mathbf{W}_p$, is always a permutation matrix, which performs the reversed bit memory location reordering.

Theilheimer [1969] gives rules for obtaining a factorization similar to (6.44). The matrices for the Cooley–Tukey factorization, when $N = 2^p$, are easily developed. For the specific example of $N = 2^3$, the matrices are developed in McCowan [1966] and are

$$
\mathbf{W}_0 = \begin{bmatrix}
1 & 0 & 0 & 0 & W^0 & 0 & 0 & 0 \\
0 & 1 & 0 & 0 & 0 & W^0 & 0 & 0 \\
0 & 0 & 1 & 0 & 0 & 0 & W^0 & 0 \\
0 & 0 & 0 & 1 & 0 & 0 & 0 & W^0 \\
1 & 0 & 0 & 0 & W^4 & 0 & 0 & 0 \\
0 & 1 & 0 & 0 & 0 & W^4 & 0 & 0 \\
0 & 0 & 1 & 0 & 0 & 0 & W^4 & 0 \\
0 & 0 & 0 & 1 & 0 & 0 & 0 & W^4
\end{bmatrix}
$$

$$
\mathbf{W}_1 = \begin{bmatrix}
1 & 0 & W^0 & 0 & 0 & 0 & 0 & 0 \\
0 & 1 & 0 & W^0 & 0 & 0 & 0 & 0 \\
1 & 0 & W^4 & 0 & 0 & 0 & 0 & 0 \\
0 & 1 & 0 & W^4 & 0 & 0 & 0 & 0 \\
0 & 0 & 0 & 0 & 1 & 0 & W^2 & 0 \\
0 & 0 & 0 & 0 & 0 & 1 & 0 & W^2 \\
0 & 0 & 0 & 0 & 1 & 0 & W^6 & 0 \\
0 & 0 & 0 & 0 & 0 & 1 & 0 & W^6
\end{bmatrix}
$$

$$
\mathbf{W}_2 = \begin{bmatrix}
1 & W^0 & 0 & 0 & 0 & 0 & 0 & 0 \\
1 & W^4 & 0 & 0 & 0 & 0 & 0 & 0 \\
0 & 0 & 1 & W^2 & 0 & 0 & 0 & 0 \\
0 & 0 & 1 & W^6 & 0 & 0 & 0 & 0 \\
0 & 0 & 0 & 0 & 1 & W^1 & 0 & 0 \\
0 & 0 & 0 & 0 & 1 & W^5 & 0 & 0 \\
0 & 0 & 0 & 0 & 0 & 0 & 1 & W^3 \\
0 & 0 & 0 & 0 & 0 & 0 & 1 & W^7
\end{bmatrix}
$$

The term W^0 is, of course, the same as unity. It was used rather than 1 to illustrate the symmetry. When the programming is specialized to take advantage of the specific forms of the matrices (i.e., do not multiply by zeroes or ones), the time savings of the algorithm result.

Cooley–Tukey Version

If we denote the vector of data values after the lth matrix multiplication by A_l, then the specific programming equation for the Cooley–Tukey version of the algorithm becomes

$$
A_l(k_0, k_1, \ldots, k_{l-2}, \overset{\overset{\textstyle k_{l-1}}{\downarrow}}{0}, i_{p-l-1}, \ldots, 0)
$$

$$
= A_{l-1}(k_0, k_1, \ldots, k_{l-2}, \overset{\overset{\textstyle i_{p-l}}{\downarrow}}{0}, i_{p-l-1}, \ldots, i_0)
$$

$$
+ A_{l-1}(k_0, k_1, \ldots, k_{l-2}, 1, i_{p-l-1}, \ldots, i_0)
$$

$$
\times W^{(k_{l-2}2^{l-2} + \cdots + k_0)\, \overset{\overset{\textstyle i_{p-l}}{\downarrow}}{1}\, \cdot 2^{p-l}} \qquad l = 1, 2, \ldots, p \qquad (6.45a)
$$

$$
A_l(k_0, k_1, \ldots, k_{l-2}, \overset{\overset{\textstyle k_{l-1}}{\downarrow}}{0}, i_{p-l-1}, \ldots, i_0)
$$

$$
= A_{l-1}(k_0, k_1, \ldots, k_{l-2}, \overset{\overset{\textstyle i_{p-l}}{\downarrow}}{0}, i_{p-l-1}, \ldots, i_0)
$$

$$
- A_{l-1}(k_0, k_1, \ldots, k_{l-2}, 1, i_{p-l-1}, \ldots, i_0)
$$

$$
\times W^{(k_{l-2}2^{l-2} + \cdots + k_0)\, \overset{\overset{\textstyle i_{p-l}}{\downarrow}}{1}\, \cdot 2^{p-l}} \qquad l = 1, 2, \ldots, p \qquad (6.45b)
$$

These equations simplify considerably when implemented in a FORTRAN program (see Figure 6.16). There we note that the innermost portion of the loop (statement numbers 48 and 49 of Figure 6.16) becomes

$$X(IJ) = X(IJ) + X(II)*CXCS$$

$$X(II) = X(IJ) - X(II)*CXCS \tag{6.46}$$

where

$$CXCS = W^{(k_{l-2}2^{l-2} + \cdots + k_0)2^{p-l}}$$

$$IJ = (k_0, k_1, \ldots, k_{l-2}, 0, i_{p-l-1}, \ldots, i_0)$$

$$II = (k_0, k_1, \ldots, k_{l-2}, 1, i_{p-l-1}, \ldots, i_0)$$

We further observe that (6.46) is the equation for a two-point Fourier transform (see Exercise 6.5) except for the complex exponential factor. The reader should recognize the following characteristics:

- The innermost loop is a two-point Fourier transform modified by a complex exponential and corresponds in form to the double-length formula given by (6.19).
- The original data is the array A_0 and the time index is decomposed into its binary components and the transform works on one of these components at a time in each stage of the recursion.
- The recursion begins with the high-order bit of the time index (i_{p-1}) and transforms it to the low-order component of the frequency index (k_0).
- The effect of the reversal of the order of the components of the index is that the final array is

$$A_l(k_{p-1}, k_{p-2}, \ldots, k_0) = X(k_0, k_1, \ldots, k_{p-1}) \tag{6.47}$$

That is, the data must be unscrambled according to the bit reversal by permuting the components of the array if the frequency values are to occur in natural order for printing and plotting.

The algorithm for bit reversal used in the FFT program of Figure 6.16 is the following:

- Test leading bits of the previous index, setting them equal to 0 until a zero bit is found.
- Set this zero bit to a one bit, and this is the desired index. For example, when $p = 3$, we begin with $000_2 = 0_{10}$. Obtained from this is $100_2 = 4_{10}$, which is $001_2 = 1_{10}$ with bits reversed. Obtained next is $010_2 = 2_{10}$, etc.

```
      SUBROUTINE FFTRAN (SIGN,T,X,NPOW)                              90010
C                                                                    90020
C         COOLEY-TUKEY METHOD OF FOURIER TRANSFORM                   90030
C         INCLUDES SINE COSINE COMPUTATION AND                       90040
C         REARRANGING DATA ACCORDING TO REVERSE BIT ADDRESSSES       90050
C                                                                    90060
C         SIGN = FOURIER DIRECTION TRANSFORM FLAG                    90070
C              = -1. FOR DIRECT TRANSFORM                            90080
C              = 1. FOR INVERSE TRANSFORM                            90090
C         T    = DELTA TIME                                          90100
C         X    = LOCATION OF FOURIER TRANSFORM BLOCK                 90110
C         NPOW = POWER OF 2 (BLOCK SIZE =2**NPOW)                    90120
C                                                                    90130
      DIMENSION X(1), CS(2), MSK(13)                                 90140
      COMPLEX X,CXCS,HOLD,XA                                         90150
      EQUIVALENCE (CXCS,CS)                                          90160
      NMAX=2**NPOW                                                   90170
      ZZ=6.283185306*SIGN/FLOAT(NMAX)                                90180
      DELTA=T                                                        90190
      IF (SIGN) 10,10,5                                              90200
   5  DELTA=1./(T*FLOAT(NMAX))                                       90210
  10  MSK(1)=NMAX/2                                                  90220
      DO 15 I=2,NPOW                                                 90230
  15  MSK(I)=MSK(I-1)/2                                              90240
      NN=NMAX                                                        90250
      MM=2                                                           90260
C                                                                    90270
C         LOOP OVER NPOW LAYERS                                      90280
C                                                                    90290
      DO 45 LAYER=1,NPOW                                             90300
      NN=NN/2                                                        90310
      NW=0                                                           90320
      DO 40 I=1,MM,2                                                 90330
      II=NN*I                                                        90340
C                                                                    90350
C         CXCS = CEXP(2*PI*NW*SIGN/NMAX)                             90360
C                                                                    90370
      W=FLOAT(NW)*ZZ                                                 90380
      CS(1)=COS(W)                                                   90390
      CS(2)=SIN(W)                                                   90400
C                                                                    90410
C         COMPUTE ELEMENTS FOR BOTH HALVES OF EACH BLOCK             90420
C                                                                    90430
      DO 20 J=1,NN                                                   90440
```

Figure 6.16a Fast Fourier transform routine, part I. Routine written by L. D. Enochson, Howard Nathans, and R. K. Otnes.

(We have been told that computer instructions exist to accomplish this, but know of no specific computers.) Both the C–T and S–T versions require bit reversals to rearrange the final results in the natural method of implementing the algorithms. Recall, however, that tricks such as rearranging the order of the data according to bit-reversed addresses can result in alternative ways to implement the algorithms.

The above is accomplished in lines 55 to 61 of Figure 6.16. The IF statement in line 57 is the testing of leading bits. The same code is repeated

```
         II=II+1                                          90450
         IJ=II-NN                                         90460
         XA=CXCS*X(II)                                    90470
         X(II)=X(IJ)-XA                                   90480
   20    X(IJ)=X(IJ)+XA                                   90490
                                                          90500
C            BUMP UP SERIES BY 2                          90510
C                                                         90520
C            COMPUTE REVERSE ADDRESSS                     90530
C                                                         90540
         DO 25 LOC=2,NPOW                                 90550
         LL=NW-MSK(LOC)                                   90560
         IF (LL) 30,35,25                                 90570
   25    NW=LL                                            90580
   30    NW=MSK(LOC)+NW                                   90590
         GO TO 40                                         90600
   35    NW=MSK(LOC+1)                                    90610
   40    CONTINUE                                         90620
                                                          90630
C            DO FINAL REARRANGEMENT                       90640
C            ALSO MULTIPLY BY DELTA                       90650
C                                                         90660
   45    MM=MM*2                                          90670
         NW=0                                             90680
         DO 80 I=1,NMAX                                   90690
         NW1=NW+1                                         90700
         HOLD=X(NW1)                                      90710
         IF (NW1-I) 60,55,50                              90720
   50    X(NW1)=X(I)*DELTA                                90730
   55    X(I)=HOLD*DELTA                                  90740
                                                          90750
C            BUMP UP SERIES BY 1                          90760
C            COMPUTE REVERSE ADDRESS                      90770
C                                                         90780
   60    DO 65 LOC=1,NPOW                                 90790
         LL=NW-MSK(LOC)                                   90800
         IF (LL) 70,75,65                                 90810
   65    NW=LL                                            90820
   70    NW=MSK(LOC)+NW                                   90830
         GO TO 80                                         90840
   75    NW=MSK(LOC+1)                                    90850
   80    CONTINUE                                         90860
         RETURN                                           90870
         END                                              90880
```

Figure 6.16b Fast Fourier transform routine, part II.

in lines 79 to 85. The first occurrence is for the computation of sine/cosine arguments, and the second for the final unscrambling of the data.

Further aspects of the FFT of Figure 6.16 are the following:

- Sines and cosines of the complex exponential are computed from FORTRAN library subroutines (code lines 39 and 40).
- The dt and df from the Fourier integral are included in the computation. These are the T and b of (6.2) and (6.13), respectively (code lines 73 and 74).

This algorithm is to be used to solve the even-numbered exercises at the end of the chapter.

An alternative FFT is the Sande–Tukey version, which is derived in Otnes and Enochson [1972]. The recursion equations are the following:

$$\hat{A}_l(k_0, k_1, \ldots, k_{l-2}, \overset{\overset{\displaystyle k_{l-1}}{\downarrow}}{0}, i_{p-l-1}, \ldots, i_0)$$

$$= [\hat{A}_{l-1}(k_0, k_1, \ldots, k_{l-2}, \overset{\overset{\displaystyle i_{p-l}}{\downarrow}}{0}, i_{p-l-1}, \ldots, i_0)$$

$$+ \hat{A}_{l-1}(k_0, k_1, \ldots, k_{l-2}, 1, i_{p-l-1}, \ldots, i_0)]$$

$$\times W^{(i_{p-l-1}2^{p-l-1} + \cdots + i_0)(0)\,2^{l-1}} \quad \overset{\overset{\displaystyle k_{l-1}}{\downarrow}}{} \tag{6.48a}$$

$$\hat{A}_l(k_0, k_1, \ldots, k_{l-2}, \overset{\overset{\displaystyle k_{l-1}}{\downarrow}}{1}, i_{p-l-1}, \ldots, i_0)$$

$$= [\hat{A}_{l-1}(k_0, k_1, \ldots, k_{l-2}, \overset{\overset{\displaystyle i_{p-l}}{\downarrow}}{0}, i_{p-l-1}, \ldots, i_0)$$

$$- A_{l-1}(k_0, k_1, \ldots, k_{l-2}, 1, i_{p-l-1}, \ldots, i_0)]$$

$$\times W^{(i_{p-l-1}2^{p-l-1} + \cdots + i_0)(1)\,2^{l-1}} \quad \overset{\overset{\displaystyle k_{l-1}}{\downarrow}}{} \tag{6.48b}$$

The innermost loop in a FORTRAN program would appear slightly different from the C–T version:

$$X(IJ) = X(IJ) + X(II)$$

$$X(II) = (X(IJ) - X(II)) * CXCS$$

In the S–T case the complex exponential is

$$CXCS = W^{(i_{p-l-1}2^{p-l-1} + \cdots + i_0)2^{l-1}}$$

Again we have a two-point Fourier transform modified by a complex exponential.

In principle, the two versions require the same amount of arithmetic. In practice, the Sande–Tukey version is often simpler for data arranged in natural order because of the exponent for W. Likewise, the C–T version can be simpler for scrambled data [Otnes and Enochson, 1972, p. 154]. In both the C–T and S–T versions, from (6.45) and (6.48) it is seen that the index required for A_l or $\hat{A}_l$ can be broken into two parts:

$$\textit{Part 1}$$

$$\overbrace{k_0 2^{p-1} + k_1 2^{p-2} + \cdots + k_{l-2} 2^{p-l-3} + k_{l-1} 2^{p-l-2}}$$

$$(6.49)$$

$$\textit{Part 2}$$

$$\overbrace{+ i_{p-l-1} 2^{p-l-1} + \cdots + i_0}$$

Note that exponent $(k_{l-1} 2^{l-1} + \cdots + k_0) i_p 2^{p-l}$ in the C–T twiddle factor is a bit-reversed version of the first part of the index equation (6.49) multiplied by a power of 2. In the S-T version, the exponent $(i_{p-l-1} 2^{p-l-1} + \cdots + i_0) 2^{p-1}$ is the second part of the index equation (6.49)—not bit-reversed and multiplied by a power of 2. Thus in some instances it is easier to perform the tally necessary to obtain the complex exponential argument for the S-T version than for the C-T version.

The C–T version is often referred to as "decimation in time." If we inspect the diagram of Figure 6.17, termed a signal flow graph, we observe that the algorithm begins with complex exponential values spaced by $N/2$ locations. Hence the data is decimated in time by a factor $N/2$. Likewise,

INDEX	BINARY	ARRAY	W_3	REVERSED	INDEX
0	000	X(0)	A(0)	000	0
1	001	X(1)	A(1)	100	1
2	010	X(2)	A(2)	010	2
3	011	X(3)	A(3)	110	3
4	100	X(4)	A(4)	001	4
5	101	X(5)	A(5)	101	5
6	110	X(6)	A(6)	011	6
7	111	X(7)	A(7)	111	7

Figure 6.17 Cooley–Tukey algorithm diagram, $N=8$, $p=3$ [McCowan, 1966].

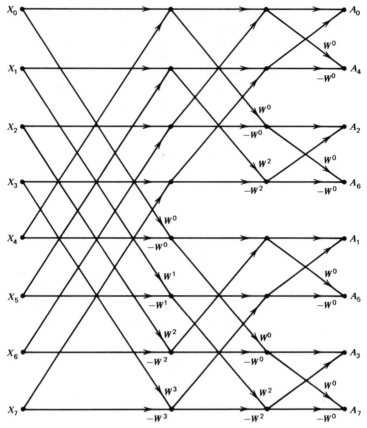

Figure 6.18 Sande–Tukey signal flow graph. From "What Is the Fast Fourier Transform," *IEEE Transactions on Audio Electroacoustics* Vol. AU-15, No. 2, pp. 45–55, 1969.

the flow graph of Figure 6.18 illustrates the S–T algorithm and we complete the algorithm with complex exponential values spaced by $N/2$ locations, hence "decimation in frequency."

MAC Algorithm

The FORTRAN program of Figure 6.16 is a straightforward version of the C–T algorithm, performed on data in natural order and unscrambled at the completion. It performs either a forward or inverse transform on $N = 2^p$ complex data points. In addition to the direction of the transform and the location of the data, the routine must also be provided with T and p. In this routine p is restricted to a maximum of 13.

The following statements define data arrays:

```
15          DIMENSION X(1), CS(2), MSK(13)
16          COMPLEX X, CXCS, HOLD, XA
17          EQUIVALENCE (CXCS, CS)
```

This statement evaluates $N = 2^p$, given $p \leqslant 13$:

```
18          NMAX = 2**NPOW
```

The following computes $ZZ = 2\pi / N$ for use in the complex exponential:

```
19          ZZ = 6.283185306*SIGN/FLOAT(NMAX)
```

For the direct transform DELTA = T, for the inverse transform DELTA $= b = 1/NT$

```
20          DELTA = T
21          IF (SIGN) 10, 10, 5
22     5    DELTA = 1./(T*FLOAT(NMAX))
```

A set of test bits for use in the bit reversal are generated next.

```
23    10    MSK(1) = NMAX/2
24          DO 15 1 = 2, NPOW
25    15    MSK(I) = MSK(I-1)/2
```

This array becomes

$$
\begin{array}{ll}
\text{MSK (1)} = & 10\text{-}\text{-}\text{-}\text{-}0 \\
\text{MSK (2)} = & 010\text{-}\text{-}\text{-}0 \\
\quad \vdots & \quad \vdots \\
\text{MSK (p)} = & \underbrace{000\text{-}\text{-}01}_{p \text{ bits}}
\end{array}
$$

The following instructions form the innermost loop of the FFT computation:

```
44          DO 20 J = 1, NN
45          II = II + 1
46          IJ = II - NN
47          XA = CXCS*X(II)
48          X(II) = X(IJ) - XA
49    20    X(IJ) = X(IJ) + XA
```

In the above, CXCS is the complex exponential

$$W^{(k_{l-2}2^{l-2}+\cdots+k_0)2^{p-l}}$$

and lines 48 and 49 are (6.45b) and (6.45a), which amount to a two-term Fourier transform modified by the rotation factor. Notice that the addresses of the data are spaced by the factor NN (bit i_{p-l} or k_{l-1}), which is also the number of times this inner loop is executed. The computation of $II = II + 1$ is to adjust for the fact that FORTRAN indices go from 1 to N and our equation indices go from 0 to $N-1$.

The following statements initialize the argument for the complex exponential (NW=0), compute the complex exponential, determine the reversed bit address needed in the complex exponential argument, and control the loop over the high order portion of the data index. Thus I is Part 1 of (6.49) whereas J in the innermost loop is Part 2 of (6.49).

```
31              NN = NN/2
32              NW = 0
33              DO 40 I = 1, MM, 2
34              II = NN*I
35      C
36      C          CXCS = CEXP(2*PI*NW*SIGN/NMAX)
37      C
38              W = FLOAT(NW)*ZZ
39              CS(1) = COS(W)
40              CS(2) = SIN(W)
 :               :
 :               :
50      C
51      C       BUMP UP SERIES BY 2
52      C
53      C       CONTINUE REVERSE ADDRESS
54      C
55              DO 25 LOC = 2, NPOW
56              LL = NW - MSK(LOC)
57              IF (LL) 30, 35, 25
58      25      NW = LL
59      30      NW = MSK(LOC) + NW
60              GO TO 40
61      35      NW = MSK(LOC + 1)
62      40      CONTINUE
```

In (6.45) it appears that we require a multiply by 2^{p-l} in the sine/cosine argument computation. This says shift the bits $p - l$ places to the left. We avoid this by generating this index from the high-order bit position and then work down. Hence this multiply is incorporated directly.

The new reversed bit address NW is determined by the previously mentioned rules, which involve testing the high-order bits of the previous reversed bit address NW. Note the use of the array MSK.

Note that NN, which controls the number of times through the inner loop, is divided by 2 each time at statement 31. Therefore, we start with $N/2$ passes and end up with one pass through the inner loop.

The following statements initialize the limits of the indices, NN for the inner loop, MM for the middle loop. The outermost loop index, LL, which corresponds to the l subscript in (6.45) runs from 1 to p.

```
26              NN = MAX
27              MM = 2
28    C
29    C              LOOP OVER NPOW LAYERS
30              DO 45 LAYER = 1, NPOW
 :                     :
63    45        MM = MM*2
```

We observe that MM, which controls the number of executions of the middle loop begins at 2 and doubles each time and is stepped by 2. Thus the central computation done at lines 47–49 is accomplished N_{ops} times given by

$$N_{ops} = \frac{MM}{2} \times \frac{NN}{2}$$

$$N_{ops} = \underbrace{\frac{2}{2} \cdot \frac{N}{2} + \frac{4}{2} \cdot \frac{N/2}{2} + \cdots + \frac{N}{2} \cdot 1}_{p \text{ times}}$$

$$= p \cdot \frac{N}{2}$$

Thus we have approximately $Np/2$ complex multiplies, complex adds, and complex subtracts in the central part of the FFT.

The final operation to be done is to unscramble the data according to reversed bit addressing and multiply by T or b. Statement numbers 68 through 86 accomplish this.

```
64    C
65    C              DO FINAL REARRANGEMENT
66    C              ALSO MULTIPLY BY DELTA
67    C
```

```
68              NW = 0
69              DO 80 I = 1, NMAX
70              NW1 = NW + 1
71              HOLD = X(NW1)
72              IF(NW1 − I) 60, 55, 50
73      50      X(NW1) = X(I)*DELTA
74      55      X(I) = HOLD*DELTA
72      C
76      C                   BUMP UP SERIES BY 1
77      C                   COMPUTE REVERSE ADDRESS
78      C
79      60      DO 65 LOC = 1, NPOW
80              LL = NW − MSK(LOC)
81              IF (LL) 70, 75, 65
82      65      NW = LL
83      70      NW = MSK(LOC) + NW
84              GO TO 80
85      75      NW = MSK(LOC + 1)
86      80      CONTINUE
```

This subroutine is short and straightforward. It can be speeded slightly by scrambling the data first, which avoids the address scrambling to get the sine/cosine argument. This would also make it convenient to generate the sines and cosines recursively. However, we note that if we are willing to sacrifice storage to increase speed by picking up sines and cosines from a table, then the prescrambling offers no advantage since we can scramble the table of sine/cosines.

Further efficiencies are obtained by noting that since $NW = 0$ in the first pass through the middle loop, we do not need to multiply by CXCS, but can get by with adds and subtracts only. We leave the coding of this modification to Exercise 6.13. Attention is called to these possibilities to emphasize the fact that there are an endless number of detail modifications that can be made to the FFT to increase its efficiency. The value of these enhancements depends on the expense of computation relative to the effort involved in programming. There are certainly no general rules to guide one as to what is best for his particular purposes.

Singleton Algorithm for Powers of 2, 3, 4, and 5

Singleton [1969] has developed an FFT program for arbitrary mixed radixes. This code is most efficient when the factors are restricted to 2, 3, 4, and 5. In this form, Maynard [1973] gives the code a very high rating in both flexibility and efficiency. The major disadvantage of the code is its complexity, for it consists of some 400 FORTRAN statements. We describe the features of the algorithm here but refer the reader to the original reference or to the Maynard report for a copy of the code. Table 6.2 presents all numbers from 2 to 5000 that can be represented as powers of 2, 3, and 5. This illustrates the considerable additional denseness of these numbers as compared to powers of 2.

Singleton defines the direct transform as

$$\alpha_k = \sum_{i=0}^{N-1} x_j \exp\left[\frac{j2\pi ik}{N} \right] \qquad (6.50)$$

Hence his direct transform is our inverse except for the factor b. The user of his code must use care to distinguish this difference.

The mixed radix FFT for $N = N_1 N_2 \cdots N_p$ is based on the fact that when the Fourier transform is represented in matrix form,

$$\mathbf{X} = \mathbf{W}\mathbf{x} \qquad (6.51)$$

then $\mathbf{W}$ can be factored

$$\mathbf{W} = \mathbf{P}\mathbf{W}_p \mathbf{W}_{p-1} \cdots \mathbf{W}_2 \mathbf{W}_1 \qquad (6.52)$$

where $\mathbf{W}_i$ corresponds to factor N_i and $\mathbf{P}$ is the permutation matrix. Each $\mathbf{W}_i$ can be partitioned into N/N_i submatrices of dimension N_i. The matrices can be further factored

$$\mathbf{W}_i = \mathbf{R}_i \mathbf{T}_i$$

where $\mathbf{R}_i$ is a diagonal matrix of rotation (twiddle) factors and $\mathbf{T}_i$ is partitioned into N/N_i identical square matrices.

Singleton partitions the factors symmetrically. For example, $N = 270$ is factored as

$$3 \times 2 \times 3 \times 5 \times 3$$

He further factors the permutation to correspond to this factoring of the algorithm.

Singleton Out-of-Core Algorithm

In another major paper by Singleton [1967], a variety of ways of computing the FFT of a length of data that could not be contained in high-speed core are discussed. Singleton is somewhat more general than the algorithm to be given here. The adaptation from his article has the following limitations:

1. It is a power of 2 algorithm.
2. It is assumed that either four tape units or one or more disks that can be made to act like four I/O units are available.

Table 6.2

Integers Between 1 and 5000 Which are
of the Form $N = 2^i 3^j 5^k$

N	i	j	k	N	i	j	k	N	i	j	k
2	1	0	0	243	0	5	0	1458	1	6	0
3	0	1	0	250	1	0	3	1500	2	1	3
4	2	0	0	256	8	0	0	1536	9	1	0
5	0	0	1	270	1	3	1	1600	6	0	2
6	1	1	0	288	5	2	0	1620	2	4	1
8	3	0	0	300	2	1	2	1728	6	3	0
9	0	2	0	320	6	0	1	1800	3	2	2
10	1	0	1	324	2	4	0	1875	0	1	4
12	2	1	0	360	3	2	1	1980	7	1	1
15	0	1	1	375	0	1	3	1944	3	5	0
16	4	0	0	384	7	1	0	2000	4	0	3
18	1	2	0	400	4	0	2	2025	0	4	2
20	2	0	1	405	0	4	1	2048	11	0	0
24	3	1	0	432	4	3	0	2160	4	3	1
25	0	0	2	450	1	2	2	2187	0	7	0
27	0	3	0	480	5	1	1	2250	1	2	3
30	1	1	1	486	1	5	0	2304	8	2	0
32	5	0	0	500	2	0	3	2400	5	1	2
36	2	2	0	512	9	0	0	2430	1	5	1
40	3	0	1	540	2	3	1	2500	2	0	4
45	0	2	1	576	6	2	0	2560	9	0	1
48	4	1	0	600	3	1	2	2592	5	4	0
50	1	0	2	625	0	0	4	2700	2	3	2
54	1	3	0	640	7	0	1	2880	6	2	1
60	2	1	1	648	3	4	0	2916	2	6	0
64	6	0	0	675	0	3	2	3000	3	1	3
72	3	2	0	720	4	2	1	3072	10	1	0
75	0	1	2	729	0	6	0	3125	0	0	5
80	4	0	1	750	1	1	3	3200	7	0	2
81	0	4	0	768	8	1	0	3240	3	4	1
90	1	2	1	800	5	0	2	3375	0	3	3
96	5	1	0	810	1	4	1	3456	7	3	0
100	2	0	2	864	5	3	0	3600	4	2	2
108	2	3	0	900	2	2	2	3645	0	6	1
120	3	1	1	960	6	1	1	3750	1	1	4
125	0	0	3	972	2	5	0	3840	8	1	1
128	7	0	0	1000	3	0	3	3888	4	5	0
135	0	3	1	1024	10	0	0	4000	5	0	3
144	4	2	0	1080	3	3	1	4050	1	4	2
150	1	1	2	1125	0	2	3	4096	12	0	0
160	5	0	1	1152	7	2	0	4320	5	3	1
162	1	4	0	1200	4	1	2	4374	1	7	0
180	2	2	1	1215	0	5	1	4500	2	2	3
192	6	1	0	1250	1	0	4	4608	9	2	0
200	3	0	2	1280	8	0	1	4800	6	1	2
216	3	3	0	1296	4	4	0	4860	2	5	1
225	0	2	2	1350	1	3	2	5000	3	0	4
240	4	1	1	1440	5	2	1				

When the four tape units are discussed in this algorithm, it should be understood that all four could be storage areas on a single disk drive.

Suppose that there are $N=2^p$ complex values in the series to be transformed, and that the data is to be written in blocks of size 2^r complex numbers, where 2^r is considerably smaller than 2^p. As it turns out, $2p-r-2$ passes must be made through the data to complete the transform and rearrange the data. There are two phases: the first consists of $p-r$ computing passes followed by $p-r-2$ permutation passes; the second phase has r computing passes.

For example, if $N=2^{15}$, and $2^r=256=2^8$ (that is, 512 real words per record), then there would be

Phase I	7 computing passes
	5 permutation passes
Phase II	8 computing passes

The computation is initiated by putting the first $N/2$ complex values to be transformed onto the first tape, and the second $N/2$ values onto the second tape. All four tapes are rewound.

In the first phase, one block each is read from tapes 1 and 2 and put into separate arrays in core storage. A complex value is sequentially taken from each array and transformed and then written over the original values. The formulas are

$$Y(k)=X(k)+X(k+N/2)\exp\left[-j\pi\left(\frac{2\left(\frac{k}{p-q}\right)}{2^{q-1}}\right)\right]$$

$$Y\left(k+\frac{N}{2}\right)=X(k)-X(k+N/2)\exp\left[-j\pi\left(\frac{2\left(\frac{k}{p-q}\right)}{2^{q-1}}\right)\right] \quad (6.53)$$

where

$$X(k)=k\text{th value on tape 1, } k=0,\ldots,N/2$$

$$X(k+N/2)=k\text{th value on tape 2, } k=0,\ldots,N/2$$

$$Y(k)=\text{replacement for } X(k)$$

$$Y(k+N/2)=\text{replacement for } X(k+N/2)$$

$$q=\text{the computational stage, } q=1,2,\ldots,m$$

It is important to do the integer arithmetic as indicated with the parentheses as shown.

These calculations are the same for all the m computational passes.

When each of the 2^r values in the two blocks has been processed, the records are written out onto tapes 3 and 4: the information originally from tape 1 goes to tape 3; that from tape 2 to tape 4.

The next block from each of tapes 1 and 2 is then read and the above process is again done. This continues until all the information from the two tapes has been read in, processed, and written out onto tapes 3 and 4. This completes the computational part of a phase I pass.

The permutation part of the phase I pass consists of rewinding the four tapes and permuting the data in the following manner:

1. Tape three is processed first: blocks are read, and the first half of tape 3 is written on tape 1; the second half of the tape is written on tape 2.
2. After tape 3 is finished, the same procedure is employed with tape 4.

This is for $q=1$. For subsequent permutation passes, each one done after a computational pass, the number of blocks consecutively taken from tapes 3 and 4 is $2^{p-r-1-q}$. That is,

q	Number of Blocks Consecutively Written
1	2^{p-r-2}
2	2^{p-r-3}
$\vdots$	$\vdots$
$p-r-2$	2
$p-r-1$	$\left.\begin{matrix}- \\ -\end{matrix}\right\}$ no permutation pass
$p-4$	

Thus for the example where $N=2^{15}$, $r=8$, and $p=15$,

q	Number of Blocks Consecutively Written
1	32
2	16
3	8
4	4
5	2
6	$\left.\begin{matrix}- \\ -\end{matrix}\right\}$ no permutation pass
7	

That is, for the last two computational passes for phase I, no permutation passes are made.

There could be a permutation pass after the computational pass for step $q = p - r - 1$ ($q = 6$ in the example). Instead, the next computational step, $q = p - r$, is modified to include it. This is done by reading pairs of blocks from tape 1 rather than a block each from tapes 1 and 2. The processing is done as before. When tape 1 is exhausted, tape 2 is also processed two blocks at a time. As noted, this procedure is only done at computational step $p - r$, the last step in phase I.

In phase II, computation and permutation are combined into a single pass, with a total of r passes being made. In each pass in this phase, the data is handled in exactly the same way: the input data is read one block at a time starting with the beginning of the first current input tape to the end of the second current input tape. Three data arrays are required of size 2^r (complex), one more such array than was needed for Phase I. One of these is used for the current input record; the other two are for two records being built up for the current output tapes.

The permutation in the qth computational step, where now $p - r - 1 \leqslant q < p$, is done in the following manner: pairs of complex values 2^{p-q} entries apart in the input block are chosen for processing. In the example, with $q = 8$, the first computation step in phase II, then $2^{15-8} = 2^7 = 128$. That is, the 1st and 129th values would be processed, then the 2nd and 130th, and so forth. The formulas employed are still the same as given for phase I. The results are stored in sequence in the two output arrays: the $Y(k)$ term goes to the first array, the $Y(k + N/2)$ to the second. When both output arrays are full, they are written out to the first and second output tapes. Thus the data is processed in pairs of input blocks; it requires two input blocks to fill up the two output arrays.

When each such phase II pass is completed, the tapes are rewound and the output units become the input units.

When all r passes of phase II have been completed, then the Fourier transformed data is on the last output units, and may be read by sequentially reading in the data from the first and then the second tape.

If the original function was real, that is to say, its imaginary part was 0, then the result on tape is the correct Fourier transform, and nothing remains to be done.

On the other hand, if the complex function consisted of two real functions, say, $x(i)$ as the real part and $y(i)$ as the imaginary part, then they must be separated. In order to do this, the same algorithm as given in (6.17) and (6.18) is employed.

The combined transform is processed as follows:

1. Process the first block of the first tape with the last block of the second tape.
2. Process the second block of the first tape with the next to the last block of the second tape.
3. And so forth.

In other words, it is necessary to read to the end of the second tape and then backspace.

Another problem is that the overlap of the blocks is not perfect; it is off by one complex value. This may be seen from the following.

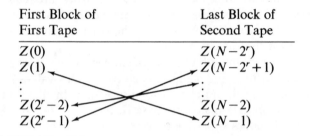

First Block of First Tape	Last Block of Second Tape
$Z(0)$	$Z(N-2^r)$
$Z(1)$	$Z(N-2^r+1)$
$\vdots$	$\vdots$
$Z(2^r-2)$	$Z(N-2)$
$Z(2^r-1)$	$Z(N-1)$

The arrows indicate the terms that are combined to yield $X(k)$ and $Y(k)$. The first term in the first block is used by itself. The first term in the last block must be saved to be used with the next pair of blocks processed. This increases the complexity of the code somewhat.

6.3   EXAMPLES

In this section we illustrate the result of certain Fourier transform computations, summarized as follows:

1. The Fourier transform of a sum of sines and cosines.
2. The Fourier transform of a stationary random process.
3. The Fourier transform of a time history of recorded accelerometer vibration data.
4. The Fourier transform of a transient signal.

5. The use of the Fourier transform to accomplish interpolation of a numerical function.
6. The general interpolative effects of zero padding data.
7. The appearance of narrow band random noise to distinguish it from the wide band example above.

We hope these examples will provide the reader with a "feeling" for the Fourier transform, its appearance under typically encountered situations, an indicator of its value in practical problems, and an example of the distortions induced by typical errors in data.

Sum of Sines and Cosines

From Chapter 1 we know that the Fourier transform of a sinusoid of frequency f_0 is a pair of delta functions at $\pm f_0$. By linearity, a sum of sinusoids is a sum of pairs of delta functions. We further know that a finite, discrete Fourier transform will be a sum of aliased $(\sin x)/x$ functions. Consider the sum of three discrete sinusoids.

$$x(i) = \sum_{k=1}^{3} a_k \cos(2\pi i T f_k + \varphi_k) \qquad i = 0, 1, 2, \dots, N-1 \qquad (6.54)$$

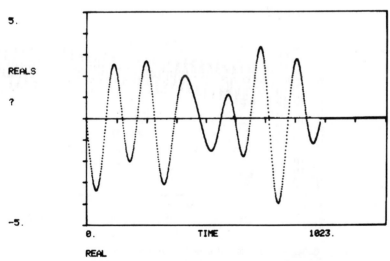

Figure 6.19   Plot of three out of phase sinusoids.

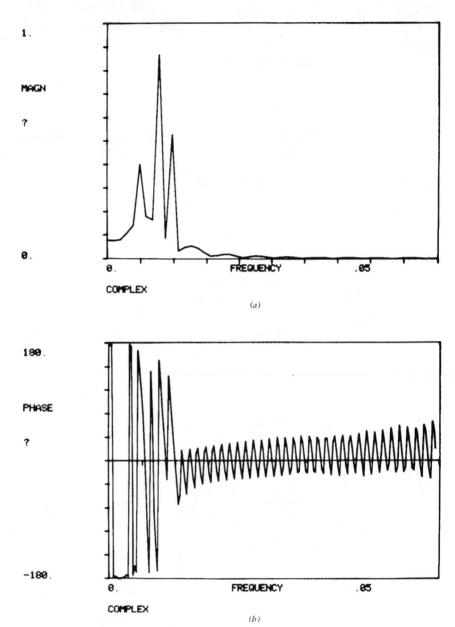

Figure 6.20 Fourier transformed time history of Figure 6.19.

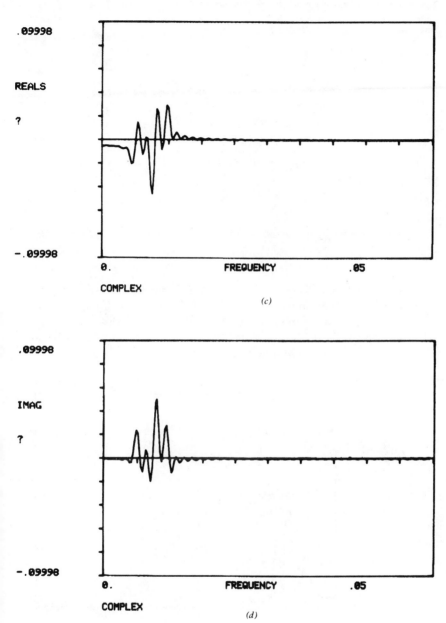

.09998

REALS

?

−.09998

0.   FREQUENCY   .05

COMPLEX

(c)

.09998

IMAG

?

−.09998

0.   FREQUENCY   .05

COMPLEX

(d)

Figure 6-20   (*Continued*).

263

with the following frequencies and phases:

k	a_k	f_k	φ_k
1	0.986	$F/16=1/8T$	$\pi/3=60°$
2	1.225	$F/8=1/4T$	$\pi/5=36°$
3	0.707	$3F/16=3/8T$	$\pi/4=45°$

We generate 128 points of (6.54) on the computer with the slightly different equation

$$x(i) = \sum_{k=1}^{3} a(k)\cos\left(\frac{2\pi k}{16}i + \varphi_k\right) \qquad i=0,1,2,\ldots,127 \qquad (6.55)$$

This time history has been generated on the digital computer and plotted in Figure 6.19. The Fourier transform of Equation (6.55) is plotted in Figure 6.20 in terms of both Cartesian and polar coordinates. In Figure 6.21 we repeat the polar coordinate plot by computing a 1024-point Fourier transform to cause interpolation in the frequency domain.

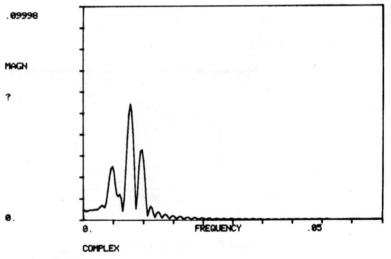

Figure 6.21   Fourier transform of (6.51) but padded with 896 zeroes.

Stationary Random Noise

We illustrate the Fourier transform of a stationary random process in this section. The time history is generated by digitizing the output of an analog Gaussian, white random noise generator. We take 1024 time points and obtain 513 frequency domain points. The random noise has $\mu_x = 0$, $\sigma_x^2 = 1$ and the data points are approximately independent of one another. The real and imaginary parts of the Fourier transform points are Gaussian and have mean and variance

$$E[X_R(k)] = E[X_I(k)] = 0 \qquad (6.56)$$

$$\text{Var}[X_R(k)] = \text{Var}[X_I(k)] = \frac{1}{2NT}$$

In Figure 6.22 we show the digitized time history and in Figure 6.23 is the Fourier transform. This is a chi variable $[\chi(2)]$ with 2 d.f. A $\chi(n)$ variable is the square root of a $\chi^2(n)$ variable and is usually known as a Rayleigh distributed variable.

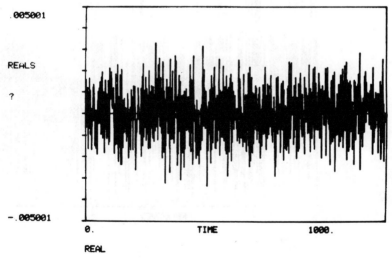

Figure 6.22 Digitized output of Gaussian, white, random noise generator.

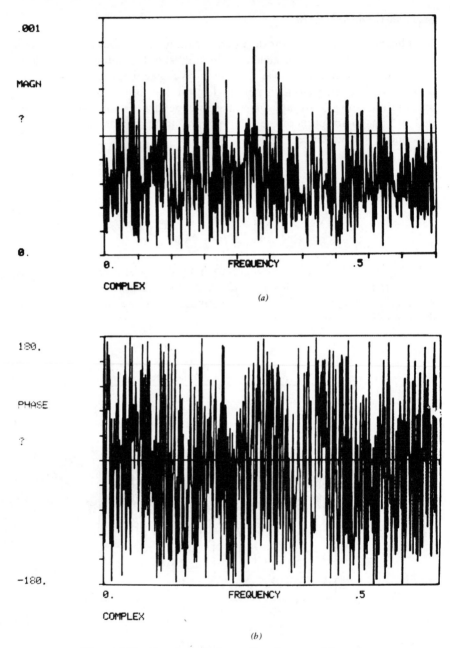

Figure 6.23   Fourier transform of stationary white noise.

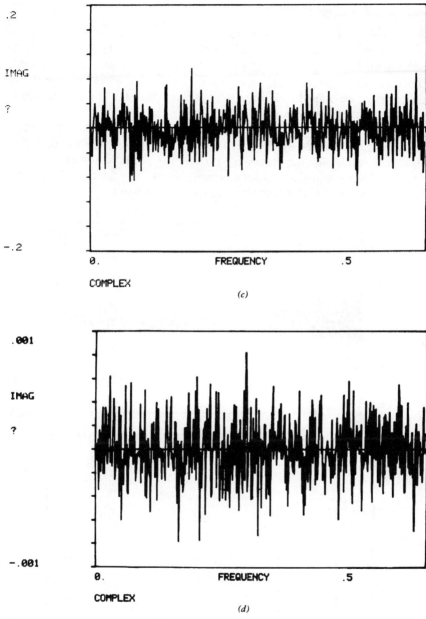

Figure 6.23 (*Continued*).

267

Recorded Transient Acceleration Data

An accelerometer was attached to the head of a small hammer and the hammer was used to strike a turbine blade structure. This is intended to provide an impulsive load (delta function) so that the frequency response function can be derived. This problem is discussed more in Chapter 9. For the moment we want to illustrate the appearance of the Fourier transform of a transient (nonstationary) time history.

The data was digitized at a rate of 4000 sps. The plot of the time history is given in Figure 6.24. Its Fourier transform is shown in Figure 6.25. The statistical results for the stationary process do not hold for the transient process. Many statistical difficulties arise from the fact that there is no longer statistical independence between frequency bands.

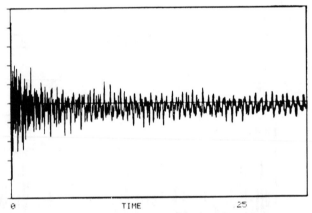

Figure 6.24   Transient acceleration time history.

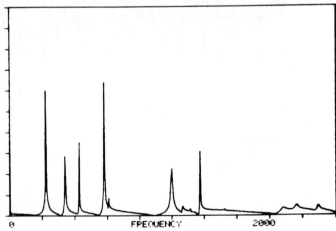

Figure 6.25   Fourier transform absolute value of acceleration transient.

Interpolation of a Bandlimited Function

In this section we demonstrate interpolation of a bandlimited discrete function using a stress distribution obtained from the output of a structural analysis of masonry block panels.

Figure 6.26 shows a two-dimensional plane stress problem subjected to

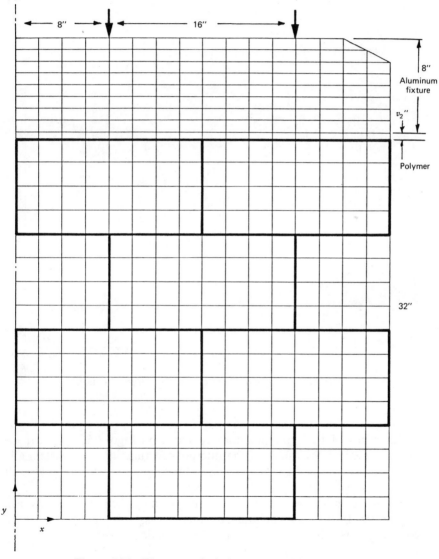

Figure 6.26 Fixture analysis for masonry block panels.

dynamic point loads. The vertical stress is computed using the finite element technique, where the stress is determined only at discrete points. The basic character of the stress distribution is determined from the analysis; however, a continuous stress distribution is not provided. Figure 6.27 shows the distribution of vertical stress at 1.5 in. below the loaded surface. The peak values under the loads at the 1.5-in. level are not available from the analysis; and methods are sought to obtain the missing values.

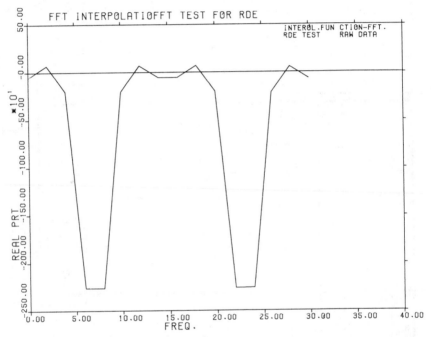

Figure 6.27 Original discrete values of stress function.

The results of FFT interpolation are shown in Figure 6.28. As can be seen, the peak stress values of the interpolated function are substantially greater in magnitude than the maxima of the original function, a key result in this analysis.

The interpolation was accomplished by padding the Fourier transform with zeroes. In this case the original function was 16 points and the final was 128 points. That is, an 8 to 1 padding was done.

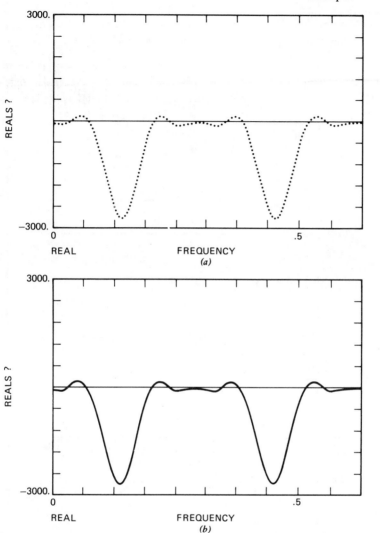

Figure 6.28 Result of FFT interpolation of stress function 8 to 1 zero padding.

Narrow Band Random Noise

In Figure 6.29*a–e*, we illustrate the appearance of narrow band noise. As can be seen in part *a*, the time history bears considerable resemblance to a modulated sine wave. However, we note the narrow band appearance of the spectral plots and in particular the randomness of the phase. This distinguishes it considerably from a sine wave.

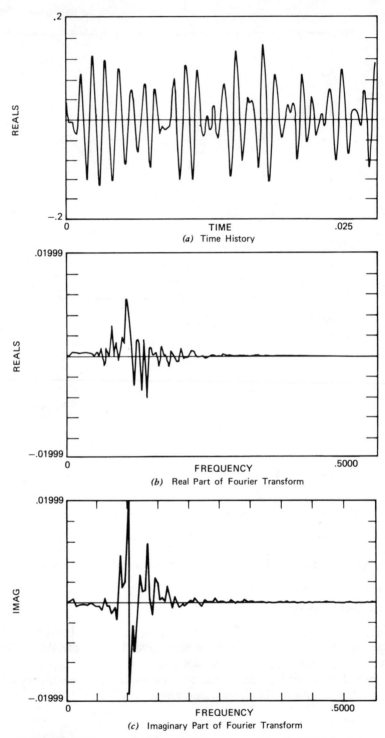

Figure 6.29 Narrow band random process and its Fourier transform.

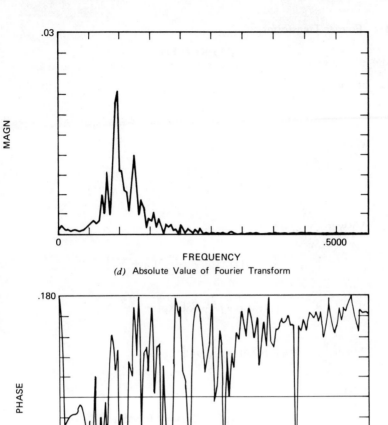

MAGN

FREQUENCY

(d) Absolute Value of Fourier Transform

PHASE

.180

−.180

0   .5000

FREQUENCY

(e)   Phase of Fourier Transform

Figure 6.29   (*Continued*).

EXERCISES

6.1. Prove

$$Z(N+k)=Z(k)$$

where

$$Z(k)=T\sum_{i=0}^{N-1}z(i)\exp\left(-j\frac{2\pi}{N}ik\right)$$

Answer:

$$z(i)\exp\left(-j\frac{2\pi}{N}2[k+N]\right)$$

$$=z(i)\exp\left(-j\frac{2\pi}{N}ik\right)\exp\left(-j\frac{2\pi}{N}iN\right)$$

$$=z(i)\exp\left(-j\frac{2\pi}{N}ik\right)$$

since

$$\exp(-j2\pi i)=1 \text{ for all } i$$

Hence

$$Z(k+N)=T\sum z(i)\exp\left(-j\frac{2\pi}{N}i[k+N]\right)$$

$$=T\sum z(i)\exp\left(-j\frac{2\pi ik}{N}\right)$$

6.2. Compute transform of a real time history of $N=128$ points. Use only 64-point complex array.

6.3. Prove $X(k)=X^*(N-k)$ if $x(i)$ is real.

6.4. Compute inverse transform of Fourier transform computed in Exercise 6.2. Use only 64-point array.

6.5. Prove that the Fourier transform of $(x(0),x(1))$ is $X(0)=(x(0)+x(1))T$ and $X(1)=(x(0)-x(1))T$.

6.6. Compute transform of Exercise 6.2 using 32-point array.

6.7. Prove $X(0)=T\sum_{i=0}^{N-1}x(i)$

6.8. Convert the result of Exercise 6.2 to absolute value and phase.

6.9. If N is even, prove $X(N/2) = \sum_{i=0}^{N-1} x(2i) - \sum_{i=0}^{N-1} x(2i+1)$.

6.10. Straighten the phase of the Fourier transform of Exercise 6.8.

6.11. Derive Euler's formula

$$\sin n\alpha = 2\sin(n-1)\alpha \cdot \cos\alpha - \sin(n-2)\alpha$$

$$\cos n\alpha = 2\cos(n-1)\alpha \cdot \cos\alpha - \cos(n-2)\alpha$$

6.12. Generate a pseudo-random white noise process and compute and plot its Fourier transform. Use TRAND or equivalent.

6.13. Rewrite the FFT subroutine to avoid multiplies in the first iteration. How much arithmetic does this save?

6.14. Generate a narrow band process by modifying the Fourier transform of Exercise 6.12 and doing an inverse FFT. Plot the time history.

6.15. Complete the derivation of (6.55) from (6.54):

Answer:

$$\sum a_k \cos(2\pi i T f_k + \varphi_k)$$

Since $f_k = k/16T$,

$$\sum a_k \cos\left(2\pi i T \frac{k}{16T}\right) = \sum a_k \cos\left(2\pi k \frac{i}{16} + \varphi_k\right)$$

$$= \sum a_k \cos\left(\frac{2\pi k}{16}i + 16\varphi_k\right)$$

6.16. Duplicate the result of Figure 6.29 by using the results of Exercise 6.14.

6.17. Explain the results of (6.56).

Answer:
a. Fourier transform is a linear transform and $E[L(x)] = LE(x) = 0$.

b. The integral of the square of the Fourier transform must be σ_x^2, since

$$\Delta f = b = \frac{1}{NT}, \quad E|X^2|\frac{1}{NT} = \sigma_x^2$$

and

$$E\frac{X_R^2}{NT} + E\frac{X_I^2}{NT} = \sigma_x^2$$

But

$$EX_R^2 = EX_I^2$$

so

$$2E\frac{X_R^2}{NT} = \sigma_x^2 \qquad \text{QED.}$$

6.18. Prove that

$$|S(f) + a\exp[-j2\pi ft]|$$

has a sinusoidal term added in.

Answer:

$$|S(f) + ae^{-j\omega t}|^2 = |S(f)|^2 + a^2 + 2\operatorname{Re}[aS(f)e^{-j\omega t}]$$

$$= |S(f)|^2 + a^2 + 2a\{\operatorname{Re}[S(f)\cos\omega t]$$

$$+ \operatorname{Im}[S(f)\sin\omega t]\}$$

CHAPTER 7

COVARIANCE AND CONVOLUTION FUNCTIONS

7.1 BACKGROUND AND THEORY

This chapter contains a discussion of covariance and convolution functions. They are lumped together because from a computational standpoint they are obtained in a nearly identical manner. However, they play different roles in many applications.

The term correlation function is often used synonymously with covariance function in time series analysis. However, covariance is an established statistical term and correlation is reserved to refer to a normalized quantity that ranges between plus and minus 1. In this chapter we follow statistical terminology.

Covariance (correlation) functions have wide applications in shock and vibration analysis, communication problems, radar detection, control systems, oceanographic data analysis, and in fact in any field where spectral analysis is pertinent owing to the relationship via Fourier transforms. When power or cross spectra can be applied to the analysis of a problem, the corresponding correlation functions can, in principle, be used in an equivalent manner, since they are Fourier transform pairs. In practice, there may be a strong reason for choosing one or the other. For example, the time delay between two signals can be determined from the phase of a cross spectrum, but would often show up in a more natural manner in the (cross) covariance function. The adjective "cross" is redundant in referring to covariance, but we often employ it to distinguish it from autocovariance.

The same wide base of applications can be stated for convolution functions. However, most applications can be phrased in terms of digital filtering since the convolution of a time history with the impulse response function of a linear filter gives the response (output) of the filter. Convolution functions are therefore useful in such problems as smoothing (lowpass filtering) data and generating a random process with a specified spectral shape in simulation studies and detecting signals (matched filter). We demonstrate many of these applications in Section 7.3.

Covariance

Covariance functions define the degree of "alikeness" between two time histories as a function of time shift (cross covariance) or the degree to which a function is correlated with itself as a function of time delay (autocovariance). The estimated cross covariance between $x(i)$ and $y(i)$, $i = 0, 1, 2, \ldots, N-1$, is mathematically defined by the equation

$$s_{xy}(i) = \frac{1}{N-i} \sum_{p=0}^{N-i-1} x(p)y(p+i) \qquad i = -m, \ldots, -1, 0, 1, \ldots, m \quad (7.1)$$

where we always assume the sample means are removed. The index i is termed "lag" and m is termed the maximum lag. If T is the sampling interval then

$$\tau_{\max} = mT \tag{7.2}$$

is the maximum lag time or delay time. Typical useful maximum delays seldom exceed 10% of the record length. If $y(i) = x(i)$ then $s_{xx}(i)$ is termed an autocovariance function and is symmetric about $i = 0$, so it need be evaluated only for positive lag values. A summary of some elementary facts regarding the covariance function is as follows:

$$s_{xy}(-i) = s_{yx}(i) \tag{7.3}$$

$$s_{xx}(-i) = s_{xx}(i) \tag{7.4}$$

$$s_{xx}(0) = s_x^2 \tag{7.5}$$

$$s_{xy}(i) + s_{xy}(-i) = A_{xy}(i) \text{ is an even function} \tag{7.6}$$

$$s_{xy}(i) - s_{xy}(-i) = B_{xy}(i) \text{ is an odd function} \tag{7.7}$$

$$s_{xx}(i) \to 0 \text{ as } i \to \infty \text{ for random data}$$

$$s_{xy}(i) \to 0 \text{ as } i \to \infty \text{ for random data}$$

$$\left| \rho_{xy}(i) = \frac{\sigma_{xy}(i)}{\sigma_x \sigma_y} \right| \leqslant 1 \tag{7.8}$$

where $\sigma_{xy}(i)$ is the "true" or "population" covariance function.

An important fact is that for finite record length data, the sample correlation

$$r_{xy}(i) = \frac{s_{xy}(i)}{s_x s_y} \tag{7.9}$$

is not necessarily bounded by unity as would be suspected from (7.8). This relation is especially likely to be violated when $r > N/10$. An alternative, slightly different definition of the sample cross correlation function is

$$s'_{xy}(i) = \frac{1}{N} \sum_{p=0}^{N-1} x(p) y(p+i) \tag{7.10}$$

This estimate of $\sigma_{xy}(i)$ has slightly smaller variance than $s_{xy}(i)$ (according to Parzen [1961]) and always satisfies (7.8). However, it is a biased estimate and the bias can be of an annoying magnitude for moderately large lags. Because of the unbiasedness of (7.8) it is the preferable estimate since its variance is not much larger than (7.10) for reasonable lag values. We illustrate that this is particularly annoying for deterministic data in Section 7.2.

The discovery of the FFT has made it economical from a computational standpoint to obtain correlation functions indirectly. The discrete form of the Wiener–Khinchine theorem states

$$S_{xy}(k) = T \sum_{i=0}^{N-1} s_{xy}(i) \exp\left(-j\frac{2\pi i k}{N}\right) \qquad k = 0, 1, 2, \ldots, N-1 \tag{7.11}$$

$$s_{xy}(i) = b \sum_{k=0}^{N-1} S_{xy}(k) \exp\left(j\frac{2\pi i k}{N}\right) \qquad i = 0, 1, 2, \ldots, N-1 \tag{7.12}$$

Hence we may determine the cross (auto) covariance from the cross (power) spectrum, where the cross (power) spectrum is computed appropriately. This is discussed in Section 7.2.

Almost all applications of cross covariance functions relate to the determination of time delays. This is true since, if $y(i)$ is identical to $x(i)$, but shifted in time, then $s_{xy}(i)$ attains a maximum at the lag value i corresponding to the amount of the time shift. It turns out that the convolution function sometimes gives better time delay estimates; this is discussed in Section 7.3.

Suppose $y(i)$ is a time delayed version of $x(i)$ plus extraneous noise.

Then

$$y(i) = x(i+k) + n(i) \tag{7.13}$$

and the covariance function is

$$s_{xy}(i) = \frac{1}{N-i} \sum_{i=0}^{N-1-i} \left[x(p)x(p+k+i) + x(p)n(p+i) \right]$$

$$= s_{xy}(k+i) + s_{xn}(i) \tag{7.14}$$

Since $s_{xn}(i)$ is 0 on the average, the cross covariance is a time-translated autocovariance, distorted by the cross covariance of $x(i)$ with the noise $n(i)$. This cross covariance will go to 0 for large N. Hence $s_{xy}(i)$ may be searched for its maximum and the corresponding lag time will be the amount of time delay. In Section 7.3 we shall see the practical problems involved.

Cross correlation (or covariance) functions also are useful in determining equivalence of time histories. The maximum value of the normalized cross correlation function provides a quantitative, repeatable, index of "alikeness." That is, if two functions are identical, except for a time shift, the maximum value of $\rho_{xy}(i)$ will be unity. If they are completely independent (uncorrelated) then $\rho_{xy}(i)$ is 0. The quantity

$$s_e = \sqrt{1 - \rho_{xy}^2(i)_{max}} \tag{7.15}$$

is a measure of "goodness of fit" between $x(i)$ and $y(i)$ and is the rms of the difference usually termed "standard error" or "standard error of the estimate."

Autocovariance functions contain the same information, in principle, as the power spectrum since they are Fourier transform pairs. As a general rule, the PSD is usually most easily interpreted in engineering applications. However, the autocorrelation occasionally depicts results in a more graphic manner. For example, if one desires coefficients for a forecasting equation (extrapolate future values of a time history from its past values) then the autocorrelation function provides the required information.

Convolution

The formula for discrete transient* convolution differs very little from covariance. The only differences are no averaging and a change of sign in

---

*We employ the term transient to distinguish from circular convolution. This is amplified in Section 7.5.

one time index. The formula is

$$
c_{xy}^t(i) = \begin{cases} T \displaystyle\sum_{p=0}^{i} x(p)y(i-p) & i=0,1,\ldots,N-1 \\[2mm] T \displaystyle\sum_{p=1}^{N-l} x(p+l)y(N-p) & i=l+N,\, l=0,1,\ldots,N-1 \end{cases} \tag{7.16}
$$

This is diagramatically illustrated below:

$$c_{xy}^t(0) = x(0)y(0)$$

$$c_{xy}^t(1) = x(0)y(1) + x(1)y(0)$$

$$c_{xy}^t(k) = x(0)y(k) + x(1)y(k-1) + \cdots + x(k)y(0)$$

$$x(0), x(1), \ldots, x(N-1)$$

$i = N-1$

$$y(N-1), y(N-2), \ldots, y(0)$$

$$c_{xy}^l(N-1) = x(0)y(N-1) + x(1)y(N-2) + \cdots + x(N-1)y(0)$$

$$x(0), \quad x(1), x(2), \ldots, x(N-1)$$

$i = N (l=0)$

$$y(N-1), y(N-2), \ldots, y(1), \quad y(0)$$

$$c_{xy}^l(N) = x(1)y(N-1) + x(2)y(N-2) + \cdots + x(N-1)y(1)$$

$$x(0), \ldots, \quad x(l+1), x(l+2), \ldots, x(N-1)$$

$i = N+l$

$$y(N-1), y(N-2), \ldots, y(l+1), \quad y(l), \ldots, y(0)$$

$$c_{xy}^l(N+1) = x(l+1)y(N-1) + x(l+2)y(N-2) + \cdots + x(N-1)y(l+1)$$

$$x(0), x(1), \ldots, x(N-1)$$

$i = 2N-1 (l=N-1)$

$$y(N-1), y(N-2), \ldots, y(0)$$

$$c_{xy}^l(2N-1) = 0$$

Convolution can be viewed as flipping the y function end for end and computing a cross covariance.

As mentioned above, this function is usually now referred to as the *transient* convolution, denoted by superscript t. The distinction has been made since the advent of the FFT and its use in determining discrete convolutions via the *convolution theorem* of Fourier analysis (i.e., compute FFTs, multiply, compute inverse FFT to obtain a convolution, which is described in considerable detail shortly).

Convolutions are fundamental to time series data analysis. First of all, the discussion in Chapter 1 shows that all linear systems are completely characterized by their impulse response functions. Furthermore, the response of the linear system to any input is given by the convolution with the impulse response function. Digital filters are linear systems and hence digital filtering can be accomplished with convolutions. One problem discussed in Chapter 4 is finite impulse response (FIR) filter design which are then implemented via convolution.

Any smoothing operation can be characterized as a lowpass filter and hence can be implemented by a convolution. Moving averages, which are often used for smoothing, are given by the formula

$$\bar{x}(i) = \frac{1}{2M+1} \sum_{j=-M}^{M} x(i-j) \qquad i = M, M+1, \ldots, N-M-1 \quad (7.17)$$

(Note: the first M and last M points are sometimes defined by assuming the data values to be 0 outside the range 0 to $N-1$).

We note that we can view $\bar{x}(i)$ as the convolution of $x(i)$ with the constant function

$$a(i) = \frac{1}{2M+1} \qquad \text{for all } i \qquad (7.18)$$

If we view the moving average in this manner, then the concept of moving average is easily generalized to

$$\bar{x}(i) = T \sum_{j=-M}^{M} a(j) x(i-j) \qquad (7.19)$$

where

$$T \sum_{j=-M}^{M} a(j) = 1$$

In Section 7.6 we deduce the frequency response of the moving average given by (7.17) and immediately see its inadequacies.

Equation (7.19) leads to a special convolution known as *symmetric convolution*. We define

$$c_{ax}(i) = T \sum_{j=-M}^{M} a(j)x(i-j)$$

$$= Ta(0)x(i) + T \sum_{j=1}^{M} a(j)\big[x(i-j) + x(i+j)\big] \qquad (7.20)$$

$$i = 0, 1, 2, \ldots, N-1$$

where

$$a(j) = a(-j) \qquad j = 0, 1, \ldots, M \qquad (7.21)$$

Again in (7.20) we interpret data values to be 0 outside the range 0 to $M-1$. We could extend the range of definition to $i = -M$, $-(M-1), \ldots,$ that is,

$$i = -M, -(M-1), \ldots, -1, 0, 1, \ldots, N-1, N, N+1, \ldots, N+M-1 \quad (7.22)$$

In general, if N_1 point and N_2 point functions are convolved we can define the convolution result to be $N_1 + N_2$ points in length

In Chapter 8 we see that modification of Fourier transforms to reduce leakage can be accomplished with a frequency domain convolution. In general, convolution is inextricably intertwined in almost all digital time series analysis. However, it is viewed in a multitude of ways and we rarely think of a convolution as a specific parameter to be computed and interpreted.

7.2 DIFFERENCES BETWEEN COVARIANCE AND CONVOLUTION

A covariance computation implies an averaging operation is accomplished. That is, it is a mean cross product. The convolution operation does not entail averaging. Both can be thought of as counterparts of integration operations and hence a scaling to account for the dt in the integral is necessary. This is automatically taken care of in covariance since $T/NT = 1/N$. However, the sampling interval, T, must be specifically incorporated into the discrete convolution equation.

Although the basic cross product looks nearly identical for both convolution and covariance, there is one key difference. The negative sign on the time index for $y(i)$ in the first part of (7.16) amounts to flipping $y(i)$ end for end.

Thus, up to a scale factor, if we flip $y(i)$ end for end, and compute the covariance function between the two time histories, we obtain the convolution of the two time histories. In equation form,

$$y'(i) = y(-i)$$

$$s_{xy'}(i) = \frac{1}{N-i} \sum_{p=0}^{N-1} x(p) y'(i+p) \qquad i = 0, 1, 2, \ldots, N-1 \text{ positive lags}$$

$$\tag{7.23}$$

$$= \frac{1}{N-i} c_{xy}^t(i) \qquad i = N-1, N-2, \ldots, 0$$

$$s_{y'x}(i) = \frac{1}{N-i} \sum_{p=0}^{N-1} y'(p) x(i+p) \qquad i = 1, 2, \ldots, N-1 \text{ negative lags} \quad (7.24)$$

$$= \frac{1}{N-i} c_{xy}^t(i) \qquad i = N, N+1, \ldots, 2N-1$$

Note that we obtain the transient convolution in two parts, but the first set of values is obtained in reverse order whereas the last half is obtained in correct order. Also, we have omitted the zero negative lag since it would repeat a middle value of the convolution. Later we see in Section 7.5 that the equation for convolution can be simplified in terms of the circular convolution and padding with zeroes.

7.3 LONG RECORD LENGTHS AND BASIC COVARIANCE COMPUTATIONS

The covariance equation is usually divided into two parts, one for positive lags and one for negative lags.

$$s_{xy}(i) = \frac{1}{N-i} \sum_{p=0}^{N-1} x(p) y(p+i) \tag{7.25}$$

$$s_{yx}(i) = \frac{1}{N-i} \sum_{p=0}^{N-1} y(p) x(p+i) \qquad i = 0, 1, \ldots, m$$

We note that the zero lag in the second equation is redundant.

This equation is easily adapted to large values of N. A total storage of $4(m+1)$ cells is required for input data plus $2(m+1)$ for accumulation of cross products. One establishes four blocks of memory, each $m+1$ cells long. The steps are as follows:

1. Read $m+1$ data values for each $x(i)$ and $y(i)$ into the first two blocks.
2. Accumulate $m+1$ cross products for lag 0, $m+1-1$ for lag 1,..., 1 for lag m.
3. Read the next $m+1$ data values into the second pair of blocks.
4. Accumulate $m+1$ cross products for all lag values.
5. Read the next $m+1$ data values into the first pair of data blocks.
6. Accumulate $m+1$ cross products for all lag values.
7. Repeat steps 3–6 until the last block is read.
8. Accumulate one cross product for lag 0, two for lag 1,..., $m+1$ for lag m.
9. Divide accumulated cross products by $N-i$. This completes the computation.

One-Bit Quantization, or Extreme Clipping Method

A relation between the correlation function of the extremely clipped signal

$$y(t)=\operatorname{sgn}x(t)=\begin{cases} 1 & x(t)\geqslant 0 \\ 1 & x(t)<0 \end{cases} \tag{7.26}$$

and an original Gaussian zero mean process from which it is obtained gives the normalized correlation function (correlation coefficient), $\rho_x(\tau)$, in terms of the correlation coefficient function of the clipped signal $\rho_y(\tau)$. It is

$$\rho_x(\tau)=\sin\left[\frac{\pi}{2}\rho_y(\tau)\right] \tag{7.27}$$

where $\rho_x(\tau)$ and $\rho_y(\tau)$ are defined as

$$\rho_x(\tau)=\frac{s_x(\tau)}{s_x(0)} \qquad \rho_y(\tau)=\frac{s_y(\tau)}{s_y(0)} \tag{7.28}$$

See Weinreb [1963] for a derivation of this relation and Hinich [1967] for theoretical work on the spectrum estimation question. The original derivation of this dates back to 1898, however, according to Kendall and Stuart [1961]. Clearly, when the one-bit quantization is performed, the multiplications that must be accomplished become trivial in that only plus or minus 1 is involved. Various ways exist for taking advantage of this trivial multiplication.

There are certain problems connected with the use of the clipping methods for correlation computations. The problem is that requirements for increased record length are traded for computational speed, assuming a constant statistical accuracy is desired. Weinreb [1963] shows that the variance of an autocorrelation function estimate is increased by a maximum factor of roughly $\pi^2/4\approx2.5$. This variance is proportional to P, so if the variance is to be kept constant, record lengths are required that are two-and-a-half times as long as those needed if all the information available in the data is to be used. The work of Hinich [1967] extended the results and is applicable to spectrum computations. The theoretical results of Hinich show that the wide band (uncorrelated data points) is a worst case. For narrow band data, less increase in variance is shown. The factor reduces from 2.5 to 1.1 in typical cases. This is certainly plausible since narrow band data would be much like a sinusoid. In the limit, a covariance computation for a sinusoid would have zero statistical variability.

In general, this result demonstrates a fact well known to random process theory researchers. Namely, there is a tremendous amount of information in the zero crossings of a random process. However, we note that one of several assumptions is involved in the use of the hard clipping method:

1. A Gaussian distribution.
2. A sinusoid.
3. A sinusoid plus Gaussian noise.

Equation (7.27) applies to data with these characteristics. Note that any periodic function (i.e., the same zero crossings) would give the same

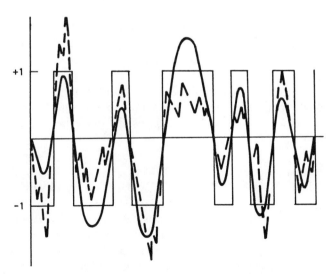

Figure 7.1   Two time series having an identical extremely clipped version.

clipped correlation function as that of a sine wave whose clipped correlation function is a triangular wave prior to applying (7.27). Consider, for example, Figure 7.1 to illustrate this idea. Thus caution must be used when applying the clipped correlation ideas to various types of data.

Only normalized correlation functions are directly obtained by this method. Hence the mean square value must be calculated separately for use as a scale factor. Also, the nonlinear effects that distort probability density functions to non-Gaussian shapes will be masked completely when such a computing method is used.

Sum of Squares and Quarter-Square Method

An additional technique that has been suggested [Schmid, 1965] takes advantage of the finite quantization of the data and expresses the product as a sum of squares. The relation employed here expresses the fact that a cross product may be expressed as a linear combination of squares by the following relation:

$$xy = \tfrac{1}{2}\left[(x+y)^2 - x^2 - y^2\right] \tag{7.29}$$

This is very similar to the fairly well-known "quarter-square" method used in construction of analog multipliers (see Kelly et al. [1966]). The quarter-square multipliers are based on the relation

$$xy = \tfrac{1}{4}\left[(x+y)^2 - (x-y)^2\right] \tag{7.30}$$

We leave it for an exercise (see 7.1 and 7.2) to rewrite these equations for covariance functions.

The key point in using such an indirect relation is that products may now be obtained by table look-up procedures. Tables of squares of two sets of data take up much less storage space than tables of cross products for the same number of data points. For example, say 10-bit quantization is being used so that a table of size 2^{20} cells could be required if all possible cross products were to be stored. The same table of squares of the sum of the data points would only take up 2^{11} cells; 2^{11} might be a very reasonable size, whereas 2^{20} is not.

7.4   COVARIANCE AND CONVOLUTION VIA FFT's

The covariance or convolution functions can be obtained from the power or cross spectral density function. The Wiener–Khinchine relations are applied for this approach. Since spectra can be obtained from Fourier transforms of time histories, the FFT can be applied to obtain correlation functions. Even though this appears to be a roundabout method, it proves to be from 5 to 100 times faster, depending on the maximum lag value desired. One can always obtain N lags of the covariance function nearly as fast as m lags, even though m is considerably smaller than N. Considerable detail is given in Sande [1965] concerning this procedure.

Basic Method

The basic method for autocovariance is as follows:

1. Compute the transform $X(k)$ of time series $x(i)$; $i, k = 0, 1, \ldots, N-1$.
2. Compute the "raw" spectrum $\hat{S}_x(k) = (1/P)|X(k)|^2$.
3. Compute the inverse FFT to obtain the autocovariance function

$$s_x(i) = \mathcal{F}^{-1}\big[S_x(k)\big]$$

Considerable amplification is necessary to illustrate the problems with this procedure. Some explanation is given here and is amplified in the next section. Since covariance functions and convolution functions are closely related the discussion applies to both.

Certain modifications that are not obvious must be made to this approach. It is shown in Sande [1965] that the usual *covariance* function is not obtained after step 3 above, but rather a "circular" autocovariance function $s_x^c(i)$ defined by the relation

$$s_x^c(i) = \frac{N-i}{N} s_x(i) + \frac{i}{N} s_x(N-i) \qquad (7.31)$$

which is illustrated in Figure 7.2.

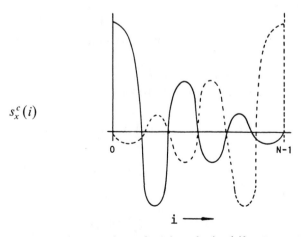

Figure 7.2   Two parts of a covariance function obtained if zeroes are not added.

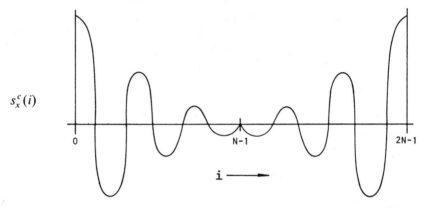

$s_x^c(i)$

0   N-1   2N-1

i ⟶

Figure 7.3   Effect on circular covariance function when N zeroes are added.

The effect on the covariance function of adding zeroes to the data is to spread apart the two portions of the circular covariance function. If N zeroes are attached, the two pieces spread as illustrated in Figure 7.3.

The preceding computational sequence can easily be modified to obtain the noncircular covariance function. If the length of the original sequence of data is a power of 2, $N = 2^p$, then N zeroes would be added to obtain all N lags. If the sequence length is not a power of 2, then the sequence could be filled with N_z zeroes until the first power of 2 was reached. The number of unbiased lag values obtained would be N_z in this case. If more were necessary, the sequence length would have to be doubled by augmenting with 2^p additional zeroes. The modified computational sequence follows:

1. Augment original time series $x'(i)$, $i = 0, 1, \ldots, N-1$, with N zeroes to obtain sequence $x(i)$, $i = 0, 1, \ldots, 2N-1$.
2. Compute the $2N$-point FFT, $X(k)$, $k = 0, 1, \ldots, 2N-1$.
3. Compute the "raw" spectrum $\hat{S}_x(k) = (T/N)|X(k)|^2$, for $k = 0, 1, \ldots, 2N-1$.
4. Compute the inverse FFT of $\hat{S}_x(k)$ and multiply the first N values by $N/(N-i)$ to obtain the correct divisor,

$$s_x(i) = \frac{N}{N-i} \mathcal{F}^{-1}[S_x(k)] \qquad i = 0, 1, \ldots, N-1 \qquad (7.32)$$

For general covariance functions, the same approach applies. In this case (7.31) generalizes to

$$s_{xy}^c(i) = \frac{N-i}{N} s_{xy}(i) + \frac{i}{N} s_{xy}(i) \qquad (7.33)$$

Detailed Method for Covariance and Convolution

The covariance or convolution function is obtained from the product of two Fourier transforms. Hence two FFT's are involved rather than one. The computational steps are as follows:

1. Store $x(i)$ in the real part and $y(i)$ in the imaginary part, $z(i) = x(i) + jy(i)$; $i = 0, 1, \ldots, N-1$.

2. Compute the N-point FFT of $z(i)$ and denote it by $Z^e(k)$:

$$Z^e(k) = \text{FFT}[z(i)] \qquad k = 0, 1, 2, \ldots, N-1 \qquad (7.34)$$

3. Read $z(i)$; $i = 0, 1, 2, \ldots, N-1$ and multiply by

$$W_{2N}^{i/2} \qquad (7.35)$$

4. Compute the N-point FFT of $z(i)W_{2N}^{i/2}$, and denote it by $Z^o(k)$:

$$Z^o(k) = \text{FFT}[z(i)W_{2N}^{i/2}] \qquad k = 0, 1, 2, \ldots, N-1 \qquad (7.36)$$

5. The full $2N$-point FFT is given by

$$Z(2k) = Z^e(k)$$

$$Z(2k+1) = Z^o(k) \qquad k = 0, 1, 2, \ldots, N-1 \qquad (7.37)$$

6. Compute the "raw" cross spectrum for covariance

$$\tilde{S}_{xy}(k) = \frac{1}{P} X^*(k) Y(k)$$

$$= \frac{1}{P} \left[\frac{Z(k) + Z^*(2N-k)}{2} \right]^* \left[\frac{Z(k) - Z^*(2N-k)}{2j} \right]$$

$$k = 0, 1, 2, \ldots, N \qquad (7.38)$$

Compute the product of the two Fourier transforms for convolution

$$C_{xy}(k) = X(k)Y(k)$$

$$= \left[\frac{Z(k) + Z^*(2N-k)}{2} \right] \left[\frac{Z(k) - Z^*(2N-k)}{2j} \right] \qquad (7.39)$$

7. The full first half of the cross spectrum, which is a Hermitian function, is

$$\tilde{S}_{xy}(2k) = S_{xy}^{e}(k)$$

$$\tilde{S}_{xy}(2k+1) = S_{xy}^{o}(k) \qquad k = 0, 1, 2, \dots, \frac{N}{2} - 1 \qquad (7.40)$$

8. We now obtain the N-point noncircular convolution or covariance function by implementing the special inverse transform described in Chapter 6. Compute

$$S_{xy}'(k) = \tilde{S}_{xy}(k) + \tilde{S}_{xy}^{*}(N-k) + j\left[\tilde{S}_{xy}(k) - \tilde{S}_{xy}^{*}(N-k)\right]W_{2N}^{-k/2}$$

$$k = 0, 1, 2, \dots, N-1 \qquad (7.41)$$

Note that this computation must be done in pairs for locations k and $(N-k)$ simultaneously in order to avoid the necessity for extra memory.

9. Compute the N-point inverse FFT of $S_{xy}'(k)$

$$s_{xy}'(i) = \text{FFT}^{-1}\left[S_{xy}'(k)\right] \qquad r = 0, 1, 2, \dots, N-1 \qquad (7.42)$$

10. Finally, we have the $2N$-point noncircular covariance or convolution function

$$s_{xy}(2i) = \frac{N}{N-i}\,\text{Re}\left[s_{xy}'(i)\right]$$

$$s_{xy}(2i+1) = \frac{N}{N-i}\,\text{Im}\left[s_{xy}'(i)\right] \qquad (7.43)$$

Note that in the usual way of computer storage of complex numbers in a FORTRAN program $s_{xy}(i)$ is obtained in natural order without any rearranging.

The method described above limits storage requirements to the length of the data sequence input. One can simplify the method by actually augmenting the data with zeroes, and computing a double-length transform in both directions, which will require more time and storage.

When zero padding is employed, the sequence of the results can be altered. For example, if the two sequences are arranged as follows:

$$x(0), x(1), x(2), \dots, x(N-1), 0(N), 0(N+1), \dots, 0(2N-1)$$

$$y(0), y(1), y(2), \dots, y(N-1), 0(N), 0(N+1), \dots, 0(2N-1)$$

then the covariance result obtained via FFT's is

$$s_{xy}(0), s_{xy}(1), \ldots, s_{xy}(N-1), s_{yx}(N), s_{yx}(N-1), \ldots, s_{yx}(1)$$

If the arrangement of zeroes is modified so that the x sequence has trailing zeroes and the y sequence has leading zeroes, then the entire covariance function from $s_{yx}(N)$ to $s_{xy}(N-1)$ is obtained. If the sequence is arranged as

$$x(0), x(1), x(2), \ldots, x(N-1), 0(N), 0(N+1), \ldots, 0(2N-1)$$

$$0(0), 0(1), 0(2), \ldots, 0(N-1), y(0), y(1), y(2), \ldots, y(N-1)$$

then the covariance result obtained is

$$s_{yx}(N), s_{yx}(N-1), \ldots, s_{yx}(1), s_{xy}(0), s_{xy}(1), \ldots, s_{xy}(N-1)$$

Since $s_{yx}(i) = s_{xy}(N-i)$, the entire covariance function is obtained in proper sequence from $i = -N$ to $i = (N-1)$.

This time shift can be accomplished by a frequency domain rotation. The time shift (rotation actually) can be accomplished if $S_{xy}(k)$ is multiplied by a factor

$$W_{2N}^{kpN} = \exp\left[-j\frac{2\pi k}{2N}(pN)\right] = \exp(-j2\pi kp) \qquad (7.44)$$

where $p = i/N$ represents the fraction of the total number of lag values to be plotted. If $p = 1$ ($i = N$) then $s_{xy}(i)$ will appear with negative lag values first and positive lag values last with $s_{xy}(0)$ appearing at the center (the Nth + 1 point). If $p = 0.10$ then $0.10N$ negative lag values would appear first, followed by all the positive lag values, in turn followed by the

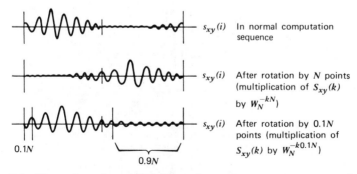

$s_{xy}(i)$ In normal computation sequence

$s_{xy}(i)$ After rotation by N points (multiplication of $S_{xy}(k)$ by W_N^{-kN})

$s_{xy}(i)$ After rotation by $0.1N$ points (multiplication of $S_{xy}(k)$ by $W_N^{-k0.1N}$)

Figure 7.4   Illustration of covariance function sequence rearrangement for plotting.

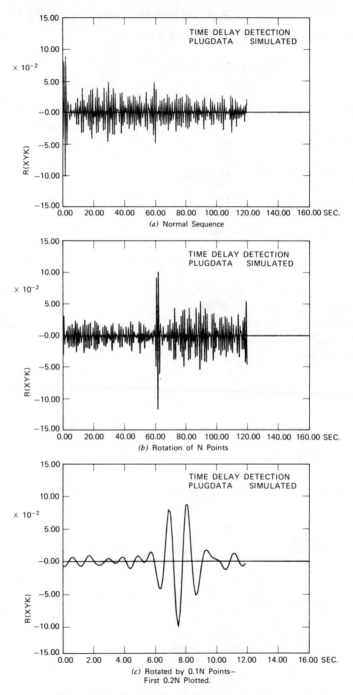

Figure 7.5 Illustration of rotated covariance.

remaining $0.90N$ negative lag values. The quantity $p = i/N$ must be chosen so that i is an integer. Figures 7.4 and 7.5 illustrate the rotated covariance value sequence for $p = 1$ and $p = 0.1$.

In summary the basic Fourier transform formulas for convolution and covariance are as follows:

Convolution:

$$c_{xy}(i) = T \sum_{p=0}^{N-1} x(p) y(p-i) \qquad i = 0, 1, 2, \ldots, N-1$$

$$c_{xy}(i) = \text{FFT}^{-1}\left[C_{xy}(k) = X(k) Y(k) \right] \tag{7.45}$$

Covariance:

$$s_{xy}(i) = \frac{1}{N-i} \sum_{p=0}^{N-1} x(p) y(p+1) \qquad i = 0, 1, 2, \ldots, N-1$$

$$s_{xy}(i) = \frac{N}{N-i} \text{FFT}^{-1}\left[S_{xy}(k) = \frac{1}{P} X^*(k) Y(k) \right] \qquad i = 0, 1, 2, \ldots, N-1$$

$$= \frac{N}{i-N} \text{FFT}^{-1}\left[S_{xy}(k) = \frac{1}{P} X^*(k) Y(k) \right] \qquad i = N+1, N+2, \ldots, 2N-1$$

$$\tag{7.46}$$

In both instances it is tacitly assumed that the last half of the time histories involved have been padded with zeroes in order to avoid circularity biases and to obtain the correct transient covariance or convolution function.

7.5   WRAPAROUND AND ALIASING EFFECTS

Now it is clearly recognized that if the FFT is employed to compute convolutions, a circularity effect is encountered (originally encountered with rotating drum types of analog correlation analyzers). The equation for such a convolution is

$$c_{xy}(i) = \sum_{p=0}^{N-1} x(p) y\left[(i-p) \bmod N \right] \qquad i = 0, 1, 2, \ldots, N-1 \tag{7.47}$$

where $(i-p) \bmod N$ means the index $(i-p)$ is interpreted cyclicly with a cycle of N. That is,

$$a = (i-p) \bmod N$$

which is read "a is congruent to $(i-p)$ modulo N." This means a is the remainder after division of $(i-p)$ by N.

This can be seen to be the sum of the first N and the last N values of $c_{xy}^t(i)$. Denote the last N values as the circular part, $c_{xy}^c(p)$. Then

$$c_{xy}(i) = c_{xy}^t(i) + c_{xy}^c(p) \qquad i=0,1,2,\ldots,N-1 \tag{7.48}$$

This can be written as

$$c_{xy}(i) = \sum_{p=0}^{k} x(p)y(i-p) + \sum_{p=0}^{N-i-2} x(p+i+1)y(N-p-i-1)$$

$$i=0,1,2,\ldots,N-1 \tag{7.49}$$

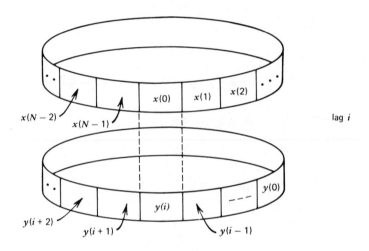

lag i

The circularity terminology arises because the data can be viewed as on a drum, as was pointed out in Chapter 1. In this case there are two segments to the sum:

$$x(0)y(i) + x(1)y(i-1) + \cdots + x(i)y(0)$$

and

$$x(l+1)y(N-1) + \cdots + x(N-1)y(l+1)$$

The circularity phenomena can be eliminated by defining new time histories with N zeroes. Then (7.47) is defined for $2N$ point sequences and the zeroes cause the circular part of (7.48) to be zero. This is illustrated in the drum diagram.

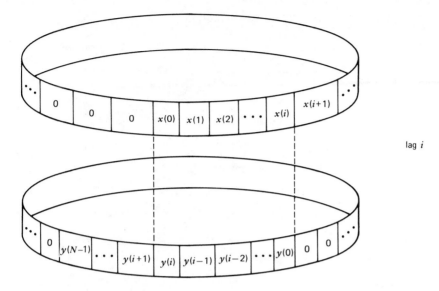

lag i

In Chapter 6 we discuss how zero padding is equivalent to interpolation with Fourier series (harmonic interpolation) on the frequency domain functions. Thus if convolution is attempted with frequency domain functions that have not been properly interpolated, then the circularity phenomena appear and represent a bias in the results. We discuss this point further, shortly.

In viewing convolution from the correlation standpoint, a problem arises with respect to definition of the time reference. Suppose there are an odd number of points $2M+1$ where M is even and assume time zero is at the middle, so that we have $x(i)$, $y(i)$ and the time index is $i=-M,\ldots,$ $-1,0,1,\ldots,M$. Now reverse $y(i)$ in time and it makes sense to compute positive lags and negative lags:

$$x(-M),\ldots,x(-1),x(0),x(1),\ldots,x(M)$$

$$y(M),\ldots,y(1),y(0),y(-1),\ldots,y(-M)$$

$x(-M)y(M)+\cdots+\qquad x(-1)y(1)+x(0)y(0)+x(1)y(-1)+\cdots+x(M)y(-M)\qquad$ lag 0

$x(-M+1)y(M)+\cdots+\qquad x(-1)y(2)+x(0)y(1)+x(1)y(0)+\cdots+x(M)y(-M+1)\quad$ lag 1

$x(-M)y(M-1)+\cdots+\qquad x(-1)y(0)+x(0)y(-1)+x(1)y(-2)+\cdots+x(M-1)y(-M)$

$x(-M+k)y(M)+\cdots+\qquad x(-1)y(k+1)+x(0)y(k)+x(1)y(k-1)+\cdots+x(M)y(-M+k)\quad$ lag k

$x(-M)y(M-k)+\cdots+x(-1)y(-k+1)+x(0)y(-k)+x(1)y(-k-1)+\cdots+x(M-k)y(-M)$

In equation form we have for convolution

$$c_{xy}^t(i) = T \sum_{P=-M+i}^{M} x(p)y(i-p) \qquad i=0,1,2,...,2M \qquad (7.50)$$

$$c_{xy}^t(i) = T \sum_{P=-M}^{M-p} x(p)y(k-p) \qquad i=-1,-2,...,-2M \qquad (7.51)$$

If we think of viewing convolution as a covariance of $x(i)$ with a time reversed version of $y(i)$, then we have

$$x(i) \qquad i=0,1,2,...,N-1$$

$$y(i) \qquad i=0,1,2,...,N-1$$

$$y(N-i)=z(i)$$

$$Ns_{xz}^t(i) = \sum_{p=0}^{N-i-1} x(p)z(p+i) \qquad i=-N,...,-1,0,1,...,N-1 \quad (7.52)$$

$$s_{xz}(i) = s_{xz}^t(i) + s_{xz}^t(N-i) \qquad i=0,1,...,N-1 \qquad (7.53)$$

Negative covariance lags correspond to positive time advances in the convolution, however. The circular convolution therefore is the sum of two sets of lag values of the convolution. The first N values of the convolution corresponds to the positive covariance lags, reversed in time. If we substitute the convolution in (7.53), then the convolution becomes

$$c_{xy}(i-1) = c_{xy}^t(N-i-1) + c_{xy}^t(i-1) \qquad i=1,2,...,N \qquad (7.54)$$

where

$$c_{xy}^t(N-i-1) = Ns_{xz}^t(i) \qquad i=1,...,N-1 \qquad (7.55)$$

$$c_{xy}^t(i-1) = Ns_{xz}^t(N-i) \qquad i=1,2,...,N \qquad (7.56)$$

and for $i=N$

$$c_{xy}^t(-1) = Ns_{xz}^t(N) = 0 \qquad (7.57)$$

Hence cross correlating $x(i)$ with a time reversed version of $y(i)$ gives $c_{xy}(i)$ shifted by one lag value.

Wraparound as Aliasing

We note that the definition of transient convolution (or covariance for that matter) results in a time history of $2N$ data points being generated from two N-point time histories. When we apply the sampling theorem in the frequency domain we note that we require the following sampling interval to avoid aliasing.

$$b' = \frac{1}{2NT} \qquad (7.58)$$

However, the Fourier transforms of $x(i)$ and $y(i)$ give us frequency spacing of

$$b = 2b' = \frac{1}{NT} \qquad (7.59)$$

which is inadequate by a factor of 2.

Hence when the product

$$C_{xy}(k) = X(k)Y(k) \qquad (7.60)$$

is computed, followed by the inverse transform, we come to the realization that we will encounter aliasing of the time domain convolution. If we apply our previous aliasing ideas, interpreted as sums of segments of length T, we find that wraparound error is exactly the same as aliasing error.

The solution is to obtain $X(k)$ and $Y(k)$ at intervals of b rather than b'. Hence we must interpolate these two Fourier transforms, or equivalently pad $x(i)$ and $y(i)$ with N zeroes, before transforming. This will give us the interpolated values of $X(k)$ and $Y(k)$. Note that we cannot interpolate $C_{xy}(k)$ since

$$\left(\widetilde{X(k)Y(k)} \right) \neq \tilde{X}(k)\tilde{Y}(k)$$

where the tilde denotes interpolated value.

Convolutional Filtering

First we cast filtering in the form of convolution. In the continuous case, if $h(\tau)$ is the impulse response function of a constant parameter linear system, then the response $y(t)$ of a linear system (filter) to any specified input $x(t)$ is given by the convolution integral, namely,

$$y(t) = \int_{-\infty}^{\infty} x(\tau)h(t-\tau)\,d\tau \qquad (7.61)$$

The finite discrete version which we refer to as the "circular" convolution is

$$y^c(i) = T \sum_{p=0}^{N-1} x(p) h[(i-p) \bmod N] \qquad i = 0, 1, \ldots, N-1 \qquad (7.62)$$

One usually wants a "transient" convolution, which is defined by (7.6).

One way to obtain (7.6) via the FFT method is to pad each time history with N zeroes. Then $y^c(i)$ will be identical with $y(i)$ over the $2N$ values. The computational time now is effectively doubled. Also, the storage required is doubled. The special "tricks" described in Chapter 6 and used in sections of this chapter can reduce the required storage and also the computational time. If we have a complex sequence $z(i)$, $i = 0, 1, \ldots, N-1$, and we want the FFT which corresponds to the FFT of $x(i)$ padded to length $2N$ where the last half is zeroes, then

$$Z(2k) = \text{FFT}\{z(i)\}$$

$$Z(2k+1) = \text{FFT}\{z(i) W_N^{i/2}\} \qquad k = 0, 1, 2, \ldots, N-1$$

Further, it was shown in Chapter 6 that we can obtain $y(i)$, $i = 0, 1, 2, \ldots, 2N-1$ by an N-point inverse FFT of

$$U(k) = [V(k) + V^*(N-k)] + j[V(k) - V^*(N-k)] W_{2N}^{-k/2}$$

$$k = 0, 1, 2, \ldots, N-1$$

where

$$V(k) = X(k) H(k) \qquad k = 0, 1, 2, \ldots, N-1$$

and $X(k)$ and $H(k)$ are obtained by splitting apart the transform $Z(k)$, which is

$$Z(k) = \text{FFT}[z(i) = x(i) + jh(i)] \qquad k = 0, 1, 2, \ldots, N-1 \qquad (7.63)$$

The final result $y(i)$ is obtained with the even indexed portion appearing as the real part of $u(i)$ and the odd indexed portion the imaginary part. In equation form,

$$y(2i) = \text{Re FFT}^{-1}[U(k)]$$

$$y(2i+1) = \text{Im FFT}^{-1}[U(k)] \qquad i = 0, 1, 2, \ldots, N-1$$

Thus we obtain $y(i)$ with three (complex) N-point FFT's instead of two (complex) $2N$-point FFT's. Since the number of arithmetic operations (for $N=2^p$) is proportional to $N\log_2 N$, we have

$$\frac{3N\log_2 N}{2\times 2N\log_2 2N} = \frac{3p}{4(p+1)}$$

Thus the computational time is reduced by about $\frac{3}{4}$ and the storage by $\frac{1}{2}$.

Chapter 3 defines a method for designing digital filters with finite length impulse response functions. It is usually computationally efficient to employ the FFT and the convolution theorem method described above to accomplish this filtering. The trade-off point usually occurs if the impulse response is between 50 and 100 points in length.* This conclusion is arrived at in the following way:

Number of operations for direct method of transient convolution, (7.6):

$$N_d = 2(1+2+3+\cdots+N) = 2\frac{N(N+1)}{2} = N(N+1) \qquad (7.64)$$

Number of operations for FFT method (assume $N=2^p$) and $4Np$ operations for each FFT:

$$N_{\text{FFT}} = 2\,(4Np)\ +\ 4Np\ =\ 12Np \qquad (7.65)$$

1 complex
FFT plus
1 extra for
interpolated
values

1 inverse
FFT using
special
inverse
method

We neglect the cross product computation and the extra operations necessary for the special inverse FFT for the moment. The ratio is

$$\frac{N_d}{N_{\text{FFT}}} = \frac{N(N+1)}{12Np} = \frac{N+1}{12p} \qquad (7.66)$$

Note that if $N=2^7=128$ then

$$\frac{N_d}{N_{\text{FFT}}} = \frac{129}{84} > 1$$

*And no decimation is being performed.

whereas if $N = 2^6 = 64$ then

$$\frac{N_d}{N_{FFT}} = \frac{65}{72} < 1$$

The specific values for the number of operations depend somewhat on the method of programming, and the above conclusion varies somewhat depending on computational method. Also, we neglected some of the operations for the FFT method. However, it is a very reasonable guideline.

It is possible to apply a "short" impulse response function to an arbitrarily long time history by a method known as "overlap adding." It can be shown [Stockham, 1966] that if the time history $x(i)$ is divided into segments the same length as $h(i)$, and the method just described is applied,

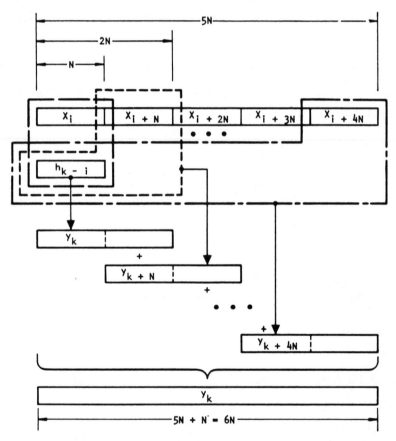

Figure 7.6 Illustration of overlap add method of convolution filter for the special case of x six times as long as h.

then if the last half of the resulting segment of $y(i)$ is saved and added to (point by point) to the first half of the next segment of $y(i)$, we obtain the entire (exact) convolution of $x(i)$ with $h(i)$. This operation, which is illustrated in Figure 7.6, allows convolutional filtering to be a practical and useful method. It would be quite inconvenient if we were restricted to time histories that are restricted in length to the maximum available high-speed core storage. It is clear in this case that we need only compute the FFT of the impulse response function one time. Then the speed ratio will be closer to

$$\frac{N_c}{N_{FFT}} = \frac{N+1}{8p} \tag{7.67}$$

since one direct FFT is not needed.

Now we note that $N = 2^6 = 64$ gives

$$\frac{N_c}{N_{FFT}} = \frac{65}{48}$$

so the break-even point is probably less than 50.

7.6 HOW TO COMPUTE COVARIANCE AND CONVOLUTION FUNCTIONS

Record Length and Number of Lags for Correlation Function

It is quite difficult to make precise quantitative statements regarding the accuracy of covariance functions for noisy data. The situation is just the opposite for that of spectral density functions where quite useful quantitative results are relatively easily derived. The reason is that the time domain covariance functions are highly correlated from point to point (except for pure white noise), whereas the power spectrum points are very nearly uncorrelated from point to point. Any attempt to derive statistical results for the covariance function inevitably lead to a result involving the true covariance function. Hence one needs to a priori know the result one is trying to estimate.

For an individual point on a *correlation* function, there is a very useful result known in statistics as the "Fisher Z-transform." This is the inverse hyperbolic tangent of $r(i)$, which is

$$\hat{z} = \tanh^{-1}[r(i)] = \frac{1}{2} \log \frac{1 + \hat{r}(i)}{1 - \hat{r}(i)} \tag{7.68}$$

It can be shown that $\hat{z}$ is approximately normally distributed with mean

$$\mu_{\hat{z}} = \tanh^{-1}\left[\rho(i)\right] \qquad (7.69)$$

and variance

$$\sigma_{\hat{z}}^2 = \frac{1}{N - 2 - i} \qquad (7.70)$$

Hence one can obtain confidence limits for any individual value, but these would not be correct bounds for the entire set of estimated function values.

As a rule of thumb, one would rarely employ correlation function values for lag values $i \geqslant 0.5N$. This is demonstrated in Akaike [1962]. One can illustrate this erratic behavior for large lags quite easily. A good rule is to not compute lag values greater than 10% of the record length. That is,

$$i \leqslant 0.1N$$

Since most applications of correlation functions are for time delay detection, one should obtain record lengths that are about 10 times as long as the expected time delays.

7.7 IMPULSE RESPONSE LENGTH AND BANDWIDTH FOR CONVOLUTION FILTERING

There are two methods for convolution filtering with FFT's.

Case 1. Time history $x(i)$ and impulse response $h(i)$

1. Impulse response of length M_1 is input and zeroes added if necessary to make a power of 2, $M = 2^p$. An additional M zeroes are effectively added and an FFT of length $2M$ is computed. Since $h(i)$ is real, the transform can be uniquely represented by $M + 1$ values. (The others are complex conjugates.) Denote this by $H(k)$.
2. A segment of $x(i)$ of length M is read, effectively augmented with M zeroes, and $2M$-point FFT is computed. Again, only $M + 1$ values are retained. Denote this by $X'(k)$.
3. The product $H(k)X'(k) = Y'(k)$ is computed.
4. The inverse $2M$-point FFT of $Y'(k)$ is computed after effectively generating the necessary $M - 1$ additional complex conjugate values. Denote this by $y'(i)$.
5. The real time history segment of $y'(i)$ is $2M$ points in length. The first M became the first M points of the final output time history $y(i)$. The second M points are saved.

6. Steps 2–4 are repeated. Denote the new segment $y^l(i)$. The next M points of $y(i)$ are obtained by adding the M points of $y^{l-1}(i)$ which have been saved to the first M points of $y^l(i)$. The second M points of $y^l(i)$ are saved.

7. Step 6 is repeated until the last segment of the input $x(i)$ is input. If it is less than M points, it is augmented with zeroes to make up a segment of M points in length. Steps 2–4 are repeated and a final segment $y^L(i)$ is obtained. The first M points of $y^L(i)$ are added to the points saved of $y^{L-1}(i)$ and output. The second M points are output directly to conclude the process.

We comment that the length M_1 of the impulse response function induces certain limitations on the filtering action. Namely, the effective bandwidth B_e of the filter is limited by

$$B_e \geqslant \frac{1}{M_1 T} \tag{7.71}$$

In practice B_e would be considerably larger and the computational bandwidth, b, would be

$$b = \frac{1}{M_1 T} \tag{7.72}$$

Case 2.   Time history $x(i)$ and frequency response $H(k)$

This method is identical to Case 1 except that step 1 is skipped since $H(k)$ is available directly. [If $H(k)$ is given as gain and phase it is converted first to real and imaginary parts. If phase is omitted, it could be assumed to be zero.]

Note that certain tacit restrictions exist for $H(k)$.

1. It must be $M+1$ points in length. If it is $M_1 < M$ in length, then it is padded with zeroes to become $M+1$ points (where M is the smallest power of 2 greater than M_1).

2. The transform of the M point ($P = MT$) segment of $x(i)$ is padded with zeroes and thus the frequency interval is

$$b = \frac{1}{2P} = \frac{1}{2MT} = \frac{S}{2M} = \frac{F}{M} \tag{7.73}$$

where $S =$ sampling rate and $F =$ folding frequency (Nyquist rate).

3. Any $H(k)$ which is supplied must be at a frequency spacing of $b = F/M = S/2M$.

4. Moreover, any $H(k)$, $k = 0, 1, \ldots, M$ that is utilized must represent a discrete transform whose odd indexed points are those interpolated points resulting when a transform is computed with M zeroes added to the M data points. Contrast this with the usual transform of an M-point real function which is M points in length of which $M/2 + 1$ are unique. Thus the usual spacing is $b = F/M/2 = 2F/M = S/M$.

Item 4 is a key point in performing convolutional filtering with a frequency domain specified function. The interpolated points could be obtained by the "upwards decimation" procedure specified in Section 10 of Chapter 5. Also, they would be obtained by computing the inverse Fourier transform, padding with zeroes, and transforming back. Severely distorted and incorrect results are obtained if resolutions are not compatible.

7.8 NORMALIZATION AND MEAN REMOVAL IN COVARIANCE COMPUTATIONS

The normalizations for correlation function computations can be done in a manner that causes apparent paradoxes to occur in some instances. The zero lag values of the appropriate sample autocorrelation functions can be employed in the normalization since

$$s_x(0) = s_x^2$$

$$s_y(0) = s_y^2 \tag{7.74}$$

Then the correlation function is

$$r_{xy}(i) = \frac{s_{xy}(i)}{\sqrt{s_x(0)s_y(0)}} \qquad i = 0, 1, \ldots, m \tag{7.75}$$

Suppose the mean values have inadvertently not been removed from the time histories. In this case the zero lag values of the apparent autocovariance functions are

$$s_x(0) = s_x^2 + \bar{x}^2 \tag{7.76}$$

$$s_y(0) = s_y^2 + \bar{y}^2$$

The resulting normalization is then in error.

Consider the effect of mean removal and normalization. Suppose

$$x(i) = \Delta x(i) + \bar{x}$$

$$y(i) = \Delta y(i) + \bar{y} \tag{7.77}$$

Then the apparent covariance function is

$$s_{xy}(i) = \frac{1}{N-i} \left[\sum_{p=0}^{N-i-1} \Delta x(p)\Delta y(p+i) + \bar{y} \sum_{p=0}^{N-i-1} \Delta x(i) \right.$$

$$\left. + \bar{x} \sum_{p=0}^{N-i-1} \Delta y(p+i) + (N-i)\,\overline{xy} \right] \tag{7.78}$$

$$= \hat{\mathrm{cov}}(x,y) + \overline{xy} + \bar{x}\Delta\bar{x}_f + \bar{y}\Delta\bar{y}_l \tag{7.79}$$

where $\Delta\bar{x}_f$ and $\Delta\bar{y}_l$ represent sample means of the first and last $N-i$ points of the respective residual time histories. The normalized quantity is the correlation function

$$r_{xy}(i) = \frac{s_{xy}(i)}{\sqrt{s_{xx}(0)s_{yy}(0)}} = \frac{\hat{\mathrm{cov}}(x,y) + xy + x\Delta x_f + y\Delta y_l}{\sqrt{(s_x^2 + \bar{x}^2)(s_y^2 + \bar{y}^2)}}$$

$$= \frac{\hat{\mathrm{cov}}(x,y)}{s_x s_y} \frac{1}{A} + \frac{\overline{xy}}{s_x s_y} \frac{1}{A} + K$$

$$= \frac{\hat{\mathrm{cov}}(x,y)}{s_x s_y} = r_{xy}(i)A - \frac{\overline{xy}}{s_x s_y} \tag{7.80}$$

The quantity A is always less than unity, which says the mean removed data gives a smaller correlation value. If the mean values are both positive or both negative, then the correlation function from data with the mean removed is smaller yet. However, if the means differ in sign the bias can go in the other direction. In general, the cross correlation of time histories without the mean values removed are biased to an artificially high value. This is not true if the sample means were of opposite sign, however.

Normalizing with variances computed over a lesser amount of data does not give a predictable bias. The sample variance computed from a shorter segment of data can be either larger or smaller than the autocorrelation function zero lag value.

7.9 EXAMPLES OF THE USE OF COVARIANCE AND CONVOLUTION

Determination of Time Delays

The convenient normalization of cross correlation functions so that they are bounded in absolute value by unity makes them more useful in applications. Almost all applications of cross correlation functions reduce to time delay detection of some form or the other. Most potential applications of autocorrelation functions are more conveniently interpreted in terms of their frequency domain counterpart, the power spectral density function.

We illustrate the use of the cross correlation in the detection of noise sources. We construct an experiment with a noise source located at three different positions relative to a pair of microphones, as diagrammed in Figure 7.7. The three different cross correlation functions are shown in Figure 7.8. It is easily seen that when the noise source is on the left, then $y(t)$ lags $x(t)$; when the source is in the middle we have a peak at essentially zero delay; and when the source is on the right, $x(t)$ lags $y(t)$, $[y(t)$ leads $x(t)]$ as indicated by the peak at the negative lag value. We note that the speed of sound is about 1100 ft/sec and the microphones are

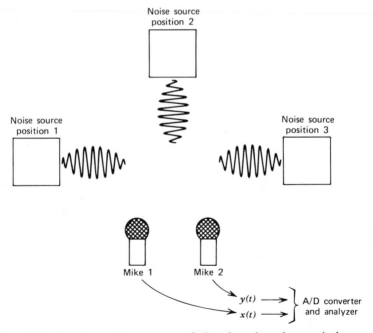

Figure 7.7   Experiment for cross correlation detection of acoustical sources.

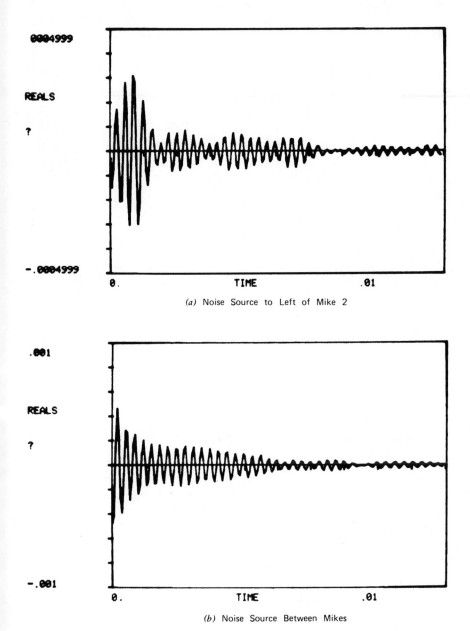

(a) Noise Source to Left of Mike 2

(b) Noise Source Between Mikes

Figure 7.8 Three cross correlation functions for three noise source position.

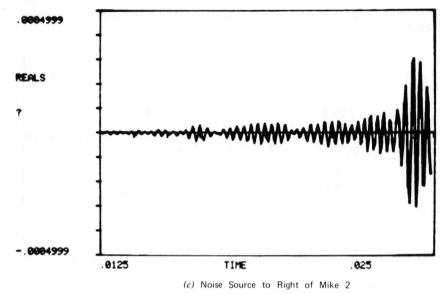

(c) Noise Source to Right of Mike 2

Figure 7.8   (*Continued*).

about 1 ft apart in this case. The time delay is seen to be about 1 msec. The sampling interval in this case is $S = 50,000$ sps, $T = 0.020$ msec so that the lag value at the peak $i = 50$, well within our recommended 10% maximum lag value.

Simulation of a Linear System Response with Convolutional Filtering

If we can estimate the frequency response function of a sensibly linear system, such as most structures, then we can simulate the response of these structures to a reasonable degree of accuracy. Suppose $\hat{H}_{xy}(k)$ is the estimated frequency response and $x(i)$ is an input for which we would like to know the response of the system. Then the estimated response, $\hat{y}(i)$, is given by

$$\hat{y}(i) = \mathcal{F}^{-1}\left[X(k)\hat{H}_{xy}(k)\right] \qquad i = 0, 1, 2, \ldots, N-1 \qquad (7.81)$$

assuming that we have taken care of the circularity problem. Equation (7.81) is equivalent to

$$\hat{y}(i) = T \sum_{p=0}^{N-1} x(p)h(p-i) \qquad i = 0, 1, 2, \ldots, N-1 \qquad (7.82)$$

where $(p - i)$ is interpreted mod N.

The continuous counterpart of (7.82) is usually referred to as Duhamel's integral in structural analysis.

This type of simulation is of interest in a variety of applications. For example, suppose we have a radar building housing delicate electronic equipment. Further, suppose we can determine the frequency response functions from the exterior to the interior.

Then, a problem that occurs in "hardness" studies is what happens at the interior when the exterior is subjected to a given air blast atmospheric overpressure, such as would occur in a nearby bomb blast. Given that we know the time history of a typical expected shock wave generated by a bomb blast, we can estimate the response with (7.81). This was accomplished by Kennedy and Safford [1974] and Masri and Safford [1976].

Illustration of Wraparound (Time Domain Aliasing)

The effect of wraparound manifests itself in distinctively different ways for periodic (deterministic) or random data. The effect of dividing by N or $N - i$ also has a substantially different effect.

For example, in Figure 7.9 we have the autocorrelation function of a sinusoid computed in three different ways:

a. No zero padding, division by N.
b. Zero padding, division by N.
c. Zero padding, division by $N - i$.

We note that we have an apparent distortion in parts b and c, and the distortion is opposite. The wraparound (aliasing) has no effect due to the periodicity of the function. Hence the information that is wrapped around is the correct information. As a result, the division by N gives the unbiased result since N correct cross products appear in the summation. This is contrasted with the zero padded data appearing in parts b and c. In these cases we prevent the wraparound and hence only $N - i$ products appear in the summation. The result is biased downward in a triangular weighted manner when division by N is performed and the result is unbiased when division by $N - i$ is used.

Division by $N - i$ gives unbiased results, but division by N maintains values less than ± 1. Our conclusion is that, if lag values are maintained so that $m \leqslant 0.1/N$, then zero padding and division by $N - i$ avoid bias and there is sufficient sample size to avoid excessive statistical variability in the random data case. We note the problem that occurs for lags near N where we come very close to dividing by zero.

The data we have presented in the plots is artificial, but we emphasize that the results faithfully reflect the effects that occur in practice.

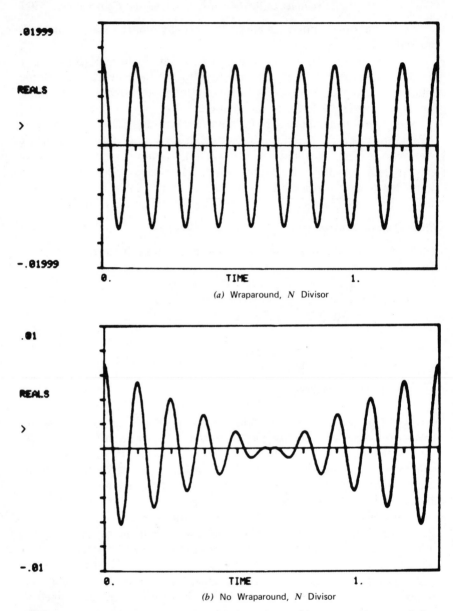

Figure 7.9 Illustration of wraparound bias for a sinusoid in computing correlation functions.

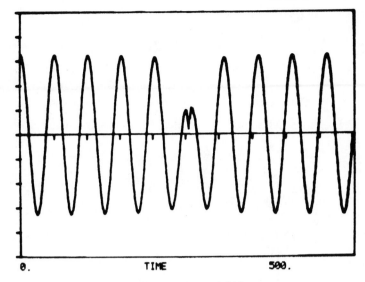

(c) No Wraparound, $N - i$ Divisor

Figure 7.9   (*Continued*).

EXERCISES

7.1. Rewrite covariance equation using (7.29).

Answer:

$$\hat{s}_{xy}(i) = \frac{1}{2N}\left(\sum_{p=1}^{N-r} \left[x(p) + y(p+i) \right]^2 \right.$$

$$\left. - \sum_{p=1}^{N-r} x^2(p) - \sum_{i=1}^{N-r} y^2(p+i) \right)$$

7.2. Rewrite covariance equation using (7.30).

Answer: See 7.1.

7.3. Prove $\mathscr{F}[s_{xy}(\tau)] = \mathscr{F}[X^*(t)\,Y(t)]$.

Answer:

$$\mathscr{F}\left[s_{xy}(\tau) \right] = \int_{-\infty}^{\infty}\int_{-\infty}^{\infty} x(t)\,y(t+\tau)\,e^{-j2\pi f\tau}\,dt\,d\tau$$

Make the change of variable:

$$u = t + \tau \qquad \tau = u - t \qquad d\tau = du$$

then we have

$$\int_{-\infty}^{\infty}\int_{-\infty}^{\infty} x(t)y(u)e^{-j2\pi f(u-t)}\,dt\,du$$

$$= \int_{-\infty}^{\infty} x(t)e^{j2\pi ft}\,dt \int_{-\infty}^{\infty} y(u)e^{-j2\pi fu}\,du = X(f)*Y(f)$$

7.4. Prove delay plots as negative linear sloping phase:

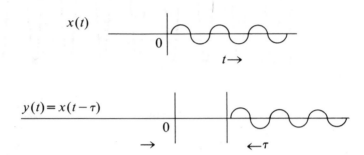

that is, delay is defined so that for $t=\tau$, $x(\tau)$ corresponds to $y(\tau)$ which is $x(\tau-\tau)=x(0)$

Answer:

$$y(\tau)=x(0)$$

Since at $t=\tau$

$$y(t)=x(t-\tau)=x(0)$$

$$\int x(t-\tau)e^{-j2\pi ft}\,dt = \int x(u)e^{-j2\pi f(u+\tau)}\,du$$

where the change of variables are made:

$$u=t-\tau \qquad t=u+\tau \qquad dt=du$$

$$=e^{-j2\pi f\tau}X(f) \qquad \varphi=-2\pi f\tau$$

7.5. Write a computer program to do the following:
  a. Generate a function equal to 0.1 for $i=0,\ldots,2^p-1$, and equal to 0 for $i=2^p,\ldots,127$. The p parameter will be varied from $p=1,\ldots,7$.
  b. Compute the circular correlation function of the above for all 7 cases, and plot using the printer plotting routine.
  c. Comment on the results.

7.6. Repeat 7.5, but modify the program to add uncorrelated Gaussian noise with 0 mean and unit variance (generate this noise by adding 12 successive outputs of TDRAND and subtracting 6 from the sum). Explain the results.

7.7. Repeat 7.6, but do a cross correlation: generate identical step functions but different Gaussian noise for each of the two functions. Explain the results.

CHAPTER 8

POWER AND
CROSS SPECTRAL
DENSITIES

8.1 GENERAL CONSIDERATIONS IN COMPUTING SPECTRA

Definition

A power spectral density function (PSD) is the distribution of variance (mean square value) of a time history over frequency. The term originated in the field of electrical engineering, where power dissipated in an electrical circuit is proportional to the mean square voltage applied, hence the term power. The adjective spectral denotes a function of frequency. The power in an infinitesimal frequency interval is divided by the width of that interval, which results in a density. The application of the concept to many fields besides electrical engineering has resulted in a tendency in some circles to use the term "auto" spectral density.

The PSD is analogous to variance of classical statistics. The natural extension to covariance as a function of frequency leads to the cross spectral density function (CSD). The CSD is defined between a pair of time histories, one usually thought of as the input to a system and the other an output. The CSD is a stepping stone to transfer functions and coherence functions.

The analogies with classical statistics continue, with transfer function being the counterpart of regression coefficient and coherence the counterpart of the squared correlation coefficient.

316

Computational Definitions

Spectral density functions can be computed in three ways. The different methods are based on three different computational definitions of PSD all of which are asymptotically equivalent. Other methods involve prewhitening which is not covered in this volume. However, Volume 2 discusses prewhitening and the application of linear predictive coding (LPC), Prony's method, autoregressive moving averages (ARMA) and maximum entropy spectral analysis (MESA), and so on, to the PSD Estimation Problem. The three methods we refer to here are:

The Fourier Transform Method

PSD $\quad \hat{S}_{xx}(f) = \frac{1}{P} \overline{|X(f)|^2}$ $\qquad\qquad$ (8.1)

CSD $\quad \hat{S}_{xy}(f) = \frac{1}{P} \overline{X^*(f)Y(f)}$ $\qquad\qquad$ (8.2)

The Correlation Function (Blackman–Tukey) Method

PSD $\quad \hat{S}_{xx}(f) = \int_{-P/2}^{P/2} \hat{R}_{xx}(\tau)\cos 2\pi f\tau \, d\tau$ $\qquad$ (8.3)

CSD $\quad \hat{S}_{xy}(f) = \int_{-P/2}^{P/2} \hat{R}_{xy}(\tau)\exp(-j2\pi f\tau) \, d\tau$ $\qquad$ (8.4)

The Bandpass Filter Method

PSD $\quad \hat{S}_{xx}(f) = \frac{1}{B_e} E[x^2(t,f,B_e)]$ $\qquad\qquad$ (8.5)

CSD $\quad \text{Re}[\hat{S}_{xy}(f)] = C_{xy}(f) = \frac{1}{B_e} E[x(t,f,B_e)y(t,f,B_e)]$ $\qquad$ (8.6)

$\quad\text{Im}[\hat{S}_{xy}(f)] = Q_{xy}(f) = \frac{1}{B_e} E[x_q(t,f,B_e)y_q(t,f,B_e)]$ $\qquad$ (8.7)

where

$E[\ ]$ = averaging (expectation) operation

$x(t,f,B_e)$ = the result of bandpass filtering $x(t)$

f = center frequency

B_e = filter bandwidth

$x_q(t,f,B_e) = x(t,f,B_e)$ phase shifted by 90° (quadrature filter)

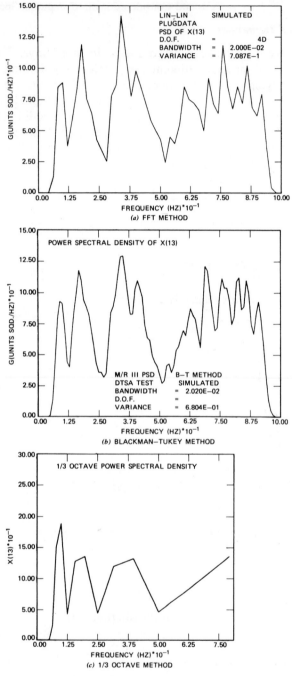

Figure 8.1 Three types of PSD.

Figure 8.1 illustrates the results of the three different methods on the same time history.

The B–T method has been largely replaced by the Fourier transform procedure. Because there are some significant differences in notation, the B–T method is taken up in Appendix B only. The filter method is covered in Chapter 5 on filter applications. In this chapter we discuss the Fourier transform method.

8.2   CONCEPT OF DENSITY

The PSD and CSD are all density functions. A fundamental notion in understanding PSD computations is that densities can never be exactly measured. This applies to any density, for example:

- The density of chalk on a chalkboard.
- The density of mass in a piece of metal.
- The density of the atmosphere.
- Pressure (psi) (in the sense of force per unit area).

In any of these measurements the amount of material in a finite area or volume must be determined and then divided by that area or volume. Hence it is an average that is actually measured over the area or volume employed. This is exactly the interpretation of PSDs.

Equations (8.1), (8.3), and (8.5) are all equivalent if infinitely long record lengths and infinitely narrow bandwidths are used. However, finite record lengths and necessarily finite bandwidths must be employed. In random process theory we would conceptually visualize a set or ensemble of time histories constituting the random process. Then depending on experimental conditions such as the time of day or the phase of the moon, we would select one or more of these which would statistically have the same characteristics at any instant. If we recorded a sufficient number of samples of the process we could perform "ensemble averaging" at any instant of time to determine our statistical characteristics including the PSD. For various reasons including recording costs and convenience it is likely that we will record a single time history. Random process theory says that we conceive of this as a single representation of the infinitely many possible samples we might have recorded had conditions been slightly different. In this case we utilize the property often attributed to random processes called ergodicity, which was discussed in Chapter 2. This says that for the right kind of process (one that is stationary, among other more general requirements) we are able to determine statistical properties with time averages. The time average is necessarily of finite duration. This brings us to our basic problems of finite bandwidths, limited statistical stability, and the other aspects of PSD computations.

As can be seen from the above discussion the concept of PSD is intimately linked to the idea of a stationary random process. However, transient processes exhibit many characteristics of frequency content similar to that of a stationary process. As a result, Fourier transforms and power spectra of transient processes are very useful concepts in data analysis also. Minor modifications in computational approach are required; these will be pointed out.

8.3   EFFECTIVE RESOLUTION BANDWIDTH

A fundamental computational concept is that of effective resolution bandwidth, B_e. It applies to all three formulas and if bandwidth, B_e, and record length, P, are matched, the three different methods will give identical answers for almost all practical purposes. A major idea is that we are only able to measure average power within the finite bandwidth. This bandwidth affects statistical stability in a crucial way which is discussed in Section 8.5.

The three methods typically have effective filter shapes as indicated in Figure 8.2. Consult Otnes and Enochson [1972, Chapters 6–8] for additional details.

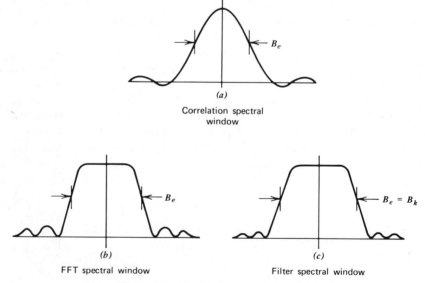

(a)

Correlation spectral window

(b)

FFT spectral window

(c)

Filter spectral window

Figure 8.2 Typical spectral windows.

It is possible to define bandwidth in many ways. The frequency distance between the half-power points on the power transfer function (spectral window) is usually used. Filters are usually designed with half-power point as a fundamental design parameter. For correlation and FFT methods, B_e can be approximately obtained from the following formulas:

Correlation bandwidth $$B_e = \frac{1}{\tau_{max}} \tag{8.8}$$

$\tau_{max} = mT$, where m = maximum lag value and τ_{max} is the maximum time delay value in correlation computation.

FFT bandwidth $$B_e = \frac{1}{P} = \frac{m}{NT}$$

where P is the record length, N the number of sampled data values, and m the number of elementary components averaged.

Filter bandwidth B_e is defined by half-power point bandwidth of digital filter employed.

Different spectral windows are possible in either method with the widest potential variation in the FFT method. Useful spectral windows are described in Section 8.8.

Difference between Resolution and Computational Bandwidth

When points on a spectral function are computed at a frequency spacing of B_e, then the spectral values are (approximately) statistically independent (orthogonal). This is strictly true only for stationary processes. It is possible to compute points at a finer frequency spacing. Strictly speaking these additional points add very little additional information (at least in the sense of information theory). However, it can be shown that one must compute points at a spacing $b = B_e/2$ in order to be able to reconstruct certain time functions from inverse Fourier transforms without a "wraparound" phenomenon occurring. This may be viewed as a frequency domain sampling requirement. In this sense a frequency domain spacing of $B_e/2$ is optimum. In particular this bandwidth is necessary if one wants to compute a transfer function that is usable in doing convolutions via FFT's. In order to avoid the circularity phenomenon, one must add N_s zeroes to each segment in order to obtain $b = B_e/2$. See Chapters 1 and 7 for a complete discussion on the circularity phenomenon.

One has the further practical consideration that smoother, neater plots may be obtained by computing the spectral function at a finer frequency spacing. This computation is in fact equivalent to interpolation with a Fourier series. It can be accomplished by augmenting a function with zeroes. For example, one could interpolate every other point in a table of a mathematical function by the following:

- Compute a Fourier transform (N points long).
- Add N zeroes to the transformed function.
- Finally, compute the inverse Fourier transform.

We generally refer to B_e as "resolution bandwidth" and b as "computational bandwidth." We distinguish between the two because of the reasons cited in this section. The spacing usually employed in B–T spectra is $b = B_e/2$ since this was recommended by Blackman and Tukey in their classic 1958 book. The usual FFT PSD spacing is $b = B_e$ since that is the minimum spacing that gives approximately nonoverlapping, independent frequency values.

8.4   RESOLUTION LIMITS

A question often posed is, "What is the frequency range for digital spectral computations?" This is not meaningful for digital computations in one sense. The reason is that once the data is digitized (sampled) the computer does not know if the data was sampled at intervals of 1 month or $1\,\mu\text{sec}$. The A/D conversion equipment may be limited but once the data is digitized there is the induced frequency range of

$$F = \frac{1}{2T} = \frac{S}{2}$$

The quantity F is the folding or Nyquist frequency and it changes at any time the sampling range is changed–through decimation, for example. The ZOOM procedures discussed in Volume 2 affect this.

If we discuss "real-time" processing, then the above question makes sense. In this case the speed of the A/D converters, the instruction execution speed of the computer and the speed at which displays or peripheral devices can accept data will all affect the speed at which data can be handled. Also, the setting of the sampling rate relative to the frequency bandwidth of the data affects the rate. For example, we process

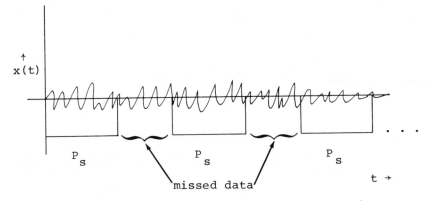

Figure 8.3 Illustration of missed data in real time processing.

data with a sampling rate of $S = 4000$ Hz. This can represent a sampling factor of 4 points per cycle of the highest frequency for 1000 Hz data. It could also be 2000 Hz bandwidth data with sampling rate of a factor of 2 points per cycle. In either case, the number of points to process is the same. However, in one case we are processing 2000-Hz bandwidth, and in the other case, 1000-Hz bandwidth data.

We tacitly assume in the above that all data is being processed. If A/D converters, computer memory speed, and the computer program data handling rate are adequate, high sampling rate data can be input to the computer. However, the FFT, PSD, and other processing may not be able to be done at that rate. In this case a time segment is acquired and processed, a time segment may be missed, and then another time segment processed as illustrated in Figure 8.3.

Often the basic minicomputer is augmented with a high-speed FFT device. Processing speed capabilities range for minicomputer based systems (at the time of this writing), from a few hundred up to about 50,000 sps when augmented with high-speed processors. Hardwired devices can attain higher rates, up to 100,000 sps in many instances. Fast processors are becoming widely available that can handle 1,000,000 sps. Undoubtedly, multi-megahertz rates will become common.

A resolution limitation exists also which is related to the number of memory cells available for data storage. One might note that the limitation is in the form of a $B_e P$ product. In equation form,

$$B_e \geqslant \frac{1}{P}$$

or

$$B_e P \geqslant 1$$

$$B_e NT \geqslant 1$$

$$\frac{NB_e}{S} \geqslant 1$$

For example, if $S = 4096$ sps and $N = 4096$, then the resolution $B_e \geqslant 1$ Hz. If $S = 4.096$ and $N = 4096$, then $B_e \geqslant 0.001$ Hz.

8.5 STATISTICAL STABILITY

Two parameters affect statistical stability:

*   Resolution bandwidth, B_e.
*   Record length $P = NT$.

It can be shown (see Otnes and Enochson [1972, Chapter 5] for example), that under reasonable conditions, PSD estimates approximately follow a chi-square (χ_n^2) distribution with n d.f., where

$$n = 2 B_e P \tag{8.9}$$

Furthermore, for n moderately large, say, $n \geqslant 30$, the χ^2 distribution approximates a Gaussian (normal) distribution. In this case, the normalized standard deviation (standard deviation relative to the value being estimated, i.e., percentage error, or in statistical terminology the "coefficient of variation") is given by

$$\varepsilon_0 = \frac{1}{\sqrt{B_e P}} \tag{8.10}$$

The quantity ε_0 is referred to as the "standard error." Proofs and additional details may be found in Otnes and Enochson [1972, Chapter 5].

The d.f. and associated standard error for the three methods are shown in Table 8.1.

The effect of increasing the d.f. is illustrated in Figure 8.4. All five plots are PSD's of bandpass filtered random noise with a sine wave added at the output.

Table 8.1

Degrees of Freedom

PSD Type	d.f. $n = 2B_e P$	$\varepsilon_0 = \sqrt{1/B_e P}$
B-T correlation	$n = 2N/m$	$\sqrt{m/N}$
FFT	$n = 2M$	$\sqrt{1/M}$
Filter	$n = 2B_k P$	$\sqrt{1/B_k P}$

Where
N = total number of data points
m = maximum lag value in correlation function
M = number of complex Fourier coefficients averaged
B_k = half-power-point bandwidth of digital filter
$P = NT$ = record length

The d.f. is $n = 2$ in the first plot, $n = 8$ in the second, 32 in the third, 128 in the fourth, and 512 in the fifth. The standard errors are as follows:

	d.f.	$\varepsilon_0 = 1/\sqrt{B_e P}$
Plot 1	2	1.0
Plot 2	8	.3
Plot 3	32	.2
Plot 4	128	.09
Plot 5	512	.05

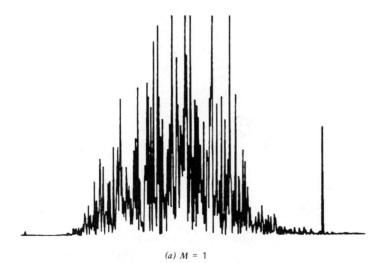

(a) $M = 1$

Figure 8.4 Example of statistical stability.

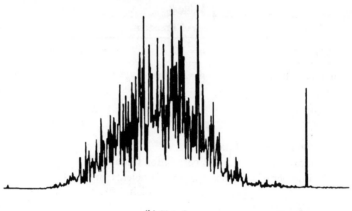

(b) M = 4

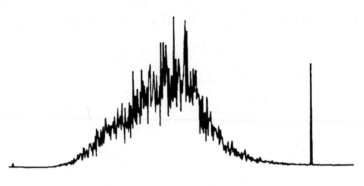

(c) M = 16

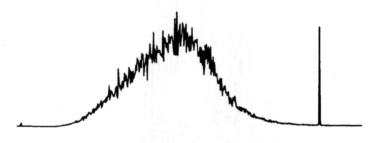

(d) M = 64

Figure 8.4 (*Continued*).

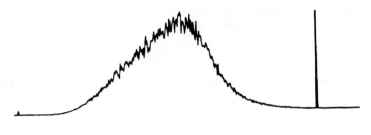

(e) $M = 256$

Figure 8.4   (*Continued*).

Power spectrum confidence limits are easily determined by reference to either χ^2 distribution tables or Gaussian distribution tables depending on n. For example, for $n = 10$, suppose

$$T = \tfrac{1}{2} \text{ sec}, \qquad N = 4000$$

Then

$$P = 2000 \text{ sec}$$

$$F = 1 \text{ Hz}$$

$$B_e = \frac{1}{400} = 0.0025$$

so that

$$n = 2 B_e P = 2 \frac{2000}{400} = 10$$

From page 217 of Otnes and Enochson [1972], if we desire $90\% = 100p$ confidence limits, then

$$\text{Upper confidence limit} = \frac{n\hat{S}(k)}{\chi^2_{n;\,1-\alpha/2}} \qquad (8.12a)$$

$$\text{Lower confidence limit} = \frac{n\hat{S}(k)}{\chi^2_{n;\,\alpha/2}} \qquad (8.12b)$$

where $\alpha = 1 - p$. From Table 5.4 in Otnes and Enochson [1972] we find

$$\chi^2_{10;\,.975} = 3.25$$

$$\chi^2_{10;\,.025} = 20.48$$

Therefore the upper and lower limits are

$$UCL = \frac{10 \, \hat{S}(k)}{3.25} \approx 3 \, \hat{S}(k)$$

$$LCL = \frac{10 \, \hat{S}(k)}{20.48} \approx 0.5 \, \hat{S}(k)$$

Example of Smearing Effect of Finite Resolution

The choice of B_e that is wide with respect to the bandwidth of responses causes a smearing to occur. Statistically speaking this is a bias related to a parameter in the estimation procedure. It is very difficult to categorize and quantify this effect. However, the distortion that occurs is very real and can be demonstrated qualitatively. This is demonstrated in Figure 8.5. The same bandpass filter that was employed for Figure 8.4 is used to filter pseudo-random white Gaussian noise and the sine wave is added to the output. We notice very clearly the loss of detail for a broad resolution. The sine wave is nearly totally lost for 128-point resolution. It progressively appears in a sharper and sharper form as resolution is increased to a maximum of $N=4096$ data points. The higher resolution data appears to have greater statistical variability. This is artificial. The statistical stability is the same, but the plotting of more points in the same space results in the appearance of greater variability.

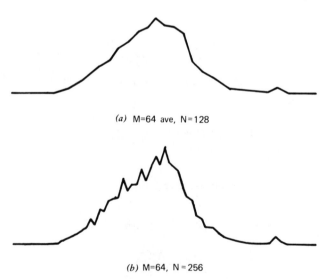

(a) M=64 ave, N=128

(b) M=64, N=256

Figure 8.5 Illustration of bias (smearing) effect due to too wide resolution.

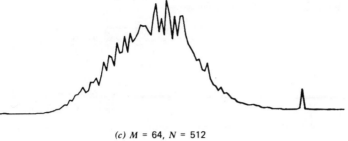

(c) $M = 64$, $N = 512$

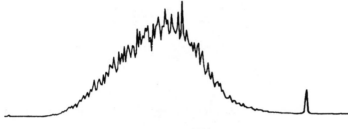

(d) $M = 64$, $N = 1024$

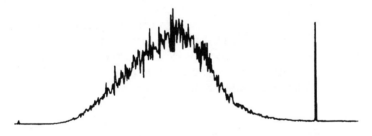

(e) $M = 64$, $N = 2048$

(f) $M = 64$, $N = 4096$

Figure 8.5 *(Continued)*.

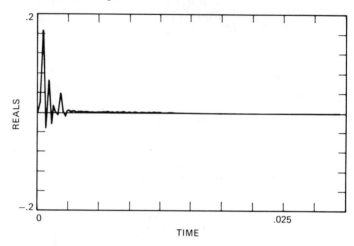

Figure 8.6   Transient time history with zero "offset" but nonzero mean.

Mean Removal

As a rule of thumb, it is good practice in spectral analysis to compute a sample mean value and subtract it from the time history involved. This is true for the analysis of stationary processes. However, it is not true for transient data analysis. Consider the example of Figure 8.6. Although the "offset" is zero, the mean value would be positive owing to the contribution of the transient. Hence the subtraction of the mean would cause an undesirable distortion.

When the time segment averaging technique is employed as discussed later in this chapter, two computational possibilities exist. One is to remove a mean based on the entire time history and the other is to remove the mean of each segment. Removal of the mean from each segment would force the value of $\hat{S}(f)$ at $k=0$ to be zero. Otherwise, the value of $S(0)$ will be

$$E(\bar{x}_s - \bar{x})^2 = \hat{S}(0) \tag{8.13}$$

That is, (8.13) represents the average squared deviation of the segment mean from the overall mean. This may or may not be a significant effect.

8.6   LEAKAGE

Spectral windows will be discussed considerably in the next section. The object of spectral windows is to deal with the phenomenon referred to as "leakage." This leakage can occur in either direction. We can have power "leak out" of a spectral bandwidth to bias power estimates downward or it can "leak in" so that a spectral estimate can be distorted upwards (or downwards if the leakage occurs with negative weighting).

Let us first demonstrate outward leakage. Consider the discrete PSD of a sinusoid of amplitude A and of frequency $f = nb$. This implies we have an integral number of cycles of the sinusoid. From the theory of Chapters 1 and 2, we know the PSD is

$$S_x(k) = \begin{cases} \dfrac{A^2}{4} P & k = \pm n \\ 0 & k \neq \pm n \end{cases} \tag{8.14}$$

which is shown in Figure 8.7. We further know that the function more generally is

$$S_x(k) = \frac{PA^2}{4} \left[\frac{\sin \pi(n-k)}{N \sin[\pi(n-k)/N]} + \frac{\sin \pi(n+k)}{N \sin[\pi(n+k)/N]} \right]^2 \tag{8.15}$$

which can be computed by padding the original time history with zeroes prior to transforming.

Note that if we integrate $S_x(k)$ of (8.14) we obtain $A^2/2$, which is the mean square value of the sinusoid. We also note in this case that the entire mean square value is obtained at the two points at $k = \pm n$.

Suppose we have the same frequency sine wave but instead of an integral number of cycles we have an extra half cycle. Then we have the PSD illustrated in Figure 8.8. This is (8.15), but evaluated at different points. We can view this spectrum as power that has leaked out from the frequency at $(n + \frac{1}{2})b$. If we had another sinusoid at any of the frequency points, then this power that leaked out from the frequency $(n + \frac{1}{2})b$ would add in to the power of this second sinusoid. In this sense it would be power leaking in. We note that *we still recover the total mean square value by integrating over frequency.*

The application of spectral windows can modify the Fourier transforms in a way to reduce and minimize this leakage. The penalty will be broadened resolution and loss of orthogonality, resulting in a loss of degrees of freedom.

In the senses we have described above we avoid leakage if we have integral numbers of cycles in our data window. We must always be careful to remember, however, that we have an underlying spectral window of approximately the $(\sin x)/x$ shape which limits the resolution to no better than $b = 1/P$. We also must keep in mind that when we are dealing with random data, it will be randomly made up of frequency components with

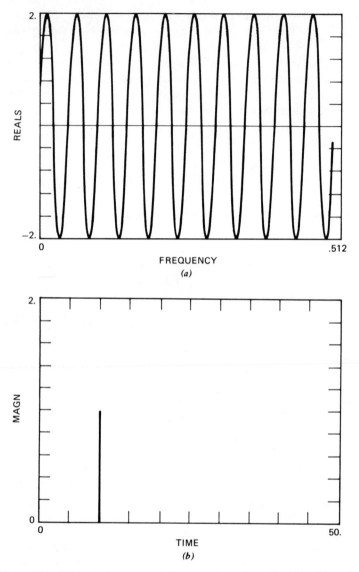

Figure 8.7 PSD of sine wave with integral number of cycles (10 cycles).

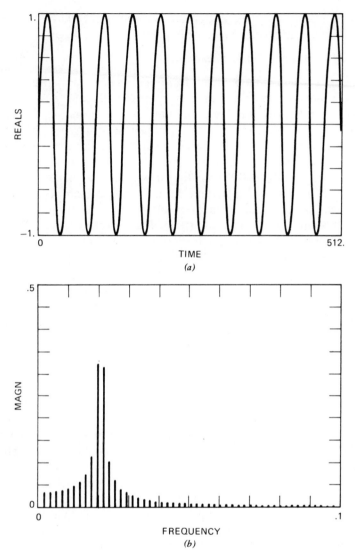

Figure 8.8 PSD of sine wave with integral number of cycles plus half cycle (10.5 cycles).

random numbers of cycles, and hence we will rarely have an integral number of cycles and will always be concerned with leakage.

Relation of Leakage to Gibbs Phenomena

The $(\sin x)/x$ phenomenon arises from the truncation to finite record length. The boxcar function truncates in a discontinuous way. The computation of the Fourier transform amounts to approximating, or fitting, a function with a linear combination of sines and cosines. The Gibbs phenomenon is a statement of the fact that there is always the $(\sin x)/x$ oscillation associated with fitting a discontinuity. If the discontinuity is smoothed, or "rounded off," then the fit will have a smaller error. This rounding off is the multiplication in the time domain by a suitable function. By the convolution theorem of Fourier transforms, this multiplication becomes a convolution (termed a "spectral window") in the frequency domain. This concept is clarified in the subsequent discussion on spectral windows.

8.7   HOW TO COMPUTE SPECTRAL FUNCTIONS

The computation of power and cross spectra was systematized and standardized with the methods of Blackman and Tukey [1958] which are described in Appendix B. These methods utilize the Wiener–Khinchine relation to obtain the spectrum as the Fourier transform of the correlation function. One of the major reasons for this approach was computational efficiency, since a satisfactory spectrum could be determined from a truncated correlation function. Thus with a digital time series of length N, a correlation function of length m is computed in about Nm multiply–add operations rather than the N^2 operations that had been previously necessary in obtaining the spectrum from the Fourier transform of the original data. The use of Fourier transform to obtain spectra was not widely used owing to its cumbersome computational aspects, and thus the practical problems of its implementation were never thoroughly dealt with.

The speed of the FFT algorithms now makes the formerly discarded method the fastest. Although some writers have advanced the use of the FFT to obtain the correlation function and then proceed with the Blackman–Tukey method, it is not often necessary to do this. There seems to be no good reason not to obtain the spectrum directly in the frequency domain without ever resorting to correlation functions. One obtains mathematically different results, but for almost all practical purposes, they are identical. Certain subtleties regarding this are discussed in Volume 2.

The FFT approach requires about $4Np$ operations, where $N = 2^p$. The number of lags for the correlation function is typically chosen to be about

$0.1N$ to $0.05N$. For $N = 4096$, $p = 12$; thus the speed advantage might range from about $100/12$ to $50/12$ or about 8 or 4 to 1 for this example. This is the primary reason for the direct use of the FFT, but certain other potential advantages accrue with regard to smoothing the spectrum; these are discussed in the following sections.

Different FFT algorithms were discussed in Chapter 6. They were for N a power of 2; N a power of 2, 3, 4, and 5; and N a power of 2 but adapted to handle arbitrarily large values of N. The power of 2 algorithm is almost universally implemented on minicomputer based Fourier analysis systems and related hardwired FFT devices, for example, Time Data and Hewlett-Packard minicomputer systems and Spectral Dynamics and Nicolet Scientific hardwired systems.* The power of 2, 3, 4, 5 algorithms are sometimes implemented in larger computer software systems, for example, University Software Systems.[†]

Restrictions on the length of the sequence give rise to special considerations. In principle, a program can be written to handle time series of arbitrary length N, and the computational speed will increase if N is any composite number not a prime. In practice, programs are often written for series of length $N = 2^p$. Thus records of data of lengths that are not integral powers of 2 must be truncated to appropriate lengths or zeroes must be attached. An alternative approach is to subdivide the time history into shorter (possibly overlapping) time histories and average the final results. In many other instances, however, digitized time histories of relatively inconvenient lengths might already be available, and discarding data might amount to throwing away expensive information. Furthermore, the requirement of collecting a certain number of data points presents an additional constraint to the data analyst.

Inconvenient spectral line spacing can arise in the frequency domain also. Suppose, as is not unusual, a sampling rate of

$$S = 1000 \text{ sps}$$

is employed in A/D conversion. Then a segment length of 1024 points, for example, is 1.024 sec and gives

$$B_e = \frac{1}{1.024} = 0.977 \text{ Hz}$$

*Time Data, "TDA Time Series Analysis Systems," Santa Clara, Calif., 1973; Hewlett-Packard, "HP2451 Fourier Analysis System," Santa Clara, Calif., 1973; Spectral Dynamics, "SD501 FFT Analyzer," San Diego, Calif., 1974; Nicolet Scientific, "Omniferous® FFT Analyzer," Northvale, N.J., 1974.
[†]University Software Systems, "MAC/RAN III, User Information Brochure," El Segundo, Calif., 1973.

rather than a more convenient 1.00 Hz. Some of the minicomputer based systems recognize this and build in sampling rates of

$$S = 256 \text{ sps, } 512 \text{ sps, } 1024 \text{ sps, etc.}$$

for example, (or powers of 10 thereof) and obtain more suitable spectral resolutions as a result.

The estimation of power, cross spectra and related spectral functions of random data is usually accomplished in one of these ways:

- Frequency band averaging.
- Ensemble averaging.
- A combination of the two.

By *frequency band averaging* is meant the averaging together of neighboring "raw" spectral estimates. By *ensemble averaging* is meant the averaging together of complete power or cross spectral functions, each computed from different time segments of a time history or pair of time histories.

The basic considerations of resolution bandwidth, record length, and degrees of freedom remain the same whichever method is employed. There will, however, be detailed differences in the effective filter shape, and identical results are never obtained by the two methods. Nevertheless, from a practical engineering standpoint, the results would generally be equivalent if resolution and d.f. are matched.

The combination of the two methods can be accomplished in either sequence. That is, one can smooth individual spectra and then average together sets of spectra, or sets of spectra may be averaged followed by smoothing of the final averaged spectra. We discuss the detailed considerations of the methods in the following sections.

8.8   TAPERING FUNCTIONS—DATA WINDOWS

It is often desirable to taper a random time series at each end to enhance certain characteristics of the spectral estimates. Tapering is multiplying the time series by a "data window," analogous to multiplying the correlation function by a lag window. Thus tapering the time series is equivalent to applying a convolution operation (see Chapter 7) to the "raw" Fourier transform. The purpose of tapering when viewed from its frequency domain effect is to suppress large side lobes in the effective filter obtained with the raw transform. When looked at from the time domain, the object of tapering is to "round off" potential discontinuities at each end of the finite segment of the time history being analyzed.

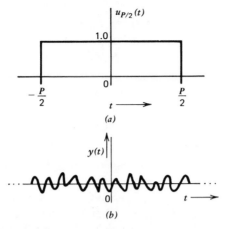

Figure 8.9 (a) Boxcar function for the FFT. (b) Sample time history of length P.

As with the correlation function, one can view a finite-length, random time series as the product of a finite-length boxcar $u_{P/2}(t)$ (Figure 8.9a) and an infinitely long time history $y(t)$ (Figure 8.9b). Thus the finite transform of $x(t)$ may be considered as the transform

$$X(f) = \int_{-P/2}^{P/2} x(t) \exp(-j2\pi ft)\, dt$$

$$= \int_{-\infty}^{\infty} y(t) u_{P/2} \exp(-j2\pi ft)\, dt \tag{8.16}$$

Because products transform to convolutions, we have

$$X(f) = Y(f) * U_{P/2}(f)$$

where

$$U_{P/2}(f) = \int_{-P/2}^{P/2} u_{P/2}(t) \exp(-j2\pi ft)\, dt$$

The effective filter shape with no tapering is illustrated in Figure 8.10. Note that the width of the boxcar function is P, where P is the record length.

Because of the large side lobes, power existing in the data at values other than at integral multiples of $1/P$ will be averaged in the value centered at $f = 0$. By sacrificing some resolution, one can improve the side lobe characteristics.

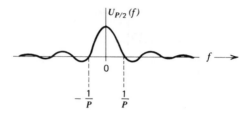

Figure 8.10   Effective filter shape with no tapering.

Sloane [1969] warns against tapering the time history (termed a "linearly modified" estimate) for Gaussian random data. He allows merit for the "signal-like" case for leakage suppression, but points to a loss of degrees of freedom for the pure random case. These comments are accurate but our position is that typical noisy data still tends to be "signal-like" to a large degree and hence some form of tapering is recommended for the typical case. We believe that data encountered in practical problems is often signal-like even though the data is Gaussian. Vibration, acoustics, seismic, and much economics data, for example, exhibit erratically shaped spectra in which distortion of estimates due to leakage is a severe problem. We can state that in our experience, distortion due to leakage and finite bandwidth smearing is at least as severe a problem as lack of available degrees of freedom in data. Thus we find the opposite of Sloane's conclusion, where it is stated that "linear modification results in a decrease in resolution without a compensating decrease in variance." The decrease in variance is seldom a problem, and leakage suppression is a valuable bias reducing property.

Using a cosine taper over $1/10$ of each end of the data rather than $u_{P/2}(t)$ is suggested in Bingham et al. (1967). Such a tapering procedure is shown in Figure 8.11. In equation form, $u_{P/2}^{(2)}(t)$ is

$$u_{P/2}^{(2)}(t) = \begin{cases} \cos^2 \dfrac{5\pi t}{T} & -\dfrac{P}{2} \leqslant t < -\dfrac{4P}{10} \\[2mm] 1 & -\dfrac{4P}{10} \leqslant t < \dfrac{4P}{10} \\[2mm] \cos^2 \dfrac{5\pi t}{T} & \dfrac{4P}{10} \leqslant t < \dfrac{P}{2} \\[2mm] 0 & \text{otherwise} \end{cases} \tag{8.17}$$

On the other hand, multiplying by a full cosine bell has the form

$$u_{P/2}^{(3)}(t) = \frac{1}{2}\left(1 + \cos \frac{2\pi t}{T}\right) \qquad -\frac{P}{2} \leqslant t \leqslant \frac{P}{2} \tag{8.18}$$

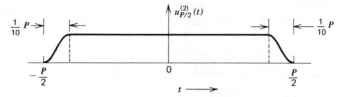

Figure 8.11   Cosine taper data window $u_{P/2}(t)$.

and can be shown to be equivalent to using discrete convolution weights
$(\frac{1}{4}, \frac{1}{2}, \frac{1}{4})$. That is, $U^{(3)}_{P/2}(f)$ is given by

$$U^{(3)}_{P/2}\left(-\frac{1}{P}\right) = \frac{1}{4}$$

$$U^{(3)}_{P/2}(0) = \frac{1}{2} \tag{8.19}$$

$$U^{(3)}_{P/2}\left(\frac{1}{P}\right) = \frac{1}{4}$$

and is 0 at all other multiples of $1/P$, which are the positions at which the
finite discrete Fourier transform is evaluated. Reducing the taper to only
$(1/10)P$ from each end point changes this, however. The approximate
shape of the effective filter is shown in Figure 8.12.

Sloane points out that both windows are members of a cosine–arch class
given in the frequency domain by

$$U_{P/2}(\omega, m) = \frac{\sin\left(\dfrac{2m-1}{2m}\right)\dfrac{\omega P}{2}}{\left(\dfrac{2m-1}{2m}\right)\dfrac{\omega}{2}} \left\{ \frac{\left(\dfrac{2\pi m}{T}\right)^2}{\left[\left(\dfrac{2\pi m}{T}\right)^2 - \omega^2\right]} \right\} \cos\frac{P}{4m} \tag{8.20}$$

When $m=5$ we have $U^{(2)}_{P/2}(\omega)$ and when $m=1$ (8.20) gives $U^{(3)}_{P/2}(\omega)$.

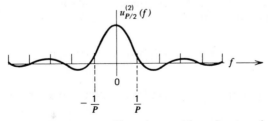

Figure 8.12   Effective filter shape with cosine tapering.

The selection of a tapering function is in many respects analogous to engineering design of an electrical filter. Two special windows have been designed based on compromises between amount of allowable leakage, resolution loss, and corresponding loss in degrees of freedom. These are discussed in the following section.

The Goodman–Enochson–Otnes (GEO) Window

The first window, designed when smoothing over a reasonably wide frequency band is to be performed, is termed the GEO window. This was designed for application as a smoothing function in the frequency domain rather than as a tapering function in the time domain. From a computational expense standpoint, there seems to be little to choose between tapering in time or smoothing in frequency.

The tapering (multiplication) becomes a convolution operation in the frequency domain. In order to minimize computational expense, it is desirable to have the number of smoothing coefficients as small as possible. On the basis of somewhat arbitrary judgment, it was decided to use seven weights. This seems a reasonable compromise between computational complexity and flexibility in selection of smoothing procedures. The smoothing equation is

$$\tilde{X}(k) = \sum_{l=-3}^{3} a(l) X(k+l) = X(k) + \sum_{l=1}^{3} a(l)(X(k-l) + X(k+l))$$

$$(8.21)$$

where

$$a(0) = 1$$

$$a(-3) = a(3)$$

$$a(-2) = a(2)$$

$$a(-1) = a(1) \qquad (8.22)$$

The next constraint imposed on these weights is that they suppress the leakage. A constraint of the form

$$a(0) - 2a(1) + 2a(2) - 2a(3) = 0 \qquad (8.23)$$

will reduce the power leakage from long distance in a manner proportional to $1/f^4$.

The coefficients (8.22) for the GEO window are*

$$a(0) = 1.0$$

$$a(1) = 0.1817$$

$$a(2) = -0.1707$$

$$a(3) = 0.1476 \tag{8.24}$$

These coefficients result in a spectral window that is 10% wider than the $(\sin x)/x$ window. Hence there is a loss of about 10% in d.f. This seems a

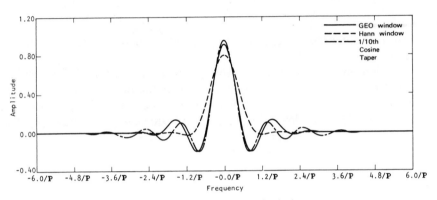

Figure 8.13 Basic spectral window.

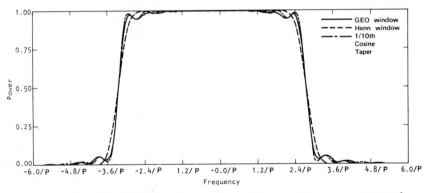

Figure 8.14 Effective PSD window when 12 basic estimates are averaged.

*The time origin is chosen at the center of the data in this formulation. If the origin is chosen at the beginning, then the odd indexed values change in sign since a rotation of 180° takes place.

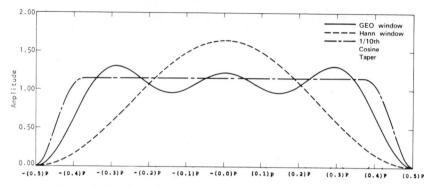

Figure 8.15 Time domain representations of the three windows.

reasonable compromise to obtain the advantage of the increased attenuation of side lobes.

Comparisons (where possible) with some of the other candidates for smoothing are illuminating. Figure 8.13 shows the basic spectral windows for GEO, Hann, and 1/10th cosine taper smoothing. Figure 8.14 illustrates the effective PSD window when 12 estimates are averaged (which provides 24 d.f. in a spectral estimate). Finally, Figure 8.15 shows the equivalent window operations in the time domain.

Leakage Figure of Merit

An additional figure of merit was investigated to estimate the relative amount of power that leaked in via side lobes. This figure of merit is the ratio of the total power in the sum of 12 spectral windows to the power in the main lobe of the composite window. The sum of 12 gives a 24 d.f. spectral estimate which is felt to be near the typical minimum d.f. which would occur in a reasonable spectral analysis.

This figure of merit was easily reduced to negligible values. It will only get smaller for larger d.f. spectral estimates. The value for the GEO window is 0.0073 (0.73%) and for the Hanning it is 0.0022 (0.22%).

A further detail must be taken care of if the property of variance invariance is to be maintained in the results. All data windows change the variance (or power) in the data, since unequal weight is given to different portions of the time history. In effect, data are thrown away. The result is a loss of d.f. and a decrease in variance. The magnitude of the reduction is calculated by computing the ratio in the square of the area of the data window function to the "boxcar" window. For the Hanning window the factor, when the first coefficient is set to 1.0, is 0.375, for the Tukey interim recipe the result is 0.875, and for the GEO window the factor is 1.267. The power spectrum must be multiplied by the reciprocal of the appropriate factor if the area under the power spectrum is to remain invariant. Equivalently, the time history or its Fourier transform can be multiplied by the square root of the appropriate factor.

Window for Ensemble Averaging

When a power (or cross) spectrum is to be computed from the average of spectra computed over individual time history segments, then window design criteria are somewhat different. It is now more important to reduce "nearby" leakage. This was taken care of in the previous design, since it was assumed that smoothing over a frequency band would take place. Thus the relatively large first two side lobes were reduced to a very small percentage of the main lobe after smoothing. This occurs because the main lobe broadens and becomes larger, whereas the side lobes retain effectively their original size.

This does not occur when no frequency smoothing is done. In ensemble averaging the main lobe is averaged with the main lobe, and the side lobe is averaged with the side lobe; the same relative magnitude is maintained. Thus we want a window design with much greater local side lobe suppression. We will sacrifice d.f. to obtain this and assume the d.f. can be regained through longer record lengths or by making the time history segments overlapping rather than contiguous.

By overlapping the segments we use part of the data twice, which is equivalent to multiplying by a factor of 2.0. Suppose the tail of the data had been reduced by a factor of 0.5 with the tapering. The factors of 2.0 and 0.5 would cancel the effect on each other, and the loss in d.f. is therefore overcome. Of course, a penalty in computation time is paid which may or may not be important.

The before and after spectral windows are illustrated in Figure 8.16.

A spectral window (informally suggested by Goodman) for time-slice (ensemble) averaging (to be discussed in the following section), based on a less formal design procedure than that for the GEO window, has weights

$$b(0) = 1.0$$

$$b(1) = b(-1) = 0.35$$

$$b(2) = b(-2) = -0.875$$

$$b(3) = b(-3) = 0.0625 \qquad (8.25)$$

Leakage is kept at about 2%; the coherence between neighboring estimates is about 30%. Local side lobes are reduced to about 2% of the height of the main lobe, however. The shape of this (the Goodman window) is shown in Figure 8.17. The equivalent time domain function is given in Figure 8.18.

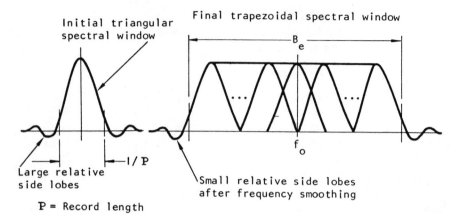

Initial triangular spectral window

Final trapezoidal spectral window

B_e

f_o

Large relative side lobes

Small relative side lobes after frequency smoothing

P = Record length

Before and after frequency smoothing
d.f = 2ℓ, ℓ = Number of raw frequency components averaged

(a)

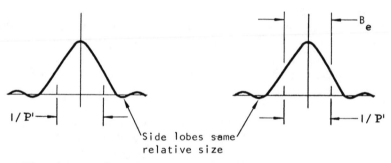

B_e

Side lobes same relative size

1/P'

P' = Segment length

Before and after time-slice spectrum averaging
d.f. = $2m$, m = Number of time slices averaged

(b)

Figure 8.16 Smoothing of FFT-generated PSDs. (a) Frequency band averaging. (b) Ensemble averaging.

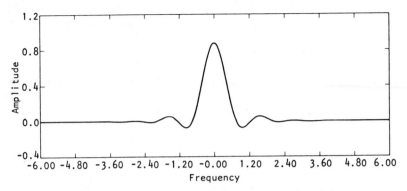

Figure 8.17   Goodman window (frequency domain).

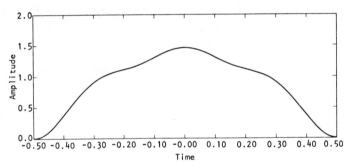

Figure 8.18   Goodman window (time domain).

Zero Padding and Frequency Spacing

The spacing of discrete Fourier transform value is

$$b = \frac{1}{P} = \frac{1}{NT} \qquad (8.26)$$

The spacing between the first zero crossings on both sides of the main lobe for $U_{P/2}$ is $B_e = 1/P$. When zeroes are attached to the sequence, nothing is contributed to the basic shape of $U_{P/2}(f)$, and hence the width of the main lobe is unchanged. However, because of the nature of the computational formula, the spacing of the estimates is based on the augmented record length and is

$$b' = \frac{1}{(N + N_z)T} \qquad (8.27)$$

where N_z is the number of zeroes attached. For example, if an equal

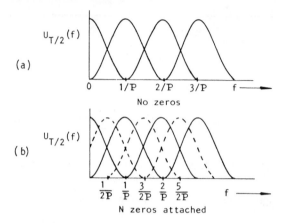

Figure 8.19   Effect on spacing of spectral averages when zeroes are added.

number of zeroes, $N_z = N$, is attached, the spacing is halved and appears as in Figure 8.19. This change in spacing leads to unusual effects, since the effective convolution applied to the raw Fourier transform may or may not lead to the desired side lobe cancellation. In fact, the side lobes might be enlarged. The problems of modifying Fourier transforms when arbitrary numbers of zeroes must be added is essentially that of empirical filter design. The effect of padding with zeroes is left for Exercise 8.7.

Power spectra are obtained from the Fourier transform by the formula

$$\tilde{S}_x(k) = \frac{T}{N}|X(k)|^2$$

$$= \frac{T}{N}\left(\{\text{Re}[X(k)]\}^2 + \{\text{Im}[X(k)]\}^2\right) \tag{8.28}$$

where the tilde ~ indicates "raw" or "unsmoothed" estimate.

If the number of data points is N, then the spacing of the raw estimates is illustrated in Figure 8.20. In statistical terms, the raw power spectra $\tilde{S}_x(k)$ can be shown (as discussed earlier in this chapter) to be approximately χ^2 variables with 2 d.f. That is, if the data are Gaussian, then each spectrum point is the sum of two independent, squared Gaussian variables. The standard error of the unsmoothed spectrum estimates is shown in Section 8.4 to be

$$\varepsilon = \left(\frac{2n}{n^2}\right)^{1/2} = \left(\frac{2\cdot2}{2\cdot2}\right)^{1/2} = 1$$

or 100%. This is not satisfactory for most purposes. If the spectrum is

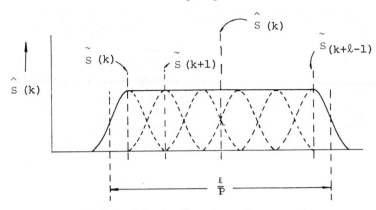

Figure 8.20   Effective filter shape after averaging.

locally smooth, the estimates at the spacing of $1/P$ are approximately uncorrelated (the correlation is the overlap between neighboring estimates as indicated in Figure 8.19a).

Computational Recipes

There are three methods to attain greater d.f. thereby reducing statistical variability:

1. Frequency averaging.
2. Ensemble averaging.
3. A combination of the two.

We explain these methods in the following sections.

Frequency Averaging

If l neighboring estimates are averaged, then the smooth estimate

$$S(k) = \frac{1}{l}\big(\tilde{S}(k) + \tilde{S}(k+1) + \cdots + \tilde{S}(k+l-1)\big) \qquad (8.29)$$

is a χ^2 variable with roughly $2l$ d.f. (and the caret denotes a smoothed estimate) by the χ^2 addition theorem. The effective filter shape is then roughly trapezoidal, since adding together triangles that overlap at half-power points gives a trapezoid as indicated in Figure 8.20. Note that the effective bandwidth is now approximately

$$B_e = lb = \frac{l}{P} \qquad (8.30)$$

The estimate $S(k)$ may be considered as representing the midpoint of the frequency interval from kb to $(k+l-1)b$. We refer to this method of smoothing to obtain additional d.f. as "frequency averaging."

The final estimates $\hat{S}(k)$ can be spaced in any manner desired. If it is satisfactory to have final estimates that overlap at half-power points, then one would average and decimate to obtain N/l final estimates that contain considerable correlation between any contiguous pair of estimates.

Equation (8.29) can be generalized from a simple moving arithmetic average to a more general convolution. Namely,

$$\hat{S}_x(k) = \sum_{i=-m}^{m} a(i)\tilde{S}_x(k-i) \qquad k=0,1,2,\ldots,\frac{N}{2} \tag{8.31}$$

A simple example is Hanning, where the weights are

$$m=1$$
$$a(0) = \tfrac{1}{2} \tag{8.32}$$
$$a(-1) = a(1) = \tfrac{1}{4}$$

if the spacing of the raw estimates is $b=1/P$ where no zeroes have been padded. Hanning may be thought of as a special case of binomial smoothing where the weights (unnormalized) are

$$
\begin{array}{ccccc}
 & 1 & 2 & 1 & \\
1 & 3 & 3 & 1 & \\
1 & 4 & 6 & 4 & 1 \\
 & \cdot & \cdot & \cdot &
\end{array} \tag{8.33}
$$

In the limit, these weights would be calculated as ordinates of the Gaussian probability density function. Since the Fourier transform of a Gaussian function is Gaussian, the time window would also be a Gaussian shape.

Note that another simple smoothing candidate would be a digital RC (exponential) filter. That is, we can view the sequence of PSD values $\tilde{S}(0), \tilde{S}(1), \tilde{S}(2),\ldots$ as a time series. Then we smooth recursively with the formula

$$\hat{S}(k) = \alpha\tilde{S}(k) + (1-\alpha)\hat{S}(k-1) \qquad k=0,1,2,\ldots,\frac{N}{2} \tag{8.34}$$

Typical values for α are 0.05 and 0.10. A recursive filter such as this averages in a way so that high-frequency values would be smoothed by averaging with lower-frequency values only. Also, a frequency shift (the equivalent of a time delay if the filter is applied in the time domain) would be induced. Hence (8.34) by itself is unsatisfactory for spectrum smoothing. However, if we apply (8.34) and then reverse the operation,

$$\hat{\hat{S}}(k) = \alpha \hat{S}(k) + (1-\alpha)\hat{\hat{S}}(k+1) \qquad k = \frac{N}{2}, \frac{N}{2} - 1, \dots, 0 \qquad (8.35)$$

will remove the phase shift. The smoothing effect will be increased in the sense that the filter roll-off is doubled.

In general any recursive filter could be applied to smooth a spectrum, but it should be applied in both directions to eliminate the phase shift and make its effect symmetric. FIR filters designed to have symmetric weights (zero phase shift) would be applied in one direction only. In either case we use the periodicity of the PSD to define the smoothing at the ends of the spectrum.

We call attention to further properties of the spectral estimates if general convolutions (kernels) are employed for smoothing. We can design a smoothing kernel by thinking in terms of the time domain operation—in this case the lag window. If we choose a "good" lowpass filter shape, then the convolution kernel will have the shape of typical impulse response functions as described in Chapters 4 and 5. We note that these have both negative and positive values. Hence we may encounter the classical paradox in the B–T method of negative spectral estimates. This can happen if we encounter erratically shaped spectra. Although this can be disturbing, it is of no cause for concern and it provides us with the information that our spectrum is rapidly varying, or very small, in the vicinity of the negative values.

Method for Frequency Averaging. Reasonable spectral estimates can be obtained for sequences of length N by the following procedure:

1. First fill out the data sequence with zero data points to obtain $2N$ total data points if this spectrum is later to be inverse-transformed to obtain a correlation function. (We will assume this is not done.)

2. Compute the finite Fourier transform of the data sequence:

$$\tilde{X}(k) = \sum_{i=0}^{N-1} x(i) W_N^{ik} \qquad k = 0, 1, \dots, N-1 \qquad (8.36)$$

3. Apply the GEO spectral window to the raw Fourier transform by the

convolution

$$X(k) = \tilde{X}(k) + \sum_{i=1}^{3} a(i)[\tilde{X}(k-1) + \tilde{X}(k+1)]$$ (8.37)

$$k = 0, 1, \ldots, N-1; \quad a(1) = -0.1817;$$

$$a(2) = -0.1707; \qquad a(3) = -0.1476$$

At the ends, use the periodicity of transform

$$\tilde{X}(N+k) = \tilde{X}(k)$$ (8.37)

to define $\tilde{X}(k)$ for values of the index less than zero or greater than $N-1$.

4. Compute the absolute value squared, scaled appropriately to obtain the "raw" power spectral estimates:

$$\tilde{S}_x(k) = \frac{1}{P}|X(k)|^2 \qquad k = 0, 1, \ldots, \frac{N}{2}$$ (8.38)

(We need a factor of 2 here if we want to account for the power at negative frequencies.)

5. Adjust the estimates for the scale factor due to GEO smoothing:

$$0.856 \tilde{S}_x(k) \rightarrow \tilde{S}_x(k) \qquad k = 0, 1, \ldots, \frac{N}{2}$$ (8.39)

This is necessary to account for the reduction in variance caused by the tapering of the spectral window. The specific numerical value depends on the fact that the central weight was normalized to unity for computational efficiency.

6. Smoothed estimates are then obtained by averaging contiguous raw estimates to yield

$$\hat{S}_x(k) = \frac{1}{2l+1} \sum_{j=-l}^{l} \tilde{S}_x(k+j) \qquad k = 0, 2l+1, 2(2l+1), \ldots, m(2l+1)$$

(8.40)

The spectrum values $\hat{S}_x(k)$ are interpreted as being at frequency values

$$f = 0, (2l+1)b, 2(2l+1)b, 3(2l+1)b, \ldots, m(2l+1)b$$

We note that this final smoothing could be replaced with a more general convolution, and the spacing could be selected to be at a finer interval than B_e. Depending on computational considerations relative to evaluating such a convolution, we may end up with a B–T approach. This is true since convolution in the frequency domain can sometimes be more efficiently implemented by multiplication of functions (a lag window in this case times the covariance function) in the time domain. Hence we could inverse transform to obtain the correlation function, multiply by an appropriate lag window and transform to obtain the smoothed spectrum and perhaps decimate the spectral function.

We now turn our attention to the alternative method of computations.

Ensemble Averaging

For long record lengths of data, an acceptable method is to segment the overall time history and compute an average spectrum which was referred to earlier as ensemble averaging. The terminology is, strictly speaking, misleading since we do not have an ensemble (set) of sample functions from a random process over which to determine statistical averages. Rather we have a set of time histories which are segments from a single time history (sample function of a random process). This is the method most often implemented on minicomputer based Fourier analysis systems or hardwired digital systems.

Because we average statistics of segments together we are tacitly assuming we have stationary processes. In practice, we can adjust our methods to allow for time varying processes, assuming the statistical characteristics do not change too rapidly with respect to segment length.

A reasonable approach is to base the segment length on resolution requirements. That is, if $B_e = b$ is specified, then the segment length is $P_s = 1/b$, which is then padded with zeroes to the nearest power of 2. The spectral window suggested is the Goodman window with small side lobes to account for the problem depicted in Figure 8.17. The computational recipe follows.

Method for Ensemble Averaging

1. Compute a trial segment length P_s' from specified resolution:

$$P_s' = \frac{1}{b} \tag{8.41}$$

Determine the smallest power of 2, p, so that

$$\frac{P_s'}{T} = N_s' \leqslant N_s = 2^p \tag{8.42}$$

If

$$2^{p-1} < N_s' \leqslant 1.25 \ 2^{p-1} \tag{8.43}$$

choose segment length $N_s = 2^{p-1}$; otherwise choose $N_s = 2^p$. If $N_s = 2^{p-1}$ is selected, recompute true resolution as

$$B_e = b = \frac{1}{2^{p-1}} \tag{8.44}$$

(The factor of .25 is arbitrary but reasonable based on the authors' experience.)

2. Compute the total number of segments

$$m < \left[\frac{N}{N_s} + 1 \right] \tag{8.45}$$

where the brackets indicate the largest integer value less than the term within the brackets. If we are dealing with a fixed record length, there will usually be one "short" segment of length

$$N_m = N - (p-1)N_s \tag{8.46}$$

This last segment will be padded with extra zeroes as necessary to bring it to length N_s.

3. Determine weights for each spectrum in final average. The first $(m-1)$ spectra are given weight

$$w = \frac{N_s}{mN_s'} \tag{8.47}$$

The last segment is given weight

$$w_m = \frac{N_s}{mN_m} \tag{8.48}$$

If all segments are equal then all weights are $1/m$.

4. Compute the finite Fourier transform of the first N_s'-point sequence, augmented with zeroes if necessary, to bring it to length $N_s = 2^p$:

$$\tilde{X}_l(k) = \sum_{i=0}^{N_s-1} x_l(i) W^{ik} \qquad l = 1 \tag{8.49}$$

where l indicates the segment number.

5. Apply the Goodman spectral window to the raw Fourier transform:

$$X_l(k) = \tilde{X}(k) + \sum_{i=1}^{3} b(i)[\tilde{X}_l(k-i) + \tilde{X}_l(k+i)]$$

$$k = 0,1,2,\ldots,N_s-1; \quad b(1) = -0.35;$$

$$b(2) = -0.0875; \quad b(3) = -0.0625 \tag{8.50}$$

6. Compute the absolute value squared, scaled appropriately, to obtain "raw" spectral estimates:

$$\tilde{S}_x(k) = \frac{1}{P_s}|X(k)|^2 \qquad k = 0,1,\ldots,\frac{N_s}{2} \tag{8.51}$$

7. Adjust the estimates for the scale factor due to Goodman smoothing:

$$(1.267)\,\tilde{S}_x(k) \to \tilde{S}_x(k)$$

8. Repeat steps 4–7 for segments $l = 2,3,\ldots,m$.
9. Compute final smoothed estimates by averaging the m raw spectra:

$$\hat{S}_x(k) = \frac{1}{w}\sum_{l=1}^{m-1}\tilde{S}_{sl}(k) + \frac{1}{w_m}\tilde{S}_{xm}(k) \qquad k = 0,1,\ldots,\frac{N_s}{2}-1 \tag{8.52}$$

One obtains $N_s/2$ spectrum estimates (possibly correlated) interpreted as located at frequency values

$$f = 0, b, 2b, 3b, \ldots, \left(\frac{N_s}{2}\right)b$$

each having approximately

$$n = 2m \text{ d.f.}$$

The preceding method is often implemented in on-line experimental situations when the available record length is arbitrarily long for all practical purposes. Then segment length can usually be adjusted along with sampling rate to provide desired resolutions. Also, sampling rates can be adjusted so the B_e will take on convenient integral values. For example, if $N = 256$ and $S = 256$ sps then

$$P = N\frac{1}{S} = 1 \text{ sec}$$

and

$$B_e = \frac{1}{P} = 1 \text{ Hz}$$

Similarly we might select $S = 2.56$, 25.6, 2560 sps or integral multiples of these in order to obtain convenient resolutions. Other values of 2^P would lead to other values for sampling rates. Finally, in this real time environment the segment weights will always be equal and be

$$w = \frac{1}{m}$$

where m is the total number of segments.

Combined Method

The two previously defined methods, frequency averaging and ensemble averaging, are both linear operations in the general sense. Hence they may both be applied, in either sequence, and the result is a linear (averaging) operation.

If we average over m segments and then further average l neighboring spectral estimates we obtain final spectral estimates with

$$n \approx 2lm \text{ d.f.} \tag{8.53}$$

and resolution

$$B_e \approx \frac{l}{P_s} \tag{8.54}$$

Since the linear averaging operations commute, it makes no difference in which sequence we perform the operations; the results will be the same (except for roundoff error).

There are two questions to answer:

1. How should segment length be selected.
2. What spectral window should be employed.

No truly optimum answer exists. A reasonable criteria is to select the segment length that minimizes computational time. A close approximation is to select a segment size that minimizes the number of zeroes to be added to a segment and yet obtains a resolution as close as possible to that selected by the analyst. A better match to requested resolution can generally be attained with the power of 2, 3, 4, 5 algorithm rather than the power of 2 version.

Let us consider an example: suppose the requested bandwidth is

$$B_e = 15 \text{ Hz}$$

and the sampling rate provided is

$$S = 10,000 \text{ Hz}$$

The minimum possible segment length is

$$P_s = \frac{1}{B_e} = \frac{1}{15} = 0.0667 \text{ sec}$$

The corresponding number of points is

$$N_s = \frac{P_s}{T} = P_s S = 0.0667 \times 10,000 = 667$$

If we have a 2^p algorithm, then 1024 would be the smallest number we could deal with and we would have to pad each segment with $1024 - 667 = 357$ zeroes. As another possibility we note that $3 \times 667 = 2001$. In this case we could pad with 23 zeroes and frequency smooth three adjacent spectral values to attain very nearly the requested resolution. Our frequency spacing of the final spectrum would be

$$3b = 3\frac{10,000}{2048} = 14.65$$

The actual resolution would be slightly wider and is approximately

$$B_e = 2b + 5 \approx 14.76$$

This is because the end spectral components contribute slightly more to the overall width. Our final d.f. would depend on our total record length and would be attained by ensemble averaging as many spectra as needed (or available). We note that we need do the frequency averaging only one time after all ensemble averaging is complete. This results in a slight computational time saving.

Our algorithm for segment size becomes:

1. Compute $P_s = 1/B_e$ where B_e is requested resolution.
2. Compute a trial number of points $N_s = P_s/T$.
3. Compare integral multiples of $kN_s (k = 1, 2, ...)$ with 2^p.
4. Select smallest value of p which gives smallest number of zeroes. The number of frequency bands to average over will be the corresponding k.

If the available FFT algorithm is for powers of 2,3,4,5, then step 3 is replaced with comparisons of the values from Table 6.2. In practice, it would be rare when a power of 2,3,4,5 would not fit the requested segment length directly.

Cross Spectra, Transfer Function, and Coherence

The computational technique for cross spectra is essentially identical to that for the power spectra. Transfer functions and coherence functions are discussed thoroughly in Chapter 9 but the basic computation is simple and is reviewed here.

If cross spectral density functions are desired, a second Fourier transform $Y(k)$ is obtained. Then the "raw" cross spectra spectral density estimate is obtained from the equation

$$\tilde{S}_{xy}(k) = \frac{1}{P} X^*(k) Y(k)$$

$$= \tilde{C}_{xy}(k) - j\tilde{Q}_{xy}(k) \qquad k = 0, 1, 2, \ldots, \frac{N}{2} \tag{8.55}$$

We assume that the Fourier transforms have been modified if necessary for leakage suppression.

It is often convenient to obtain two transforms at a time employing (6.17) and (6.18).

Final smoothing will be accomplished in either of the three methods described for PSDs, frequency averaging, ensemble averaging, or the combination.

For cross spectra, the absolute value $|\hat{S}_{xy}(k)|$, or the squared absolute value, $|\hat{S}_{xy}(k)|^2$, and the phase (in degrees), $\hat{\theta}_{xy}(k)$, will normally be the final results given by

$$\left|\hat{S}_{xy}(k)\right|^2 = \hat{C}_{xy}^2(k) + \hat{Q}_{xy}^2(k)$$

$$\hat{\theta}_{xy}(k) = \frac{360}{2\pi} \arctan\left[\hat{Q}_{xy}(k)/\hat{C}_{xy}(k)\right] \text{ (in degrees)}$$

$$|\hat{S}_{xy}(k)| = \sqrt{|\hat{S}_{xy}(k)|^2} \qquad k = 0, 1, 2, \ldots, \frac{N}{2} \tag{8.56}$$

The cross spectrum is rarely an end result by itself. Rather it is usually an intermediate step in obtaining the closely related transfer function and coherence function. The transfer function is given by

$$\hat{H}_{xy}(k) = \frac{\hat{S}_{xy}(k)}{\hat{S}_x(k)} \qquad k = 0, 1, 2, \ldots, \frac{N}{2} \tag{8.57}$$

It is usually expressed in terms of absolute value, referred to as *gain*, or absolute value squared and phase. The gain is

$$|\hat{H}_{xy}(k)| = \frac{|\hat{S}_{xy}(k)|}{\hat{S}_x(k)} \qquad k = 0, 1, 2, \ldots, \frac{N}{2} \qquad (8.58)$$

The phase is identical to the cross spectrum phase and hence is given by (8.56). The transfer function defines the complex valued relationship between two time histories as a function of frequency. This complex relationship is normally stated in polar coordinate form, that is, gain (absolute value) and phase. See Chapter 9 for a comprehensive discussion.

The coherence function is also closely related to the cross spectrum and is given by

$$\hat{\gamma}_{xy}^2(k) = \frac{|\hat{S}_{xy}(k)|^2}{\hat{S}_x(k)\hat{S}_y(k)} \qquad k = 0, 1, 2, \ldots, \frac{N}{2} \qquad (8.59)$$

In some cases the phase is also associated with the coherence function. In other instances, the positive square root is taken. When this is done, we have a generalization of the correlation coefficient of basic statistics. A $0°$ phase shift corresponds to positive correlation; a $180°$ phase shift corresponds to negative correlation. Other phases have no counterpart in elementary statistics. Consult Chapter 9 for an amplification of these points.

Linear Averaging

The above types of PSD smoothing procedures are all of the *quadratic* averaging class. Under certain circumstances it is possible to attain more accurate spectral estimates by ensemble averaging time segments. That is,

$$\bar{x}(i) = \frac{1}{m}\sum_{l=1}^{m} x(i) \qquad i = 0, 1, 2, \ldots, N-1 \qquad (8.60)$$

If the segments were statistically independent, this method would be nonsensical since we would quickly arrive at the mean value of the process, which would be 0 in the case of a zero mean process! We shall see that in important practical situations, the segments are not statistically independent and we obtain an advantage from linear averaging.

We note that (8.60) is equivalent to averaging Fourier transforms since

$$\bar{X}(k) = \mathscr{F}[\bar{x}(i)] = \mathscr{F}\left[\frac{1}{m}\sum x(i)\right]$$

$$= \frac{1}{m}\sum \mathscr{F}[x(i)]$$

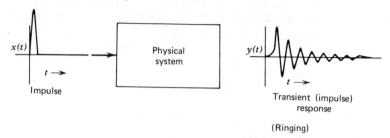

Figure 8.21   Impulse in and transient response of linear system.

That is, both are linear operations and hence are commutative. With this in mind it is simpler to see why linear averaging is effective. We discuss this from an intuitive viewpoint and refer the reader to Norin and Sloane [1975] for a more complete discussion.

Consider the response of a physical system to an impulsive input. It is clear that the system "rings"; that is, a transient response occurs which takes some time to decay as depicted in Figure 8.21. The ringing of a bell when struck by a hammer is an extreme example of this. We can view a time history as a sequence of impulses at an infinitesimally small spacing as illustrated in Figure 8.22. Thus when we truncate a pair of time histories to some finite time segment to obtain spectral estimates, we always miss portions of the transient response of the output due to the final portion of the input. The longer the segment length relative to the length of the transient response, the smaller the error due to this truncation.

The frequency domain interpretation of the above discussion is the error due to a resolution bandwidth that is too wide. However, the crucial point is that even if resolution is too wide, we can recover the bias error due to smearing by linear averaging!

We cannot obtain any more points on the spectral functions, and hence cannot improve the resolution past the basic limitation imposed by the segment length. However, we can minimize the error at the points where the spectra are computed. In addition to reducing smearing errors *we*

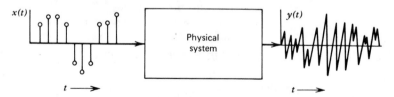

Figure 8.22   Response to time history as sequence of impulse.

obtain the added advantage of reducing variability! This is because extraneous independent noise is smoothed by the linear averaging.

In a statistical sense, the estimates of PSD's and CSD's are second-order (quadratic) functions and the analogies are variance and covariance. The linear average then is the counterpart of estimating the mean value. If we did things with uncorrelated data samples, our mean value estimate would merely converge to zero. When we deal with correlated samples, however, we obtain a better estimate of the impulse response.

Recall from the aliasing discussion that if we compute the inverse transform of a frequency function (here in particular, we are primarily concerned with transfer functions), then we obtain a biased (circular) time function. That is, we obtain

$$h'(i) = \sum_{n=-\infty}^{\infty} h(i-nP) \qquad P=NT \tag{8.61}$$

In this case

$$h'(i) = b \sum_{k=0}^{N-1} H(k) W_N^{-ik} \qquad k=0,1,2,\dots,N-1$$

and we assume $H(k)$ is the exact transfer function at the points at which it is computed; see Figure 8.23. If we reason in reverse, we see that if our time segment is short relative to the decay time of the impulse response, then when we compute our transfer function, we will be in error if we leave off these segments. Furthermore we can recover our error by linearly adding in segments as defined by (8.61). This is the rationale behind linear averaging.

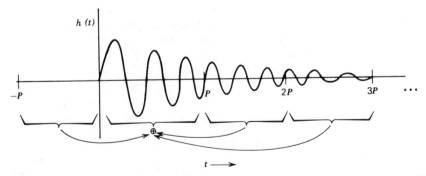

Figure 8.23 A biased impulse response function. Segments of length P are all added into the base segment from 0 to P.

8.9 EXAMPLES OF THE USE OF PSD FUNCTIONS

Fast Frequency Response Measurements

Since white noise has all frequencies at the same intensity it can be applied to one port of a two port system. This is the drive signal. The second port can be analyzed with a PSD analyzer and the output spectrum is the frequency response of the two port system.

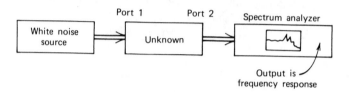

Typical sweep oscillators take several minutes to produce a 10–20 Hz frequency response. A real time (R.T.) spectrum analyzer can speed this up considerably. Sweep oscillators also are limited in their ability to cover very low frequency. R.T. spectrum analyzers go to DC so the noise generator is the limiting low frequency factor.

Measurement of Acoustic Transmission / Loss Properties

Often it is important to test materials to see what types of transmission characteristics they exhibit. This may mean testing a metal structure like a plate of steel or glass to see what frequencies excite this structure and cause it to vibrate. More commonly, materials specifically designed to attenuate noise like sound-deadening panels are tested. This type of material is usually supplied with an attenuation curve which specifies the amount and frequency of loss through the panel.

Measurements can be made on the loudspeaker side as well and then subtracted from the measurements made on the other side. This corrects for inaccuracy caused because of frequency responses of the power amplifier and loudspeaker.

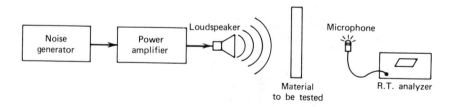

Measurements of Harmonic Distortion in Audio Frequency Systems

Audio circuits are designed to be distortion free, but all electronics have distortion due to nonideal characteristics. It is important to measure this distortion and determine if products meet design objectives and are usable. Usually harmonic distortion is caused by the third harmonic of a fundamental. A simple measurement technique for measurement of this harmonic distortion can be made with a real time R.T. analyzer and a sine wave oscillator.

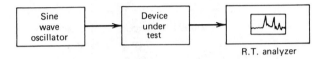

R.T. analyzer

The approximate percentage distortion is found by finding the D level between the fundamental and third harmonic, that is:

$$D \text{ level} = 40 \text{ dB} = 1\% \text{ distortion}$$

$$D \text{ level} = 60 \text{ dB} = 0.1\% \text{ distortion}$$

Other harmonics can be power summed and compared for exact harmonic distortion but little improvement in accuracy is obtained.

EXERCISES

8.1. Why is the statement made that binomial smoothing weights have a Gaussian limiting shape?

Answer:

Fundamental central limit of statistics says that limit of binomial distribution is the Gaussian.

8.2. Suppose we want to analyze vibration data with maximum expected frequency components of $3k$ Hz and we decide to use $S = 10,000$ sps. Also suppose the narrowest response band is expected to be about 40 Hz and we select a resolution of $B_e = 10$ Hz. What are

$$\text{Nyquist frequency} = F =$$

$$\text{Segment period} = P_s =$$

$$\text{Segment size} = N_s =$$

If we want $n = 100$ d.f., how many segments do we need?

8.3. In the discussion of frequency averaging in Section 8.8 we state that the Fourier transform of a Gaussian function is a function with Gaussian shape. Prove this statement.

8.4. The scale factor $PA^2/4$ occurs in (8.15) of a finite discrete PSD of a sine wave of frequency nb, prove the scale factor is consistent with T/N used elsewhere.

8.5. Derive (8.15).

8.6. Derive a formula for the time domain version of the GEO window for arbitrary N, program this formula, and generate a plot.

8.7. In the discussion of zero padding and frequency spacing in Section 8.8 we state that unpredictable effects can occur in the shape of spectral windows when zero padding is employed. Compute the shape of the GEO window (in the frequency domain) by using the results of Exercise 8.6. Fourier transform this equation after padding with $1/3N$ zeroes and $2/3N$ zeroes and plot the results.

CHAPTER 9

TRANSFER FUNCTIONS AND COHERENCE FUNCTION

9.1 PROPERTIES OF TRANSFER FUNCTIONS

In this chapter we use the term transfer function for brevity when, by most definitions, we are, strictly speaking, referring to frequency response functions. In particular we are concerned with the computation of estimates of transfer functions when a "linear" model underlies the analysis. This transfer function might be the reciprocal of a mechanical impedance function in the case of structures. In electrical circuitry, it might represent a linear filter, where filter can be interpreted very generally as any linear operation definable by a convolution integral. In a variety of situations, the transfer function might simply represent some unexplained, but useful, linear relation between two arbitrary time histories. The discussion in this chapter covers both single input and multiple input linear systems. The concepts involved for the multi-input case involve both multivariate statistics and time series analysis. As a result, much of the discussion is relatively advanced and the reader is advised to bypass it on the first reading of the text if he is not thoroughly comfortable with at least one of the two disciplines; this includes Sections 9.3 and 9.4 and parts of other sections.

The concepts are easily extended (in theory, but not necessarily in practice) to multivariate models represented as a multiple input–single output system. These are discussed in Section 9.2.

An extremely useful parameter in evaluating the accuracy of an useful-ness of linear relations is the "coherence" function which is discussed in Section 9.4.

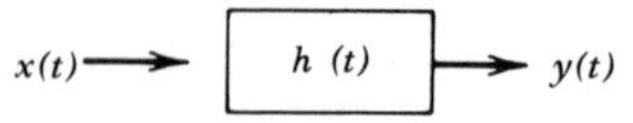

$x(t) \longrightarrow$ | $h\ (t)$ | $\longrightarrow y(t)$

Figure 9.1 Block diagram for single input–single output linear system.

Consider a physically realizable linear system such as depicted by the input/output diagram of Figure 9.1 that does not have any time-varying parameters. As discussed in Chapter 1, the weighting function $h(\tau)$ associated with this system is defined as the response (the output) function of the system to a unit impulse input function as a function of the time τ from the occurrence of the impulse. For physically realizable systems, it is necessary that $h(\tau)=0$ for $\tau<0$, since the response must follow the input. The weighting function or impulse response function concept is useful because, for an arbitrary input $x(t)$, the system output $y(t)$ is given by the convolution integral

$$y(t)=\int_0^\infty h(\tau)x(t-\tau)\,d\tau \tag{9.1}$$

That is, the value of the output $y(t)$ at any time t is given as a weighted linear (infinite) sum over the entire past history of the input $x(t)$.

The linear system may alternatively be characterized by its frequency response or transfer function $H(f)$, which is defined as the Fourier transform of $h(\tau)$. That is,

$$H(f)=\int_0^\infty h(\tau)e^{-j2\pi f\tau}\,d\tau \tag{9.2}$$

The lower limit is 0 instead of $-\infty$, since $h(\tau)=0$ for $\tau<0$.

The idea of physical realizability is important from the standpoint of the engineering analysis of real systems. However, from a mathematical, and sometimes also computational viewpoint, physically unrealizable versions of (9.1) and (9.2) are most useful. Instead of a finite lower limit, $-\infty$ is used. Thus

$$y(t)=\int_{-\infty}^\infty h(\tau)x(t-\tau)\,d\tau \tag{9.3}$$

$$H(f)=\int_{-\infty}^\infty h(\tau)e^{-j2\pi f\tau}\,d\tau \tag{9.4}$$

For example, digital FIR filters used in a digital computer need not be realizable in this sense. It is perfectly correct to use symmetrical weighting functions and have phaseless (zero phase shift) filters (see Chapter 4). The frequency response function relates the input and output variables by the formula

$$Y(f) = H(f)X(f) \qquad (9.5)$$

This is obtained by taking Fourier transforms of both sides of (9.3) and is referred to as the "convolution theorem." The frequency response function is of great interest, because it contains both amplitude magnification (or attenuation) and phase-shift information. Since $H(f)$ is complex valued, the complex exponential (polar) notation may be used. That is,

$$H(f) = |H(f)|e^{j\phi(f)}$$

$$|H(f)| = \sqrt{\left(\mathrm{Re}\left[H(f)\right]\right)^2 + \left(\mathrm{Im}\left[H(f)\right]\right)^2}$$

$$\phi(f) = \arctan\left[\frac{\mathrm{Im}\left[H(f)\right]}{\mathrm{Re}\left[H(f)\right]}\right] \qquad (9.6)$$

where the absolute value $H(f)$ is the gain and the argument $\phi(f)$ is the phase angle in radians.

The convention shown for the choice of the sign of the phase angle is an attempt to be consistent with control theory and other established fields utilizing the idea of a frequency response function. With this definition a negative time shift (time delay) will have a phase which is a straight line with a negative slope. Suppose $y(t)$ is a time-delayed version of $x(t)$. That is,

$$y(t) = x(t - \tau)$$

Then the Fourier transform of $y(t)$ is

$$Y(f) = \int_{-\infty}^{\infty} y(t)e^{-j2\pi ft}\,dt = \int_{-\infty}^{\infty} x(t - \tau)e^{-j\pi ft}\,dt$$

$$= e^{-j2\pi f\tau}\int_{-\infty}^{\infty} x(t)e^{-j2\pi ft}\,dt = e^{-j2\pi f\tau}X(f)$$

Thus the frequency response function, gain, and phase are

$$H(f) = \exp(-j2\pi f\tau), \qquad |H(f)| = 1, \qquad \phi(f) = -2\pi f\tau \qquad (9.7)$$

so phase is a straight line with slope $-2\pi\tau$. This is plotted in Figure 9.2.

We make the assumption that the system relating $x(t)$ and $y(t)$ is a "linear" system. When we say a system is linear, we mean that it satisfies

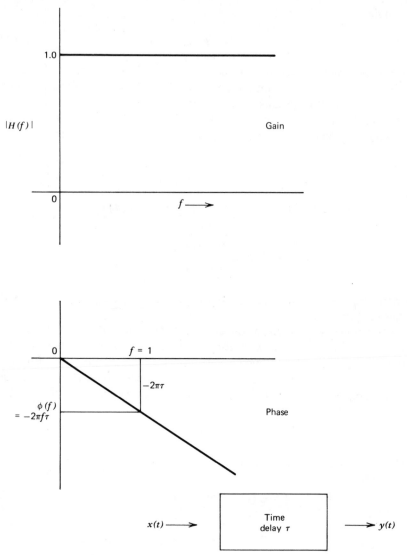

Figure 9.2   Gain and phase for system consisting of time delay only.

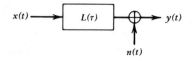

Figure 9.3   Block diagram for single input–single output system with extraneous noise $n(t)$.

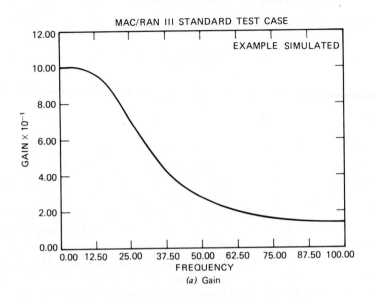

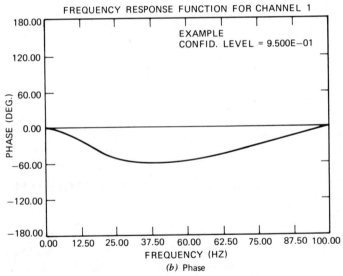

Figure 9.4 (*a*) Gain and (*b*) phase plot of numerical filter.

the rules for a linear operator L. That is,

$$y(t) = L\left[a_1 x_1(t) + a_2 x_2(t)\right]$$
$$= a_1 L\left[x_1(t)\right] + a_2 L\left[x_2(t)\right]$$
$$= a_1 y_1(t) + a_2 y_2(t) \tag{9.8}$$

In words, the additive rule, which states that the sum of two inputs produces the sum of the corresponding outputs, is satisfied, as well as the homogeneity rule, which states that if an input is multiplied by a constant then the corresponding output is multiplied by that constant.

It must be kept in mind that a system can be linear even though its "gain" $|H_{xy}(f)|$ and "phase" $\phi_{xy}(f)$ are nonlinear functions when plotted versus frequency. The shape of the gain merely states which frequency components are transferred with what gain (or attenuation). The shape of the phase plot may be interpreted as the amount of delay a signal component of frequency f experiences as determined by the formula

$$\text{delay at frequency } f = -\tau = \frac{\phi_{xy}(f)}{2\pi f} \tag{9.9}$$

which is obtained by solving for τ in (9.7) and recalling that we consider positive delay as a negative time translation. Figure 9.3 is a general block diagram for the linear system with noise.

Typical plots of gain (in linear units, not decibels) and phase for a (linear) digital lowpass filter are shown in Figure 9.4.

9.2   SPECTRAL RELATIONSHIPS FOR SINGLE INPUT SYSTEM

Assume that a linear system with a clearly defined, single input and single output is subjected to a random input x, which is a representative member from a stationary random process with a zero mean value. Then the output y will have the same properties, as shown in Bendat and Piersol [1971]. Two relations between the power and the cross spectral density functions $S_x(f)$, $S_y(f)$, and $S_{xy}(f)$ are

$$S_y(f) = |H(f)|^2 S_x(f) \tag{9.10}$$

$$S_{xy}(f) = H(f) S_x(f) \tag{9.11}$$

Therefore, with knowledge of the input power spectrum and the spectrum cross power, the frequency response function for a linear system is completely determined including both gain and phase.

The coherence function $\gamma_{xy}^2(f)$ is a real-valued quantity defined as

$$\gamma_{xy}^2(f) = \frac{\left|S_{xy}(f)\right|^2}{S_x(f)S_y(f)} \tag{9.12}$$

Some authors define the positive square root $\gamma_{xy}(f)$ as coherence. The cross power spectral density function $S_{xy}(f)$ may be shown to satisfy the inequality (see Jenkins and Watts [1968, p. 467].

$$\left|S_{xy}(f)\right|^2 \leqslant S_x(f)S_y(f) \tag{9.13}$$

which implies that

$$0 \leqslant \gamma_{xy}^2(f) \leqslant 1 \tag{9.14}$$

It is quite instructive to compare (9.10), (9.11), and (9.12) with the regression and correlation discussion of Chapter 2. We see for example that $H(f)$ is the counterpart of the regression coefficient β and that the power and cross spectra are counterparts of the variance and covariance, respectively. Furthermore, the coherence is the counterpart of the square of the correlation coefficient. If we consider the *complex coherence*

$$\gamma_{xy}(f) = \sqrt{\frac{\left|S_{xy}(f)\right|}{S_x(f)S_y(f)}} \; e^{\phi_{xy}(f)} \tag{9.15}$$

we then have a generalization of the correlation coefficient where positive correlation corresponds to $0°$ phase shift ("in phase") and negative correlation corresponds to $180°$ phase shift ("out of phase").

Throughout this chapter we see that the understanding of many deep results is considerably simplified by relating the frequency domain results back to relatively elementary concepts of basic statistics. We are able, for stationary processes, to perform an independent statistical analysis in each narrow frequency band. This is due to the orthogonalizing property of the Fourier transform. Hence, in addition to the engineering appeal of working in the frequency domain in order to characterize such important parameters as resonant frequency and the like, there is also considerable mathematical-statistical motivation owing to the simplification of the analysis.

Now consider the measurement of the CSD for ideal, no noise, linear systems. For this case, $\gamma_{xy}^2 = 1$. Hence the coherence function attains a theoretical maximum of unity at all frequencies for the case of linear systems. If the coherence function is less than unity, one possible cause may be the lack of complete linear dependence between the input and the output for the system in question; that is, the system is nonlinear.

Given discrete time histories x_i and y_i, $i = 0, 1, \ldots, N-1$, (9.11) and (9.12) are directly applied to compute transfer and coherence function estimates. These might be considered as "natural" estimating formulas, but they can easily be derived from least-squares considerations also (see Jenkins and Watts [1968, p. 432], for example).

One method of deriving (9.11) and (9.12) is the following (which happens to work for all least-squares problems). We begin with the convolution theorem equation

$$Y(f) = H(f)X(f)$$

Then we multiply through by $X^*(f)$ (where the asterisk indicates complex conjugate), and then average by taking expected values and obtain

$$E[X^*(f)Y(f)] = E[X^*(f)H(f)X(f)] \qquad (9.16)$$

Since $H(f)$ is a fixed characteristic of the linear system, it factors out. Then, by definition, we have cross spectra on the left and power spectra on the right

$$S_{xy}(f) = H(f)S_{xx}(f)$$

This amounts to a calculation of the covariance of the input with the output. If we calculate the mean square of both sides we have

$$E|Y(f)|^2 = E\left[|H(f)X(f)|^2\right]$$

or

$$S_{yy}(f) = |H(f)|^2 S_{xx}(f)$$

All the formulas have their counterparts in terms of discrete spectral functions for finite record lengths. There is no essential difference between the discrete and the continuous except that if errors such as aliasing occur in the Fourier transform, they also occur in the functions derived from them.

9.3 SPECTRAL RELATIONSHIPS FOR MULTIPLE INPUT LINEAR SYSTEMS

A model of a linear system responding to multiple inputs is now considered. It is assumed that p inputs exist, and a single output is measured. Three types of coherence functions, ordinary, multiple, and partial, play an important role in this analysis, and their evaluation is discussed in Section 9.4.

Consider a linear system with time-invariant parameters and p inputs $x_l(t)$, $l=1,2,\ldots,p$. That is,

$$y(t)= \sum_{l=1}^{p} y_l(t) \tag{9.17}$$

where $y_l(t)$ is defined as that part of the output produced by the lth input, $x_l(t)$, when all the other inputs are 0 (see Figure 9.5). The function h_{ly} in Figure 9.5 is defined as the weighting function associated with the linear system between the input $x_l(t)$ and the partial output $y_l(t)$. Hence $y_l(t)$ is

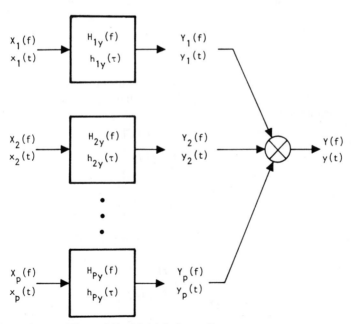

Figure 9.5 Multiple input linear system.

given as follows:

$$y_I(t) = \int_{-\infty}^{\infty} h_{Iy}(\tau) x_I(t-\tau) d\tau \qquad (9.18)$$

The Fourier transform of (9.18) gives

$$Y_I(f) = H_{Iy}(f) X_I(f) \qquad (9.19)$$

where $Y_I(f)$ and $X_I(f)$ are the Fourier transforms of $Y_I(t)$ and $x_I(t)$, respectively. Then the Fourier transform $Y(f)$ for the total output is

$$Y(f) = \sum_{I=1}^{p} Y_I(f) = \sum_{I=1}^{p} H_{Iy}(f) X_I(f) \qquad (9.20)$$

The statistician reading this material should immediately note that (9.20) is a multiple regression equation for zero mean variables similar to the single input case defined before. The dependent variable is Y, the independent variables are X_I, and the regression coefficients are H_{Iy}. Thus electrical or mechanical engineering frequency domain transfer function concepts can be interpreted by the statistician via regression analysis of complex random variables. This concept is delved into in considerable detail by Akaike [1965]. The gist of it is that we can treat each frequency band independently, and by accomplishing many complex variable multiple regression analyses (one for each frequency band) we obtain the entire frequency domain functions.

As in multiple regression analysis, the preceding relations can be expressed more concisely in matrix notation, and many results become more readily apparent. First, define a p-dimensional input column vector of the Fourier transforms:

$$\mathbf{X}(f) = \begin{bmatrix} X_1(f) \\ X_2(f) \\ \vdots \\ X_p(f) \end{bmatrix} \qquad (9.21)$$

Also define a p-dimensional transfer function column vector:

$$\mathbf{H}(f) = \begin{bmatrix} H_{1y}(f) \\ H_{2y}(f) \\ \vdots \\ H_{py}(f) \end{bmatrix} \qquad (9.22)$$

Next, define a p-dimentional cross power spectrum column vector of the output $y(t)$ with the inputs $x_l(t)$:

$$\mathbf{S}_{xy}(f) = \begin{bmatrix} S_{1y}(f) \\ S_{2y}(f) \\ \vdots \\ S_{py}(f) \end{bmatrix} \tag{9.23}$$

where

$$S_{ly}(f) \equiv S_{x_l y}(f) \qquad l = 1, 2, \ldots, p \tag{9.24}$$

Finally, define the $(p \times p)$ matrix of the power and cross spectra of all the inputs $x_l(t)$:

$$\mathbf{S}_{xx}(f) = \begin{bmatrix} S_{11}(f) & S_{12}(f) & \cdots & S_{1p}(f) \\ S_{21}(f) & S_{22}(f) & \cdots & S_{2p}(f) \\ \vdots & \vdots & & \vdots \\ S_{p1}(f) & S_{p2} & \cdots & S_{pp}(f) \end{bmatrix} = E\left[\mathbf{X}^*(f)\mathbf{X}^T(f)\right] \tag{9.25}$$

where the asterisk denotes conjugate and T denotes transpose. For simplicity we adopt the notation

$$S_{ij} = S_{x_i x_j}(f) \qquad i, j = 1, 2, \ldots, p \tag{9.26}$$

The matrix $\mathbf{S}_{xx}$ is Hermitian, since it equals its conjugate transpose. This implies, for example, that the eigenvalues of $\mathbf{S}_{xx}(f)$ are real numbers. These parameters are of interest in certain applications.

The system of linear equations to obtain a least-squares solution for the $H_{ly}(f)$ of (9.22) is the matrix equation

$$\mathbf{S}_{xy} = \mathbf{S}_{xx}\mathbf{H} \tag{9.27}$$

This is equivalent to

$$\begin{bmatrix} S_{1y} \\ S_{2y} \\ \vdots \\ S_{py} \end{bmatrix} = \begin{bmatrix} S_{11} & S_{12} & \cdots & S_{1p} \\ S_{21} & S_{22} & \cdots & S_{2p} \\ \vdots & \vdots & & \vdots \\ S_{p1} & S_{p2} & \cdots & S_{pp} \end{bmatrix} \begin{bmatrix} H_{1y} \\ H_{2y} \\ \vdots \\ H_{py} \end{bmatrix} \tag{9.28}$$

The solution to this system of equations is

$$H = S_{xx}^{-1} S_{xy} \tag{9.29}$$

For the practical situation, we estimate the spectra and cross spectra in (9.28) with the procedures described in Chapter 8.

9.4   ORDINARY, MULTIPLE, AND PARTIAL COHERENCE FUNCTIONS

For the single input system we have one type of coherence, which is the ordinary coherence function defined by (9.12). It was mentioned at that time that coherence has its counterpart in the square of the correlation coefficient of basic statistics. We now note that the concept of coherence generalizes to the multi-input case and we have two other types of coherence, multiple and partial, which are counterparts of the squared multiple correlation coefficient and the square of the partial correlation coefficient.

In order to unify the ideas of these three different coherence functions we rewrite (9.12) in a different form which relates the input power and the linearly "predictable" output power. We note in Figure 9.3 that output $y(t)$ is made up of two independent (by assumption) components, and hence the power spectrum has two components. Namely,

$$S_y = S_n + S_u \tag{9.30}$$

where we define $U(f)$ as the noisefree output of the system

$$U(f) = H(f)X(f) \tag{9.31}$$

We note that (9.10) applies, so that

$$S_u = |H|^2 S_x$$

which implies that S_u is the portion of the total power related to the input. We now compute the fraction of power which is

$$\frac{S_u}{S_y} = \frac{|H|^2 S_x}{S_y} = \frac{|S_{xy}|^2}{S_x^2} \frac{S_x}{S_y} = \frac{|S_{xy}|^2}{S_x S_y} = \gamma_{xy}^2 \tag{9.32}$$

When the relation is written in this form we see that the ordinary coherence represents the fraction of power of the output accounted for by the linear relation with the input. It is exactly this interpretation which generalizes to the multiple and partial coherence cases.

When the system is nonlinear, then the transfer function estimate $\hat{H}(f)$ is the "least squares" approximation to the "true" nonlinear transfer function. A very interesting theorem about systems states that the output $y(t)$ can always be split into two independent parts, $u(t)$, which is perfectly coherent with the input $x(t)$, and $n(t)$, which is perfectly incoherent with the input $x(t)$. The coherence function then is the power ratio of the coherent part to the total power as given by (9.32).

There are two additional forms of coherence for $p > 1$:

$\gamma_{y \cdot x}^2(f)$ = multiple coherence. The fraction of power accounted for in the output $y(t)$ via linear relations with the inputs $x_1(t), \ldots, x_p(t)$.

$\gamma_{iy|1,2,\ldots,i-1,i+1,\ldots,p}^2(f)$ = partial coherence. The ordinary coherence between the residual of the ith input, $\Delta x_i(t)$, and the output, $\Delta y(t)$, after the linear effects of the other $p-1$ inputs have been removed.

For the multiple input case the "predicted" variance is

$$S_{yx}^T H_{xy} = S_{yx}^T S_{xx}^{-1} S_{xy} \tag{9.33}$$

Thus the multiple coherence is given by

$$\gamma_{y \cdot x}^2 = \frac{S_{yx}^T S_{xx}^{-1} S_{xy}}{S_{yy}} \tag{9.34}$$

The residual output spectrum, often termed the "conditioned"* spectrum, is

$$S_{y|x} = S_{yy} - S_{yx}^T S_{xx}^{-1} S_{xy} \tag{9.35}$$

The multiple coherence in terms of the conditional output spectrum is

$$\gamma_{y \cdot x}^2 = 1 - \frac{S_{y|x}}{S_{yy}} \tag{9.36}$$

The multiple coherence function is the fraction of power in the output

*The term conditioning derives from conditional probabilities in probability theory. This may be roughly interpreted as "what exists given that some condition has occurred."

accounted for by simultaneous linear filter relationships with all the inputs.

To obtain the partial coherence function between any input, say, x_1, and the output conditioned on the remaining $(p-1)$ inputs, one partitions the augmented spectral matrix as indicated below:

$$
\mathbf{S}_{yxx} =
\begin{bmatrix}
S_{yy} & S_{y1} & \vdots & S_{y2} & \cdots & S_{yp} \\
S_{1y} & S_{11} & \vdots & S_{12} & \cdots & S_{1p} \\
\text{--} & \text{--} & \text{--} & \text{--} & \text{--} & \text{--} \\
S_{2y} & S_{2l} & \vdots & S_{22} & \cdots & S_{2p} \\
\vdots & \vdots & \vdots & \vdots & & \vdots \\
S_{py} & S_{p1} & \vdots & S_{p2} & \cdots & S_{pp}
\end{bmatrix}
=
\begin{bmatrix}
\boldsymbol{\Sigma}_{yy} & \boldsymbol{\Sigma}_{y1} \\
\boldsymbol{\Sigma}_{1y} & \boldsymbol{\Sigma}_{11}
\end{bmatrix}
\tag{9.37}
$$

Then compute the conditional spectral matrix*:

$$
\mathbf{S}_{xy|p} = \boldsymbol{\Sigma}_{yy} - \boldsymbol{\Sigma}_{y1} \boldsymbol{\Sigma}_{11}^{-1} \boldsymbol{\Sigma}_{1y}
\tag{9.38}
$$

The partial coherence function between the input x_1 and the output y, conditioned on the other $(p-1)$ inputs, is now computed by

$$
\gamma_{1y|p}^2 = \frac{|S_{1y|p}|^2}{S_{11|p} S_{yy|p}}
\tag{9.39}
$$

Similar results apply for x_2 by interchanging x_2 with x_1, for x_3 by interchanging x_3 with x_2, etc.

9.5   CONFIDENCE LIMITS FOR COHERENCE

The statistical distribution of coherence is closely related to the statistical distribution of correlation coefficients. The most convenient approach to the confidence limits seems to be via a normalizing transformation, that is, a transformation that makes the statistical distribution of coherence estimates become approximately normal (Gaussian). This approach was pursued by Enochson and Goodman (1965), extended and improved by Benignus (1969), and further discussed by Carter (1972). The transformation employed is termed the Fisher "z"-transform, named after a famous statistician, Sir R. A. Fisher.

*Equation (9.38) is a complex analog of multivariate regression analysis equation such as given by Anderson [1958, p. 28, equation 3].

Characteristics of Coherence Estimates

The statistical sampling theory for coherence shows that estimates are biased in addition to exhibiting statistical variability. The bias and variance are approximately

$$\sigma_z^2 = \frac{1}{n-2} \qquad (9.40)$$

$$b = \frac{1}{n-2} \qquad (9.41)$$

where

$$z = \tanh^{-1} \hat{\gamma} \qquad (9.42)$$

Since n, the d.f., appears in the denominator for small d.f. the bias is extremely large. In particular, for 2 d.f., as is shown by Enochson and Otnes [1972, Chapter 9],

$$\hat{\gamma}_{xy}^2(f) = 1.0$$

for all f.

A second type of bias occurs for which the theory has not been worked out. Hence only a qualitative discussion is presented in Section 9.12. Any spectral estimate is subject to a "smearing bias" if the resolution bandwidth, B_e, is wide relative to the actual peak in a spectrum.

Such bias is not uncommon. Also, for some reason, such smearing seems to have a substantially greater effect on coherence. The authors have observed changes from $\hat{\gamma}^2 = 0.4$ to $\hat{\gamma}^2 = 0.9$ in several cases where B_e was halved and all other parameters remained the same. It is suggested that experimentation be performed, varying B_e, in any analysis situation where one is unsure of the width of spectral peaks that will be encountered.

At least part of the reason for such behavior of coherence can be attributed to the effect of time delays in a system. Large delays are manifested as a rapidly varying phase function. This in turn implies rapidly varying real and imaginary parts of the cross spectrum. Hence it is likely that severe bias will occur in many practical situations owing to the rapidly varying cross spectral functions.

An estimation procedure is given by Cleveland and Parzen [1975] for aiding in the elimination of the bias.

The transformation that leads to an accurate normal (Gaussian) approximation for the distribution of sample coherence functions is shown by

Enochson and Goodman [1965] to be given by

$$z = \tanh^{-1}\hat{\gamma} = \frac{1}{2} \ln\left[\frac{1+\hat{\gamma}}{1-\hat{\gamma}}\right] \tag{9.43}$$

where $\hat{\gamma}$ is the positive square root of the sample coherence estimate $\hat{\gamma}^2$. The mean value and variance associated with z are approximated by

$$\mu_z = \tanh^{-1}\gamma + \left(\frac{p}{n-2p}\right) \tag{9.44}$$

$$\sigma_z^2 = \frac{1}{n-2p} \tag{9.45}$$

where $n = 2B_e P$.

The improvements developed by Benignus (1969) are both bias and variability. The estimate $\hat{\gamma}^2$ of coherence can be improved by a bias correction

$$B(\hat{\gamma}^2) = \frac{1}{2n}(1-\hat{\gamma}^2) \tag{9.46}$$

Then a corrected coherence estimate is utilized in (9.43):

$$\tilde{\gamma}^2 = \hat{\gamma}^2 - B(\hat{\gamma}^2) \tag{9.47}$$

The correction for the variance to be utilized instead of (9.45) is based on a curve fit to improve the estimate of σ_z^2 when $\hat{\gamma}^2 < 0.3$. The curve developed is

$$E(\sigma_z) = 1 - 0.004^{(1.6\hat{\gamma}^2 + 0.22)} \tag{9.48}$$

Then instead of σ_z from (9.45) we use

$$\sigma_z = \left(\sqrt{\frac{1}{n-2p}}\right)[E(\sigma_z)] \tag{9.49}$$

From the previous equations, for measured values of γ^2 and n, one can determine $(1-\alpha)$ confidence limits for the true value γ^2 by the following relation:

$$\tanh\left(z - b - \sigma_{z_{\alpha/2}}^z\right) \leqslant \gamma \leqslant \tanh\left(z - b + \sigma_{z_{\alpha/2}}^z\right) \tag{9.50}$$

where Z_α is the 100α percentage point of the normal distribution, and

$$b = \frac{p}{n - 2p} \tag{9.51}$$

The above confidence limit formula applies either to ordinary coherence functions where $p = 1$ or to the multiple coherence functions where $p > 1$.

A simple adjustment can be made to obtain partial coherence function confidence limits. In general, one must reduce the number of d.f. in the analysis by the number of conditional variables whose effects have been subtracted out. For example, in the case where the effects of $(p - 1)$ inputs are subtracted out, one used n' d.f. given by

$$n' = n - (p - 1) \tag{9.52}$$

where $n = 2B_e T$.

9.6   CONFIDENCE LIMIT COMPUTATIONS FOR TRANSFER FUNCTIONS

The confidence bands for the frequency response functions $H_{iy}(f)$, $i = 1, 2, \ldots, p$, representing the model of Figure 9.5, depend upon the sample coherence function between the output and the inputs, the sample multiple coherence function between the inputs, the sample input PSD functions, and the sample frequency response functions. The basis for these results is discussed in Bendat and Piersol [1971] and Goodman [1965].

Assume negligible bias error due to smearing in the various spectral estimates involved. Let the true gain factor be $|H_{iy}|$ and the true phase be ϕ_{iy} so that

$$H_{iy} = |H_{iy}| e^{j\phi_{iy}} \tag{9.53}$$

Then the $(1 - \alpha)$ confidence intervals for H_{iy} and ϕ_{iy} are given simultaneously at every i and at any specified frequency f (or digitally by the frequency index k):

$$\left\{ \begin{array}{l} |\hat{H}_{iy}| - \hat{r}_i < |H_{iy}| \leqslant |\hat{H}_{iy}| + \hat{r}_i \\ \hat{\phi}_{iy} - \hat{\Delta\phi}_i < \phi_{iy} \leqslant \hat{\phi}_{iy} + \hat{\Delta\phi}_i \end{array} \right\} \quad i = 1, 2, \ldots, p \tag{9.54}$$

where $|\hat{H}_{iy}|$ and $\hat{\phi}_{iy}$ are sample estimates. The square of the radial error,

$\hat{r}_i^2 \equiv \hat{r}_i^2(f)$, and the phase error, $\Delta\hat{\phi}_i \equiv \Delta\hat{\phi}_i(f)$, are computed for each i by

$$\hat{r}_i^2 = \frac{2p}{n-2p}\left(F_{n_1,n_2;\alpha}\right)\frac{\left(1-\hat{\gamma}_{y\cdot x}^2\right)\hat{S}_y}{\left(1-\hat{\gamma}_{i\cdot x}^2\right)\hat{S}_i} \tag{9.55}$$

$$\Delta\hat{\phi}_i = \sin^{-1}\left(\frac{\hat{r}_i}{|\hat{H}_{iy}|}\right) \tag{9.56}$$

The various quantities in (9.55) and (9.56) are

    p = number of inputs (excluding output)

    $n = 2B_e P$ = number of d.f. in each spectral estimate

$F_{n_1,n_2;\alpha} = 100\alpha$ percentage point of an F distribution with $n_1 = 2p$ and
    $n_2 = 2n - 2p$ d.f.

    $\hat{\gamma}_{y\cdot x}^2$ = sample estimate of the multiple coherence function between the output y and all the measured inputs

    $\hat{\gamma}_{i\cdot x}^2$ = sample estimate of the multiple coherence function between the input x_i and the other measured inputs excluding x_i

    $\hat{S}_y$ = power spectrum estimate for the output y

    $\hat{S}_i$ = power spectrum estimate for the input x_i

A polar diagram for the confidence region represented by (9.54) is shown in Figure 9.6 at the frequency f_0. Different confidence regions apply to each specified frequency f_k and to each of the possible $i = 1, 2, \ldots, p$.

Equation (9.55) gives the radial error for the most general case of multiple coherent inputs. For special situations when the p inputs are

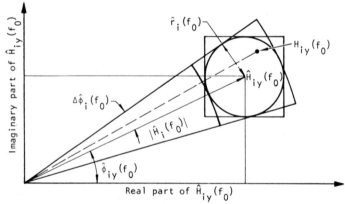

Figure 9.6   Confidence diagram for multiple frequency response functions.

coherent or there is only a single input $p = 1$, the square of the radial error takes the special form

$$\hat{r}_i^2 = \frac{2}{n-2}\left(F_{n_1,n_2;\alpha}\right)\left(1 - \hat{\gamma}_{yi}^2\right)\frac{\hat{S}_y}{\hat{S}_i} \qquad (9.57)$$

where n, $\hat{S}_y$, and $\hat{S}_i$ are the same as before, and

$F_{n_1,n_2;\alpha} = 100\alpha$ percentage point of an F distribution with $n_1 = 2$ and $n_2 = n - 2$ d.f.

    $\hat{\gamma}_{yi}^2 =$ sample estimate of the ordinary coherence function between y and x_i

The phase error $\Delta\hat{\phi}_i$ is calculated as before by (9.56); however, the $\hat{r}_i$ is obtained from (9.57) instead of (9.55) is used.

A subtle point is involved in the distinction between single and multiple input confidence limits. Suppose we had 100 multi-input systems and computed 90% confidence limits. We would expect these limits to be violated about 10 times out of 100. Suppose instead we computed confidence limits for each individual input and the output based on the single input situation. Then, of the 100 sets of confidence limits for any specific single input, we would expect to see about 10 violations. However, if we had, say, $p = 10$ inputs, then we would expect to see some larger number of violations, but we could not say exactly how many since the different sets of confidence limits for the single input models would not be independent. The point is that if we are interested in only one specific frequency response function, then we should use the single input formulas, even though it is part of a multiple input system. These confidence limits will in general be narrower in width than the multi-input limits and are preferable. However, if all confidence limits are wanted, the multiple limit formulas are wanted.

One can obtain clues as to how to optimize an experiment to measure multiple transfer functions from (9.55).

1. Make all input functions equally powerful since the output to input power ratio being small makes $\hat{r}_i(f)$ small.
2. Reduce noise at the output and make the systems linear since a large multiple coherence reduces $\hat{r}_i(f)$.
3. Make the inputs as independent as possible since a low multiple coherence among the inputs reduces $\hat{r}_i(f)$.
4. Make the d.f. as high as possible since this will both reduce the F value (for a given α) and create a larger denominator to reduce $\hat{r}_i(f)$. Keep

in mind that for a fixed record length of data, increasing d.f. requires increasing B_e, which in turn tends to create bias problems due to smearing.

These are very useful qualitative concepts and can be of considerable assistance in designing data collection programs. The key thing to note is the trade-off between degrees of freedom and high coherence. It is difficult to emphasize this sufficiently. We repeat for emphasis: "High coherence will allow very accurate estimates of transfer functions even though d.f. are small and power spectra are highly inaccurate (and vice versa)."

9.7   HOW TO COMPUTE TRANSFER FUNCTIONS

Computational considerations for the single input system are relatively minor compared with the multi-input and we shall emphasize the latter initially. In the latter examples demonstrate problems common to both.

The computational procedures necessary for the solution of (9.29) subdivide into three groups:

1.   Power and cross spectral density function computational routines.
2.   A procedure for simultaneously handling $(p + 1)$ variables to efficiently obtain the spectral density functions among all the variables.
3.   The complex variable arithmetical and matrix operations to compute the multidimensional linear system parameters.

The spectral density functions necessary would normally be generated by FFT PSD procedures. The main requirement is that all possible combinations of cross spectra are computed. Because of the Hermitian symmetry, only the diagonal and the upper right portion of the matrix need be calculated. That is,

$$S_{ij}(f) = S_{ji}^*(f) = S_{ij}(-f) \qquad (9.58)$$

The computational procedures described here are for computing parameters of a mathematical model, assuming a p input $[x_i(t), \quad i = 1, 2, \ldots, p]$ and single output $[y(t)]$ linear system. The system parameters to be computed are as follows:

1.   Transfer functions between each of the inputs and the output.
2.   Ordinary coherence functions between all pairs of variables.

3. The multiple coherence function between the output and all the inputs.
4. Partial (conditional) coherence functions between each input and the output while conditioning on the other inputs.

In the ensuing discussion we do not distinguish statistical estimates by the caret notation. The notation is sufficiently complicated without introducing additional symbols. We hope no confusion will result, since in all cases the theoretical equations or those involving statistical estimates are identical anyway.

The first operation that must be performed is a sorting procedure. The spectral density functions are normally computed as a function of frequency. A program for multiple input linear system analysis eventually must operate on the $(p+1) \times (p+1)$ spectral density matrices, one matrix for each frequency value.

The data operated on by the program are a set of spectral density matrices at frequencies indexed by k as follows:

$$\mathbf{S}_{yxx}(k) = \begin{bmatrix} S_{yy}(k) & S_{y1}(k) & S_{y2}(k) & \cdots & S_{yp}(k) \\ S_{1y}(k) & S_{11}(k) & S_{12}(k) & \cdots & S_{1p}(k) \\ \vdots & \vdots & \vdots & & \vdots \\ S_{py}(k) & S_{p1}(k) & S_{p2}(k) & \cdots & S_{pp}(k) \end{bmatrix} \qquad k=0,1,\ldots,m$$

(9.59)

The frequency index k will usually represent special frequency values

$$f_k = \frac{kF}{m} \qquad k=0,1,\ldots,m \tag{9.60}$$

where F is the Nyquist frequency. More generally, k can represent the frequency values

$$f_r = f_1 + k\Delta f \qquad k=0,1,\ldots,m$$

where

$$f_1 = \text{beginning frequency}$$

$$\Delta f = \text{frequency increment}$$

The m separate $(p+1) \times (p+1)$ spectral density matrices can be visualized in the three-dimensional form illustrated in Figure 9.7. The initial

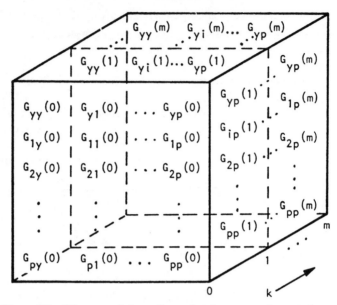

Figure 9.7 Diagram of three-dimensional storage of spectral matrix.

computation of any spectral density function provides a single-element $(m+1)$-longitudinal column of the $(p+1)\times(p+1)\times(m+1)$ block in Figure 9.7. For the frequency response computations, a single slice of the block in the horizontal–vertical plane is needed. Logistical problems arise if magnetic tape is used for intermediate storage, since then the data must have been arranged in a serial fashion. Disk file storage is convenient for the necessary rearranging that has to take place.

The p input variables and the output variable are assumed to be zero mean, stationary, Gaussian processes whenever any statistical distribution results are discussed. The functions $H_{ly}(k)$, $l=1,2,\dots,p$, are the frequency response function (transfer function) characteristics of the linear systems through which the variables are passing to make up $y(t)$.

The variables $x_l(i)$, $l=1,2,\dots,p$, and $y(i)$ are assumed to be discrete (digitized) sequences of N points each.

The matrix equation to be solved to determine the frequency response function is (9.28), where the function argument will be omitted for notational simplicity [e.g., S_{11} is written instead of $S_{11}(k)$]. The matrix and vectors in (9.28) are complex valued and hence require complex arithmetical operations for correct manipulation. In particular,

$$S_{il} = C_{il} - jQ_{il} \qquad (9.61)$$

where $C(k)$ and $Q(k)$ are the appropriate cospectral and quadspectral density functions at index value k.

The solution to (9.28) is

$$
\begin{bmatrix} H_{1y} \\ H_{2y} \\ \vdots \\ H_{py} \end{bmatrix} = \begin{bmatrix} S_{11} & S_{12} & \cdots & S_{1p} \\ S_{21} & S_{22} & \cdots & S_{2p} \\ \vdots & \vdots & \vdots & \vdots \\ S_{p1} & S_{12} & \cdots & S_{pp} \end{bmatrix}^{-1} \begin{bmatrix} S_{1y} \\ S_{2y} \\ \vdots \\ S_{py} \end{bmatrix} \tag{9.62}
$$

or, in more concise matrix notation,

$$
\mathbf{H}_{xy} = \mathbf{S}_{xx}^{-1} \mathbf{S}_{xy} \tag{9.63}
$$

We recommend following the advice of Forsythe and Moler [1971, p. 77]:

"One way to solve the system of linear equations $\mathbf{Ax} = \mathbf{b}$ is to compute the inverse of $\mathbf{A}$ and then multiply $\mathbf{A}^{-1}$ by $\mathbf{b}$....However, a set of linear equations solving procedure...can accomplish this task with fewer operations and greater accuracy."

The system of complex equations may be solved directly with complex arithmetic. Alternatively the equations may be decomposed into real and imaginary parts. Lanczos [1956] describes one method which is given in detail in Otnes and Enochson [1972, pp. 347–349]. One may also employ the isomorphism

$$
(\mathbf{C} + j\mathbf{Q}) \sim \begin{bmatrix} \mathbf{C} & -\mathbf{Q} \\ \mathbf{Q} & \mathbf{C} \end{bmatrix} \tag{9.64}
$$

which relates to $p \times p$ complex matrix to the $2p \times 2p$ real matrix on the right side of (9.64). The solution (9.63) would contain the real part in the first p elements of the $\mathbf{H}_{xy}$ vector and the imaginary part in the second p elements.

The recommended computational method is to solve the system of equations with the Forsythe and Moler procedures adapted to complex arithmetic. These amount to a careful Gaussian elimination with pivoting about maximum elements and scaling. Alternatives are procedures based on either orthogonalization of the data or orthogonalization of spectral matrix. See, for example, Longley [1967] or Wampler [1970]. The Forsythe and Moler method contains a routine for iterative refinement of the solution along with an estimate of the number of digits of accuracy in the solution. Double precision computations may be necessary, depending on the word length of the digital computer involved and the condition of the matrix.

The solution method is summarized as follows:

1. Solve the system of spectral equations employing the Forsythe–Moler method working directly in complex arithmetic.
2. Employ iterative refinement to improve the solution. Use double precision arithmetic if results are unsatisfactory.
3. Obtain multiple coherence and partial coherences with the aid of the "sweep" operator defined below.

Iterative methods which begin with a single input system and progress upward to additional variables are conceptually convenient. One such method, "the escalator method," is described in Otnes and Enochson [1972]. However, this class of techniques is by no means computationally optimum; moreover, the computational accuracy and results depend on the order in which the variables are introduced. Hence these methods are not generally recommended.

9.8   THE SWEEP OPERATOR

We assume we have solved the system of equations and have the following matrix available:

$$
\Sigma = \begin{array}{c} p \\ 1 \end{array}
\begin{array}{cc} p & 1 \end{array}
\left[
\begin{array}{c|c}
\mathbf{S}_{xx}^{-1} & \left(\mathbf{S}_{xx}^{-1}\mathbf{S}_{xy}\right)^{T} \\
\hline
-\left(\mathbf{S}_{xx}^{-1}\mathbf{S}_{xy}\right)^{*} & \mathbf{S}_{yy}-\mathbf{S}_{yx}\mathbf{S}_{xx}^{-1}\mathbf{S}_{xy}
\end{array}
\right]
\begin{array}{c} p \\ 1 \end{array}
\tag{9.65}
$$
$$
\begin{array}{cc} p & 1 \end{array}
$$

We note that the multiple coherence is

$$
\gamma_{y\cdot x}^{2} = 1 - \frac{S_{yy}-\mathbf{S}_{yx}\mathbf{S}_{xx}^{-1}\mathbf{S}_{xy}}{S_{yy}} = \frac{\mathbf{S}_{yx}\mathbf{S}_{xx}^{-1}\mathbf{S}_{xy}}{S_{yy}}
\tag{9.66}
$$

We further note that the multiple coherences among the inputs are given by

$$
\gamma_{x\cdot i|j}^{2} = 1 - \frac{1}{S_{ii}S^{ii}}
\tag{9.67}
$$

where S^{ii} is the ith diagonal elements of $\mathbf{S}_{xx}^{-1}$. These quantities are required for the confidence limit computations.

We define a *sweep* [Schatzoff et al., 1968] of the rth row and column by the following operation: Let $\mathbf{A} = (a_{ij})$ and $\mathbf{B} = (b_{ij})$ be square matrices. $\mathbf{A}$ is transformed into $\mathbf{B}$ as follows:

$$
\begin{aligned}
b_{rr} &= \frac{1}{a_{rr}} \\
b_{ir} &= -\frac{a_{ir}}{a_{rr}} \qquad && i \neq r \\
b_{rj} &= \frac{a_{rj}}{a_{rr}} \qquad && j \neq r \\
b_{ij} &= a_{ij} - \frac{a_{ir}}{a_{rr}} a_{rj} \qquad && i,j \neq r
\end{aligned}
\tag{9.68}
$$

The sweep operator is reversible; hence when we sweep Σ, for example, on the pth row and column we obtain

$$
\Sigma' = \begin{array}{c} p-1 \\ 2 \end{array} \left[\begin{array}{c:c} \Sigma_{11}^{-1} & \left(\Sigma_{11}^{-1} \Sigma_{1y} \right)^T \\ \hdashline -\left(\Sigma_{11}^{-1} \Sigma_{1y} \right)^* & \Sigma_{yy} - \Sigma_y \Sigma_{11}^{-1} \Sigma_{1y} \end{array} \right] \begin{array}{c} p-1 \\ 2 \end{array}
\tag{9.69}
$$

Thus we have effectively obtained the conditional spectral matrix $\mathbf{S}_{xy|p}$ in (9.38). Thus the ordinary coherence computed from this 2×2 matrix is the partial coherence between the pth input and the output y.

In order to obtain other partial coherence we sweep again on the pth row and column which restores the matrix Σ' to Σ. Then we sweep on other rows and columns to obtain other partial coherences.

We can considerably simplify things if only the first-order partial and multiple coherences are required. The only elements of Σ' that are required are $S_{pp|p}$, $S_{yy|p}$ and $S_{py|p}$ which correspond to b_{rr}, $b_{p+1,p+1}$ and $b_{r,p+1}$, respectively. Hence to obtain the conditional spectral matrix we compute

$$
S_{pp|p} = b_{rr} = \frac{1}{a_{rr}}
\tag{9.70}
$$

$$
S_{py|p} = b_{r,p+1} = \frac{a_{r,p+1}}{a_{rr}}
\tag{9.71}
$$

$$
S_{yy|p} = b_{pr,p+1} = a_{p+1,p+1} - \frac{a_{p+1,r}}{a_{rr}} a_{r,p+1}
\tag{9.72}
$$

$$
= a_{p+1,p+1} - \frac{|a_{r,p+1}|^2}{a_{rr}}
$$

This method of determining partial coherence and the conditional spectral matrix is undoubtedly the most efficient computationally and the most accurate numerically.

9.9   TRANSFER FUNCTION FROM SINE WAVES

The most common laboratory method in the past for determining transfer functions employed sine waves. The digital equivalent of this method has already been discussed in Section 5.2. We employ the fact that the amplitude change and phase shift gives the characteristics of the transfer function and (9.5) and (9.6):

$$Y(f) = |H(f)|e^{j\phi(f)}X(f)$$

If the input is a cosine wave at frequency f_c, which may be considered to be the real part of a complex exponential, then we have

$$x(t) = Re[Ae^{j2\pi f_c t}] = A\cos 2\pi f_c t$$

and

$$X(f) = \frac{A}{2}\left[\delta(f-f_c) + \delta(f+f_c)\right]$$

and the output is

$$Y(f) = |H(f)|e^{j\phi(f)}\frac{A}{2}\left[\delta(f-f_c) + \delta(f+f_c)\right]$$

$$= \frac{A}{2}\left[|H(f_c)|e^{j\phi(f_c)}\delta(f-f_c) + |H(f_c)|e^{j\phi(-f_c)}\delta(f+f_c)\right]$$

and

$$y(t) = A|H(f_c)|Re(e^{j[2\pi f_c t + \phi(f_c)]}) \tag{9.73}$$

Thus the real part of the output is a cosine with amplitude $A|H(f_c)|$ and a phase change of $\phi(f_c)$ relative to the input. We illustrate this in Figure 9.8. Part a of the figure is the input sinusoid and part b is the output. We note it is changed in amplitude and shifted in phase. Hence if we have a method for determining amplitude ratio and phase shift, we can completely determine the characteristics of the transfer function.

It must be noted that a sinusoid is a "steady-state" function. Even though (9.5) holds for arbitrary functions, when we make the particular

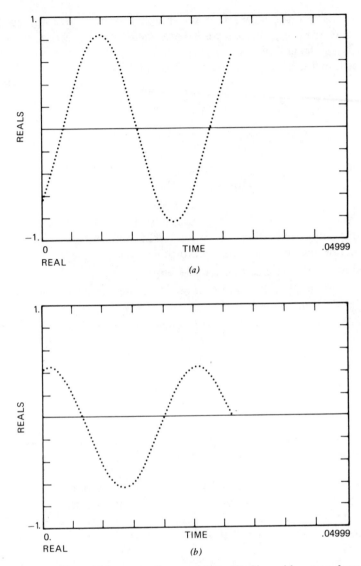

Figure 9.8 (*a*) Sinusoid input to linear system. (*b*) Sinusoid output from linear system with attenuated amplitude and shifted phase.

selection of a sine wave we must allow the system to build up to its steady-state response before we take a measurement. Since in physical systems, the length of time of their transient response P_t is about the reciprocal of their bandwidth, we can use that as a criterion. That is,

$$P_t \approx \frac{1}{B_e} \tag{9.74}$$

where B_e is the bandwidth of a response. Hence when employing sine wave testing we should wait a period of time about $2P_t$ before we record amplitude and phase.

We can summarize the method as follows.

1. Select oscillator or wave form generator to appropriate frequency.
2. Route input into filter, shaker, or whatever device is being tested to generate the sinusoidal input into this system.
3. Allow steady-state response to develop.
4. Measure amplitude ratio of output to input and phase shift of output relative to input.
5. Repeat steps 1–4 for all other frequencies across response band.

The advantages of the sine wave method for determination of transfer function are as follows:

1. All signal energy is concentrated in one frequency band so signal to noise ratios are high.
2. It is simple and straightforward and can be done with relatively simple instruments.

The disadvantages of the method center primarily around the fact that it requires an extremely long period of time to accomplish a test to completely determine a transfer function. This basic inadequacy led to the development of swept sine, and then later random inputs, to determine transfer functions.

Transfer Function from Swept Sine Wave

In order to completely determine a system transfer function one requires an input function with sufficient power at all frequencies for which significant responses would exist. The single sine wave at a time method requires excessive amounts of time. A swept sine wave is one possible way of shortening the test time. The linearly swept sine is defined as

$$x(t) = \sin \omega t$$

where

$$\omega = at + b$$

so that

$$x(t) = \sin(at^2 + bt) \tag{9.75}$$

Instantaneous frequency is the derivative of the argument of the sinusoid which is

$$\omega(t) = 2at + b$$

Thus for $t = 0$, the starting frequency is

$$\omega(0) = 2\pi f_0 = b$$

The final frequency after P sec is

$$\omega(P) = 2\pi f_1 = 2aP + b$$

Therefore the sweep rate is $2a$ where

$$2a = \frac{2\pi(f_1 - f_0)}{P} \quad \text{or} \quad a = \frac{\pi(f_1 - f_0)}{P} \,(\text{rad/sec})$$

If one desires to cover a frequency range f_1 to f_0 in P seconds, then one needs a sweep rate of

$$\frac{a}{2\pi} = \frac{(f_1 - f_0)}{2P}$$

The PSD of a typical swept sine is shown in Figure 9.9. The incorrect assumption is often made that a swept sine of constant amplitude has a "flat" spectrum. As can be seen from the plot this is not so. A "hash band" exists whose magnitude is independent of the sweep rate. An approximate formula is

$$s_{\max} = \frac{1.38\pi}{4a} = 1.38 s_{\text{ave}} \tag{9.76}$$

If the input were perfectly constant in spectral density then one would not need to employ the Fourier transform of the input, but one could just look at the square root of the PSD to obtain transfer function gain.

If one employs the cross spectral method or ratio of Fourier transforms then the same problem does not exist. One then encounters the standard

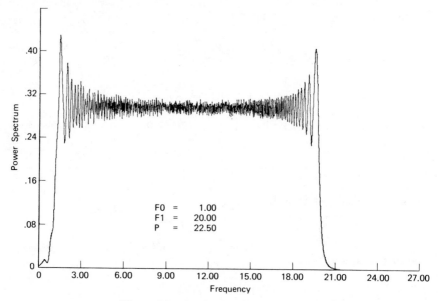

Figure 9.9 Swept sine wave spectrum.

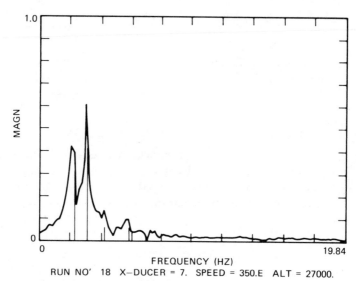

RUN NO' 18   X–DUCER = 7.   SPEED = 350.E   ALT = 27000.

Figure 9.10 AFFTC flutter test results: transfer function magnitude (27,000 ft = 8230 m).

limitations of resolution and d.f. (if substantial noise exists). A subtle problem exists in that power in the swept sine in given frequency bands exists over only short periods of time. There is some evidence to suggest that, at least in structural applications, structural modes are not excited to their full steady values if the sweep is "too fast." One must experiment with his own particular application and test at several sweep rates to ensure this is not a problem.

Figure 9.10 is the transfer function of a portion of the Rockwell B-1 bomber structure obtained in flight flutter tests. A swept sine excitation is employed in these tests.

9.10   TRANSFER FUNCTION FROM RANDOM INPUTS

The relationship defined by (9.5) relates an arbitrary input function to an output function. Effectively no restrictions are placed on the input. In particular the input function can be a sample function from a random process. It boils down to the fact that if we have a perfect linear system, and no extraneous noise, then a *single measurement* is adequate to *perfectly* estimate the transfer function of a system.

In particular, a white noise input function contains power at all frequencies and is a very appropriate candidate for an input function. We of course must contend with the fact that we in fact do have extraneous noise, and hence must perform some averaging in order to average out the effect of the noise. However, the fact that we have a steady-state function (on the average) with equal power at all frequencies (again on the average) makes a white noise input function an overwhelming choice as the most suitable choice for an input function for transfer function measurements.

The advantages of the white noise random input function are the following:

1. It contains equal power, on the average, at all frequencies.
2. For a given amount of extraneous noise it is very convenient to average over a suitably long record length or to average in frequency over a wider band to increase the d.f. and thus increase the accuracy of the estimate.
3. For a given desired resolution and extraneous noise, one needs merely to extend the time of the test in order to obtain a specified accuracy.

The disadvantages of random inputs relate more to tradition. Owing to the lack of understanding in the past, there has been limited development of

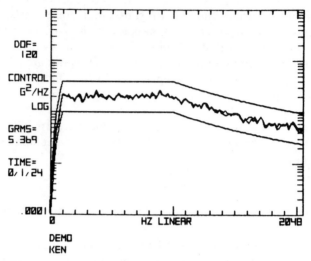

DOF=
1 20

CONTROL
G²/HZ
LOG

GRMS=
5.369

TIME=
0/1/24

.0001

0   HZ LINEAR   2048

DEMO
KEN

Figure 9.11   Vibration control system control spectrum.

equipment capable of generating white noise inputs. However, the introduction of digital computers in transfer function estimation applications
such as vibration control testing has made the generation of random inputs
practical.

We employ the cross spectrum technique defined by (9.11) when random
noise is employed. The cross spectrum and power spectrum must be
estimated by proper techniques. If the spectral estimates are smeared
owing to inadequate resolution then so will the transfer function estimate.

The control spectrum computed in a digital vibration control loop is
shown in Figure 9.11. White noise is created with a digital random number
generator. The transfer function of the system is estimated and the input
spectrum is shaped until the output spectrum conforms to a predetermined
spectrum.

9.11   COHERENCE FUNCTION FOR $B_e = 1/P$

The coherence function is a very useful parameter to aid in understanding
of input–output systems. However it possesses what appear to be peculiar
statistical properties. If the error formulas of Section 9.5 are examined, in
particular (9.51), we can expect unusual behavior as $n \to 2$ since this bias
term goes to infinity. What happens is that coherence function becomes

identically equal to unity when $n = 2$. This is illustrated by the equation

$$\gamma_{xy}^2(k) = \frac{|S_{xy}(f)|^2}{S_x(f)S_y(k)}$$

$$= \frac{\left(\frac{1}{P}\right)^2 X(k)Y^*(k)X^*(k)Y(k)}{\frac{1}{P}X^*(k)X(k)\frac{1}{P}Y^*(k)Y(k)} \equiv 1$$

The second line holds since if $n = 2$ (or $B_e = 1/P$) then no averaging has occurred. In general, of course, the average of a ratio is not equal to the ratio of averages and thus the coherence is not unity in the usual situation.

We can understand the preceding phenomenon if we recall the interpretation of coherence in terms of a linear relation. If we have a Fourier transform, $X(f)$, then at a single frequency it defines one point in the complex plane. If we have a second Fourier transform, $Y(f)$, then a second point on the complex plane is defined. As illustrated in Figure 9.12, since we have only two points, a single straight line is exactly defined; hence there is a perfect linear relation and coherence must therefore be unity.

If instead we have several estimates of the Fourier transform, each with some error, then we would have groupings about some average values of

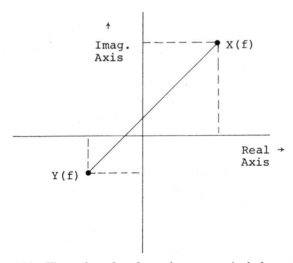

Figure 9.12   Illustration of perfect coherence at single frequency.

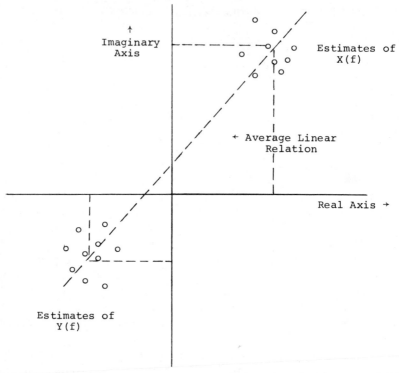

Figure 9.13 Average linear relation between clusters of $X(f)$ estimates and $Y(f)$ estimates.

$X(f)$ and $Y(f)$. In this case, we would have a line that would connect the averages on a minimum mean square basis. Then the coherence is a measure of the goodness of fit of the line. This is illustrated in Figure 9.13.

Also, as is demonstrated in a simple manner by Koopmans [1973, p. 309], coherence can also be severely biased due to smearing effects if too wide resolution. This is particularly true in an area of rapidly varying phase which occurs at resonances in mechanical structures, for example.

9.12 EXAMPLES OF TRANSFER FUNCTION COMPUTATIONS

Digital Filter

If we construct a digital filter we have a perfectly coherent linear system and it is simple to obtain good estimates of the transfer function. This is illustrated in Figure 9.14. There we have the transfer function of a low pass

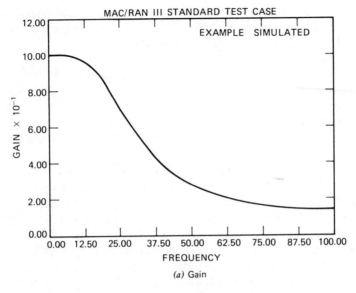

(a) Gain

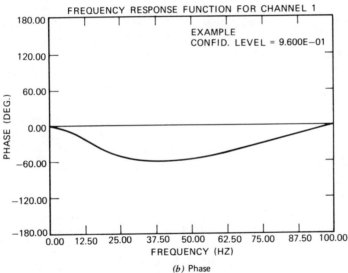

(b) Phase

Figure 9.14 (a) Gain and (b) phase plot of numerical filter.

recursive (Butterworth) filter obtained from cross spectrum computations.

As can be seen from Figure 9.14, both gain and phase are quite smooth. Only very small statistical inaccuracies are present.

Effect of Adding Noise

If we take a simple electrical filter and add independent white noise to the output we have a demonstration of the effects of extraneous noise. In Figures 9.15–9.17, we have added 0%, 10% and 50% extraneous noise. In every case, the analysis is performed with $n = 128$ d.f. It should be noted that we have added white noise which by definition is constant across the frequency band. The output power is not constant, however. The bandpass filter shape passes more power at the passband than at other frequencies. As a result the signal to extraneous noise ratio is greater in the area outside of the passband. This is reflected in the statistical variability, which is much higher outside the passband.

The coherence function is a very important companion to the transfer function because of the key role it plays in the statistical accuracy of the results. The confidence limit calculations provide the quantitative statistical accuracy but there are some qualitative judgments based on experience that are useful and are described now. Figures 9.18–9.22 which are $\hat{G}_{xx}(f)$, $\hat{G}_{yy}(f)$, $|\hat{H}_{xy}(f)|$, $\hat{\phi}_{xy}(f)$, and $\hat{\gamma}^2_{xy}(f)$ respectively, where $x(t)$ is the pseudorandom white noise, and $H_{xy}(f)$ represents a bandpass digital filter.

The coherence plot illustrates the fact that when true coherence is high in the passband of the filter (near 0.8 in this case since we added extraneous noise) then the coherence estimate comes close to the true value. On the other hand, when true coherence is low (near zero outside the passband) then the estimate exhibits high variability. Note that the overall view of the function is important. We see a very clear band of high coherence at lower frequencies and tend to "believe" that in fact true coherence is high (from about 0.2 Hz on we begin to see very erratic behavior). Thus even though we see a fairly high individual peak of $\hat{\gamma} = 0.4$ at about 0.5 Hz we tend to discount its importance because of the "global" erraticism of the function. As a result we tend to put considerable faith in the transfer function gain and phase plots in about the range from 0.05 to 0.15 and less faith outside that band. Unfortunately we know of no way to describe this type of behavior in a more quantitative manner. However, this type of situation does often occur in practice and such judgments are useful.

Example for Multi-Input System

We generate an artificial two input system according to the diagram of Figure 9.23. The two transfer functions are for eight-pole bandpass filters,

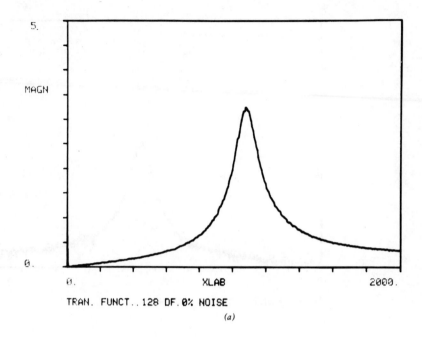

TRAN. FUNCT..128 DF.0% NOISE

(a)

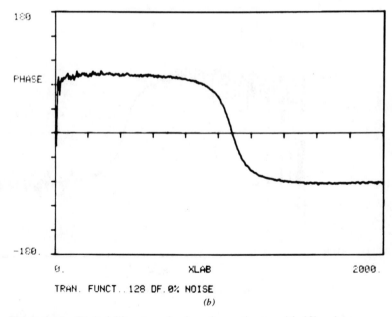

TRAN. FUNCT..128 DF.0% NOISE

(b)

Figure 9.15 Digital filter transfer function estimate with 0% noise.

399

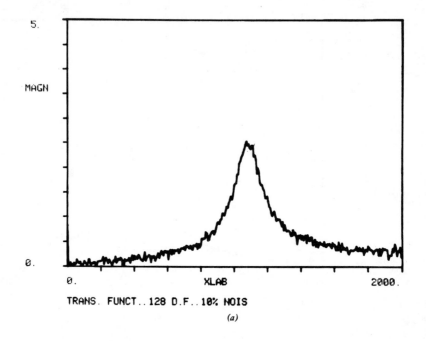

TRANS. FUNCT..128 D.F..10% NOIS

(a)

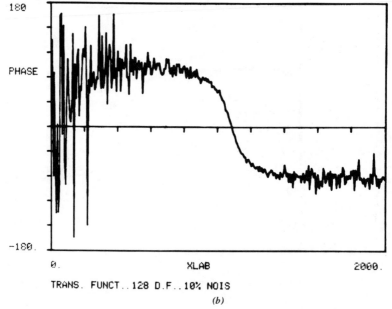

TRANS. FUNCT..128 D.F..10% NOIS

(b)

Figure 9.16 Digital filter transfer function estimate with 10% noise.

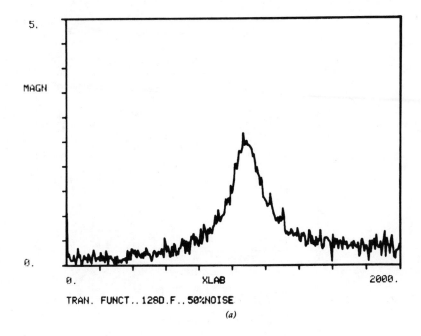

TRAN. FUNCT..128D.F..50%NOISE

(a)

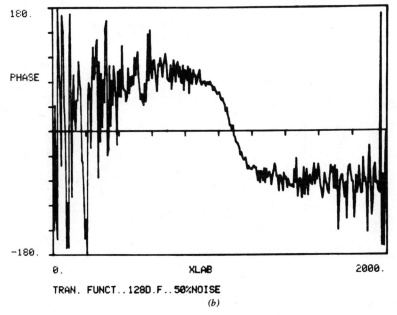

TRAN. FUNCT..128D.F..50%NOISE

(b)

Figure 9.17 Digital filter transfer function estimate with 50% noise.

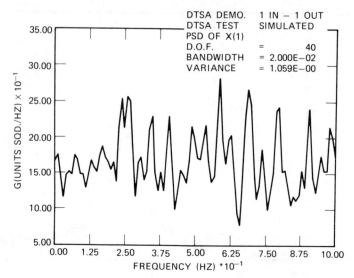

Figure 9.18 Input PSD, $\hat{G}_{xy}(f)$.

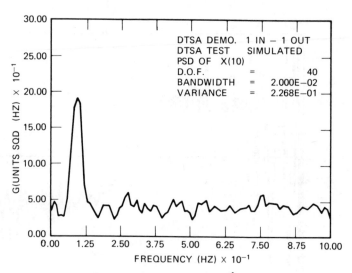

Figure 9.19 Output PSD, $\hat{G}_{yy}(f)$.

402

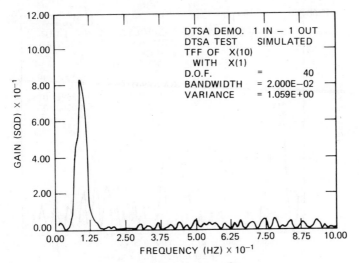

Figure 9.20 Filter gain, $|\hat{H}_{xy}(f)|$.

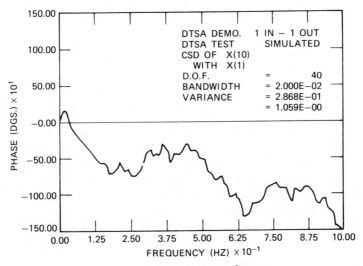

Figure 9.21 Filter phase, $\hat{\varnothing}_{xy}(f)$.

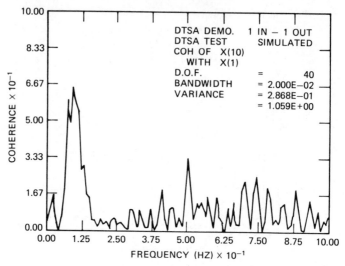

Figure 9.22   Coherence, $\hat{\gamma}_{xy}^2(f)$.

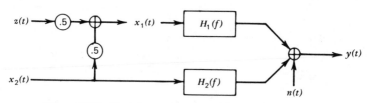

Figure 9.23   Two input systems with correlated inputs.

the first from 0.07 to 0.12 Hz and the second from 0.14 to 0.24 Hz. Correlated inputs are simulated by the fact that $x_1(t)$ includes half of $x_2(t)$. If the two inputs were completely independent then the single input solutions for $H_1(f)$ and $H_2(f)$ would be adequate. The existence of correlation in the input functions requires the multi-input solution involving a matrix inverse to obtain unbiased results.

Examinations of the plots in Figures 9.24–9.32 allow one to draw the expected conclusions:

1. The bandpass filter characteristics can at least be roughly deduced from the gain plots.

2. The multiple coherence shows that the output is made up of data highly linearly related to inputs in the frequency range dictated by the two bandpass filter gains. As will be seen from the confidence limit

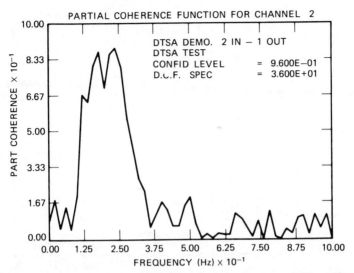

Figure 9.24 Multi-input example. Partial coherence for second filter. Shows that effects coming through the first passband are almost all removed but effects through second passband are retained.

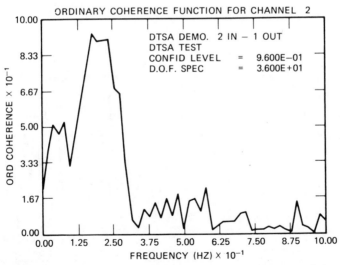

Figure 9.25 Mult-input example. Ordinary coherence for second input came through passband of first filter also at about $\frac{1}{2}$ the power level (coherence is about 0.5).

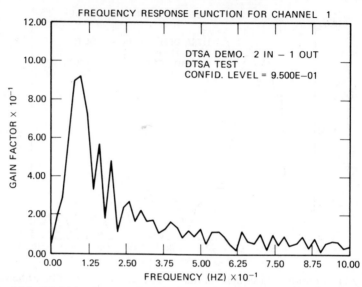

Figure 9.26 Multi-input example. Gain of first filter passband about 0.07–0.12 Hz.

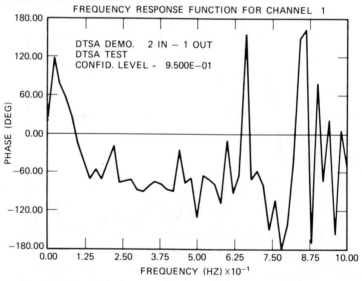

Figure 9.27 Multi-input example. Sample-phase of first filter.

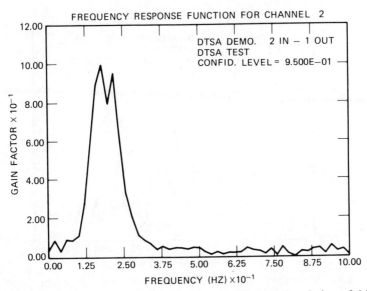

Figure 9.28 Multi-input example. Gain of second filter passband about 0.14–0.24 Hz.

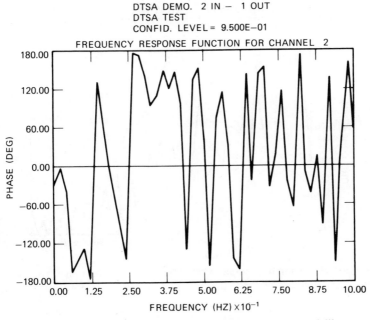

Figure 9.29 Multi-input example. Sample-phase of second filter.

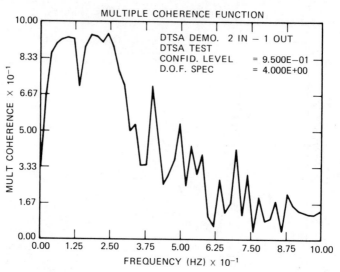

Figure 9.30 Multi-input example. Multiple coherence function. Note high coherence in the filter passbands.

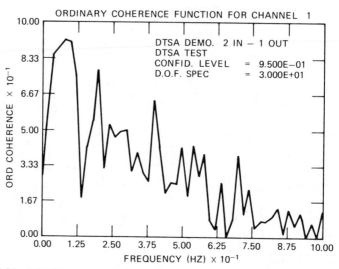

Figure 9.31 Multi-input example. Ordinary coherence for first filter. Note high coherence in passband of first filter and some erratic high coherence in band of second filter.

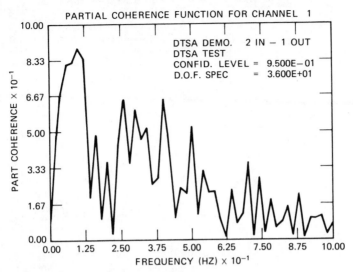

Figure 9.32 Multi-input example. Partial coherence for first filter. Note most of coherence in area of passband is removed but first remains.

formulas we tend to trust transfer function results in the areas of high multiple coherence. Experience tells us to treat the individual coherence peaks in the higher frequency range with caution owing to the "global" erratic behavior.

3. The relation of the ordinary and partial coherences of the two-channels suggests that the linear relations of the individual channels are restricted to the bands of about 0.03–0.10 Hz and 0.13–0.26 Hz for channels 1 and 2, respectively. This is indicated since apparent power is the higher band in the first case, and the lower band in the second case is removed by the partial coherence computation.

This example serves to illustrate the type of useful deductions that can be made from multi-input computations of transfer functions and the various coherence functions. The results can be much more effective if they can be related to physical information. For example, if we were able to make the advance hypothesis that we expect the two transmission channels to be bandpass filters, the observed results would tend to back up that hypothesis is every respect.

Some Plotting Considerations

Transfer functions in the field of control theory have traditionally been plotted in terms of "dB" with a logarithmic frequency scale. We prefer

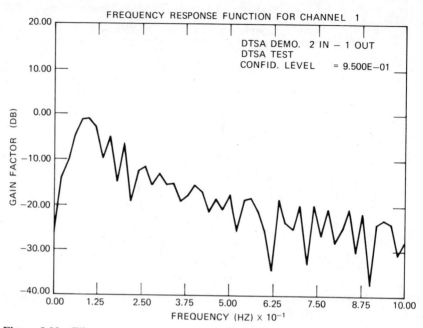

Figure 9.33 Filter gain for channel 1 plotted (dB scale). Compare with Figure 9.26.

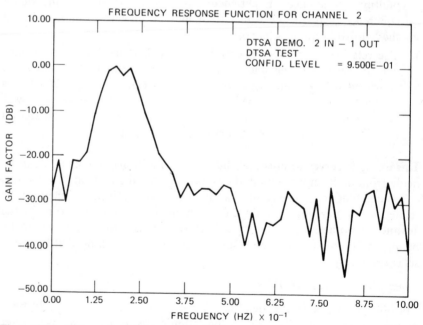

Figure 9.34 Filter gain for channel 2 plotted (dB scale). Compare with Figure 9.26.

410

linear–linear plots but there are reasons for either mode. The abbreviation dB stands for decibel from acoustics and is defined by

$$dB = 10\log\frac{x}{ref} \qquad (9.77)$$

where ref stand for some reference value of the variable x. Usually it relates to voltage levels in control theory:

$$dB = 20\log\frac{v_1}{v_2} \qquad (9.78)$$

or for power ratios,

$$dB = 10\log\frac{v_1^2}{v_2^2} = 20\log\frac{v_1}{v_2}$$

since power is proportional to the square of voltage.

In transfer function gains we reference to a gain of unity and have

$$|H| \text{ in } dB = 10\log\frac{|H(f)|^2}{1} = 20\log|H(f)| \qquad (9.79)$$

We reference to unity since a physical system cannot amplify (unless outside power is used for amplifiers) and thus unity gain would be a filter that passes all frequencies perfectly. This corresponds to a dB level of 0 and attenuations are represented by negative values.

The logarithmic transformation has the effect of broadening the range that can appear on a plot. This is illustrated in Figures 9.33 and 9.34, which are the same as those in Figures 9.26 and 9.28 but in dB units. Note that the log scale is relabeled in linear units by the dB transformation. Keep in mind that 10 dB represents a change by the multiplicative factor of 10. Almost all the concepts stem from acoustics because the human ear tends to judge the loudness of sound in a logarithmic manner. That is, a 100 to 1 increase in a sound level tends to seem only twice as loud.

The logarithmic transformation of the frequency axis spreads the lower and compresses the upper end. Many physical systems tend to act in a broader bandwidth at higher frequencies. The log transformation would make high- and low-frequency bands appear of constant width in this case.

EXERCISES

9.1. Fill in missing steps for (9.16).

9.2. Prove that (9.32) and (9.12) are equivalent.

9.3. Prove (9.72).

9.4. Write (9.70)–(9.72) in their simplest form in terms of elements of the spectral matrix.

9.5. Derive (9.5) from (9.3) by computing the Fourier transform of (9.3). Assume all appropriate mathematical conditions for the existence of the transforms, etc., are satisfied.

Almost all linear systems formulas can be derived by doing complex variable analogies on the Fourier-transformed variables (at each frequency value f) with classical statistics. Define variance as $E[X^*X]$, and covariance as $E[X^*Y]$. Let the PSD be analogous to variance and the cross spectrum to covariance. Use these facts in Exercises 9.6–9.8.

9.6 Derive (9.10) as the analogy of the statistical equation

$$\sigma_y^2 = \beta^2 \sigma_x^2 \qquad y = \beta + \varepsilon$$

where ε is a zero mean independent noise.

9.7. Derive (9.11) as the analogy of the statistical equation

$$\sigma_{xy} = \beta_{xy} \sigma_x^2$$

where $\sigma_{xy} = \text{cov}[x,y]$.

9.8 What is the classical statistical analogy of ordinary coherence, (9.12)?

9.9 Derive the special equations for a two input—single output system.

9.10 Derive $y(t)$, the inverse Fourier transform of (9.73).

APPENDIX A

COMPUTER SUBROUTINES
FOR TIME SERIES ANALYSIS

A.1 INTRODUCTION

The purpose of these subroutines is to provide the student with the capability of working certain of the exercises.

The code was written in a simplified subset of FORTRAN so that it will run on most machines having FORTRAN compilers.

Because the objectives we set when writing the routines were clarity and generality rather than efficiency, it is very likely that the code could be made to run faster or occupy less computer storage. Therefore, the user should not be surprised when he finds code that would appear gross by his own standards.

At the other extreme, we would like to caution the students that although the code as given will be useful in solving the problems in this text, it will not solve all the problems to be found in time series work. Rather, the code will give the student an elementary capability in dealing with problems of this type. Almost two orders of magnitude more code are required for a general time series capability.

The following subroutines are included:

TDRAND	Uniform random number generator
PRPLOT	Printer plotting routine
FFTRAN	Fast Fourier transform
LPSB	Routine for generating the weights for lowpass Butterworth filters
TTRAN	Routine for computing the transfer function of digital filters

413

Additionally, there is a short program which partially tests the routines. It is recommended that this test program be run and the answers checked before attempting to work any of the problems. It is all too easy to enter a character incorrectly and then spend hours attempting to solve a problem when it cannot be done because of an error in a subroutine. The results of running the test case are given, so that this basic check is easy to do. However, please remember that the check case is not exhaustive; it may run correctly even though there have been errors in keypunching or design.

Another point to note is that the subroutines do *not* check the ranges of input parameters for validity. If bad values are given for some of the parameters, it is quite possible that an arithmetic error will occur of such a nature so as to cause the program to be aborted on some operating systems.

A.2   RANDOM NUMBER GENERATOR

Subroutine TDRAND (Figure A.1) generates a single, uniformly distributed, pseudo-random number for each entry. The calling sequence is of the form

CALL TDRAND (X)

where X is the resulting random number. It is uniformly distributed in the range $(0, 1)$ and has expected mean $\frac{1}{2}$ and variance $\frac{1}{12}$.

The procedure is essentially Algorithm 266 [G5] by M. C. Pike and J. D. Hill, as modified by L. Hanson (Reference [Pike, 1965]).

There is no way to reinitialize TDRAND.

Figures A.2 and A.3 show the result of computing 1000 pseudo-random numbers from TDRAND, subtracting $\frac{1}{2}$ to give a zero mean, and then computing their histogram and power spectral density.

The histogram has 20 equally spaced pockets. In the unlikely event that there were exactly 50 values in each pocket, then the probability would be 0.05 for all pockets. As can be seen, the results are fairly close to this.

The PSD of the 1000 points would theoretically be the constant $8.3333.10^{-4}$ in this case. Note how the computed PSD does in fact vary about this value.

```
SUBROUTINE TDRAND (X)
DATA I/783637/
I=125*I
I=I-(I/2796203)*2796203
X=FLOAT(I)/2796202.
RETURN
END
```

Figure A.1   Uniform random number generator.

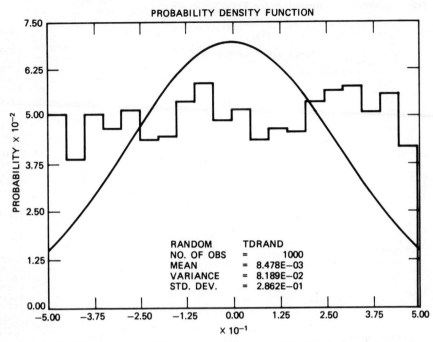

Figure A.2 Histogram of 1000 values generated by TDRAND. One-half has been subtracted from each output in order to make the histogram symmetric about 0.

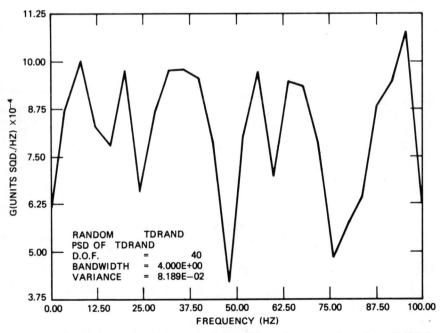

Figure A.3 Power spectral density of the 1000 points. A value of $T=0.005$ is assumed.

415

```
      SUBROUTINE PRPLOT (Y,N,FIRST,DX,JSKIP)                    100010
      DIMENSION Y(1), A(26), SYM(4)                             100020
      DATA BLNK/4H    /,SYM(1)/4H+   /,SYM(2)/4H +  /,           100030
     1SYM(3)/4H  + /,SYM(4)/4H   +/,IPRINT/6/                    100040
      ISKIP=JSKIP                                               100050
      IF (ISKIP.LE.0) ISKIP=1                                   100060
      DO 5 I=1,26                                               100070
5     A(I)=BLNK                                                 100080
      ZERO=FIRST                                                100090
      C=Y(1)                                                    100100
      D=C                                                       100110
      DO 10 I=2,N                                               100120
      LOC=1+ISKIP*(I-1)                                         100130
      E=Y(LOC)                                                  100140
      IF (E.GT.D) D=E                                           100150
      IF (E.LT.C) C=E                                           100160
10    CONTINUE                                                  100170
      IGT=1                                                     100180
      IF (D.GT.9999.) IGT=2                                     100190
      IF (C.LT.-9999.) IGT=2                                    100200
      IF (D.LT.0.1.AND.C.GT.-0.1) IGT=2                         100210
      DMC=D-C                                                   100220
      AA=(DMC)/100.                                             100230
      BB=(D+C)/2.                                               100240
      WRITE (IPRINT,45) C,BB,D                                  100250
      IF (ABS(DMC).GT.1.E-20) GO TO 15                          100260
      WRITE (IPRINT,50)                                         100270
      GO TO 40                                                  100280
15    DO 35 I=1,N                                               100290
      LOC=1+ISKIP*(I-1)                                         100300
      XP=Y(LOC)                                                 100310
      J=(XP-C)/AA+0.5                                           100320
      J4=J/4                                                    100330
      JU=J-J4*4+1                                               100340
      J4=J4+1                                                   100350
      A(J4)=SYM(JU)                                             100360
      GO TO (20,25),IGT                                         100370
20    WRITE (IPRINT,55) ZERO,XP,A                               100380
      GO TO 30                                                  100390
25    WRITE (IPRINT,60) ZERO,XP,A                               100400
30    ZERO=ZERO+DX                                              100410
      A(J4)=BLNK                                                100420
35    CONTINUE                                                  100430
40    RETURN                                                    100440
C                                                               100450
C                                                               100460
C                                                               100470
45    FORMAT (20X,F10.2,35X,F10.2,36X,F10.2)                    100480
50    FORMAT (26HODATA ALL EQUAL...NO PLOT.,//)                 100490
55    FORMAT (1X,F8.4,F10.4,1X,26A4)                            100500
60    FORMAT (1X,F7.4,E11.4,1X,26A4)                            100510
      END                                                       100520
```

Figure A.4 Printer plotting routine PRPLOT. Written by R. K. Otnes.

A.3   PLOTTING ON THE PRINTER

Subroutine PRPLOT (Figure A.4) is a simple subroutine which may be used to plot equally spaced data on a printer. The calling sequence is

CALL SUBROUTINE PRPLOT (Y,N,FIRST,DX,ISKIP)

These parameters are:

> Y = the data (dependent variable). Dimensioned and at equally spaced intervals of size DX
> N = total number of points to be plotted
> FIRST = X_0, the initial value of the independent variable usually 0
> DX = the increment between successive values of X
> ISKIP ⩽ 1 = plot all values of Y
> > 1 = plot N values of Y starting with $Y(1)$, but skip ISKIP-1 between each plotted value

This routine does not eject a page before starting to plot. The user should print one or more lines before going to PRPLOT for identification and should include in the header information the carriage control for ejecting a page.

The skipping option, last parameter, is included so that the real and imaginary parts of complex data may be plotted separately without having to separate the parts of the complex variable from the way in which they are naturally stored. Note that the routine is set up to print out on *unit 6*. Many systems will require that this be changed.

A.4   FAST FOURIER TRANSFORM

Subroutine FFTRAN, shown in Figure A.5, computes the Fourier Transform of equally spaced complex data using the Cooley–Tukey method. The calling sequence is

CALL FFTRAN (SIGN,T,X,NPOW)

where

> SIGN = −1.   for time to frequency
> > 1.   for frequency to time
> T = the sampling interval in the time domain
> X = the data
> NPOW = power of 2 of the length of the data. That is, $N = 2^{NPOW}$

This routine assumes that there are $N = 2^{NPOW}$ complex values of data stored in the dimensioned variable X. Thus the dimension of X must be at least 2*(2**NPOW) for X real.

T is always the sampling interval in the time domain. When required, b, the frequency interval is computed from T and NPOW as $b = 1/NT$.

```
      SUBROUTINE FFTRAN (SIGN,T,X,NPOW)                                      9001
C                                                                            9002
C         COOLEY-TUKEY METHOD OF FOURIER TRANSFORM                           9003
C         INCLUDES SINE COSINE COMPUTATION AND                              9004
C         REARRANGING DATA ACCORDING TO REVERSE BIT ADDRESSSES              9005
C                                                                            9006
C         SIGN = FOURIER DIRECTION TRANSFORM FLAG                           9007
C              = -1. FOR DIRECT TRANSFORM                                   9008
C              = 1. FOR INVERSE TRANSFORM                                   9009
C         T    = DELTA TIME                                                 9010
C         X    = LOCATION OF FOURIER TRANSFORM BLOCK                        9011
C         NPOW = POWER OF 2 (BLOCK SIZE =2**NPOW)                           9012
C                                                                            9013
      DIMENSION X(1), CS(2), MSK(13)                                        9014
      COMPLEX X,CXCS,HOLD,XA                                                9015
      EQUIVALENCE (CXCS,CS)                                                 9016
      NMAX=2**NPOW                                                          9017
      ZZ=6.283185306*SIGN/FLOAT(NMAX)                                       9018
      DELTA=T                                                               9019
      IF (SIGN) 10,10,5                                                     9020
    5 DELTA=1./(T*FLOAT(NMAX))                                              9021
   10 MSK(1)=NMAX/2                                                         9022
      DO 15 I=2,NPOW                                                        9023
   15 MSK(I)=MSK(I-1)/2                                                     9024
      NN=NMAX                                                               9025
      MM=2                                                                  9026
C                                                                            9027
C         LOOP OVER NPOW LAYERS                                             9028
C                                                                            9029
      DO 45 LAYER=1,NPOW                                                    9030
      NN=NN/2                                                               9031
      NW=0                                                                  9032
      DO 40 I=1,MM,2                                                        9033
      II=NN*I                                                               9034
C                                                                            9035
C         CXCS = CEXP(2*PI*NW*SIGN/NMAX)                                    9036
C                                                                            9037
      W=FLOAT(NW)*ZZ                                                        9038
      CS(1)=COS(W)                                                          9039
      CS(2)=SIN(W)                                                          9040
C                                                                            9041
C         COMPUTE ELEMENTS FOR BOTH HALVES OF EACH BLOCK                    9042
C                                                                            9043
      DO 20 J=1,NN                                                          9044
```

Figure A.5 Fast Fourier transform routine. Written by L. D. Enochson, Howard Nathans, and R. K. Otnes.

418

```
      II=II+1                                            90450
      IJ=II-NN                                           90460
      XA=CXCS*X(II)                                      90470
      X(II)=X(IJ)-XA                                     90480
20    X(IJ)=X(IJ)+XA                                     90490
C                                                        90500
C          BUMP UP SERIES BY 2                           90510
C                                                        90520
C          COMPUTE REVERSE ADDRESSS                      90530
C                                                        90540
      DO 25 LOC=2,NPOW                                   90550
      LL=NW-MSK(LOC)                                     90560
      IF (LL) 30,35,25                                   90570
25    NW=LL                                              90580
30    NW=MSK(LOC)+NW                                     90590
      GO TO 40                                           90600
35    NW=MSK(LOC+1)                                      90610
40    CONTINUE                                           90620
C                                                        90630
C          DO FINAL REARRANGEMENT                        90640
C          ALSO MULTIPLY BY DELTA                        90650
C                                                        90660
45    MM=MM*2                                            90670
      NW=0                                               90680
      DO 80 I=1,NMAX                                     90690
      NW1=NW+1                                           90700
      HOLD=X(NW1)                                        90710
      IF (NW1-I) 60,55,50                                90720
50    X(NW1)=X(I)*DELTA                                  90730
55    X(I)=HOLD*DELTA                                    90740
C                                                        90750
C          BUMP UP SERIES BY 1                           90760
C          COMPUTE REVERSE ADDRESS                       90770
C                                                        90780
60    DO 65 LOC=1,NPOW                                   90790
      LL=NW-MSK(LOC)                                     90800
      IF (LL) 70,75,65                                   90810
65    NW=LL                                              90820
70    NW=MSK(LOC)+NW                                     90830
      GO TO 80                                           90840
75    NW=MSK(LOC+1)                                      90850
80    CONTINUE                                           90860
      RETURN                                             90870
      END                                                90880
```

Figure A.5   (*Continued.*)

The formulas for computation are

$$X(k) = T \sum_{i=0}^{N-1} x(i) \exp\left(\frac{-j2\pi ik}{N}\right)$$

where $N = 2^{\text{NPOW}}$.

Both $x(i)$ and $X(k)$ are complex. Storage of these variables is as follows

Time Function	Program Storage	Frequency Function	Program Storage
$x(0)$	X(1)	$X(0)$	X(1), X(2)
$x(1)$	X(3)	$X(1)$	X(3), X(4)
$\vdots$	$\vdots$	$\vdots$	$\vdots$
$x(i)$	X(2i+1)	$X(k)$	X(2k+1), X(2k+2)
$\vdots$	$\vdots$	$\vdots$	$\vdots$
$x(N-1)$	X(2N-1)	$X(N-1)$	X(2N-1), X(2N)

For many problems it is simpler to

1. Transform one function at a time.
2. Use a two variable dimension for x.

By the latter is meant something of the form

DIMENSION X(2,1024)

Here $N = 1024$ and the function to be transformed is stored as follows:

$$x(i) \rightarrow X(1, \text{I or } i+1) \qquad I = 1, \ldots, N$$
$$0 \rightarrow X(2, \text{I or } i+1) \qquad i = 0, \ldots, N-1$$

After transformation, the result is stored as follows:

	Frequency
Re$[X(0)]$ is in X(1, 1)	
	0
Im$[X(0)]$ is in X(2, 1)	
$\vdots$	
Re$[X(k)]$ is in X(1, K or $k+1$)	
	kb
Im$[X(k)]$ is in X(2, K or $k+1$)	
$\vdots$	
Re$[X(N/2)]$ is in X(1, N/2+1)	
	F
Im$[X(N/2)]$ is in X(2, N/2+1)	

Remember that the correspondence between k and K is

$$k: \quad 0 \quad k \qquad \frac{N}{2}$$

$$K: \quad 1 \quad k+1 \quad \frac{N}{2}+1$$

A.5 GENERATION OF LOWPASS FILTER WEIGHTS

Subroutine LPSB, shown in Figure A.6, generates the coefficients to be employed in lowpass filtering. In particular the weights are of the sine Butterworth variety. The calling sequence is

$$\text{CALL LPSB (M,T,BW,A1,A2,BZERO)}$$

The definitions of these parameters are as follows:

Input

M = the order of the filter; should be limited to the range $1 \leqslant M \leqslant 20$, with M = 6 a typical value

T = the sampling interval in seconds

BW = cutoff (half-power point) of the filter in Hz; must be on the range $0 < BW < 1/2T$

Output

A1 = the a_{1p} term in the filter, $p = 1, \ldots, P$; P is defined by

$$P = \frac{M}{2} \qquad (M \text{ even})$$

$$P = \frac{M+1}{2} \qquad (M \text{ odd})$$

A2 = the a_{2p} term in the filter; there are P of these if M is even; if M is odd, the last (Pth) one is 0

BZERO = a constant; the b_0 term for all stages of the filter

The filtering convention for the pth stage of the filter is

$$y^{(P)}(i) = b_0 y^{(p-1)}(i) - a_{1p} y^{(p)}(i-1) - a_{2p} y^{(P)}(i-2)$$

In pictorial form,

```
      SUBROUTINE LPSB (MM,T,BW,A1,A2,BZERO)
C
C     THIS ROUTINE COMPUTES SINE BUTTERWORTH LOWPASS FILTERS
C
C     FROM... APPLIED TIME SERIES ANALYSIS...
C
C     BY ROBERT K. OTNES AND LOREN ENOCHSON
C
C     COPYRIGHT 1977, WILEY INTERSCIENCE, NEW YORK
C
C     CONVENTION IS...
C
C     Y(I)=-A1*Y(I-1)-A2*Y(I-2)+BZERO*X(I)
C
      DIMENSION A1(1), A2(1)
      DOUBLE PRECISION A,B,C,D,E,F,G,H,FN,FACT,WEDGE,SECTOR,ANG
      FACT=3.14159265*T*BW
      FACT=DSIN(FACT)
      F=1.D0
      M=MM
      M1=M/2
      M3=M1
      IF (M1.EQ.0) GO TO 10
      M2=M
      A=M2
      SECTOR=3.14159265D0/A
      WEDGE=SECTOR/2.D0
      DO 5 I=1,M1
      FN=I-1
      B=FACT*DSIN(FN*SECTOR+WEDGE)
      C=1.D0-FACT*FACT
      D=0.5D0*(-C+DSQRT(C*C+4.D0*B**2))
      E=DSQRT(D+1.D0)+DSQRT(D)
      G=2.D0*((2.D0*B*B/D)-1.D0)/(E**2)
      H=-1.D0/(E**4)
      F=F*(1.D0-G-H)
      A1(I)=-G
      A2(I)=-H
    5 CONTINUE
   10 IT=M-2*M1
      IF (IT.EQ.0) GO TO 15
      M3=M1+1
      A=FACT*FACT
      G=2.D0*A+1.D0-2.D0*FACT*DSQRT(A+1.D0)
      A1(M3)=-G
      A2(M3)=0.
      F=F*(1.D0-G)
   15 A=M3
      BZERO=F**(1.D0/A)
      RETURN
      END
```

Figure A.6 Routine for generating the weights for lowpass Butterworth filtering.

Note that $y^{(p-1)}(i)$ is the input at each stage and $y^{(p)}(i)$ is the output. Also,

$$y^{(0)}(i) = x(i) \quad \text{(initial input)}$$

$$y^{(P)}(i) = y(i) \quad \text{(final output)}$$

A.6   TRANSFER FUNCTION OF A DIGITAL FILTER

Subroutine TTRAN, shown in Figure A.7. computes the transfer function of a digital filter for a specified set of frequencies given the filter weights. The routine expects the filter to be in cascade form.

The calling sequence of this subroutine is

CALL TTRAN (A1,A2,B0,B1,B2,M,NPO,T,FREQ,ABZ,PHS)

```
        SUBROUTINE TTRAN (A1,A2,B0,B1,B2,M,NPO,T,FREQ,ABZ,PHS)
        DIMENSION A1(1),A2(1),B0(1),B1(1),B2(1),FREQ(1),ABZ(1),
       1PHS(1)
        FACT=6.2831853*T
        IP=M-M/2
        ADD=0.
        PREV=0.
        DO 10 I=1,NPO
        FD=FREQ(I)*FACT
        S1=SIN(FD)
        C1=COS(FD)
        A=2.*FD
        S2=SIN(A)
        C2=COS(A)
        ABSA=1.
        PHSA=0.
        DO 5 J=1,IP
        AR=B0(J)+B1(J)*C1+B2(J)*C2
        AI=-B1(J)*S1-B2(J)*S2
        ANM=AR**2+AI**2
        PND=0.
        IF (AI.NE.0..OR.AR.NE.0.) PND=ATAN2(AI,AR)
        AR=1.+A1(J)*C1+A2(J)*C2
        AI=-A1(J)*S1-A2(J)*S2
        ABSA=ABSA*ANM/(AR**2+AI**2)
        DUM=0.
        IF (AI.NE.0..OR.AR.NE.0.) DUM=ATAN2(AI,AR)
    5   PHSA=PHSA+PND-DUM
        ABZ(I)=10.*ALOG10(ABSA+1.E-30)
        ANG=PHSA*180./3.14159265
        CUR=ANG+ADD
        TEST=CUR-PREV
        IF (ABS(TEST).LT.180.) GO TO 9
        IF (TEST.LT.0.) GO TO 7
        ADD=ADD-360.
        CUR=CUR+360.
        GO TO 9
    7   ADD=ADD+360.
        CUR=CUR-360.
    9   PREV=CUR
        PHS(I)=CUR
   10   CONTINUE
        RETURN
        END
```

Figure A.7   Routine for computing the transfer function of a digital filter in terms of gain in dB and phase in degrees.

The definitions of these terms are as follows:

Input to the routine

> A1 = a_{1p} terms (dimension P or greater)
> A2 = a_{2p} terms (dimension P or greater)
> BO = b_{0p} terms (dimension P or greater)
> B1 = b_{1p} terms (dimension P or greater)
> B2 = b_{2p} terms (dimension P or greater)
> M = number of recursive terms in the filter
> NPO = number of output points desired in the computed transfer function
> T = the sampling interval in seconds
> FREQ = the table of frequencies for which the transfer function is to be computed; frequencies are to be in Hz (FREQ must be of dimension NPO or greater)

Output from the routine

> ABZ = the absolute value squared of the transfer function in dB (ABZ must be of dimension NPO or greater)
> PHS = the phase of the transfer function in degrees (PHS must be of dimension NPO or greater)

It is assumed that there are P stages, where

$$P = \begin{cases} \dfrac{M}{2} & (M \text{ even}) \\ \dfrac{M+1}{2} & (M \text{ odd}) \end{cases}$$

The pth stage of the filter has the form

$$y^{(p)}(i) = b_{0p}y^{(p-1)}(i) + b_{1p}y^{(p-1)}(i-1) + b_{2p}y^{(p-1)}(i-2)$$
$$- a_{1p}y^{(p)}(i-1) - a_{2p}y^{(p)}(i-2) \qquad p = 1,\ldots,P$$

As with the previous routine, the original input to the filter, $x(i)$, is also designated by $y^{(0)}(i)$ and $y(i)$. The final output from the filter is also denoted $y^{(P)}(i)$.

This routine allows for much more general nonrecursive terms than are output by subroutines LPSP. To find the transfer of a filter whose weights were generated by LPSB, the A1, A2, M, and T would be exactly as employed with that routine. The B0, B1, and B2 would be defined by

$$BZERO \rightarrow BO(I)$$

$$0. \rightarrow B1(I)$$

$$0. \rightarrow B2(I) \qquad \text{for all } I = 1, \ldots, P$$

Note that BZERO is a scalar in LPSB, whereas B0 is dimensioned in TTRAN.

A.7 TEST CASE AND RESULTS

A simple test case for the subroutines is shown in Figure A.8.
It is divided into four parts:

Test Case	Lines	Function
1	4–21	Generates 10,000 pseudo-random numbers in TDRAND and computes their mean and variance
2	22–42	Sets up a symmetrical pulse and then computes and plots its Fourier transform
3	43–58	Computes and prints the filter weights for a five-pole lowpass Butterworth filter
4	59–69	Computes the transfer function of the filter whose weights were generated in the preceding stage

The program and subroutines were compiled and run on various computers. Job control language (JCL) for that computer had to be added. It is not shown because it is specific to that computer. The JCL will generally be quite different for different manufacturers, so it did not seem worthwhile to reproduce it. Note that all printing is done on unit IPRINT, which is defined by the data statement to be 5. This will have to be modified on some machines.

The results from running the code are shown in Figures A.9–A.11.

Because of the broad range of computer word sizes, the results vary from computer to computer. However, they should be approximately the same as shown.

Figure A.9 shows the output from test case 1 of the program. The expected values of the parameters shown therein are 0., $\frac{1}{12}$ (.083333...) and

```
          DIMENSION A1(3),A2(3),B0(3),B1(3),B2(3),FREQ(101),X(101),Y(101)
          DOUBLE PRECISION D,SUM,SUMS
          DATA IPRINT /6/
          WRITE (IPRINT,1000)
1000   FORMAT (13H1TEST CASE 1.,/,
      *54HOCHECK OF STATISTICS OF THE FIRST 10,000 POINTS OUT OF,/,
      *29H THE RANDOM NUMBER GENERATOR.)
          SUM=0.D0
          SUMS=0.D0
          DO 10 I=1,10000
          CALL TDRAND (A)
          D=A-0.5
          SUM=SUM+D
10        SUMS=SUMS+D*D
          SUM=SUM/10000.D0
          SUMS=(SUMS-10000.D0*SUM*SUM)/9999.D0
          A=1.D0/SUMS
          WRITE (IPRINT,1001) SUM,SUMS,A
1001   FORMAT (25HOMEAN                  =,F12.6,/,
      *25HOVARIANCE              =,F12.6,/,
      *25HORECIPROCAL OF VARIANCE =,F12.6)
          DO 20 I=1,64
20        X(I)=0.
          X(1)=1.
          X(3)=1.
          X(5)=1.
          X(61)=1.
          X(63)=1.
          CALL FFTRAN (-1.,1.,X,5)
          WRITE (IPRINT,1002)
1002   FORMAT (13H1TEST CASE 2.,/,
      *47HOREAL PART OF THE FOURIER TRANSFORM OF A PULSE.)
          CALL PRPLOT (X,17,0.,1.,2)
          WRITE (IPRINT,1003)
1003   FORMAT (30H1IMAGINARY PART OF THE FOURIER,/,
      *24H TRANSFORM OF THE PULSE.)
          CALL PRPLOT (X(2),17,0.,1.,2)
          CALL FFTRAN (1.,1.,X,5)
          WRITE (IPRINT,1004)
1004   FORMAT (29H1INVERSE FOURIER TRANSFORM OF,/,
      *23H THE TRANSFORMED PULSE.)
          CALL PRPLOT (X,32,0.,1.,2)
          WRITE (IPRINT,1005)
1005   FORMAT (13H1TEST CASE 3.,/,
      *26HOFIVE POLE LOWPASS FILTER.,/,
      *18HOFILTER WEIGHTS...,/,
      *37HO      I          A1              A2,
      *15H            B0,//)
          T=0.005
          BW=5.
          M=5
          CALL LPSB (M,T,BW,A1,A2,BZERO)
          DO 30 I=1,3
          B0(I)=BZERO
          B1(I)=0.
          B2(I)=0.
30        WRITE (IPRINT,1006) I,A1(I),A2(I),B0(I)
1006   FORMAT (1H ,I6,3F15.8)
          DO 40 I=1,101
40        FREQ(I)=I-1
          CALL TTRAN (A1,A2,B0,B1,B2,M,101,T,FREQ,X,Y)
          WRITE (IPRINT,1007)
1007   FORMAT (30H1GAIN OF THE TRANSFER FUNCTION,/,
      *21H OF THE FILTER IN DB.)
          CALL PRPLOT (X,101,0.,1.,1)
          WRITE (IPRINT,1008)
1008   FORMAT (31H1PHASE OF THE TRANSFER FUNCTION,/,
      *26H OF THE FILTER IN DEGREES.)
          CALL PRPLOT (Y,101,0.,1.,1)
          STOP
          END
```

Figure A.8 Program with four simple test cases for the routines. part I. Note: do not punch square bracketed terms in formats 1001 and 1005. They indicate the number of blanks in the long empty areas.

426

```
TEST CASE 1.

CHECK OF STATISTICS OF THE FIRST 10,000 POINTS OUT OF
THE RANDOM NUMBER GENERATOR.

MEAN                     =     0.000974

VARIANCE                 =     0.083891

RECIPROCAL OF VARIANCE = 11.920185
```

Figure A.9 Results from the test case for the pseudo-random number generator.

```
TEST CASE 2.

REAL PART OF THE FOURIER TRANSFORM OF A PULSE.
                        -1.24                            1.88                        5.00
   0.0       5.0000                                                                    +
   1.0000    4.8093                                                                 +
   2.0000    4.2620                                                           +
   3.0000    3.4283                                                    +
   4.0000    2.4142                                          +
   5.0000    1.3458                              +
   6.0000    0.3512                      +
   7.0000   -0.4576            +
   8.0000   -1.0000    +
   9.0000   -1.2379  +
  10.0000   -1.1796  +
  11.0000   -0.8765     +
  12.0000   -0.4142           +
  13.0000    0.1024                  +
  14.0000    0.5665                      +
  15.0000    0.8862                          +
  16.0000    1.0000                            +
```

Figure A.10a

```
IMAGINARY PART OF THE FOURIER
TRANSFORM OF THE PULSE.
                        -0.00                           -0.00                       0.00
   0.0       0.0
   1.0000 0.1848E-05                                            +
   2.0000 0.1431E-05                                                    +
   3.0000 0.2325E-05                                                +
   4.0000 0.4172E-06                                         +
   5.0000 0.5960E-07                                    +
   6.0000-0.4768E-06                              +
   7.0000-0.1729E-05                      +
   8.0000 0.0                                    +
   9.0000-0.1550E-05              +
  10.0000-0.1431E-05                 +
  11.0000-0.2444E-05 +
  12.0000-0.1252E-05                   +
  13.0000-0.2325E-05        +
  14.0000-0.1132E-05                 +
  15.0000-0.1609E-05          +
  16.0000 0.0                                        +
```

Figure A.10b This part should be nearly zero, as it is in this case. This plot varies considerably from machine to machine.

```
INVERSE FOURIER TRANSFORM OF
THE TRANSFORMED PULSE.
                     -0.00                                    0.50                                      1.00
   0.0      1.0000                                                                                       +
   1.0000   1.0000                                                                                       +
   2.0000   1.0000                                                                                       +
   3.0000   0.0000 +
   4.0000   0.0000 +
   5.0000   0.0000 +
   6.0000   0.0000 +
   7.0000   0.0000 +
   8.0000   0.0    +
   9.0000   0.0000 +
  10.0000   0.0000 +
  11.0000   0.0000 +
  12.0000  -0.0000 +
  13.0000   0.0000 +
  14.0000   0.0000 +
  15.0000   0.0000 +
  16.0000   0.0000 +
  17.0000   0.0000 +
  18.0000   0.0000 +
  19.0000  -0.0000 +
  20.0000  -0.0000 +
  21.0000  -0.0000 +
  22.0000   0.0000 +
  23.0000   0.0000 +
  24.0000   0.0    +
  25.0000   0.0000 +
  26.0000   0.0000 +
  27.0000   0.0000 +
  28.0000   0.0000 +
  29.0000   0.0000 +
  30.0000   1.0000
  31.0000   1.0000
```

Figure A.10c   The skipping option in PRPLOT was employed so that only the real part is plotted.

TEST CASE 3.

FIVE POLE LOWPASS FILTER.

FILTER WEIGHTS...

I	A1	A2	B0
1	-1.88388157	0.90733629	0.04194543
2	-1.75400639	0.77569389	0.04194543
3	-0.85491133	0.0	0.04194543

Figure A.11a   The parameters were $T=0.005$ and $B=5$ Hz. Thus the frequencies are directly in percentages of the folding frequency.

GAIN OF THE TRANSFER FUNCTION
OF THE FILTER IN DB.
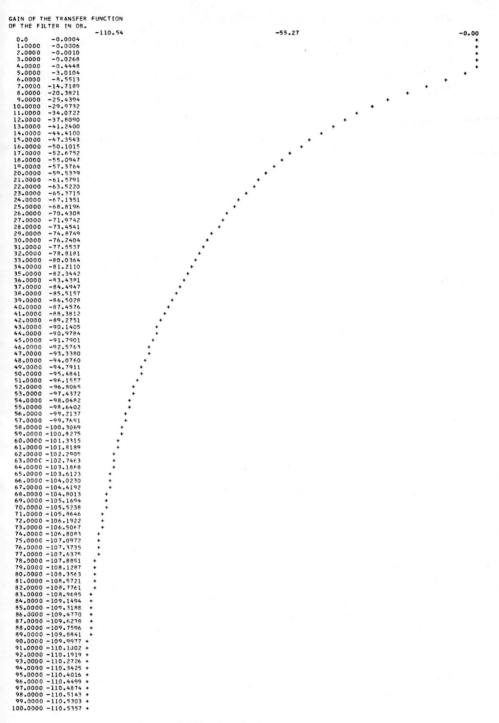

-110.54	-55.27 -0.00

```
   0.0       -0.0004
   1.0000    -0.0006
   2.0000    -0.0010
   3.0000    -0.0268
   4.0000    -0.4448
   5.0000    -3.0104
   6.0000    -8.5513
   7.0000   -14.7189
   8.0000   -20.3821
   9.0000   -25.4394
  10.0000   -29.9732
  11.0000   -34.0722
  12.0000   -37.8090
  13.0000   -41.2400
  14.0000   -44.4100
  15.0000   -47.3543
  16.0000   -50.1015
  17.0000   -52.6752
  18.0000   -55.0947
  19.0000   -57.3764
  20.0000   -59.5339
  21.0000   -61.5791
  22.0000   -63.5220
  23.0000   -65.3715
  24.0000   -67.1351
  25.0000   -68.8196
  26.0000   -70.4308
  27.0000   -71.9742
  28.0000   -73.4541
  29.0000   -74.8749
  30.0000   -76.2404
  31.0000   -77.5537
  32.0000   -78.8181
  33.0000   -80.0364
  34.0000   -81.2110
  35.0000   -82.3442
  36.0000   -83.4381
  37.0000   -84.4947
  38.0000   -85.5157
  39.0000   -86.5028
  40.0000   -87.4576
  41.0000   -88.3812
  42.0000   -89.2751
  43.0000   -90.1405
  44.0000   -90.9784
  45.0000   -91.7901
  46.0000   -92.5763
  47.0000   -93.3380
  48.0000   -94.0760
  49.0000   -94.7911
  50.0000   -95.4841
  51.0000   -96.1557
  52.0000   -96.8065
  53.0000   -97.4372
  54.0000   -98.0482
  55.0000   -98.6402
  56.0000   -99.2137
  57.0000   -99.7691
  58.0000  -100.3069
  59.0000  -100.8275
  60.0000  -101.3315
  61.0000  -101.8189
  62.0000  -102.2905
  63.0000  -102.7463
  64.0000  -103.1868
  65.0000  -103.6123
  66.0000  -104.0230
  67.0000  -104.4192
  68.0000  -104.8013
  69.0000  -105.1694
  70.0000  -105.5238
  71.0000  -105.8646
  72.0000  -106.1922
  73.0000  -106.5067
  74.0000  -106.8083
  75.0000  -107.0972
  76.0000  -107.3735
  77.0000  -107.6375
  78.0000  -107.8891
  79.0000  -108.1287
  80.0000  -108.3563
  81.0000  -108.5721
  82.0000  -108.7761
  83.0000  -108.9685
  84.0000  -109.1494
  85.0000  -109.3188
  86.0000  -109.4770
  87.0000  -109.6238
  88.0000  -109.7596
  89.0000  -109.8841
  90.0000  -109.9977
  91.0000  -110.1002
  92.0000  -110.1919
  93.0000  -110.2726
  94.0000  -110.3425
  95.0000  -110.4016
  96.0000  -110.4499
  97.0000  -110.4874
  98.0000  -110.5143
  99.0000  -110.5303
 100.0000  -110.5357
```

Figure A.11*b*   Results from test case 4.

12, respectively. The actual results are well within allowable statistical variability.

Figures A.10a, A.10b, and A.10c show the results from test case 2 of the program. The objective was to compute the Fourier transform of a rectangular pulse. A total of 32 complex points were used with

$$x(i) = \begin{cases} 1 & i = -2, -1, 0, 1, 2 \\ 0 & \text{otherwise} \end{cases}$$

In the storage arrangement employed, the correspondence was

i	-2	-1	0	1	2
I	61	63	1	3	5

The value for T was taken to be 1. Thus, making use of symmetry and formulas in Appendix B,

$$X(k) = \sum_{i=-2}^{2} e^{-j\frac{2\pi ik}{32}}$$

$$= \sum_{i=-2}^{2} \cos\left(\frac{\pi ik}{16}\right)$$

$$= \sin\left(\frac{5\pi k}{32}\right) / \sin\left(\frac{\pi k}{32}\right)$$

As a test, take $k = 8$. This yields

$$X(8) = \sin\left(\frac{5\pi}{4}\right) / \sin\left(\frac{\pi}{4}\right)$$

$$= -1.$$

Figure A.10a shows Re[$X(k)$] and $X(8)$ is equal to -1. The other values will also be found to check.

Because the chosen function is symmetric, Im[$X(f)$] should be identically 0. Owing to computer roundoff during floating point arithmetic operations, it will not turn out to be precisely 0. This will be seen in Figure A.10b, which shows the plot of Im[$X(f)$]. Some of the answers are 0, with the rest of them small in magnitude when compared to 5. the largest value for Re[$X(f)$]. This is a plot of roundoff error, and varies considerably with different computers. It is unlikely that this picture will be the same with the other computers.

The inverse Fourier transform was taken and the results were plotted as shown in Figure A.10c. The skipping option in PRPLOT was employed, so that only the real part of the time history is shown.

Figure A.11a shows the results from test case 3, which requested a five-pole lowpass filter with cutoff at 5% of the Nyquist folding frequency. Note that the a_{23} term is 0, as (5 Hz in this case) would be expected in a five-pole filter.

Figure A.11b, which is test case 4, has the plot of the data resulting from inputting the above filter to subroutine TTRAN in order to compute its transfer function. Only its gain in dB is shown. Note that the transfer function is equal to -3.0103 dB at 5 Hz as would be expected.

APPENDIX B

BLACKMAN–TUKEY COMPUTATIONAL PROCEDURE FOR PSD'S

B.1 INTRODUCTION

The feasibility of computing PSD's from covariance functions was shown by Wiener and Khintchine, and was later turned into a practical digital procedure by Blackman and Tukey [1958]. Their book was a milestone in time series analysis.

Although they have been largely superseded by DFT methods, it is still worthwhile to review the algorithms and understand the problems involved.

First of all, let us define the autocovariance function of $x(t)$, denoted by $s_{xx}(\tau)$, by

$$s_{xx}(\tau) = \lim_{P \to \infty} \frac{1}{2P} \int_{-P}^{P} x(t) x(t+\tau) \, d\tau$$

It is assumed that $x(t)$ has zero mean.

The power spectral density, $S_{xx}(f)$, is then given by

$$S_{xx}(f) = \lim_{P \to \infty} \int_{-P}^{P} s_{xx}(\tau) \exp(-j2\pi f \tau) \, d\tau$$

$$= \lim_{P \to \infty} \int_{-P}^{P} s_{xx}(\tau) \cos 2\pi f \tau \, d\tau$$

$$= \lim_{P \to \infty} 2 \int_{0}^{P} s_{xx}(\tau) \cos 2\pi f \tau \, d\tau$$

The last two steps can be made owing to the fact that $s(\tau)$ is symmetric.

In actual practice, the limit of integration is finite, as the data gathered is itself finite. Thus

$$\hat{s}_{xx}(\tau) = \frac{1}{2P} \int_{-P'}^{P'} x(t)x(t+\tau)\,dt \qquad -P \leqslant \tau \leqslant P$$

$$\hat{S}_{xx}(f) = \int_{-P}^{P} s_x(\tau)\cos 2\pi f \tau \, d\tau$$

where the caret notation indicates a finite sample, and the length of $2P'$ of the original data is to be larger than $2P$, the length of autocovariance employed in computing $\hat{s}_{xx}(f)$.

If P' is large enough so that $\hat{s}_{xx}(\tau)$ is a good estimate of $s_{xx}(\tau)$, then the sample spectrum can be modeled in the following manner:

$$\hat{S}_{xx}(f) = \int_{-\infty}^{\infty} v(\tau)s_{xx}(\tau)\exp(-j2\pi f \tau)\,d\tau$$

where

$$v(\tau) = \begin{cases} 1 & -P \leqslant \tau < P \\ 0 & \text{otherwise} \end{cases}$$

This $v(\tau)$ function is almost the same as $u(t)$, the boxcar function defined in Chapter 1. There is one very important difference: $v(\tau)$ is twice as wide as $u(t)$. Therefore, $V(f)$, its Fourier transform, turns out to be

$$V(f) = \frac{2\sin 2\pi f P}{2\pi f}$$

Thus for equal size P, $V(f)$ is twice as high as $U(f)$, and with main lobe half as wide.

The observed PSD is then the convolution of $S_x(f)$ and $V(f)$:

$$\hat{S}_{xx}(f) = \int_{-\infty}^{\infty} S_{xx}(\eta)V(f-\eta)\,d\eta$$

Note that it is $V(f)$ rather than $V^2(f)$ which appears in this expression. $V(f)$ is negative for some values of f, and, as will be seen, this makes possible observed negative power in some circumstances.

For example, suppose $x(t)$ is a sinusoid

$$x(t) = A\sin(2\pi f_0 t + \phi)$$

As has been shown earlier, the autocovariance function for this case is

$$s_{xx}(\tau) = \frac{A^2}{2} \cos 2\pi f_0 \tau$$

and the power spectral density is

$$S_{xx}(f) = \frac{A^2}{4} \left[\delta(f - f_0) + \delta(f + f_0) \right]$$

As a model for $\hat{S}_{xx}(f)$, suppose this $s_{xx}(\tau)$ is used for $\hat{s}_{xx}(\tau)$, and that $\hat{S}_{xx}(f)$ is computed using the finite interval $(-P, P)$, so that

$$\hat{S}_{xx}(f) = \int_{-\infty}^{\infty} S_{xx}(\eta) V(f - \eta) d\eta$$

$$= \int_{-\infty}^{\infty} \frac{A^2}{4} \left[\delta(\eta - f_0) + \delta(\eta + f_0) \right] \frac{2 \sin 2\pi(f - \eta) p}{2\pi(f - \eta) P} d\eta$$

$$= \frac{A^2}{4} \left\{ \frac{2 \sin \left[2\pi(f - f_0) P \right]}{2\pi(f - f_0) P} + \frac{2 \sin \left[2\pi(f + f_0) P \right]}{2\pi(f + f_0)} \right\}$$

The original PSD $S_{xx}(f)$ consists of two delta functions located at $\pm f_0$ Hz. The observed PSD consists of two $(\sin x / x$ functions also centered at $\pm f_0$ Hz. As $P \to \infty$ these $(\sin x)/x$ functions in the limit will go to delta functions.

For finite P there is a noticeable spreading or *smearing* of the PSD. The power that is observed away from the place it is supposed to be ($\pm f_0$ Hz in this case) is termed *leakage*.

The *window* $v(\tau)$ or its frequency counterpart $V(f)$ can be varied to reduce this leakage. A number of window functions were devised as solutions to this and other forms of the leakage problem.

B.2   COMPUTATIONAL FORMULAS

This section summarizes the formulas employed in computing $B–T$ PSD's digitally.

1. Assume that $x(i)$ is a sequence of N points having a zero mean. If the mean is not 0, it should be calculated and removed from the data. This step might include the removal of subharmonic terms.

2. The sample autocovariance function of $x(i)$ is computed for $(m+1)$ values:

$$s_{xx}(i) = \frac{1}{N-i-1} \sum_{p=0}^{N-i-1} x(p)x(p+i) \qquad i=0,\ldots,m$$

3. A window is selected. Possible candidates are
    a. Hann

$$v_m^{(1)}(i) = \frac{1}{2}\left(1+\cos\frac{\pi i}{m}\right)$$

    b. Hamming

$$v_m^{(2)}(i) = 0.54 + 0.46\cos\frac{\pi i}{m}$$

    c. Parzen

$$v_m^{(3)}(i) = \begin{cases} \left(1-6\frac{i}{m}\right)^2\left(1-\frac{i}{m}\right) & i<\frac{m}{2} \\[2ex] 2\left(1-\frac{i}{m}\right)^3 & i>\frac{m}{2} \end{cases}$$

One of these is applied to the correlation, resulting in a new correlation, $\hat{s}_x(i)$

$$\tilde{s}_x(i) = s_x(i)v_m^{I}(i)$$

4. The PSD is calculated for various frequencies using trapezoidal integration,

$$\hat{S}_{xx}(f) = T\left(\tilde{s}_x(0) + 2\sum_{i=1}^{m-1}\hat{s}_x(i)\cos 2\pi f i T + \hat{s}_{xx}(i)\cos 2\pi f m T\right)$$

The "standard" set of frequencies is

$$f_k = \frac{k}{2mT} \qquad k=0,1,\ldots,m$$

This produces $(m+1)$ equally spaced, overlapping PSD estimates. The preceding equation can be rewritten as

$$\hat{S}_{xy}(k) = T\left(\tilde{S}_x(0) + 2\sum_{i=1}^{m-1}\tilde{S}_x(i)\cos\frac{\pi i k}{m} + \tilde{S}_x(m)\cos\pi i\right)$$

$$k=0,1,\ldots,m$$

Any prewhitening would be done before step 2, and the corresponding postdarkening accomplished after step 4.

If the PSD is calculated at the frequencies $k/2mT$, $k=0,1,\dots,m$, then it is possible to change the order of the computations. Step 3 in the above is deleted, and a new one is added at the end. It consists of weighting the PSD in the following manner:

$$S_x(k) = \begin{cases} D_0\tilde{G}_{x(k-1)} + D_1\tilde{G}_{xk} + D_0\tilde{G}_{x(k+1)} & k \neq 0, m \\ D_1\tilde{G}_{x0} + 2D_0\tilde{G}_{x1} & k = 0 \\ D_1\tilde{G}_{xm} + 2D_0\tilde{G}_{x(m-1)} & k = m \end{cases}$$

The values for D_0 and D_1 are

$$D_0 = \begin{cases} \frac{1}{2} & \text{Hann} \\ 0.54 & \text{Hamming} \end{cases}$$

$$D_1 = \begin{cases} \frac{1}{4} & \text{Hann} \\ 0.23 & \text{Hamming} \end{cases}$$

There does not seem to be any real gain in doing the lag window operation in this manner. Compared with the expense of computing the autocorrelation and Fourier transform, the lag window computations require an insignificant amount of time. This formulation is therefore included only because the reader is likely to encounter it in the course of reviewing the computations as done by some organizations.

Step 4, which is essentially that of computing the Fourier cosine transformation, could be accomplished using the FFT techniques described in Chapter 6. On the other hand, if a small number of lag values is used, the complication of the FFT may not be merited. The fact that the desired frequency spacing may not be able to be attained with the FFT can also be a disadvantage. If the FFT is not utilized, one of several recursive sine/cosine computing methods can be implemented as a cost saving procedure.

The method described in Section 4.3 is applicable. The recursive relation takes the form

$$c_1 = hc_{i-1} - c_{i-2}$$

$$h = 2\cos 2\pi Tf_0$$

This relation will yield either sines or cosines, depending on what is used to start the recursion. In particular,

$$c_0 = \begin{cases} 1 & \text{cosine generation} \\ 0 & \text{sine generation} \end{cases}$$

$$c_{-1} = \begin{cases} \cos 2\pi T f_0 & \text{cosine generation} \\ -\sin 2\pi T f_0 & \text{sine generation} \end{cases}$$

B.3   PROCEDURE FOR CROSS SPECTRA

The last topic of this appendix is the calculation of cross spectral density (CSD). The lag window considerations for the CSD are identical to those for the PSD, so that only the definitions and computational procedure need be discussed. In the continuous case, the cross covariance function is

$$s_{xy}(\tau) = E\big[x(t)y(t+\tau)\big]$$

The time average definition is

$$s_{xy}(\tau) = \lim_{P \to \infty} \frac{1}{2P} \int_{-P}^{P} x(t)y(t+\tau)\,d\tau$$

The CSD is the Fourier transform of the latter:

$$S_{xy}(f) = \int_{-\infty}^{\infty} s_{xy}(\tau)\exp(-j2\pi f\tau)\,d\tau$$

Another formulation in terms of real and imaginary parts is

$$S_{xy}(f) = C_{xy}(f) + jQ_{xy}(f)$$

The C_{xy} function is the *cospectral density* or *cospectrum*, and Q_{xy} is the *quadrature spectral density* or *quadspectrum*. The definitions of these two expressions are

$$C_{xy}(f) = \int_{0}^{\infty} \big[s_{xy}(\tau) + s_{xy}(-\tau)\big]\cos 2\pi f\tau\,d\tau$$

$$Q_{xy}(f) = \int_{0}^{\infty} \big[s_{xy}(\tau) - s_{xy}(-\tau)\big]\sin\pi 2\tau f\,d\tau$$

The digital procedure would be much the same as for the PSD:

1. The variables $x(i)$ and $y(i)$ are assumed to be zero mean sequences of N points. If the means were not 0, they would be calculated and removed.

2. Sample covariance functions are computed for $(m+1)$ values:

$$\hat{S}_{xy}(i)=\frac{1}{N-i-1}\sum_{p=0}^{N-i-1}x(p)y(p+i)$$

$$\hat{S}_{yx}(i)=\frac{1}{N-i-1}\sum_{p=0}^{N-i-1}x(p+i)y(p)\qquad i=0,1,\ldots,m$$

3. An appropriate lag window is selected as above, and two new covariance functions are computed:

$$\tilde{S}_{xy}(i)=v_m^l(i)\hat{S}_{xy}(i)$$

$$\tilde{S}_{yx}(i)=v_m^l(i)\hat{S}_{yx}(i)\qquad i=0,1,\ldots,m$$

4. The intermediate quantities $A_{xy}(i)$ and $B_{xy}(i)$ are computed:

$$A_{xy}(i)=\tilde{S}_{xy}(i)+\tilde{S}_{yx}(i)$$

$$B_{xy}(i)=\tilde{S}_{xy}(i)-\tilde{S}_{yx}(i)\qquad i=0,1,\ldots,m$$

5. The cospectra and quadspectra are computed for various frequencies using trapezodial integrations:

$$\hat{C}_{xy}(f)=\frac{T}{2}\left[A_{xy}(0)+2\sum_{i=1}^{m-1}A_{xy}(i)\cos 2\pi fiT\right.$$

$$\left.+A_{xy}(m)\cos 2\pi fmT\right]$$

$$\hat{Q}_{xy}(f)=\frac{T}{2}\left[B_{xy}(0)+2\sum_{r=1}^{m-1}B_{xy}(i)\sin 2\pi fiT\right.$$

$$\left.+B_{xy}(m)\sin 2\pi fmT\right]$$

As in the case for the PSD, a standard set of frequencies can be used:

$$f_k=\frac{k}{2mT}\qquad k=0,1,\ldots,m$$

6. There are various ways of displaying different forms of output for

$\hat{C}_{xy}(f)$ and $\hat{Q}_{xy}(f)$. Some commonly calculated additional information is the following.

a.   The absolute value of the CSD,

$$|\hat{S}_{xy}(f)| = \sqrt{\hat{C}_{xy}^2(f) + \hat{Q}_{xy}^2(f)}$$

b.   The phase angle of the CSD (in degrees)

$$\hat{\phi}(f) = \frac{360}{2\pi} \arctan\left[\frac{\hat{Q}_{xy}(f)}{\hat{C}_{xy}(f)}\right]$$

Note that the quadrant is always known, so that $\hat{\phi}$ ranges over 360°. The most usual span is -180 to 180°. A test using the signs of $\hat{Q}_{xy}$ and $\hat{C}_{xy}$ has to be made to determine the proper quadrant. Many routines that compute arctangents are designed to take care of this problem.

c.   The transfer function between x and y,

$$\hat{H}(f) = \frac{\hat{C}_{xy}(f) + j\hat{Q}_{xy}(f)}{\hat{G}_{xx}(f)}$$

This is also usually rewritten in terms of the modulus and the phase angle. The modulus is

$$|\hat{H}(f)| = \sqrt{\frac{\hat{C}_{xy}^2(f) + \hat{Q}_{xy}^2(f)}{\hat{G}_{xx}^2(f)}}$$

The phase angle is the same as for the CSD.

B.4   COMMENTS

There are some precautionary statements that should be kept in mind when employing or reviewing PSD's computed in this manner:

1.   It is usually $G_x(k)$, rather than $S_x(k)$, that is produced. $G_x(k)$, known as the "one-sided PSD," is defined by

$$G_x(k) = \begin{cases} 2S_x(k) & k \geqslant 0 \\ 0 & k < 0 \end{cases}$$

2.   The frequency interval $f_k = k/2mT$ produces spectral estimates that overlap each other. There are two results from this:
   a.   If the PSD is integrated in order to obtain the variance, the result must be divided in two because of this redundancy; otherwise, the result will be twice as high as it should be.
   b.   There is no circularity effect as is found with the Fourier transform method when no zeroes are added; taking the inverse Fourier transform of $S_x(k)$ will yield $s_x(i)$ except for roundoff.
3.   The number of degrees of freedom for each spectral estimate for the white noise case is

$$d = \frac{2N}{m}$$

When put into the familiar bP form, it is

$$d = 2bP$$

where $b = 1/mT$ and $P = NT$.

4.   This form of PSD is "energy preserving," whereas the Fourier transform method is not. The total energy is carried in $s_x(0)$ term, which is the same as the sample variance. All the window functions employed are equal to unity at $\tau = 0$, so that the total energy in the PSD is not changed by employing a window. This is not necessarily the case for PSD's computed via the Fourier transform procedure where windowing is performed.

REFERENCES

Abramowitz, M. and I. A. Stegun, *Handbook of Mathematical Functions*, U.S. Government Printing Office, Washington, D.C., 1964.

Akaike, H., "Undamped Oscillation of the Sample Autocovariance Function and the Effect of Prewhitening Operation," *Annals of the Institute of Statistical Mathematics*, Vol. 13, pp. 127–144, 1962.

Akaike, H., "On the Statistical Estimation of the Frequency Response Function of a System Having Multiple Input," *Annals of the Institute of Statistical Mathematics*, Vol. 17, No. 2, 1965.

Balakrishnan, A. V. "On the Problem of Time Jitter in Sampling," *IRE Transactions on Information Theory*, Vol. IT-8, No. 3, pp. 226–236, April 1962.

Bendat, J. S. and A. G. Piersol, *Random Data: Analysis and Measurement Procedures*, Wiley, New York, 1971.

Benignus, V. A., "Estimation of the Coherence Spectrum and Its Confidence Interval Using the Fast Fourier Transform," *IEEE Transactions on Audio and Electroacoustics*, Vol. AU-17, No. 2, 1969.

Bingham, C., M. D. Godfrey, and J. W. Tukey, "Modern Techniques of Power Spectrum Estimation," *IEEE Transactions on Audio and Electroacoustics*, Vol. AU-15, No. 2, pp. 56–66, 1967.

Blackman, R. B. and J. W. Tukey, *The Measurement of Power Spectra from the Point of View of Communications Engineering*, Dover, New York, 1958.

Bracewell, R. M., *The Fourier Transform and Its Applications*, McGraw-Hill, New York, 1965.

Butterworth, S., "On the Theory of Filter Amplifiers," *Experimental Wireless*, Vol. 7, pp. 536–541, Oct. 1930.

Carter, G. C., "Estimation of the Magnitude-Squared Coherence Function," Naval Undersea Systems Center Report 4343, May 19, 1972.

Cleveland, W. S. and E. Parzen, "Estimation of Coherence, Frequency Response, and Envelope Delay," *Technometrics*, May 1975.

Cooley, J. W. and J. W. Tukey, "An Algorithm for the Machine Calculation of Complex Fourier Series," *Mathematics of Computation*, Vol. 19, p. 297, 1965.

Cramer, H., *Mathematical Methods of Statistics*, Princeton University Press, Princeton, N.J., 1946.

Dixon, W. G. and F. J. Massey, *Introduction to Statistical Analysis*, 3rd ed., McGraw-Hill, New York, 1969.

Dym, H. and H. P. McKean, *Fourier Series and Integrals*, Academic Press, New York, 1972.

Enochson, L. D. and N. R. Goodman, "Gaussian Approximations to the Distribution of Sample Coherence," AFFDL TR-65-57, Research and Technology Division, AFSC, Wright-Patterson Air Force Base, Ohio, Feb. 1965.

Fletcher, R. and M. J. D. Powell, "A Rapidly Convergent Descent Method for Minimization," *Computer Journal*, Vol. 6, No. 2, 1963.

Forsythe, G. and C. Moler, *Computer Solution of Linear Algebraic Systems*, Prentice-Hall, Englewood Cliffs, N.J., 1971.

Fraser, D. A. S., *Statistics: An Introduction*, Wiley, New York, 1958.

Gabor, D. "Theory of Communication," *Journal IEEE (London)*, Vol. 93, Part 3, No. 26, 1946.

Gentlemen, W. M. and G. Sande, "Fast Fourier Transforms for Fun and Profit," *AFIPS Conference Proceedings*, Vol. 29, 563–578, 1966.

Goodman, N. R., "Measurement of Matrix Frequency Response Functions and Multiple Coherence Functions," AFDL TR-65-56, Research and Technology Division, AFSC, Wright Patterson Air Force Base, Ohio, Feb. 1965.

Gray, A. H., Jr. and J. D. Markel, "A Spectral-Flatness Measure for Studying the Autocorrelation Method of Linear Speech Analysis," *IEEE Transactions on Speech Acoustics and Signal Processing*, pp. 207–271, 1974.

Gray, A. H., Jr. and J. D. Markel, "Digital Lattice and Ladder Filter Synthesis," *IEEE Transaction on Audio and Electroacoustics*, Dec. 1973.

Guilleman, E. A., *Synthesis of Passive Networks*, Wiley, New York, 1957.

Hastings, C., *Approximations for Digital Computers*, Princeton University Press, Princeton, N.J., 1955.

Hinich, M., "Estimation of Spectra after Hard Clipping of Gaussian Processes," *Technometrics*, Vol. 9, p. 391, 1967.

Holtz, H., "The Synthesis of Linear Recursive Digital Filters Optimal in a Minimax Sense," *Seventh Asilomar Conference on Circuits, Systems, and Computers*, Pacific Grove, Calif., pp. 513–517, Nov. 1973.

Hsu, H. P., *Fourier Analysis*, rev. ed., Simon and Schuster, New York, 1970.

Jackson, L. B., "Roundoff Noise Analysis for Fixed Point Digital Filters Realized in Cascade or Parallel Form," *IEEE Transactions on Audio and Electroacoustics*, June 1970.

Jenkins, G. M. and D. G. Watts, *Spectral Analysis and Its Applications*, Holden-Day, San Francsico, 1968.

Jullien, G. A. and M. A. Sid-Ahmed "A Computer Program for Filter Design Having Arbitrary Magnitude Specifications in the Frequency Domain," *International Journal of Numerical Methods (Great Britain)*, Vol. 6, No. 2, pp. 275–285, 1973.

Jury, E. I., "A Stability Test for Linear Discrete Systems Using a Simple Division," *Proceedings of the IRE*, Dec. 1961.

Jury, E. I. and J. Blanchard, "A Stability Test for Linear Discrete Systems in Table Form," *Proceedings of the IRE*, Dec. 1961.

Kaiser, J. F., "Design Methods for Sampled Data Filters (Z-transform)," *Proceedings of the First Annual Allerton Conference on Circuit and System Theory*, Nov. 1963.

Kelly, R. D., L. D. Enochson, and L. A. Rondinelli, "Techniques and Errors in Measuring Cross-Correlation and Cross-Spectral Density Functions," NASA CR-74505, Feb. 1966.

Kendall, M. G. and A. G. Stuart, *The Advanced Theory of Statistics*, Hafner, London, 1961.

Kennedy, J. E. and F. B. Safford, "The Use of Vibration/Impedance Measurements to Predict Blast Induced Structural Vibrations," *Fourth International Symposium on Military Applications of Blast Simulation*, Atomic Weapon Research Establishment, Foulness, England, Sept. 1974.

Koopmans, L. H., *The Spectral Analysis of Time Series*, Academic Press, New York, 1974.

Lanczos, C., *Applied Analysis*, Prentice-Hall, Englewood Cliffs, N.J., 1956.

Liu, B. (Ed.), *Digital Filters and the Fast Fourier Transform*, Dowden, Hutchinson, and Ross, Stroudsburg, PA., 1975.

Longley, J. W., "An Appraisal of Least Squares Computer Programs for the Electronic Computer from the Point of View of the User," *JASA*, Vol. 62, pp. 819–841, 1967.

McClellan, J. H., T. W. Parks, and L. R. Rabiner, "A Computer Program for Designing Optimum FIR Linear Filters," *IEEE Transactions on Audio and Electroacoustics*, Dec. 1973.

McCowan, D. W., "Finite Fourier Transform Theory and Its Application to the Computation of Convolutions, Correlations, and Spectra," Research Department Technical Memorandum No. 8-66, Earth Sciences Division, Teledyne, Inc., Dec. 1966.

Magrab, E. D. and D. S. Blomquist, *The Measurement of Time-Varying Phenomena*, Wiley, New York, 1971.

Masri, S. F. and F. B. Safford, "Dynamic Environment Simulation by Pulse Techniques," *Journal of the Engineering Mechanics Division*, American Society of Civil Engineers, EM1, 11923, Feb. 1976.

Maynard, H. W., "An Evaluation of Ten Fast Fourier Transfer Programs," Army Electronics Command, White Sands Missile Range, March 1973.

Mitra, S. K. and R. J. Sherwood, "Digital Ladder Networks," *IEEE Transactions on Audio and Electroacoustics*, Feb. 1973.

Norin, R. and E. Sloane, "A New Algorithm for Improving Digital Random Control System Speed and Accuracy," *IES Proceedings*, pp. 46–52, 1975.

Nyquist, H. "Certain Factors Affecting Telegraph Speed," *Bell Systems Journal*, Vol. 3, April 1924.

Oliver, B. M., J. R. Pierce, and C. E. Shannon, "The Philosophy of PCM," *Proceedings of IRE*, Nov. 1948.

Oppenheim, A. V. et al. (Eds.), *Selected Papers in Digital Signal Processing, II*, IEEE Press, New York, 1976.

Ormsby, J. F. "Design of Numerical Filters with Applications to Missile Data Processing," *Journal of the Association for Computing Machinery*, Vol. 8, No. 3, July 1961.

Otnes, R. K. and L. Enochson, *Digital Time Series Analysis*, Wiley-Interscience, New York, 1972.

Otnes, R. K. and L. P. McNamee, "Instability Thresholds in Digital Filters Due to Coefficient Rounding," *IEEE Transactions on and Audio Electroacoustics*, Vol. AU-18, pp. 456–463, 1970.

Otnes, R. K., H. A. Nathans, and L. Enochson, "A Procedure for Computing Power Spectral Density of Gust Data," AFFDL-TR-69-11, Wright Patterson Air Force Base, Ohio, March 1969.

Parks, T. W. and J. H. McClellan, "A Program for the Design of Linear Phase Finite Impulse Response Digital Filters," *IEEE Transactions on Audio and Electroacoustics*, Aug. 1972.

Parzen, E., "Mathematical Considerations in the Estimation of Spectra," *Technometrics*, Vol. 3, pp. 167–190, 1961.

Pike, M. C. and I. D. Hill, "Algorithm 266, Pseudo Random Numbers (65)," *Collected Algorithms from CACM*, July 1965.

Potter, R. W., *Compilation of Time Windows and Time Shapes for Fourier Analysis*, 02-5952-0705, Hewlett-Packard, 1971.

Rabiner, L. R. and C. M. Rader (Eds.), *Digital Signal Processing*, IEEE Press, New York, 1972.

Rabiner, L. R. and B. Gold, *Theory and Application of Digital Signal Processing*, Prentice-Hall, Englewood Cliffs, N.J., 1975.

Sande, G., "On an Alternative Method for Calculating Covariance Functions," Princeton Computer Memorandum, Princeton, N.J., 1965.

Schafer, R. W. and L. R. Rabiner, "A Digital Signal Processing Approach to Interpolation," *Proceedings of the IEEE*, Vol. 61, No. 6, June 1973.

Schatzoff, M., M. Fienberg, and S. Tsao, "Efficient Calculation of All Possible Regressions," *Technometrics*, Vol. 9, pp. 531–540, 1968.

Schmid, L. P., "Efficient Autocorrelation," *Communications of the ACM*, Vol. 8, p. 115, 1965.

Shannon, C. E., "Communication in the Presence of Noise," *Proceedings of the IRE*, Jan. 1949.

Singleton, R. C., "A Method for Computing the Fast Fourier Transform with Auxiliary Memory and Limited High-Speed Storage," *IEEE Transactions on Audio and Electroacoustics*, Vol. AU-15, No. 2, June 1967.

Singleton, R. C., "An Algorithm for Computing the Mixed Radix Fast Fourier Transform," *IEEE Transactions on Audio and Electroacoustics*, Vol. AU-17, No. 2, June 1969.

Sloane, E. A., "Comparison of Linearly and Quadratically Modified Spectral Estimates of Gaussian Signals," *IEEE Transactions on Audio and Electroacoustics*, Vol. AU-17, No. 2, 1969.

Steiglitz, K., *An Introduction to Discrete Systems*, Wiley, New York, 1974.

Stockham, T. G., "High Speed Convolution and Correlation," *AFIPS Conference Proceedings*, Vol. 28, pp. 229–233, 1966.

Storer, J. E., *Passive Network Synthesis*, McGraw-Hill, New York, 1957.

Theilheimer, F., "A Matrix Version of the Fast Fourier Transform," *IEEE Transactions on Audio and Electroacoustics*, Vol. AU-17, No. 2, 1969.

Wampler, R. N., "On the Accuracy of Least Squares Computer Programs," *JASA*, Vol. 65, p. 549, June 1970.

Weinreb, S., "A Digital Spectral Analysis Technique and Its Application to Radio Astronomy," MIT Research Laboratory of Electronics, Technical Report 412, Aug. 1963.

Wiener, N., *Extrapolation, Interpolation, and Smoothing of Stationary Time Series*, MIT Press, Cambridge, Mass., 1949.

INDEX